Business Analysis & Valuation

Using Financial Statements

Third Edition

Krishna G. Palepu, PhD

Ross Graham Walker Professor of Business Administration
Harvard University

Paul M. Healy, PhD, ACA

James R. Williston Professor of Business Administration
Harvard University

Victor L. Bernard, PhD, CPA

Late Price Waterhouse Professor of Accounting
University of Michigan

THOMSON

SOUTH-WESTERN

Australia · Canada · Mexico · Singapore · Spain · United Kingdom · United States

Business Analysis & Valuation: Using Financial Statements, 3e

Krishna G. Palepu, Paul M. Healy, and Victor L. Bernard

VP/Editorial Director:
Jack W. Calhoun

VP/Editor-in-Chief:
George Werthman

Acquisitions Editor:
Julie Lindsay

Developmental Editor:
Ken Martin

Marketing Manager:
Keith Chassé

Production Editor:
Chris Sears

Manufacturing Coordinator:
Doug Wilke

Media Developmental Editor:
Josh Fendley

Media Production Editor:
Kelly Reid

Production House:
Bay Island Books

Compositor:
John Richards

Cover Designer:
Bethany Casey

Cover Images:
© Corbis Corporation

Internal Designer:
Bethany Casey

Printer:
Quebecor World
Dubuque, IA

For permission to use material
from this text or product, contact
us by
Tel (800) 730-2214
Fax (800) 730-2215
http://www.thomsonrights.com

For more information
contact South-Western,
5191 Natorp Boulevard,
Mason, Ohio, 45040.
Or you can visit our Internet site
at: http://www.swlearning.com.

PREFACE

◆

Financial statements are the basis for a wide range of business analysis. Managers use them to monitor and judge their firms' performance relative to competitors, to communicate with external investors, to help judge what financial policies they should pursue, and to evaluate potential new businesses to acquire as part of their investment strategy. Securities analysts use financial statements to rate and value companies they recommend to clients. Bankers use them in deciding whether to extend a loan to a client and to determine the loan's terms. Investment bankers use them as a basis for valuing and analyzing prospective buyouts, mergers, and acquisitions. And consultants use them as a basis for competitive analysis for their clients. Not surprisingly, therefore, we find that there is a strong demand among business students for a course that provides a framework for using financial statement data in a variety of business analysis and valuation contexts. The purpose of this book is to provide such a framework for business students and practitioners.

The first two editions of this book have been successful well beyond our original expectations. The book has been used in Accounting and Finance departments in business schools in the U.S. and around the world.

CHANGES FROM THE SECOND EDITION

Many of our colleagues who used the second edition provided us with valuable feedback. Based on this feedback, we made the following changes:

- We rewrote the chapters dealing with accounting analysis to focus sharply on the task of the analyst. There are now two chapters on this topic. The first of these (Chapter 3) provides a conceptual approach to evaluating a firm's accounting choices and estimates with respect to assets, liabilities, entities, revenues, and expenses. The second chapter (Chapter 4) shows specific steps the analyst can take in examining assets, liabilities, revenues, and expenses, and in making adjustments to reported financial statements where needed. Our objective is that these two chapters will prepare students to identify questionable accounting practices, make adjustments, and produce a set of restated financials that are free of these accounting concerns.
- We revised the forecasting and valuation chapters (Chapters 6 and 7) to better prepare students for the task of making specific assumptions in the analysis steps. We use a real company example in both these chapters, so that students can use the material as a basis for studying the case applications.
- The chapter on management communication (Chapter 13) has been substantially revised. It now focuses heavily on the corporate governance role of financial reports and the role of key accounting institutions—auditors, audit committees of corporate boards, and top management of firms—in the governance process. The chapter is designed to address some of the issues raised in the aftermath of accounting and governance debacles at major corporations around the world.
- This new edition is accompanied by a comprehensive software model, the **BAV Tool**, to implement the analytical framework and techniques discussed in this book. This companion software allows students to import a company's reported financial

statements from any source, as long as they are in a Microsoft Excel spreadsheet format, and analyze them. The tool facilitates the following activities: (1) recasting the reported financial statements in a standard format for analysis; (2) performing accounting analysis as discussed in Chapters 3 and 4, making desired accounting adjustments, and producing restated financials; (3) computing ratios and free cash flows presented in Chapter 5; (4) producing forecasted income statement, balance sheet, and cash flow statements for as many as 15 years into the future, using the approach discussed in Chapter 6; and (5) valuing a company (either assets or equity) from these forecasts and preparing a terminal value forecast using the abnormal earnings method, the abnormal returns method, and discounted cash flow method discussed in Chapters 7 and 8. The tool also allows students to graph their assumptions and compare them with the historical performance of a large group of U.S. companies that are in the same performance range at the beginning of the forecasting period. This comparison is facilitated by a database consisting of key ratios for a comprehensive set of U.S. public companies listed on Standard & Poor's Compustat. We think that the BAV Tool will make it significantly easier for students to apply the framework and techniques discussed in the book in a real-world context.

- The third edition also includes access to ***Thomson Analytics–Business School Edition***, which is a web-based portal product that provides integrated access to Thomson financial content for the purpose of financial analysis. This new application delivers the most powerful and flexible tools available for turning critical market data into actionable intelligence for educational purposes. *Thomson Analytics–Business School Edition* is an educational version of the same financial resources used by Wall Street analysts on a daily basis.

Thomson Analytics–Business School Edition includes the following content sets:

I/B/E/S Consensus Estimate Includes consensus estimates—averages, means, and medians; analyst-by-analyst earnings coverage; analysts forecasts based on 15 industry standard measures; and current and historic coverage for the selected 500 companies that are drawn from a database of 60 established and emerging markets. Current history is five years forward and historic data is from 1976 for the U.S. and 1987 for international. Current data is updated daily and historic is updated monthly.

Worldscope Includes company profiles, financials and accounting results and market per-share data for the selected 500 companies drawn from a database of more than 55 established and emerging markets. Annual information and monthly prices going back to 1980 are all updated daily.

Disclosure SEC Database Includes company profiles, annual and quarterly company financials, pricing information, and earnings estimates for selected U.S. and Canadian companies. Annual information from 1987—quarterly data rolling 10 years—and monthly pricing are all updated weekly.

DataStream–International Equity and Index Daily Pricing Includes share price index and exchange rate data—updated daily.

ILX Systems Delayed Quotes Equities and indices, 20-minute-delayed quotes from domestic and international markets.

Comtex Real Time News Real-time feed of company and market news.

SEC Filings and ***Global Image Source Filings*** Regulatory and nonregulatory filings.

KEY FEATURES

This book differs from other texts in business and financial analysis in a number of important ways. We introduce and develop a framework for business analysis and valuation using financial statement data. We then show how this framework can be applied to a variety of decision contexts.

Framework for Analysis

We begin the book with a discussion of the role of accounting information and intermediaries in the economy, and how financial analysis can create value in well functioning markets. We identify four key components of effective financial statement analysis:

- Business Strategy Analysis
- Accounting Analysis
- Financial Analysis
- Prospective Analysis

The first of the components, business strategy analysis, involves developing an understanding of the business and competitive strategy of the firm being analyzed. Incorporating business strategy into financial statement analysis is one of the distinctive features of this book. Traditionally, this step has been ignored by other financial statement analysis books. However, we believe that it is critical to begin financial statement analysis with a company's strategy because it provides an important foundation for the subsequent analysis. The strategy analysis section discusses contemporary tools for analyzing a company's industry, its competitive position and sustainability within an industry, and the company's corporate strategy.

Accounting analysis involves examining how accounting rules and conventions represent a firm's business economics and strategy in its financial statements, and, if necessary, developing adjusted accounting measures of performance. In the accounting analysis section, we do not emphasize accounting rules. Instead we develop general approaches to analyzing assets, liabilities, entities, revenues, and expenses. We believe that such an approach enables students to effectively evaluate a company's accounting choices and accrual estimates, even if students have only a basic knowledge of accounting rules and standards. The material is also designed to allow students to make accounting adjustments rather than merely identify questionable accounting practices.

Financial analysis involves analyzing financial ratio and cash flow measures of the operating, financing, and investing performance of a company relative to either key competitors or historical performance. Our distinctive approach focuses on using financial analysis to evaluate the effectiveness of a company's strategy and to make sound financial forecasts.

Finally, under prospective analysis we show how to develop forecasted financial statements and how to use these to make estimates of a firm's value. Our discussion of valuation includes traditional discounted cash flow models as well as techniques that link value directly to accounting numbers. In discussing accounting-based valuation models, we integrate the latest academic research with traditional approaches such as earnings and book value multiples that are widely used in practice.

While we cover all four components of business analysis and valuation in the book, we recognize that the extent of their use depends on the user's decision context. For example, bankers are likely to use business strategy analysis, accounting analysis, financial analysis, and the forecasting portion of prospective analysis. They are less likely to be interested in formally valuing a prospective client.

Application of the Framework to Decision Contexts

The next section of the book shows how our business analysis and valuation framework can be applied to a variety of decision contexts:

- Securities Analysis
- Credit Analysis
- Corporate Financing Policies Analysis
- Merger and Acquisition Analysis
- Governance and Communication Analysis

For each of these topics we present an overview to provide a foundation for the class discussions. Where possible we discuss relevant institutional details and the results of academic research that are useful in applying the analysis concepts developed earlier in the book. For example, the chapter on credit analysis shows how banks and rating agencies use financial statement data to develop analysis for lending decisions and to rate public debt issues. This chapter also presents academic research on how to determine whether a company is financially distressed.

USING THE BOOK

We designed the book so that it is flexible for courses in financial statement analysis for a variety of student audiences—MBA students, Masters in Accounting students, Executive Program participants, and undergraduates in Accounting or Finance. Depending upon the audience, the instructor can vary the manner in which the conceptual materials in the chapters and end-of-chapter questions are used.

To get the most out of the book, students should have completed basic courses in financial accounting, finance, and either business strategy or business economics. The text provides a concise overview of some of these topics. But it would probably be difficult for students with no prior knowledge in these fields to use the chapters as stand-alone coverage of them.

If the book is used for students with prior working experience or for executives, the instructor can use almost a pure case approach, adding relevant lecture sections as needed. When teaching students with little work experience, a lecture class can be presented first, followed by an appropriate case or other assignment material.

Alternatively, lectures can be used as a follow-up to cases to more clearly lay out the conceptual issues raised in the case discussions. This may be appropriate when the book is used in undergraduate capstone courses. In such a context, cases can be used in course projects that can be assigned to student teams.

ACKNOWLEDGMENTS

We wish to thank Jonathan Barnett for his outstanding research assistance in the revision of the text chapters, and especially in the development of the BAV Tool; Keith MacKay of Village Software for his help with the development of the BAV Tool; our assistants Christian Douglass and Kathy Cohrs for able assistance throughout the project; Chris Allen for assistance with data on financial ratios for U.S. companies; the Division of Research at the

Harvard Business School for assistance in developing materials for this book; and our past and present MBA students for stimulating our thinking and challenging us to continually improve our ideas and presentation

We especially thank the following colleagues who gave us feedback as we wrote this edition: Jim Boatsman (Arizona State University), Wilfred Dellva (Villanova University), Frank Hodge (University of Washington), Paul Hriber (Cornell University), Duncan Kretovich (Portland State University), Thomas Omer (University of Illinois), Michael Sandretto (University of Illinois), David Shaffer (Villanova University), Billy Soo (Boston College), and Richard Willis (Duke University).

We are also very grateful to Laurie McKinzey and Deborah Marlino for their help and assistance throughout this project, to Julie Lindsay and Keith Chasse for their tireless efforts in promoting this revision, to our colleagues, and to Ken Martin, Chris Sears, and Julia Chitwood for their patient editorial and production help.

We would like to thank our parents and families for their strong support and encouragement throughout this project.

AUTHORS

Krishna G. Palepu is the Ross Graham Walker Professor of Business Administration and Senior Associate Dean and Director of Research at the Harvard Business School. During the past twenty years, Professor Palepu's research has focused on corporate strategy, governance, and disclosure. Professor Palepu is the winner of the American Accounting Association's Notable Contributions to Accounting Literature Award (in 1999) and the Wildman Award (in 1997).

Paul Healy is the James R. Williston Professor of Business Administration at the Harvard Business School and Co-Chair of the Doctoral Program. Professor Healy's research has focused on corporate governance and disclosure, mergers and acquisitions, earnings management, and management compensation. He has previously worked at the MIT Sloan School of Management, ICI Ltd., and Arthur Young in New Zealand. Professor Healy has won the Notable Contributions to Accounting Literature Award (in 1990 and 1999) and the Wildman Award (in 1997) for contributions to practice.

Vic Bernard, who passed away November 14, 1995, was a CPA and held a PhD from the University of Illinois. He was the Price Waterhouse Professor of Accounting and Director of the Paton Accounting Center at the University of Michigan and Director of Research for the American Accounting Association. His research examined issues in financial reporting, financial statement analysis, and financial economics. He received the Notable Contributions to Accounting Literature Award in 1991, 1993, and 1999, the Outstanding Accounting Educator Award in 1997, and the Wildman Award in 1997.

CONTENTS

Part 1 FRAMEWORK

1 A Framework for Business Analysis and Valuation Using
Financial Statements   1-1

The Role of Financial Reporting in Capital Markets   1-2
From Business Activities to Financial Statements   1-3
From Financial Statements to Business Analysis   1-6
Summary   1-9
Discussion Questions   1-9

Part 2 BUSINESS ANALYSIS AND VALUATION
TOOLS

2 Strategy Analysis   2-1

Industry Analysis   2-1
Applying Industry Analysis: The Personal Computer Industry 2-5
Competitive Strategy Analysis   2-7
Corporate Strategy Analysis   2-11
Summary   2-14
Discussion Questions   2-15

3 Overview of Accounting Analysis   3-1

The Institutional Framework for Financial Reporting   3-1
Factors Influencing Accounting Quality   3-4
Steps in Doing Accounting Analysis   3-6
Accounting Analysis Pitfalls   3-11
Value of Accounting Data and Accounting Analysis   3-12
Summary   3-13
Discussion Questions   3-14

4 Implementing Accounting Analysis   4-1

Recasting Financial Statements   4-1
Asset Distortions   4-5
Overstated Assets   4-7
Understated Assets   4-12

ix

Liability Distortions **4-21**

Equity Distortions **4-30**

Summary **4-33**

Discussion Questions **4-34**

Appendix: Recasting Financial Statements Into Standardized Templates **4-41**

5 Financial Analysis **5-1**

Ratio Analysis **5-1**

Cash Flow Analysis **5-22**

Summary **5-27**

Discussion Questions **5-28**

Appendix: Part A: Nordstrom, Inc. Financial Statements **5-30**

     Part B: The TJX Companies, Inc. Financial Statements **5-36**

6 Prospective Analysis: Forecasting **6-1**

Relation of Forecasting to Other Analyses **6-1**

The Techniques of Forecasting **6-1**

Making Forecasts **6-7**

Sensitivity Analysis **6-10**

Summary **6-12**

Discussion Questions **6-13**

Appendix: The Behavior of Components of ROE **6-15**

7 Prospective Analysis: Valuation Theory and Concepts **7-1**

Defining Value for Shareholders **7-2**

The Discounted Abnormal Earnings Valuation Method **7-3**

Valuation Using Price Multiples **7-5**

Shortcut Forms of Earnings-Based Valuation **7-10**

The Discounted Cash Flow Model **7-12**

Comparing Valuation Methods **7-14**

Summary **7-16**

Discussion Questions **7-17**

Appendix: Reconciling the Discounted Dividends and Discounted Abnormal Earnings Models **7-20**

8 Prospective Analysis: Valuation Implementation **8-1**

Detailed Forecasts of Performance **8-1**

Computing a Discount Rate **8-2**

Terminal Values **8-7**

Computing Estimated Values **8-11**

Summary **8-16**

Discussion Questions **8-16**

Part 3 BUSINESS ANALYSIS AND VALUATION APPLICATIONS

9 Equity Security Analysis — 9-1

Investor Objectives — 9-1
Equity Security Analysis and Market Efficiency — 9-2
Approaches to Fund Management and Securities Analysis — 9-4
The Process of a Comprehensive Security Analysis — 9-6
Performance of Security Analysts and Fund Managers — 9-10
Summary — 9-12
Discussion Questions — 9-13

10 Credit Analysis and Distress Prediction — 10-1

The Market for Credit — 10-2
The Credit Analysis Process — 10-3
Financial Statement Analysis and Public Debt — 10-9
Prediction of Distress and Turnaround — 10-13
Summary — 10-15
Discussion Questions — 10-15

11 Mergers and Acquisitions — 11-1

Motivation for Merger or Acquisition — 11-1
Acquisition Pricing — 11-5
Acquisition Financing — 11-10
Acquisition Outcome — 11-14
Summary — 11-15
Discussion Questions — 11-16

12 Corporate Financing Policies — 12-1

Factors That Determine Firms' Debt Policies — 12-1
The Optimal Long-Term Mix of Debt and Equity — 12-2
The Financing of New Projects — 12-7
Factors That Determine Dividend Policies — 12-9
Summary — 12-13
Discussion Questions — 12-14

13 Communication and Governance — 13-1

Governance Overview — 13-2
Management Communication with Investors — 13-4
Communication Through Financial Reporting — 13-6
Other Forms of Communicating with Investors — 13-9

Auditor Analysis   13-12
Audit Committee Reviews   13-17
Summary   13-18
Discussion Questions   13-19

Index   I-1

Author Index   I-13

P A R T 1

Framework

Chapter 1

**A Framework for Business Analysis and
Valuation Using Financial Statements**

A Framework for Business Analysis and Valuation Using Financial Statements

This chapter outlines a comprehensive framework for financial statement analysis. Because financial statements provide the most widely available data on public corporations' economic activities, investors and other stakeholders rely on financial reports to assess the plans and performance of firms and corporate managers.

A variety of questions can be addressed by business analysis using financial statements, as shown in the following examples:

- A security analyst may be interested in asking: "How well is the firm I am following performing? Did the firm meet my performance expectations? If not, why not? What is the value of the firm's stock given my assessment of the firm's current and future performance?"
- A loan officer may need to ask: "What is the credit risk involved in lending a certain amount of money to this firm? How well is the firm managing its liquidity and solvency? What is the firm's business risk? What is the additional risk created by the firm's financing and dividend policies?"
- A management consultant might ask: "What is the structure of the industry in which the firm is operating? What are the strategies pursued by various players in the industry? What is the relative performance of different firms in the industry?"
- A corporate manager may ask: "Is my firm properly valued by investors? Is our investor communication program adequate to facilitate this process?"
- A corporate manager could ask: "Is this firm a potential takeover target? How much value can be added if we acquire this firm? How can we finance the acquisition?"
- An independent auditor would want to ask: "Are the accounting policies and accrual estimates in this company's financial statements consistent with my understanding of this business and its recent performance? Do these financial reports communicate the current status and significant risks of the business?"

In the twentieth century, we have seen two distinct models for channeling savings into business investments. Communist and socialist market economies have used central planning and government agencies to pool national savings and to direct investments in business enterprises. The failure of this model is evident from the fact that most of these economies have abandoned it in favor of the second model—the market model. In almost all countries in the world today, capital markets play an important role in channeling financial resources from savers to business enterprises that need capital.

Financial statement analysis is a valuable activity when managers have complete information on a firm's strategies and a variety of institutional factors make it unlikely that they fully disclose this information. In this setting outside analysts attempt to create "inside information" from analyzing financial statement data, thereby gaining valuable insights about the firm's current performance and future prospects.

To understand the contribution that financial statement analysis can make, it is important to understand the role of financial reporting in the functioning of capital markets and the institutional forces that shape financial statements. Therefore we present first a brief description of these forces; then we discuss the steps that an analyst must perform to extract information from financial statements and provide valuable forecasts.

THE ROLE OF FINANCIAL REPORTING IN CAPITAL MARKETS

A critical challenge for any economy is the allocation of savings to investment opportunities. Economies that do this well can exploit new business ideas to spur innovation and create jobs and wealth at a rapid pace. In contrast, economies that manage this process poorly dissipate their wealth and fail to support business opportunities.

Figure 1-1 provides a schematic representation of how capital markets typically work. Savings in any economy are widely distributed among households. There are usually many new entrepreneurs and existing companies that would like to attract these savings to fund their business ideas. While both savers and entrepreneurs would like to do business with each other, matching savings to business investment opportunities is complicated for at least two reasons. First, entrepreneurs typically have better information than savers on the value of business investment opportunities. Second, communication by entrepreneurs to investors is not completely credible because investors know entrepreneurs have an incentive to inflate the value of their ideas.

These information and incentive problems lead to what economists call the "lemons" problem, which can potentially break down the functioning of the capital market.[1] It works like this. Consider a situation where half the business ideas are "good" and the other half are "bad." If investors cannot distinguish between the two types of business ideas, entrepreneurs with "bad" ideas will try to claim that their ideas are as valuable as the "good" ideas. Realizing this possibility, investors value both good and bad ideas at an average level. Unfortunately, this penalizes good ideas, and entrepreneurs with good ideas find the terms on which they can get financing to be unattractive. As these entrepreneurs leave the capital market, the proportion of bad ideas in the market increases. Over time, bad ideas "crowd out" good ideas, and investors lose confidence in this market.

Figure 1-1	Capital Markets

The emergence of intermediaries can prevent such a market breakdown. Intermediaries are like a car mechanic who provides an independent certification of a used car's quality to help a buyer and seller agree on a price. There are two types of intermediaries in the capital markets. Financial intermediaries, such as venture capital firms, banks, mutual funds, and insurance companies, focus on aggregating funds from individual investors and analyzing different investment alternatives to make investment decisions. Information intermediaries, such as auditors, financial analysts, bond-rating agencies, and the financial press, focus on providing information to investors (and to financial intermediaries who represent them) on the quality of various business investment opportunities. Both these types of intermediaries add value by helping investors distinguish "good" investment opportunities from the "bad" ones.

Financial reporting plays a critical role in the functioning of both the information intermediaries and financial intermediaries. Information intermediaries add value by either enhancing the credibility of financial reports (as auditors do), or by analyzing the information in the financial statements (as analysts and the rating agencies do). Financial intermediaries rely on the information in the financial statements to analyze investment opportunities, and supplement this information with other sources of information. In the following section, we discuss key aspects of the financial reporting system design that enable it to play effectively this vital role in the functioning of the capital markets.

FROM BUSINESS ACTIVITIES TO FINANCIAL STATEMENTS

Corporate managers are responsible for acquiring physical and financial resources from the firm's environment and using them to create value for the firm's investors. Value is created when the firm earns a return on its investment in excess of the cost of capital. Managers formulate business strategies to achieve this goal, and they implement them through business activities. A firm's business activities are influenced by its economic environment and its own business strategy. The economic environment includes the firm's industry, its input and output markets, and the regulations under which the firm operates. The firm's business strategy determines how the firm positions itself in its environment to achieve a competitive advantage.

As shown in Figure 1-2, a firm's financial statements summarize the economic consequences of its business activities. The firm's business activities in any time period are too numerous to be reported individually to outsiders. Further, some of the activities undertaken by the firm are proprietary in nature, and disclosing these activities in detail could be a detriment to the firm's competitive position. The firm's accounting system provides a mechanism through which business activities are selected, measured, and aggregated into financial statement data.

Intermediaries using financial statement data to do business analysis have to be aware that financial reports are influenced both by the firm's business activities and by its accounting system. A key aspect of financial statement analysis, therefore, involves understanding the influence of the accounting system on the quality of the financial statement data being used in the analysis. The institutional features of accounting systems discussed below determine the extent of that influence.

Accounting System Feature 1: Accrual Accounting

One of the fundamental features of corporate financial reports is that they are prepared using accrual rather than cash accounting. Unlike cash accounting, accrual accounting distinguishes between the recording of costs and benefits associated with economic activities and the actual payment and receipt of cash. Net income is the primary periodic performance

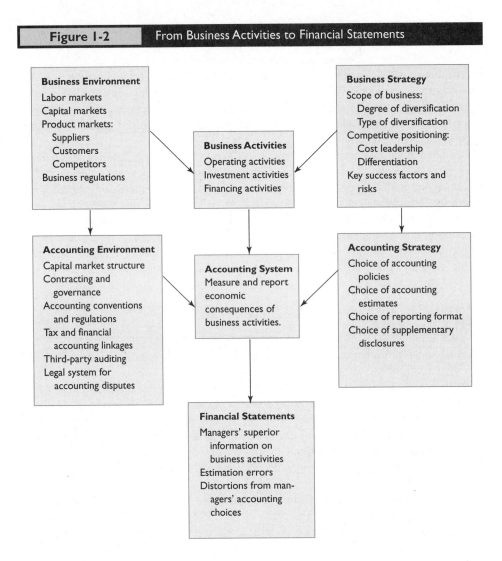

Figure I-2 From Business Activities to Financial Statements

index under accrual accounting. To compute net income, the effects of economic transactions are recorded on the basis of *expected,* not necessarily *actual,* cash receipts and payments. Expected cash receipts from the delivery of products or services are recognized as revenues, and expected cash outflows associated with these revenues are recognized as expenses.

The need for accrual accounting arises from investors' demand for financial reports on a periodic basis. Because firms undertake economic transactions on a continual basis, the arbitrary closing of accounting books at the end of a reporting period leads to a fundamental measurement problem. Since cash accounting does not report the full economic consequence of the transactions undertaken in a given period, accrual accounting is designed to provide more complete information on a firm's periodic performance.

Accounting System Feature 2: Accounting Standards and Auditing

The use of accrual accounting lies at the center of many important complexities in corporate financial reporting. Because accrual accounting deals with *expectations* of future cash consequences of current events, it is subjective and relies on a variety of assumptions. Who should be charged with the primary responsibility of making these assumptions? A firm's managers are entrusted with the task of making the appropriate estimates and assumptions to prepare the financial statements because they have intimate knowledge of their firm's business.

The accounting discretion granted to managers is potentially valuable because it allows them to reflect inside information in reported financial statements. However, since investors view profits as a measure of managers' performance, managers have incentives to use their accounting discretion to distort reported profits by making biased assumptions. Further, the use of accounting numbers in contracts between the firm and outsiders provides another motivation for management manipulation of accounting numbers. Income management distorts financial accounting data, making them less valuable to external users of financial statements. Therefore, the delegation of financial reporting decisions to corporate managers has both costs and benefits.

A number of accounting conventions have evolved to ensure that managers use their accounting flexibility to summarize their knowledge of the firm's business activities, and not to disguise reality for self-serving purposes. For example, the measurability and conservatism conventions are accounting responses to concerns about distortions from managers' potentially optimistic bias. Both these conventions attempt to limit managers' optimistic bias by imposing their own pessimistic bias.

Accounting standards, called Generally Accepted Accounting Principles (GAAP), promulgated by the Financial Accounting Standards Board (FASB) and similar standard-setting bodies in other countries, also limit potential distortions that managers can introduce into reported numbers. Uniform accounting standards attempt to reduce managers' ability to record similar economic transactions in dissimilar ways, either over time or across firms.

Increased uniformity from accounting standards, however, comes at the expense of reduced flexibility for managers to reflect genuine business differences in their firm's financial statements. Rigid accounting standards work best for economic transactions whose accounting treatment is not predicated on managers' proprietary information. However, when there is significant business judgment involved in assessing a transaction's economic consequences, rigid standards which prevent managers from using their superior business knowledge would be dysfunctional. Further, if accounting standards are too rigid, they may induce managers to expend economic resources to restructure business transactions to achieve a desired accounting result.

Auditing, broadly defined as a verification of the integrity of the reported financial statements by someone other than the preparer, ensures that managers use accounting rules and conventions consistently over time, and that their accounting estimates are reasonable. Therefore auditing improves the quality of accounting data.

Third-party auditing may also reduce the quality of financial reporting because it constrains the kind of accounting rules and conventions that evolve over time. For example, the FASB considers the views of auditors in the standard-setting process. Auditors are likely to argue against accounting standards producing numbers that are difficult to audit, even if the proposed rules produce relevant information for investors.

The legal environment in which accounting disputes between managers, auditors, and investors are adjudicated can also have a significant effect on the quality of reported numbers. The threat of lawsuits and resulting penalties have the beneficial effect of improving the accuracy of disclosure. However, the potential for a significant legal liability might also discourage managers and auditors from supporting accounting proposals requiring risky forecasts, such as forward-looking disclosures.

Accounting System Feature 3: Managers' Reporting Strategy

Because the mechanisms that limit managers' ability to distort accounting data add noise, it is not optimal to use accounting regulation to eliminate managerial flexibility completely. Therefore real-world accounting systems leave considerable room for managers to influence financial statement data. A firm's reporting strategy, that is, the manner in which managers use their accounting discretion, has an important influence on the firm's financial statements.

Corporate managers can choose accounting and disclosure policies that make it more or less difficult for external users of financial reports to understand the true economic picture of their businesses. Accounting rules often provide a broad set of alternatives from which managers can choose. Further, managers are entrusted with making a range of estimates in implementing these accounting policies. Accounting regulations usually prescribe *minimum* disclosure requirements, but they do not restrict managers from *voluntarily* providing additional disclosures.

A superior disclosure strategy will enable managers to communicate the underlying business reality to outside investors. One important constraint on a firm's disclosure strategy is the competitive dynamics in product markets. Disclosure of proprietary information about business strategies and their expected economic consequences may hurt the firm's competitive position. Subject to this constraint, managers can use financial statements to provide information useful to investors in assessing their firm's true economic performance.

Managers can also use financial reporting strategies to manipulate investors' perceptions. Using the discretion granted to them, managers can make it difficult for investors to identify poor performance on a timely basis. For example, managers can choose accounting policies and estimates to provide an optimistic assessment of the firm's true performance. They can also make it costly for investors to understand the true performance by controlling the extent of information that is disclosed voluntarily.

The extent to which financial statements are informative about the underlying business reality varies across firms and across time for a given firm. This variation in accounting quality provides both an important opportunity and a challenge in doing business analysis. The process through which analysts can separate noise from information in financial statements, and gain valuable business insights from financial statement analysis, is discussed next.

FROM FINANCIAL STATEMENTS TO BUSINESS ANALYSIS

Because managers' insider knowledge is a source both of value and distortion in accounting data, it is difficult for outside users of financial statements to separate true information from distortion and noise. Not being able to undo accounting distortions completely, investors "discount" a firm's reported accounting performance. In doing so, they make a probabilistic assessment of the extent to which a firm's reported numbers reflect economic reality. As a result, investors can have only an imprecise assessment of an individual firm's performance. Financial and information intermediaries can add value by improving investors' understanding of a firm's current performance and its future prospects.

Effective financial statement analysis is valuable because it attempts to get at managers' inside information from public financial statement data. Because intermediaries do not have direct or complete access to this information, they rely on their knowledge of the firm's industry and its competitive strategies to interpret financial statements. Successful intermediaries have at least as good an understanding of the industry economics as do the firm's managers as well as a reasonably good understanding of the firm's competitive strategy. Although outside analysts have an information disadvantage relative to the firm's managers, they are more objective in evaluating the economic consequences of the firm's investment and operating decisions. Figure 1-3 provides a schematic overview of how business intermediaries use financial statements to accomplish four key steps: (1) business strategy analysis, (2) accounting analysis, (3) financial analysis, and (4) prospective analysis.

Analysis Step 1: Business Strategy Analysis

The purpose of business strategy analysis is to identify key profit drivers and business risks, and to assess the company's profit potential at a qualitative level. Business strategy analysis involves analyzing a firm's industry and its strategy to create a sustainable competitive advantage. This qualitative analysis is an essential first step because it enables the analyst to frame the subsequent accounting and financial analysis better. For example, identifying the key success factors and key business risks allows the identification of key accounting policies. Assessment of a firm's competitive strategy facilitates evaluating whether current profitability is sustainable. Finally, business analysis enables the analyst to make sound assumptions in forecasting a firm's future performance.

Figure 1-3	Analysis Using Financial Statements

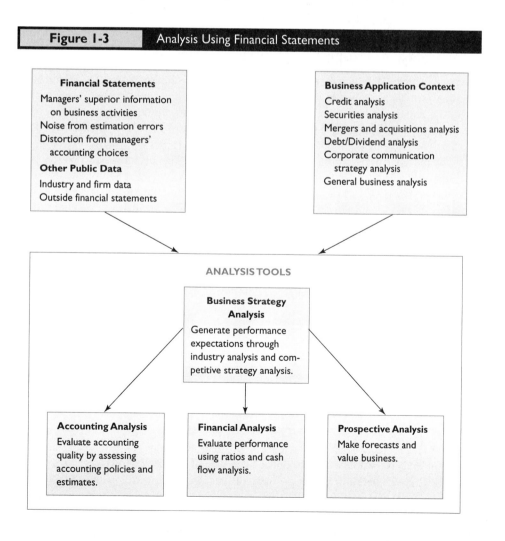

Financial Statements

Managers' superior information on business activities
Noise from estimation errors
Distortion from managers' accounting choices

Other Public Data

Industry and firm data
Outside financial statements

Business Application Context

Credit analysis
Securities analysis
Mergers and acquisitions analysis
Debt/Dividend analysis
Corporate communication strategy analysis
General business analysis

ANALYSIS TOOLS

Business Strategy Analysis

Generate performance expectations through industry analysis and competitive strategy analysis.

Accounting Analysis

Evaluate accounting quality by assessing accounting policies and estimates.

Financial Analysis

Evaluate performance using ratios and cash flow analysis.

Prospective Analysis

Make forecasts and value business.

Analysis Step 2: Accounting Analysis

The purpose of accounting analysis is to evaluate the degree to which a firm's accounting captures the underlying business reality. By identifying places where there is accounting flexibility, and by evaluating the appropriateness of the firm's accounting policies and estimates, analysts can assess the degree of distortion in a firm's accounting numbers. Another important step in accounting analysis is to "undo" any accounting distortions by recasting a firm's accounting numbers to create unbiased accounting data. Sound accounting analysis improves the reliability of conclusions from financial analysis, the next step in financial statement analysis.

Analysis Step 3: Financial Analysis

The goal of financial analysis is to use financial data to evaluate the current and past performance of a firm and to assess its sustainability. There are two important skills related to financial analysis. First, the analysis should be systematic and efficient. Second, the analysis should allow the analyst to use financial data to explore business issues. Ratio analysis and cash flow analysis are the two most commonly used financial tools. Ratio analysis focuses on evaluating a firm's product market performance and financial policies; cash flow analysis focuses on a firm's liquidity and financial flexibility.

Analysis Step 4: Prospective Analysis

Prospective analysis, which focuses on forecasting a firm's future, is the final step in business analysis. Two commonly used techniques in prospective analysis are financial statement forecasting and valuation. Both these tools allow the synthesis of the insights from business analysis, accounting analysis, and financial analysis in order to make predictions about a firm's future.

While the value of a firm is a function of its future cash flow performance, it is also possible to assess a firm's value based on the firm's current book value of equity, and its future return on equity (ROE) and growth. Strategy analysis, accounting analysis, and financial analysis, the first three steps in the framework discussed here, provide an excellent foundation for estimating a firm's intrinsic value. Strategy analysis, in addition to enabling sound accounting and financial analysis, also helps in assessing potential changes in a firm's competitive advantage and their implications for the firm's future ROE and growth. Accounting analysis provides an unbiased estimate of a firm's current book value and ROE. Financial analysis allows you to gain an in-depth understanding of what drives the firm's current ROE.

The predictions from a sound business analysis are useful to a variety of parties and can be applied in various contexts. The exact nature of the analysis will depend on the context. The contexts that we will examine include securities analysis, credit evaluation, mergers and acquisitions, evaluation of debt and dividend policies, and assessing corporate communication strategies. The four analytical steps described above are useful in each of these contexts. Appropriate use of these tools, however, requires a familiarity with the economic theories and institutional factors relevant to the context.

There are several ways in which financial statement analysis can add value, even when capital markets are reasonably efficient. First, there are many applications of financial statement analysis whose focus is outside the capital market context—credit analysis, competitive benchmarking, analysis of mergers and acquisitions, to name a few. Second, markets become efficient precisely because some market participants rely on analytical tools such as the ones we discuss in this book to analyze information and make investment decisions.

SUMMARY

Financial statements provide the most widely available data on public corporations' economic activities; investors and other stakeholders rely on them to assess the plans and performance of firms and corporate managers. Accrual accounting data in financial statements are noisy, and unsophisticated investors can assess firms' performance only imprecisely. Financial analysts who understand managers' disclosure strategies have an opportunity to create inside information from public data, and they play a valuable role in enabling outside parties to evaluate a firm's current and prospective performance.

This chapter has outlined the framework for business analysis with financial statements, using the four key steps: business strategy analysis, accounting analysis, financial analysis, and prospective analysis. The remaining chapters in this book describe these steps in greater detail and discuss how they can be used in a variety of business contexts.

DISCUSSION QUESTIONS

1. John, who has just completed his first finance course, is unsure whether he should take a course in business analysis and valuation using financial statements since he believes that financial analysis adds little value, given the efficiency of capital markets. Explain to John when financial analysis can add value, even if capital markets are efficient.

2. Accounting statements rarely report financial performance without error. List three types of errors that can arise in financial reporting.

3. Joe Smith argues that "learning how to do business analysis and valuation using financial statements is not very useful, unless you are interested in becoming a financial analyst." Comment.

4. Four steps for business analysis are discussed in the chapter (strategy analysis, accounting analysis, financial analysis, and prospective analysis). As a financial analyst, explain why each of these steps is a critical part of your job and how they relate to one another.

NOTE

1. G. Akerlof, "The Market for 'Lemons': Quality Uncertainty and the Market Mechanism," *Quarterly Journal of Economics* (August 1970): 488–500.

P A R T 2

Business Analysis and Valuation Tools

Chapter 2

Strategy Analysis

Chapter 3

Overview of Accounting Analysis

Chapter 4

Implementing Accounting Analysis

Chapter 5

Financial Analysis

Chapter 6

Prospective Analysis: Forecasting

Chapter 7

Prospective Analysis: Valuation Theory and Concepts

Chapter 8

Prospective Analysis: Valuation Implementation

Strategy Analysis

Strategy analysis is an important starting point for the analysis of financial statements. Strategy analysis allows the analyst to probe the economics of a firm at a qualitative level so that the subsequent accounting and financial analysis is grounded in business reality. Strategy analysis also allows the identification of the firm's profit drivers and key risks. This in turn enables the analyst to assess the sustainability of the firm's current performance and make realistic forecasts of future performance.

A firm's value is determined by its ability to earn a return on its capital in excess of the cost of capital. What determines whether or not a firm is able to accomplish this goal? While a firm's cost of capital is determined by the capital markets, its profit potential is determined by its own strategic choices: (1) the choice of an industry or a set of industries in which the firm operates (industry choice), (2) the manner in which the firm intends to compete with other firms in its chosen industry or industries (competitive positioning), and (3) the way in which the firm expects to create and exploit synergies across the range of businesses in which it operates (corporate strategy). Strategy analysis, therefore, involves industry analysis, competitive strategy analysis, and corporate strategy analysis.[1] In this chapter, we will briefly discuss these three steps and use the personal computer industry and Amazon.com, respectively, to illustrate the application of the steps.

INDUSTRY ANALYSIS

In analyzing a firm's profit potential, an analyst has to first assess the profit potential of each of the industries in which the firm is competing because the profitability of various industries differs systematically and predictably over time. For example, the ratio of earnings before interest and taxes to the book value of assets for all U.S. companies between 1981 and 1997 was 8.8 percent. However, the average returns varied widely across specific industries: for the bakery products industry, the profitability ratio was 43 percentage points greater than the population average, and for the silver ore mining industry it was 23 percentage points less than the population average.[2] What causes these profitability differences?

There is a vast body of research in industrial organization on the influence of industry structure on profitability.[3] Relying on this research, strategy literature suggests that the average profitability of an industry is influenced by the "five forces" shown in Figure 2-1.[4] According to this framework, the intensity of competition determines the potential for creating abnormal profits by the firms in an industry. Whether or not the potential profits are kept by the industry is determined by the relative bargaining power of the firms in the industry and their customers and suppliers. We will discuss each of these industry profit drivers in more detail below.

Degree of Actual and Potential Competition

At the most basic level, the profits in an industry are a function of the maximum price that customers are willing to pay for the industry's product or service. One of the key determinants of the price is the degree to which there is competition among suppliers of the same or similar products. At one extreme, if there is a state of perfect competition in the industry, micro-economic theory predicts that prices will be equal to marginal cost, and there will be

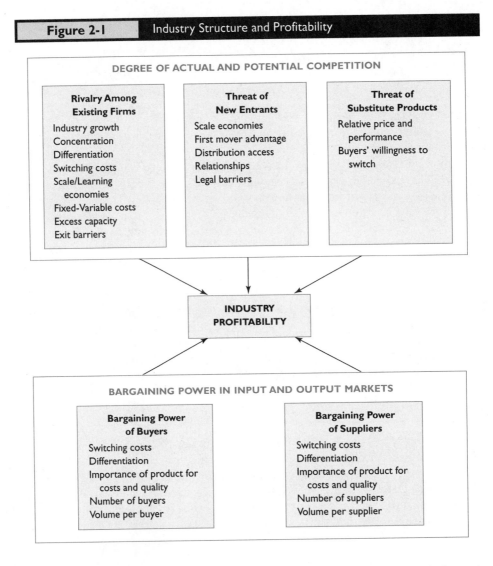

Figure 2-1   Industry Structure and Profitability

DEGREE OF ACTUAL AND POTENTIAL COMPETITION

Rivalry Among Existing Firms

Industry growth
Concentration
Differentiation
Switching costs
Scale/Learning economies
Fixed-Variable costs
Excess capacity
Exit barriers

Threat of New Entrants

Scale economies
First mover advantage
Distribution access
Relationships
Legal barriers

Threat of Substitute Products

Relative price and performance
Buyers' willingness to switch

INDUSTRY PROFITABILITY

BARGAINING POWER IN INPUT AND OUTPUT MARKETS

Bargaining Power of Buyers

Switching costs
Differentiation
Importance of product for costs and quality
Number of buyers
Volume per buyer

Bargaining Power of Suppliers

Switching costs
Differentiation
Importance of product for costs and quality
Number of suppliers
Volume per supplier

few opportunities to earn supernormal profits. At the other extreme, if the industry is dominated by a single firm, there will be potential to earn monopoly profits. In reality, the degree of competition in most industries is somewhere in between perfect competition and monopoly.

There are three potential sources of competition in an industry: (1) rivalry between existing firms, (2) threat of entry of new firms, and (3) threat of substitute products or services. We will discuss each of these competitive forces in the following paragraphs.

Competitive Force 1: Rivalry Among Existing Firms

In most industries the average level of profitability is primarily influenced by the nature of rivalry among existing firms in the industry. In some industries firms compete aggressively, pushing prices close to (and sometimes below) the marginal cost. In other industries firms do not compete aggressively on price. Instead, they find ways to coordinate their pricing, or compete on nonprice dimensions such as innovation or brand image. Several factors determine the intensity of competition between existing players in an industry:

Industry Growth Rate   If an industry is growing very rapidly, incumbent firms need not grab market share from each other to grow. In contrast, in stagnant industries the only way existing firms can grow is by taking share away from the other players. In this situation one can expect price wars among firms in the industry.

Concentration and Balance of Competitors   The number of firms in an industry and their relative sizes determine the degree of concentration in an industry.[5] The degree of concentration influences the extent to which firms in an industry can coordinate their pricing and other competitive moves. For example, if there is one dominant firm in an industry (such as IBM in the mainframe computer industry in the 1970s), it can set and enforce the rules of competition. Similarly, if there are only two or three equal-sized players (such as Coke and Pepsi in the U.S. soft-drink industry), they can implicitly cooperate with each other to avoid destructive price competition. If an industry is fragmented, price competition is likely to be severe.

Degree of Differentiation and Switching Costs   The extent to which firms in an industry can avoid head-on competition depends on the extent to which they can differentiate their products and services. If the products in an industry are very similar, customers are ready to switch from one competitor to another purely on the basis of price. Switching costs also determine customers' propensity to move from one product to another. When switching costs are low, there is a greater incentive for firms in an industry to engage in price competition.

Scale/Learning Economies and the Ratio of Fixed to Variable Costs   If there is a steep learning curve or there are other types of scale economies in an industry, size becomes an important factor for firms in the industry. In such situations, there are incentives to engage in aggressive competition for market share. Similarly, if the ratio of fixed to variable costs is high, firms have an incentive to reduce prices to utilize installed capacity. The airline industry, where price wars are quite common, is an example of this type of situation.

Excess Capacity and Exit Barriers   If capacity in an industry is larger than customer demand, there is a strong incentive for firms to cut prices to fill capacity. The problem of excess capacity is likely to be exacerbated if there are significant barriers for firms to exit the industry. Exit barriers are high when the assets are specialized or if there are regulations which make exit costly.

Competitive Force 2: Threat of New Entrants

The potential for earning abnormal profits will attract new entrants to an industry. The very threat of new firms entering an industry potentially constrains the pricing of existing firms within it. Therefore the ease with which new firms can enter an industry is a key determinant of its profitability. Several factors determine the height of barriers to entry in an industry:

Economies of Scale   When there are large economies of scale, new entrants face the choice of having either to invest in a large capacity which might not be utilized right away or to enter with less than the optimum capacity. Either way, new entrants will at least initially suffer from a cost disadvantage in competing with existing firms. Economies of scale might arise from large investments in research and development (the pharmaceutical or jet engine industries), in brand advertising (soft-drink industry), or in physical plant and equipment (telecommunications industry).

First Mover Advantage   Early entrants in an industry may deter future entrants if there are first mover advantages. For example, first movers might be able to set industry standards, or enter into exclusive arrangements with suppliers of cheap raw materials. They may also acquire scarce government licenses to operate in regulated industries. Finally, if there are learning economies, early firms will have an absolute cost advantage over new entrants. First mover advantages are also likely to be large when there are significant switching costs for customers once they start using existing products. For example, switching costs faced by the users of Microsoft's DOS operating system make it difficult for software companies to market a new operating system.

Access to Channels of Distribution and Relationships Limited capacity in the existing distribution channels and high costs of developing new channels can act as powerful barriers to entry. For example, a new entrant into the domestic auto industry in the U.S. is likely to face formidable barriers because of the difficulty of developing a dealer network. Similarly, new consumer goods manufacturers find it difficult to obtain supermarket shelf space for their products. Existing relationships between firms and customers in an industry also make it difficult for new firms to enter an industry. Industry examples of this include auditing, investment banking, and advertising.

Legal Barriers There are many industries in which legal barriers such as patents and copyrights in research-intensive industries limit entry. Similarly, licensing regulations limit entry into taxi services, medical services, broadcasting, and telecommunications industries.

Competitive Force 3: Threat of Substitute Products

The third dimension of competition in an industry is the threat of substitute products or services. Relevant substitutes are not necessarily those that have the same form as the existing products but those that perform the same function. For example, airlines and car rental services might be substitutes for each other when it comes to travel over short distances. Similarly, plastic bottles and metal cans substitute for each other as packaging in the beverage industry. In some cases, threat of substitution comes not from customers' switching to another product but from utilizing technologies that allow them to do without, or use less of, the existing products. For example, energy-conserving technologies allow customers to reduce their consumption of electricity and fossil fuels.

   The threat of substitutes depends on the relative price and performance of the competing products or services and on customers' willingness to substitute. Customers' perception of whether two products are substitutes depends to some extent on whether they perform the same function for a similar price. If two products perform an identical function, then it would be difficult for them to differ from each other in price. However, customers' willingness to switch is often the critical factor in making this competitive dynamic work. For example, even when tap water and bottled water serve the same function, many customers may be unwilling to substitute the former for the latter, enabling bottlers to charge a price premium. Similarly, designer label clothing commands a price premium even if it is not superior in terms of basic functionality because customers place a value on the image offered by designer labels.

While the degree of competition in an industry determines whether there is *potential* to earn abnormal profits, the *actual profits* are influenced by the industry's bargaining power with its suppliers and customers. On the input side, firms enter into transactions with suppliers of labor, raw materials and components, and finances. On the output side, firms either sell directly to the final customers or enter into contracts with intermediaries in the distribution chain. In all these transactions, the relative economic power of the two sides is important to the overall profitability of the industry firms.

Competitive Force 4: Bargaining Power of Buyers

Two factors determine the power of buyers: price sensitivity and relative bargaining power. Price sensitivity determines the extent to which buyers care to bargain on price; relative bargaining power determines the extent to which they will succeed in forcing the price down.[6]

Price Sensitivity Buyers are more price sensitive when the product is undifferentiated and there are few switching costs. The sensitivity of buyers to price also depends on the importance of the product to their own cost structure. When the product represents a large fraction of the buyers' cost (for example, the packaging material for soft-drink producers), the buyer is likely to expend the resources necessary to shop for a lower cost alternative. In contrast, if the product is a small fraction of the buyers' cost (for example, windshield wipers for automobile manufacturers), it may not pay to expend resources to search for lower-cost alternatives. Further, the importance of the product to the buyers' own product quality also determines whether or not price becomes the most important determinant of the buying decision.

Relative Bargaining Power Even if buyers are price sensitive, they may not be able to achieve low prices unless they have a strong bargaining position. Relative bargaining power in a transaction depends, ultimately, on the cost to each party of not doing business with the other party. The buyers' bargaining power is determined by the number of buyers relative to the number of suppliers, volume of purchases by a single buyer, number of alternative products available to the buyer, buyers' costs of switching from one product to another, and the threat of backward integration by the buyers. For example, in the automobile industry, car manufacturers have considerable power over component manufacturers because auto companies are large buyers with several alternative suppliers to choose from, and switching costs are relatively low. In contrast, in the personal computer industry, computer makers have low bargaining power relative to the operating system software producers because of high switching costs.

Competitive Force 5: Bargaining Power of Suppliers

The analysis of the relative power of suppliers is a mirror image of the analysis of the buyer's power in an industry. Suppliers are powerful when there are only a few companies and few substitutes available to their customers. For example, in the soft-drink industry, Coke and Pepsi are very powerful relative to the bottlers. In contrast, metal can suppliers to the soft drink industry are not very powerful because of intense competition among can producers and the threat of substitution of cans by plastic bottles. Suppliers also have a lot of power over buyers when the suppliers' product or service is critical to buyers' business. For example, airline pilots have a strong bargaining power in the airline industry. Suppliers also tend to be powerful when they pose a credible threat of forward integration. For example, IBM is powerful relative to mainframe computer leasing companies because of its unique position as a mainframe supplier and its own presence in the computer leasing business.

APPLYING INDUSTRY ANALYSIS: THE PERSONAL COMPUTER INDUSTRY

Let us consider the above concepts of industry analysis in the context of the personal computer (PC) industry.[7] The industry began in 1981 when IBM announced its PC with Intel's microprocessor and Microsoft's DOS operating system. By now personal computers are ubiquitous—over 136 million units were shipped worldwide in 2002 alone. Despite the spectacular growth in the sales volume in this industry, however, it was characterized by low profitability. Even the largest companies in the industry, such as IBM, Compaq, Dell, and Apple, reported poor performance in the early 1990s and were forced to undergo internal restructuring. What accounted for this low profitability? What was the computer industry's future profit potential?

Competition in the Personal Computer Industry

The competition was very intense for a number of reasons:

- The industry was fragmented, with many firms producing virtually identical products. Even though the computer market became more concentrated in the 1990s, with the top five vendors controlling close to 60 percent of the market, competition was intense, leading to routine price cuts on a monthly basis.
- Component costs accounted for more than 60 percent of total hardware costs of a personal computer, and volume purchases of components reduced these costs. Therefore there was intense competition for market share among competing manufacturers.
- Products produced by different firms in the industry were virtually identical, and there were few opportunities to differentiate the products. While brand name and service were dimensions that customers valued in the early years of the industry, they became less important as PC buyers became more informed about the technology.
- Switching costs across different brands of personal computers were relatively low because a vast majority of the personal computers used Intel microprocessors and Microsoft Windows operating systems.
- Access to distribution was not a significant barrier, as demonstrated by Dell Computers, which distributed its computers by direct mail through the 1980s and introduced Internet-based sales in the mid-1990s. The advent of computer superstores like CompUSA also mitigated this constraint, since these stores were willing to carry several brands.
- Since virtually all the components needed to produce a personal computer were available for purchase, there were very few barriers to entering the industry. In fact, Michael Dell started Dell Computer Company in the early 1980s by assembling PCs in his University of Texas dormitory room.
- Apple's Macintosh computers offered competition as a substitute product. Workstations produced by Sun and other vendors were also potential substitutes at the higher end of the personal computer market.

The Power of Suppliers and Buyers

Suppliers and buyers had significant power over firms in the industry for these reasons:

- Key hardware and software components for personal computers were controlled by firms with virtual monopoly. Intel dominated the microprocessor production for the personal computer industry, and Microsoft controlled the operating system market with its DOS and Windows operating systems.
- Buyers gained more power during the ten years from 1983 to 1993. Corporate buyers, who represented a significant portion of the customer base, were highly price sensitive since the expenditure on PCs represented a significant cost to their operations. Further, as they became knowledgeable about personal computer technology, customers were less influenced by brand name in their purchase decision. Buyers increasingly viewed PCs as commodities and used price as the most important consideration in their buying decision.

As a result of the intense rivalry and low barriers to entry in the personal computer industry, there was severe price competition among different manufacturers. Further, there was tremendous pressure on firms to spend large sums of money to introduce new products rapidly, maintain high quality, and provide excellent customer support. Both these factors led to a low profit potential in the industry. The power of suppliers and buyers reduced the profit potential further. Thus, while the personal computer industry represented a technologically dynamic industry, its profit potential was poor.

There were few indications of change in the basic structure of the personal computer industry, and there was little likelihood of viable competition emerging to challenge the domination of Microsoft and Intel in the input markets. Attempts by industry leaders like IBM to create alternative proprietary technologies have not succeeded. As a result, the profitability of the PC industry may not improve significantly any time in the near future.

Limitations of Industry Analysis

A potential limitation of the industry analysis framework discussed in this chapter is the assumption that industries have clear boundaries. In reality, it is often not easy to clearly demarcate industry boundaries. For example, in analyzing Dell's industry, should one focus on the IBM-compatible personal computer industry or the personal computer industry as a whole? Should one include workstations in the industry definition? Should one consider only the domestic manufacturers of personal computers or also manufacturers abroad? Inappropriate industry definition will result in incomplete analysis and inaccurate forecasts.

COMPETITIVE STRATEGY ANALYSIS

The profitability of a firm is influenced not only by its industry structure but also by the strategic choices it makes in positioning itself in the industry. While there are many ways to characterize a firm's business strategy, as Figure 2-2 shows, there are two generic competitive strategies: (1) cost leadership and (2) differentiation.[8] Both these strategies can potentially allow a firm to build a sustainable competitive advantage. Strategy researchers have traditionally viewed cost leadership and differentiation as mutually exclusive strategies. Firms that straddle the two strategies are considered to be "stuck in the middle" and are expected to earn low profitability.[9] These firms run the risk of not being able to attract price conscious customers because their costs are too high; they are also unable to provide adequate differentiation to attract premium price customers.[10]

Sources of Competitive Advantage

Cost leadership enables a firm to supply the same product or service offered by its competitors at a lower cost. Differentiation strategy involves providing a product or service that is distinct in some important respect valued by the customer. As an example in retailing, Nordstrom has succeeded on the basis of differentiation by emphasizing exceptionally high customer service. In contrast, Filene's Basement stores is a discount retailer competing purely on a low-cost basis.

Competitive Strategy 1: Cost Leadership
Cost leadership is often the clearest way to achieve competitive advantage. In industries where the basic product or service is a commodity, cost leadership might be the only way to achieve superior performance. There are many ways to achieve cost leadership, including

Figure 2-2	Strategies for Creating Competitive Advantage

Cost Leadership

Supply same product or service at a lower cost.

Economies of scale and scope
Efficient production
Simpler product designs
Lower input costs
Low-cost distribution
Little research and development or
    brand advertising
Tight cost control system

Differentiation

Supply a unique product or service at a cost lower than the price premium customers will pay.

Superior product quality
Superior product variety
Superior customer service
More flexible delivery
Investment in brand image
Investment in research and
    development
Control system focus on creativity
    and innovation

Competitive Advantage

- Match between firm's core competencies and key success factors to execute strategy
- Match between firm's value chain and activities required to execute strategy
- Sustainability of competitive advantage

economies of scale and scope, economies of learning, efficient production, simpler product design, lower input costs, and efficient organizational processes. If a firm can achieve cost leadership, then it will be able to earn above-average profitability by merely charging the same price as its rivals. Conversely, a cost leader can force its competitors to cut prices and accept lower returns, or to exit the industry.

Firms that achieve cost leadership focus on tight cost controls. They make investments in efficient scale plants, focus on product designs that reduce manufacturing costs, minimize overhead costs, make little investment in risky research and development, and avoid serving marginal customers. They have organizational structures and control systems that focus on cost control.

Competitive Strategy 2: Differentiation

A firm following the differentiation strategy seeks to be unique in its industry along some dimension that is highly valued by customers. For differentiation to be successful, the firm has to accomplish three things. First, it needs to identify one or more attributes of a product or service that customers value. Second, it has to position itself to meet the chosen customer need in a unique manner. Finally, the firm has to achieve differentiation at a cost that is lower than the price the customer is willing to pay for the differentiated product or service.

Drivers of differentiation include providing superior intrinsic value via product quality, product variety, bundled services, or delivery timing. Differentiation can also be achieved by investing in signals of value such as brand image, product appearance, or reputation. Differentiated strategies require investments in research and development, engineering skills, and marketing capabilities. The organizational structures and control systems in firms with differentiation strategies need to foster creativity and innovation.

While successful firms choose between cost leadership and differentiation, they cannot completely ignore the dimension on which they are not primarily competing. Firms that target differentiation still need to focus on costs so that the differentiation can be achieved at an acceptable cost. Similarly, cost leaders cannot compete unless they achieve at least a minimum level on key dimensions on which competitors might differentiate, such as quality and service.

Achieving and Sustaining Competitive Advantage

The choice of competitive strategy does not automatically lead to the achievement of competitive advantage. To achieve competitive advantage, the firm has to have the capabilities needed to implement and sustain the chosen strategy. Both cost leadership and differentiation strategy require that the firm make the necessary commitments to acquire the core competencies needed, and structure its value chain in an appropriate way. Core competencies are the economic assets that the firm possesses, whereas the value chain is the set of activities that the firm performs to convert inputs into outputs. The uniqueness of a firm's core competencies and its value chain and the extent to which it is difficult for competitors to imitate them determines the sustainability of a firm's competitive advantage.[11]

To evaluate whether a firm is likely to achieve its intended competitive advantage, the analyst should ask the following questions:

- What are the key success factors and risks associated with the firm's chosen competitive strategy?
- Does the firm currently have the resources and capabilities to deal with the key success factors and risks?
- Has the firm made irreversible commitments to bridge the gap between its current capabilities and the requirements to achieve its competitive advantage?
- Has the firm structured its activities (such as research and development, design, manufacturing, marketing and distribution, and support activities) in a way that is consistent with its competitive strategy?
- Is the company's competitive advantage sustainable? Are there any barriers that make imitation of the firm's strategy difficult?
- Are there any potential changes in the firm's industry structure (such as new technologies, foreign competition, changes in regulation, changes in customer requirements) that might dissipate the firm's competitive advantage? Is the company flexible enough to address these changes?

Applying Competitive Strategy Analysis

Let us consider the concepts of competitive strategy analysis in the context of Dell Computer Corporation. In 1998 Round Rock, Texas-based Dell Computer was the fourth largest computer maker, behind IBM, Hewlett-Packard, and Compaq. The company, founded by Michael Dell in his University of Texas dorm room, started selling "IBM clone" personal computers in 1984. From the beginning Dell sold its machines directly to end users rather than through retail outlets, at a significantly lower price than its competitors.

After rapid growth and some management hiccups, Dell firmly established itself in the personal computer industry by following a low-cost strategy. For the fiscal year ending January 31, 2003, Dell achieved $35.4 billion in revenues and $2.12 billion in net income. Dell's growth rates over the previous three years were extraordinary. Dell's stellar performance made it one of the most profitable personal computer makers in a highly competitive industry. How did Dell achieve such performance?

Dell's superior performance was based on a low-cost competitive strategy that consisted of the following key elements:

- *Direct selling.* Dell sold most of its computers directly to its customers, thus saving on retail markups. As computer users become sophisticated, and as computers become standardized on the Windows-Intel platform, the value of distribution through retailers declines. Dell was the first company to capitalize on this trend. In 1996 Dell began selling computers through its Internet web site. By 2003 the company was generating a very significant amount of its sales through on-line orders.

- *Made-to-order manufacturing.* Dell developed a system of flexible manufacturing that allowed the company to assemble and ship computers very quickly, usually within five days of receiving an order. This allowed the company to avoid large inventories of parts and assembled computers. Low inventories allowed Dell to save on working capital costs; it also reduced costly write-offs of obsolete inventories, a significant risk in the fast-changing computer industry.

- *Third-party service.* Dell used two low-cost approaches to after-sales service: telephone-based service and third-party maintenance service. Dell had several hundred technical support representatives accessible to customers by phone any time of the day. Using a comprehensive electronic maintenance system, the service representatives could diagnose problems and help customers to resolve them in the vast majority of cases. In the rare instance where on-site maintenance was required, Dell used third-party maintenance contracts with office equipment companies such as Xerox. Through this service strategy, Dell was able to avoid investing in an expensive field service network without compromising on service quality.

- *Low accounts receivable.* Dell was able to reduce its accounts receivable days to an industry minimum by encouraging its customers to pay by credit card at the time of the purchase or through electronic payment immediately after the purchase.

- *Focused investment in R&D.* Dell recognized that most of the basic innovations in the personal computer industry were led by the component suppliers and software producers. For example, two key suppliers, Intel and Microsoft, invested billions of dollars in developing new generation processors and software, respectively. Dell's innovations were primarily in creating a low-cost, high velocity organization that can respond quickly to these changes. By focusing its R&D innovations, Dell was able to minimize these costs and get high return on its investments.

As a result of the above strategy, Dell achieved a significant cost advantage over its competitors in the personal computer industry. This advantage resulted in a consistent pattern of rapid growth, increasing market share, and very high profitability in an industry that is characterized by rapid technological changes, significant supplier and buyer power, and intense competition. Further, because the strategy involved activities that are highly interrelated and involved continuous organizational innovations, Dell's business model was difficult to replicate, making its competitive advantage sustainable. In fact, Dell's success inspired several of its competitors, including Compaq and IBM, to attempt to replicate parts of its strategy. However no competitor to date has been able to replicate Dell's business model. The extraordinarily high earnings and book value multiples at which Dell's stock has been trading in recent years is evidence that investors are betting that Dell's competitive advantage and its superior profit performance is likely to be sustained for the foreseeable future.

CORPORATE STRATEGY ANALYSIS

So far in this chapter we have focused on the strategies at the individual business level. While some companies focus on only one business, many companies operate in multiple businesses. For example, the average number of business segments operated by the top 500 U.S. companies in 1992 is eleven industries.[12] In recent years, there has been an attempt by U.S. companies to reduce the diversity of their operations and focus on a relatively few "core" businesses. However, multibusiness organizations continue to dominate the economic activity in most countries in the world.

When analyzing a multibusiness organization, an analyst has to not only evaluate the industries and strategies of the individual business units but also the economic consequences—either positive or negative—of managing all the different businesses under one corporate umbrella. For example, General Electric has been very successful in creating significant value by managing a highly diversified set of businesses ranging from aircraft engines to light bulbs, but Sears has not been very successful in managing retailing together with financial services.

Sources of Value Creation at the Corporate Level

Economists and strategy researchers have identified several factors that influence an organization's ability to create value through a broad corporate scope. Economic theory suggests that the optimal activity scope of a firm depends on the relative transaction cost of performing a set of activities inside the firm versus using the market mechanism.[13] Transaction cost economics implies that the multiproduct firm is an efficient choice of organizational form when coordination among independent, focused firms is costly due to market transaction costs.

Transaction costs can arise out of several sources. They may arise if the production process involves specialized assets such as human capital skills, proprietary technology, or other organizational know-how that is not easily available in the marketplace. Transaction costs also may arise from market imperfections such as information and incentive problems. If buyers and sellers cannot solve these problems through standard mechanisms such as enforceable contracts, it will be costly to conduct transactions through market mechanisms.

For example, as discussed in Chapter 1, public capital markets may not work well when there are significant information and incentive problems, making it difficult for entrepreneurs to raise capital from investors. Similarly, if buyers cannot ascertain the quality of products being sold because of lack of information, or cannot enforce warranties because of poor legal infrastructure, entrepreneurs will find it difficult to break into new markets. Finally, if employers cannot assess the quality of applicants for new positions, they will have to rely more on internal promotions rather than external recruiting to fill higher positions in an organization. Emerging economies often suffer from these types of transaction costs because of poorly developed intermediation infrastructure.[14] Even in many advanced economies, examples of high transaction costs can be found. For example, in many countries other than the U.S., the venture capital industry is not highly developed, making it costly for new businesses in high technology industries to attract financing. Even in the U.S., transaction costs may vary across economic sectors. For example, until recently electronic commerce was hampered by consumer concerns regarding the security of credit card information sent over the Internet.

Transactions inside an organization may be less costly than market-based transactions for several reasons. First, communication costs inside an organization are reduced because confidentiality can be protected and credibility can be assured through internal mechanisms. Second, the headquarters office can play a critical role in reducing costs of enforcing agreements between organizational subunits. Third, organizational subunits can share valuable nontradable assets (such as organizational skills, systems, and processes) or nondivisible assets (such as brand names, distribution channels, and reputation).

There are also forces that increase transaction costs inside organizations. Top management of an organization may lack the specialized information and skills necessary to manage businesses across several different industries. This lack of expertise reduces the possibility of actually realizing economies of scope, even when there is potential for such economies. This problem can be remedied by creating a decentralized organization, hiring specialist managers to run each business unit, and providing these managers with proper incentives. However, decentralization will also potentially decrease goal congruence among subunit managers, making it difficult to realize economies of scope.

Whether or not a multibusiness organization creates more value than a comparable collection of focused firms is, therefore, context dependent.[15] Analysts should ask the following questions to assess whether an organization's corporate strategy has the potential to create value:

- Are there significant imperfections in the product, labor, or financial markets in the industries (or countries) in which a company is operating? Is it likely that transaction costs in these markets are higher than the costs of similar activities inside a well managed organization?
- Does the organization have special resources such as brand names, proprietary know-how, access to scarce distribution channels, and special organizational processes that have the potential to create economies of scope?
- Is there a good fit between the company's specialized resources and the portfolio of businesses in which the company is operating?
- Does the company allocate decision rights between the headquarters office and the business units optimally to realize all the potential economies of scope?
- Does the company have internal measurement, information, and incentive systems to reduce agency costs and increase coordination across business units?

Empirical evidence suggests that creating value through a multibusiness corporate strategy is hard in practice. Several researchers have documented that diversified U.S. companies trade at a discount in the stock market relative to a comparable portfolio of focused companies.[16] Studies also show that acquisitions of one company by another, especially when the two are in unrelated businesses, often fail to create value for the acquiring companies.[17] Finally, there is considerable evidence that value is created when multibusiness companies increase corporate focus through divisional spinoffs and asset sales.[18]

There are several potential explanations for the above diversification discount. First, managers' decisions to diversify and expand are frequently driven by a desire to maximize the size of their organization rather than to maximize shareholder value. Second, diversified companies often suffer from incentive misalignment problems leading to suboptimal investment decisions and poor operating performance. Third, capital markets find it difficult to monitor and value multibusiness organizations because of inadequate disclosure about the performance of individual business segments.

In summary, while companies can theoretically create value through innovative corporate strategies, there are many ways in which this potential fails to get realized in practice. Therefore, it pays to be skeptical when evaluating companies' corporate strategies.

Applying Corporate Strategy Analysis

Let us apply the concepts of corporate strategy analysis to Amazon.com, a pioneer in electronic commerce. Amazon started operations as an online bookseller in 1995 and went public in 1997 with a market capitalization of $561 million dollars. The company grew rapidly and began to pose a serious threat to the dominance of leading chain store booksellers like Barnes & Noble. Investors rewarded Amazon by increasing its market capitalization to a remarkable $36 billion dollars by April 1999.

Flush with his success in online book selling, Jeff Bezos, the founder and chief executive officer of Amazon, moved the company into many other areas of electronic commerce. Amazon claimed that its brand, its loyal customer base, and its ability to execute electronic commerce were valuable assets that can be exploited in a number of other online business areas. Through a series of acquisitions beginning in 1998, Amazon expanded into online selling of CDs, videos, gifts, prescription drugs, pet supplies, and groceries. In April 1999 Amazon announced plans to diversify into the online auction business by acquiring LiveBid.com. Bezos explained, "We are not a book company. We're not a music company. We're not a video company. We're not an auctions company. We're a customer company."[19]

Amazon's rapid expansion attracted controversy among the investment community. Some analysts argued that Amazon could create value through its broad corporate focus for the following reasons:

- Amazon has established a valuable brand name on the Internet. Given that electronic commerce is a relatively new phenomenon, customers are likely to rely on well known brands to reduce the risk of a bad shopping experience. Amazon's expansion strategy is sensible because it exploits this valuable resource.
- Amazon has been able to acquire critical expertise in flawless execution of electronic retailing. This is a general competency that can be exploited in many areas of electronic retailing.
- Amazon has been able to create a tremendous amount of loyalty among its customers through superior marketing and execution. As a result, a very high proportion of Amazon's sales comes from repeat purchases by its customers. Amazon's strategy exploits this valuable customer base.

There were also some skeptics who believed that Amazon was expanding too rapidly and that its diversification beyond book retailing was likely to fail. These skeptics questioned the value of Amazon's brand name. They argued that traditional retailers such as Barnes & Noble, Wal-Mart, and CVS, who are boosting their online efforts, also have valuable brand names, execution capabilities, and customer loyalty. Therefore these companies are likely to offer formidable competition to Amazon's individual business lines. Amazon's critics also pointed out that expanding rapidly into so many different areas is likely to confuse customers, dilute Amazon's brand value, and increase the chance of poor execution. Commenting on the fact that Amazon is losing money in all of its businesses while it is expanding rapidly, *Barron's* business weekly stated, "Increasingly, Amazon's strategy is looking like the dim-bulb businessman who loses money on every sale but tries to make it up by making more sales."[20]

Investor concerns about Amazon's corporate strategy began to affect its share price, which dropped from a high of $221 dollars in April 1999 to $118 dollars by the end of May 1999. Still, at a total market capitalization of about $19 billion dollars, many investors are betting that Amazon's corporate strategy is likely to yield rich dividends in the future.

An interesting question to examine is whether there are systematic reasons to believe that a company such as Amazon can succeed in pursuing a wide focus because its business model—on-line selling—somehow allows it to manage this diversity in a fundamentally different manner than a traditional retailer would be able to. Amazon's change in stock market fortunes from year 2000 on suggests that investors were reassessing in this respect. In response, Amazon's management was also making a series of changes in its business to make the company more cost-efficient, even though in 2003 the company was still in a wide range of product lines.

SUMMARY

Strategy analysis is an important starting point for the analysis of financial statements because it allows the analyst to probe the economics of the firm at a qualitative level. Strategy analysis also allows the identification of the firm's profit drivers and key risks, enabling the analyst to assess the sustainability of the firm's performance and make realistic forecasts of future performance.

Whether a firm is able to earn a return on its capital in excess of its cost of capital is determined by its own strategic choices: (1) the choice of an industry or a set of industries in which the firm operates (industry choice), (2) the manner in which the firm intends to compete with other firms in its chosen industry or industries (competitive positioning), and (3) the way in which the firm expects to create and exploit synergies across the range of businesses in which it operates (corporate strategy). Strategy analysis involves analyzing all three choices.

Industry analysis consists of identifying the economic factors which drive the industry profitability. In general, an industry's average profit potential is influenced by the degree of rivalry among existing competitors, the ease with which new firms can enter the industry, the availability of substitute products, the power of buyers, and the power of suppliers. To perform industry analysis, the analyst has to assess the current strength of each of these forces in an industry and make forecasts of any likely future changes.

Competitive strategy analysis involves identifying the basis on which the firm intends to compete in its industry. In general, there are two potential strategies that could provide a firm with a competitive advantage: cost leadership and differentiation. Cost leadership involves offering at a lower cost the same product or service that other firms offer. Differentiation involves satisfying a chosen dimension of customer need better than the competition, at an incremental cost that is less than the price premium that customers are willing to pay. To perform strategy analysis, the analyst has to identify the firm's intended strategy, assess whether the firm possesses the competencies required to execute the strategy, and recognize the key risks that the firm has to guard against. The analyst also has to evaluate the sustainability of the firm's strategy.

Corporate strategy analysis involves examining whether a company is able to create value by being in multiple businesses at the same time. A well crafted corporate strategy reduces costs or increases revenues from running several businesses in one firm relative to the same businesses operating independently and transacting with each other in the marketplace. These cost savings or revenue increases come from specialized resources that the firm has to exploit synergies across these businesses. For these resources to be valuable, they must be nontradable, not easily imitated by competition, and nondivisible. Even when a firm has such resources, it can create value through a multibusiness organization only when it is managed so that the information and agency costs inside the organization are smaller than the market transaction costs.

The insights gained from strategy analysis can be useful in performing the remainder of the financial statement analysis. In accounting analysis the analyst can examine whether a firm's accounting policies and estimates are consistent with its stated strategy. For example, a firm's choice of functional currency in accounting for its international operations should be consistent with the level of integration between domestic and international operations that the business strategy calls for. Similarly, a firm that mainly sells housing to low-income customers should have higher than average bad debts expenses.

Strategy analysis is also useful in guiding financial analysis. For example, in a cross-sectional analysis the analyst should expect firms with cost leadership strategy to have lower gross margins and higher asset turnover than firms that follow differentiated strategies. In a time series analysis, the analyst should closely monitor any increases in expense ratios and asset turnover ratios for low-cost firms, and any decreases in investments critical to differentiation for firms that follow differentiation strategy.

Business strategy analysis also helps in prospective analysis and valuation. First, it allows the analyst to assess whether, and for how long, differences between the firm's performance and its industry (or industries) performance are likely to persist. Second, strategy analysis facilitates forecasting investment outlays the firm has to make to maintain its competitive advantage.

DISCUSSION QUESTIONS

1. Judith, an accounting major, states, "Strategy analysis seems to be an unnecessary detour in doing financial statement analysis. Why can't we just get straight to the accounting issues?" Explain to Judith why she might be wrong?

2. What are the critical drivers of industry profitability?

3. One of the fastest growing industries in the last twenty years is the memory chip industry, which supplies memory chips for personal computers and other electronic devices. Yet the average profitability for this industry has been very low. Using the industry analysis framework, list all the potential factors that might explain this apparent contradiction.

4. Rate the pharmaceutical and lumber industries as high, medium, or low on the following dimensions of industry structure:

	Pharmaceutical Industry	Lumber Industry
Rivalry		
Threat of new entrants		
Threat of substitute products		
Bargaining power of buyers		
Bargaining power of suppliers		

Given your ratings, which industry would you expect to earn the highest returns?

5. Joe Smith argues, "Your analysis of the five forces that affect industry profitability is incomplete. For example, in the banking industry, I can think of at least three other factors that are also important; namely, government regulation, demographic trends, and cultural factors." His classmate Jane Brown disagrees and says, "These three factors are important only to the extent that they influence one of the five forces." Explain how, if at all, the three factors discussed by Joe affect the five forces in the banking industry.

6. Coca-Cola and Pepsi are both very profitable soft drinks. Inputs for these products include sugar, bottles/cans, and soft drink syrup. Coca-Cola and Pepsi produce the syrup themselves and purchase the other inputs. They then enter into exclusive contracts with independent bottlers to produce their products. Use the five forces framework and your knowledge of the soft drink industry to explain how Coca-Cola and Pepsi are able to retain most of the profits in this industry.

7. In the early 1980s, United, Delta, and American Airlines each started frequent flier programs as a way to differentiate themselves in response to excess capacity in the industry. Many industry analysts, however, believe that this move had only mixed success. Use the competitive advantage concepts to explain why.

8. What are the ways that a firm can create barriers to entry to deter competition in its business? What factors determine whether these barriers are likely to be enduring?

9. Explain why you agree or disagree with each of the following statements:
   a. It's better to be a differentiator than a cost leader, since you can then charge premium prices.
   b. It's more profitable to be in a high technology than a low technology industry.
   c. The reason why industries with large investments have high barriers to entry is because it is costly to raise capital.

10. There are very few companies that are able to be both cost leaders and differentiators. Why? Can you think of a company that has been successful at both?

11. Many consultants are advising diversified companies in emerging markets such as India, Korea, Mexico, and Turkey to adopt corporate strategies proven to be of value in advanced economies like the U.S. and the U.K. What are the pros and cons of this advice?

NOTES

1. The discussion presented here is intended to provide a basic background in strategy analysis. For a more complete discussion of the strategy concepts, see, for example, *Contemporary Strategy Analysis* by Robert M. Grant (Cambridge, MA: Blackwell Publishers, 1991); *Economics of Strategy* by David Besanko, David Dranove, and Mark Shanley (New York: John Wiley & Sons, 1996); *Strategy and the Business Landscape* by Pankaj Ghemawat (Reading, MA: Addison Wesley Longman, 1999); and *Corporate Strategy: Resources and the Scope of the Firm* by David J. Collis and Cynthia Montgomery (Burr Ridge, IL: Irwin/McGraw-Hill, 1997).

2. These data are taken from "Do Competitors Perform Better When They Pursue Different Strategies?" by Anita M. McGahan, Harvard Business School, working paper, May 12, 1999.

3. For a summary of this research, see *Industrial Market Structure and Economic Performance*, second edition, by F. M. Scherer (Chicago: Rand McNally College Publishing Co., 1980).

4. See *Competitive Strategy* by Michael E. Porter (New York: The Free Press, 1980).

5. The four-firm concentration ratio is a commonly used measure of industry concentration; it refers to the market share of the four largest firms in an industry.

6. While the discussion here uses the buyer to connote industrial buyers, the same concepts also apply to buyers of consumer products. Throughout this chapter we use the terms buyers and customers interchangeably.

7. The data on Dell and the PC industry discussed here and elsewhere in this chapter is drawn from "Dell Computer Corporation" by Das Narayandas and V. Kasturi Rangan, Harvard Business School Publishing Division, Case 9-596-058, and "Dell Online" by V. Kasturi Rangan and Marie Bell, Harvard Business School Publishing Division, Case 9-598-116.

8. For a more detailed discussion of these two sources of competitive advantage, see Michael E. Porter, *Competitive Advantage: Creating and Sustaining Superior Performance* (New York: The Free Press, 1985).

9. Ibid.

10. In recent years one of the strategic challenges faced by corporations is having to deal with competitors who achieve differentiation with low cost. For example, Japanese auto manufacturers have successfully demonstrated that there is no necessary trade-off between quality and cost. Similarly, in recent years several highly successful retailers like Wal-Mart and Home Depot have been able to combine high quality, high service, and low prices. These examples suggest that combining low cost and differentiation strategies is possible when a firm introduces a significant technical or business innovation. However, such cost advantage and differentiation will be sustainable only if there are significant barriers to imitation by competitors.

11. See *Competing for the Future* by Gary Hammel and C. K. Prahalad (Boston: Harvard Business School Press, 1994) for a more detailed discussion of the concept of core competencies and their critical role in corporate strategy.

12. Cynthia Montgomery, "Corporate Diversification," *Journal of Economic Perspectives*, Summer 1994.

13. The following works are seminal to the transaction cost economics: "The Nature of the Firm" by Ronald Coase, *Economica* 4 (1937): 386–405; *Markets and Hierarchies: Analysis and Antitrust Implications* by Oliver Williamson (New York: The Free Press, 1975); "Toward an Economic Theory of the Multi-product Firm" by David Teece, *Journal of Economic Behavior and Organization* 3 (1982): 39–63.

14. For a more complete discussion of these issues, see "Building Institutional Infrastructure in Emerging Markets" by Krishna Palepu and Tarun Khanna, *Brown Journal of World Affairs*, Winter/ Spring 1998, and "Why Focused Strategies May Be Wrong for Emerging Markets," by Tarun Khanna and Krishna Palepu, *Harvard Business Review*, July/August 1997.

15. For an empirical study which illustrates this point, see "Is Group Affiliation Profitable in Emerging Markets? An Analysis of Diversified Indian Business Groups," by Tarun Khanna and Krishna Palepu, *Journal of Finance* (April 2000): 867–91.

16. See "Tobin's q, diversification, and firm performance" by Larry Lang and Rene Stulz, *Journal of Political Economy* 102 (1994): 1248–80, and "Diversification's Effect on Firm Value" by Phillip Berger and Eli Ofek, *Journal of Financial Economics* 37 (1994): 39–65.

17. See "Which Takeovers Are Profitable: Strategic or Financial?" by Paul Healy, Krishna Palepu, and Richard Ruback, *Sloan Management Review* 38 (Summer 1997): 45–57.

18. See "Effects of Recontracting on Shareholder Wealth: The Case of Voluntary Spinoffs" by Katherine Schipper and Abbie Smith, *Journal of Financial Economics* 12 (December 1983): 437–67; "Asset Sales, Firm Performance, and the Agency Costs of Managerial Discretion" by L. Lang, A. Poulsen, and R. Stulz, *Journal of Financial Economics* 37 (January 1995): 3–37.

19. "eBay vs. Amazon.com," *Business Week*, May 31, 1999.

20. "Amazon.Bomb" by Jacqueline Doherty, *Barron's*, May 31, 1999.

Overview of Accounting Analysis

The purpose of accounting analysis is to evaluate the degree to which a firm's accounting captures its underlying business reality.[1] By identifying places where there is accounting flexibility, and by evaluating the appropriateness of the firm's accounting policies and estimates, analysts can assess the degree of distortion in a firm's accounting numbers. Another important skill is adjusting a firm's accounting numbers using cash flow and footnote information to "undo" any accounting distortions. Sound accounting analysis improves the reliability of conclusions from financial analysis, the next step in financial statement analysis.

THE INSTITUTIONAL FRAMEWORK FOR FINANCIAL REPORTING

There is typically a separation between ownership and management in public corporations. Financial statements serve as the vehicle through which owners keep track of their firms' financial situation. On a periodic basis, firms typically produce three financial reports: (1) an income statement that describes the operating performance during a time period, (2) a balance sheet that states the firm's assets and how they are financed, and (3) a cash flow statement (or in some countries, a funds flow statement) that summarizes the cash (or fund) flows of the firm. These statements are accompanied by footnotes that provide additional details on the financial statement line items, as well as by management's narrative discussion of the firm's performance in the Management Discussion and Analysis section.

To evaluate effectively the quality of a firm's financial statement data, the analyst needs to first understand the basic features of financial reporting and the institutional framework that governs them, as discussed in the following sections.

Accrual Accounting

One of the fundamental features of corporate financial reports is that they are prepared using accrual rather than cash accounting. Unlike cash accounting, accrual accounting distinguishes between the recording of costs and benefits associated with economic activities and the actual payment and receipt of cash. Net income is the primary periodic performance index under accrual accounting. To compute net income, the effects of economic transactions are recorded on the basis of *expected,* not necessarily *actual,* cash receipts and payments. Expected cash receipts from the delivery of products or services are recognized as revenues, and expected cash outflows associated with these revenues are recognized as expenses.

While there are many rules and conventions that govern a firm's preparation of financial statements, there are only a few conceptual building blocks that form the foundation of accrual accounting. The following definitions are critical to the income statement, which summarizes a firm's revenues and expenses[2]:

- **Revenues** are economic resources earned during a time period. Revenue recognition is governed by the realization principle, which proposes that revenues should be recognized when (a) the firm has provided all, or substantially all, the goods or services to be delivered to the customer and (b) the customer has paid cash or is expected to pay cash with a reasonable degree of certainty.

- **Expenses** are economic resources used up in a time period. Expense recognition is governed by the matching and the conservatism principles. Under these principles, expenses are (a) costs directly associated with revenues recognized in the same period, or (b) costs associated with benefits that are consumed in this time period, or (c) resources whose future benefits are not reasonably certain.
- **Profit** is the difference between a firm's revenues and expenses in a time period.[3]

The following fundamental relationship is therefore reflected in a firm's income statement:

Profit = Revenues − Expenses

In contrast, the balance sheet is a summary at one point in time. The principles that define a firm's assets, liabilities, equities, revenues, and expenses are as follows:

- **Assets** are economic resources owned by a firm that are (a) likely to produce future economic benefits and (b) measurable with a reasonable degree of certainty.
- **Liabilities** are economic obligations of a firm arising from benefits received in the past that (a) are required to be met with a reasonable degree of certainty and (b) whose timing is reasonably well defined.
- **Equity** is the difference between a firm's assets and its liabilities.

The definitions of assets, liabilities, and equity lead to the fundamental relationship that governs a firm's balance sheet:

Assets = Liabilities + Equity

Delegation of Reporting to Management

While the basic definitions of the elements of a firm's financial statements are simple, their application in practice often involves complex judgments. For example, how should revenues be recognized when a firm sells land to customers and also provides customer financing? If revenue is recognized before cash is collected, how should potential defaults be estimated? Are the outlays associated with research and development activities, whose payoffs are uncertain, assets or expenses when incurred? Are contractual commitments under lease arrangements or post-retirement plans liabilities? If so, how should they be valued?

Because corporate managers have intimate knowledge of their firms' businesses, they are entrusted with the primary task of making the appropriate judgments in portraying myriad business transactions using the basic accrual accounting framework. The accounting discretion granted to managers is potentially valuable because it allows them to reflect inside information in reported financial statements. However, since investors view profits as a measure of managers' performance, managers have an incentive to use their accounting discretion to distort reported profits by making biased assumptions. Further, the use of accounting numbers in contracts between the firm and outsiders provides a motivation for management manipulation of accounting numbers.

Earnings management distorts financial accounting data, making them less valuable to external users of financial statements. Therefore, the delegation of financial reporting decisions to managers has both costs and benefits. Accounting rules and auditing are mechanisms designed to reduce the cost and preserve the benefit of delegating financial reporting to corporate managers. The legal system is used to adjudicate disputes between managers, auditors, and investors.

Generally Accepted Accounting Principles

Given that it is difficult for outside investors to determine whether managers have used accounting flexibility to signal their proprietary information or merely to disguise reality, a number of accounting conventions have evolved to mitigate the problem. For example, in most countries financial statements are prepared using the historical cost convention, where assets and liabilities are recorded at historical exchange prices rather than fair values, replacement values, or values in use. This reduces managers' ability to overstate the value of the assets that they have acquired or developed, or to understate the value of liabilities. Of course, historical cost also limits the information that is available to investors about the potential of the firm's assets, since exchange prices are usually different from fair values or values in use.

Accounting standards and rules also limit management's ability to misuse accounting judgment by regulating how particular types of transactions are recorded. For example, accounting standards for leases stipulate how firms are to record contractual arrangements to lease resources. Similarly, pension and other post-employment benefit standards describe how firms are to record commitments to provide pensions and other retirement benefits for employees.

In the United States, the Securities and Exchange Commission (SEC) has the legal authority to set accounting standards. The SEC typically relies on private sector accounting bodies to undertake this task. Since 1973 accounting standards in the United States have been set by the Financial Accounting Standards Board (FASB). There are similar private sector or public sector accounting standard-setting bodies in many other countries. In addition, the International Accounting Standards Committee (IASC) has been attempting to set worldwide accounting standards, though IASC's pronouncements are not legally binding in the United States as of now.

Uniform accounting standards attempt to reduce managers' ability to record similar economic transactions in dissimilar ways either over time or across firms. Thus they create a uniform accounting language and increase the credibility of financial statements by limiting a firm's ability to distort them. Increased uniformity from accounting standards, however, comes at the expense of reduced flexibility for managers to reflect genuine business differences in a firm's accounting decisions. Rigid accounting standards work best for economic transactions whose accounting treatment is not predicated on managers' proprietary information. However, when there is significant business judgment involved in assessing a transaction's economic consequences, rigid standards are likely to be dysfunctional because they prevent managers from using their superior business knowledge. Further, if accounting standards are too rigid, they may induce managers to expend economic resources to restructure business transactions to achieve a desired accounting result.

External Auditing

Broadly defined as a verification of the integrity of the reported financial statements by someone other than the preparer, external auditing ensures that managers use accounting rules and conventions consistently over time, and that their accounting estimates are reasonable. In the U.S., all listed companies are required to have their financial statements audited by an independent public accountant. The standards and procedures to be followed by independent auditors are set by the American Institute of Certified Public Accountants (AICPA). These standards are known as Generally Accepted Auditing Standards (GAAS). While auditors issue an opinion on published financial statements, it is important to remember that the primary responsibility for the statements still rests with corporate managers.

Auditing improves the quality and credibility of accounting data by limiting a firm's ability to distort financial statements to suit its own purposes. However, as recent audit failures at companies such as Enron and Worldcom show, auditing is imperfect. Audits cannot review all of a firm's transactions. They can also fail because of lapses in quality, or because of lapses in judgment by auditors who fail to challenge management for fear of losing future business.

Third-party auditing may also reduce the quality of financial reporting because it constrains the kind of accounting rules and conventions that evolve over time. For example, the FASB considers the views of auditors in the standard-setting process. Auditors are likely to argue against accounting standards that produce numbers which are difficult to audit, even if the proposed rules produce relevant information for investors.

Legal Liability

The legal environment in which accounting disputes between managers, auditors, and investors are adjudicated can also have a significant effect on the quality of reported numbers. The threat of lawsuits and resulting penalties have the beneficial effect of improving the accuracy of disclosure. However, the potential for significant legal liability might also discourage managers and auditors from supporting accounting proposals requiring risky forecasts, for example, forward-looking disclosures. The U.S. auditing community often expresses this type of concern.

FACTORS INFLUENCING ACCOUNTING QUALITY

Because the mechanisms that limit managers' ability to distort accounting data themselves add noise, it is not optimal to use accounting regulation to eliminate managerial flexibility completely. Therefore, real-world accounting systems leave considerable room for managers to influence financial statement data. The net result is that information in corporate financial reports is noisy and biased, even in the presence of accounting regulation and external auditing.[4] The objective of accounting analysis is to evaluate the degree to which a firm's accounting captures its underlying business reality and to "undo" any accounting distortions. When potential distortions are large, accounting analysis can add considerable value.[5]

There are three potential sources of noise and bias in accounting data: (1) that introduced by rigidity in accounting rules, (2) random forecast errors, and (3) systematic reporting choices made by corporate managers to achieve specific objectives. Each of these factors is discussed below.

Noise from Accounting Rules

Accounting rules introduce noise and bias because it is often difficult to restrict management discretion without reducing the information content of accounting data. For example, the Statement of Financial Accounting Standards No. 2 issued by the FASB requires firms to expense research outlays when they are incurred. Clearly, some research expenditures have future value while others do not. However, because SFAS 2 does not allow firms to distinguish between the two types of expenditures, it leads to a systematic distortion of reported accounting numbers. Broadly speaking, the degree of distortion introduced by accounting standards depends on how well uniform accounting standards capture the nature of a firm's transactions.

Forecast Errors

Another source of noise in accounting data arises from pure forecast error, because managers cannot predict future consequences of current transactions perfectly. For example, when a firm sells products on credit, accrual accounting requires managers to make a judgment about the probability of collecting payments from customers. If payments are deemed "reasonably certain," the firm treats the transactions as sales, creating accounts receivable on its balance sheet. Managers then make an estimate of the proportion of receivables that will not be collected. Because managers do not have perfect foresight, actual defaults are likely to be different from estimated customer defaults, leading to a forecast error. The extent of errors in managers' accounting forecasts depends on a variety of factors, including the complexity of the business transactions, the predictability of the firm's environment, and unforeseen economy-wide changes.

Managers' Accounting Choices

Corporate managers also introduce noise and bias into accounting data through their own accounting decisions. Managers have a variety of incentives to exercise their accounting discretion to achieve certain objectives[6]:

- *Accounting-based debt covenants.* Managers may make accounting decisions to meet certain contractual obligations in their debt covenants. For example, firms' lending agreements with banks and other debt holders require them to meet covenants related to interest coverage, working capital ratios, and net worth, all defined in terms of accounting numbers. Violation of these constraints may be costly because it allows lenders to demand immediate payment of their loans. Managers of firms close to violating debt covenants have an incentive to select accounting policies and estimates to reduce the probability of covenant violation. The debt covenant motivation for managers' accounting decisions has been analyzed by a number of accounting researchers.[7]
- *Management compensation.* Another motivation for managers' accounting choice comes from the fact that their compensation and job security are often tied to reported profits. For example, many top managers receive bonus compensation if they exceed certain prespecified profit targets. This provides motivation for managers to choose accounting policies and estimates to maximize their expected compensation.[8]
- *Corporate control contests.* In corporate control contests, including hostile takeovers and proxy fights, competing management groups attempt to win over the firm's shareholders. Accounting numbers are used extensively in debating managers' performance in these contests. Therefore, managers may make accounting decisions to influence investor perceptions in corporate control contests.[9]
- *Tax considerations.* Managers may also make reporting choices to trade off between financial reporting and tax considerations. For example, U.S. firms are required to use LIFO inventory accounting for shareholder reporting in order to use it for tax reporting. Under LIFO, when prices are rising, firms report lower profits, thereby reducing tax payments. Some firms may forgo the tax reduction in order to report higher profits in their financial statements.[10]
- *Regulatory considerations.* Since accounting numbers are used by regulators in a variety of contexts, managers of some firms may make accounting decisions to influence regulatory outcomes. Examples of regulatory situations where accounting numbers are used include antitrust actions, import tariffs to protect domestic industries, and tax policies.[11]
- *Capital market considerations.* Managers may make accounting decisions to influence the perceptions of capital markets. When there are information asymmetries

between managers and outsiders, this strategy may succeed in influencing investor perceptions, at least temporarily.[12]

- *Stakeholder considerations.* Managers may also make accounting decisions to influence the perception of important stakeholders in the firm. For example, since labor unions can use healthy profits as a basis for demanding wage increases, managers may make accounting decisions to decrease income when they are facing union contract negotiations. In countries like Germany, where labor unions are strong, these considerations appear to play an important role in firms' accounting policy. Other important stakeholders that firms may wish to influence through their financial reports include suppliers and customers.
- *Competitive considerations.* The dynamics of competition in an industry might also influence a firm's reporting choices. For example, a firm's segment disclosure decisions may be influenced by its concern that disaggregated disclosure may help competitors in their business decisions. Similarly, firms may not disclose data on their margins by product line for fear of giving away proprietary information. Finally, firms may discourage new entrants by making income-decreasing accounting choices.

In addition to accounting policy choices and estimates, the level of disclosure is also an important determinant of a firm's accounting quality. Corporate managers can choose disclosure policies that make it more or less costly for external users of financial reports to understand the true economic picture of their businesses. Accounting regulations usually prescribe minimum disclosure requirements, but they do not restrict managers from voluntarily providing additional disclosures. Managers can use various parts of the financial reports, including the Letter to the Shareholders, Management Discussion and Analysis, and footnotes, to describe the company's strategy, its accounting policies, and its current performance. There is wide variation across firms in how managers use their disclosure flexibility.[13]

STEPS IN DOING ACCOUNTING ANALYSIS

In this section we discuss a series of steps that an analyst can follow to evaluate a firm's accounting quality.

Step 1: Identify Key Accounting Policies

As discussed in the chapter on business strategy analysis, a firm's industry characteristics and its own competitive strategy determine its key success factors and risks. One of the goals of financial statement analysis is to evaluate how well these success factors and risks are being managed by the firm. In accounting analysis, therefore, the analyst should identify and evaluate the policies and the estimates the firm uses to measure its critical factors and risks.

Key success factors in the banking industry include interest and credit risk management; in the retail industry, inventory management is a key success factor; and for a manufacturer competing on product quality and innovation, research and development and product defects after the sale are key areas of concern. One of the key success factors in the leasing business is to make accurate forecasts of residual values of the leased equipment at the end of the lease terms. In each of these cases, the analyst has to identify the accounting measures the firm uses to capture these business constructs, the policies that determine how the measures are implemented, and the key estimates embedded in these policies. For example, the accounting measure a bank uses to capture credit risk is its loan loss reserves, and the accounting measure that captures product quality for a manufacturer is its warranty expenses and reserves. For a firm in the equipment leasing industry, one of the most important accounting policies is the way residual values are recorded. Residual values influence the company's reported profits and its asset base. If residual values are overestimated, the firm runs the risk of having to take large write-offs in the future.

Step 2: Assess Accounting Flexibility

Not all firms have equal flexibility in choosing their key accounting policies and estimates. Some firms' accounting choice is severely constrained by accounting standards and conventions. For example, even though research and development is a key success factor for biotechnology companies, managers have no accounting discretion in reporting on this activity. Similarly, even though marketing and brand building are key to the success of consumer goods firms, they are required to expense all their marketing outlays. In contrast, managing credit risk is one of the critical success factors for banks, and bank managers have the freedom to estimate expected defaults on their loans. Similarly, software developers have the flexibility to decide at what points in their development cycles the outlays can be capitalized.

If managers have little flexibility in choosing accounting policies and estimates related to their key success factors (as in the case of biotechnology firms), accounting data are likely to be less informative for understanding the firm's economics. In contrast, if managers have considerable flexibility in choosing the policies and estimates (as in the case of software developers), accounting numbers have the potential to be informative, depending upon how managers exercise this flexibility.

Regardless of the degree of accounting flexibility a firm's managers have in measuring their key success factors and risks, they will have some flexibility with respect to several other accounting policies. For example, all firms have to make choices with respect to depreciation policy (straight-line or accelerated methods), inventory accounting policy (LIFO, FIFO, or Average Cost), policy for amortizing goodwill (write-off over forty years or less), and policies regarding the estimation of pension and other post-employment benefits (expected return on plan assets, discount rate for liabilities, and rate of increase in wages and health care costs). Since all these policy choices can have a significant impact on the reported performance of a firm, they offer an opportunity for the firm to manage its reported numbers.

Step 3: Evaluate Accounting Strategy

When managers have accounting flexibility, they can use it either to communicate their firm's economic situation or to hide true performance. Some of the strategy questions one could ask in examining how managers exercise their accounting flexibility include the following:

- How do the firm's accounting policies compare to the norms in the industry? If they are dissimilar, is it because the firm's competitive strategy is unique? For example, consider a firm that reports a lower warranty allowance than the industry average. One explanation is that the firm competes on the basis of high quality and has invested considerable resources to reduce the rate of product failure. An alternative explanation is that the firm is merely understating its warranty liabilities.

- Do managers face strong incentives to use accounting discretion to manage earnings? For example, is the firm close to violating bond covenants? Or are the managers having difficulty meeting accounting-based bonus targets? Does management own significant stock? Is the firm in the middle of a proxy fight or union negotiations? Managers may also make accounting decisions to reduce tax payments or to influence the perceptions of the firm's competitors.
- Has the firm changed any of its policies or estimates? What is the justification? What is the impact of these changes? For example, if warranty expenses decreased, is it because the firm made significant investments to improve quality?
- Have the company's policies and estimates been realistic in the past? For example, firms may overstate their revenues and understate their expenses during the year by manipulating quarterly reports, which are not subject to a full-blown external audit. However, the auditing process at the end of the fiscal year forces such companies to make large fourth-quarter adjustments, providing an opportunity for the analyst to assess the quality of the firm's interim reporting. Similarly, firms that depreciate fixed assets too slowly will be forced to take a large write-off later. A history of write-offs may be, therefore, a sign of prior earnings management.
- Does the firm structure any significant business transactions so that it can achieve certain accounting objectives? For example, leasing firms can alter lease terms (the length of the lease or the bargain purchase option at the end of the lease term) so that the transactions qualify as sales-type leases for the lessors. Enron structured acquisitions of joint venture interests and hedging transactions with special purpose entities to avoid having to show joint venture liabilities, and to avoid reporting investment losses in its financial statements.[14] Such behavior may suggest that the firm's managers are willing to expend economic resources merely to achieve an accounting objective.

Step 4: Evaluate the Quality of Disclosure

Managers can make it more or less easy for an analyst to assess the firm's accounting quality and to use its financial statements to understand business reality. While accounting rules require a certain amount of minimum disclosure, managers have considerable choice in the matter. Disclosure quality, therefore, is an important dimension of a firm's accounting quality.

In assessing a firm's disclosure quality, an analyst could ask the following questions:

- Does the company provide adequate disclosures to assess the firm's business strategy and its economic consequences? For example, some firms use the Letter to the Shareholders in their annual report to clearly lay out the firm's industry conditions, its competitive position, and management's plans for the future. Others use the letter to puff up the firm's financial performance and gloss over any competitive difficulties the firm might be facing.
- Do the footnotes adequately explain the key accounting policies and assumptions and their logic? For example, if a firm's revenue and expense recognition policies differ from industry norms, the firm can explain its choices in a footnote. Similarly, when there are significant changes in a firm's policies, footnotes can be used to disclose the reasons.
- Does the firm adequately explain its current performance? The Management Discussion and Analysis section of the annual report provides an opportunity to help analysts understand the reasons behind a firm's performance changes. Some firms use this

section to link financial performance to business conditions. For example, if profit margins went down in a period, was it because of price competition or because of increases in manufacturing costs? If the selling and general administrative expenses went up, was it because the firm is investing in a differentiation strategy, or because unproductive overhead expenses were creeping up?

- If accounting rules and conventions restrict the firm from measuring its key success factors appropriately, does the firm provide adequate additional disclosure to help outsiders understand how these factors are being managed? For example, if a firm invests in product quality and customer service, accounting rules do not allow the management to capitalize these outlays, even when the future benefits are certain. The firm's Management Discussion and Analysis can be used to highlight how these outlays are being managed and their performance consequences. For example, the firm can disclose physical indexes of defect rates and customer satisfaction so that outsiders can assess the progress being made in these areas and the future cash flow consequences of these actions.

- If a firm is in multiple business segments, what is the quality of segment disclosure? Some firms provide excellent discussion of their performance by product segments and geographic segments. Others lump many different businesses into one broad segment. The level of competition in an industry and management's willingness to share desegregated performance data influence a firm's quality of segment disclosure.

- How forthcoming is the management with respect to bad news? A firm's disclosure quality is most clearly revealed by the way management deals with bad news. Does it adequately explain the reasons for poor performance? Does the company clearly articulate its strategy, if any, to address the company's performance problems?

- How good is the firm's investor relations program? Does the firm provide fact books with detailed data on the firm's business and performance? Is the management accessible to analysts?

Step 5: Identify Potential Red Flags

In addition to the above analysis, a common approach to accounting quality analysis is to look for "red flags" pointing to questionable accounting quality. These indicators suggest that the analyst should examine certain items more closely or gather more information on them. Some common red flags are the following:

- *Unexplained changes in accounting, especially when performance is poor.* This may suggest that managers are using their accounting discretion to "dress up" their financial statements.[15]

- *Unexplained transactions that boost profits.* For example, firms might undertake balance sheet transactions, such as asset sales or debt for equity swaps, to realize gains in periods when operating performance is poor.[16]

- *Unusual increases in accounts receivable in relation to sales increases.* This may suggest that the company is relaxing its credit policies or artificially loading up its distribution channels to record revenues during the current period. If credit policies are relaxed unduly, the firm may face receivable write-offs in subsequent periods as a result of customer defaults. If the firm accelerates shipments to its distributors, it may either face product returns or reduced shipments in subsequent periods.

- *Unusual increases in inventories in relation to sales increases.* If the inventory build-up is due to an increase in finished goods inventory, it could be a sign that demand for the firm's products is slowing down, suggesting that the firm may be forced to cut prices (and hence earn lower margins) or write down its inventory. A build-up in work-in-progress inventory tends to be good news on average, probably signaling that managers expect an increase in sales. If the build-up is in raw materials, it could suggest manufacturing or procurement inefficiencies, leading to an increase in cost of goods sold (and hence lower margins).[17]

- *An increasing gap between a firm's reported income and its cash flow from operating activities.* While it is legitimate for accrual accounting numbers to differ from cash flows, there is usually a steady relationship between the two if the company's accounting policies remain the same. Therefore, any *change* in the relationship between reported profits and operating cash flows might indicate subtle changes in the firm's accrual estimates. For example, a firm undertaking large construction contracts might use the percentage-of-completion method to record revenues. While earnings and operating cash flows are likely to differ for such a firm, they should bear a steady relationship to each other. Now suppose the firm increases revenues in a period through an aggressive application of the percentage-of-completion method. Then its earnings will go up, but its cash flow remains unaffected. This change in the firm's accounting quality will be manifested by a *change* in the relationship between the firm's earnings and cash flows.

- *An increasing gap between a firm's reported income and its tax income.* Once again, it is quite legitimate for a firm to follow different accounting policies for financial reporting and tax accounting as long as the tax law allows it.[18] However, the relationship between a firm's book and tax accounting is likely to remain constant over time, unless there are significant changes in tax rules or accounting standards. Thus, an *increasing* gap between a firm's reported income and its tax income may indicate that financial reporting to shareholders has become more aggressive. For example, warranty expenses are estimated on an accrual basis for financial reporting, but they are recorded on a cash basis for tax reporting. Unless there is a big change in the firm's product quality, these two numbers bear a consistent relationship to each other. Therefore, a change in this relationship can be an indication either that product quality is changing significantly or that financial reporting estimates are changing.

- *A tendency to use financing mechanisms like research and development partnerships, special purpose entities, and the sale of receivables with recourse.* While these arrangements may have a sound business logic, they can also provide management with an opportunity to understate the firm's liabilities and/or overstate its assets.[19]

- *Unexpected large asset write-offs.* This may suggest that management is slow to incorporate changing business circumstances into its accounting estimates. Asset write-offs may also be a result of unexpected changes in business circumstances.[20]

- *Large fourth-quarter adjustments.* A firm's annual reports are audited by the external auditors, but its interim financial statements are usually only reviewed. If a firm's management is reluctant to make appropriate accounting estimates (such as provisions for uncollectable receivables) in its interim statements, it could be forced to make adjustments at the end of the year as a result of pressure from its external auditors. A consistent pattern of fourth-quarter adjustments, therefore, may indicate aggressive management of interim reporting.[21]

- *Qualified audit opinions or changes in independent auditors that are not well justified.* These may indicate a firm's aggressive attitude or a tendency to "opinion shop."

- *Related-party transactions or transactions between related entities.* These transactions may lack the objectivity of the marketplace, and managers' accounting estimates related to these transactions are likely to be more subjective and potentially self-serving.[22]

While the preceding list provides a number of red flags for potentially poor accounting quality, it is important to do further analysis before reaching final conclusions. Each of the red flags has multiple interpretations; some interpretations are based on sound business reasons, and others indicate questionable accounting. It is, therefore, best to use the red flag analysis as a starting point for further probing, not as an end point in itself.[23]

Step 6: Undo Accounting Distortions

If the accounting analysis suggests that the firm's reported numbers are misleading, analysts should attempt to restate the reported numbers to reduce the distortion to the extent possible. It is, of course, virtually impossible to perfectly undo the distortion using outside information alone. However, some progress can be made in this direction by using the cash flow statement and the financial statement footnotes.

A firm's cash flow statement provides a reconciliation of its performance based on accrual accounting and cash accounting. If the analyst is unsure of the quality of the firm's accrual accounting, the cash flow statement provides an alternative benchmark of its performance. The cash flow statement also provides information on how individual line items in the income statement diverge from the underlying cash flows. For example, if an analyst is concerned that the firm is aggressively capitalizing certain costs that should be expensed, the information in the cash flow statement provides a basis to make the necessary adjustment.

Financial statement footnotes also provide a lot of information that is potentially useful in restating reported accounting numbers. For example, when a firm changes its accounting policies, it provides a footnote indicating the effect of that change if it is material. Similarly, some firms provide information on the details of accrual estimates such as the allowance for bad debts. The tax footnote usually provides information on the differences between a firm's accounting policies for shareholder reporting and tax reporting. Since tax reporting is often more conservative than shareholder reporting, the information in the tax footnote can be used to estimate what the earnings reported to shareholders would be under more conservative policies.

In Chapter 4, we show how to make accounting adjustments for the some of the most common types of accounting distortions.

ACCOUNTING ANALYSIS PITFALLS

There are several potential pitfalls and common misconceptions in accounting analysis that an analyst should avoid.

1. Conservative accounting is not "good" accounting.

Some firms take the approach that it pays to be conservative in financial reporting and to set aside as much as possible for contingencies. This logic is commonly used to justify the expensing of R&D and advertising, and the rapid write-down of intangible assets such as goodwill. It is also used to support large loss reserves for insurance companies, for merger expenses, and for restructuring charges.

From the standpoint of a financial statement user, it is important to recognize that conservative accounting is not the same as "good" accounting. Financial statement users want to evaluate how well a firm's accounting captures business reality in an unbiased manner, and conservative accounting can be as misleading as aggressive accounting in this respect.

It is certainly true that it can be difficult to estimate the economic benefits from many intangibles. However, the intangible nature of some assets does not mean that they do not have value. Indeed, for many firms these types of assets are their most valued. For example, Merck's two most valued assets are its research capabilities that permit it to generate new drugs, and its sales force that enables it to sell those drugs to doctors. Yet neither is recorded on Merck's balance sheet. From the investors' point of view, accountants' reluctance to value intangible assets does not diminish their importance. If they are not included in financial statements, investors have to look to alternative sources of information on these assets.

Further, conservative accounting often provides managers with opportunities for "income smoothing," which may prevent analysts from recognizing poor performance in a timely fashion. Finally, over time investors are likely to figure out which firms are conservative and may discount their management's disclosures and communications.

2. Not all unusual accounting is questionable.

It is easy to confuse unusual accounting with questionable accounting. While unusual accounting choices might make a firm's performance difficult to compare with other firms' performance, such an accounting choice might be justified if the company's business is unusual. For example, firms that follow differentiated strategies or firms that structure their business in an innovative manner to take advantage of particular market situations may make unusual accounting choices to properly reflect their business. Therefore it is important to evaluate a company's accounting choices in the context of its business strategy.

Similarly, it is important not to necessarily attribute all *changes* in a firm's accounting policies and accruals to earnings management motives.[24] Accounting changes might be merely reflecting changed business circumstances. For example, as already discussed, a firm that shows unusual increases in its inventory might be preparing for a new product introduction. Similarly, unusual increases in receivables might merely be due to changes in a firm's sales strategy. Unusual decreases in the allowance for uncollectable receivables might be reflecting a firm's changed customer focus. It is therefore important for an analyst to consider all possible explanations for accounting changes and investigate them using the qualitative information available in a firm's financial statements.

VALUE OF ACCOUNTING DATA AND ACCOUNTING ANALYSIS

What is the value of accounting information and accounting analysis? Given the incentives and opportunities for managers to affect their firms' reported accounting numbers, some have argued that accounting data and accounting analysis are not likely to be useful for investors.

Researchers have examined the value of accounting by estimating the return that could be earned by an investor with perfect earnings foresight one year prior to an earnings announcement.[25] The findings show that by buying stocks of firms with increased earnings and selling stocks of firms with decreased earnings each year, a hypothetical investor could earn an average portfolio return of 37.5 percent in the period 1954 to 1996. This is equivalent to 44 percent of the return that could have been earned if the investor had perfect foresight of the stock price itself for one year and bought stocks with increased prices and sold stocks whose price decreased. Perfect foresight of ROE permits the investor to earn an even higher rate of return, 43 percent, than perfect earnings foresight. This is equivalent to 50 percent of the return that could be earned with perfect stock price foresight.

In contrast, cash flow data appear to be considerably less valuable than earnings or ROE information. Perfect foresight of cash flows from operations would permit the hypothetical investor to earn an average annual return of only 9 percent, equivalent to 11 percent of the return that could be earned with perfect foresight of stock prices.

Overall, this research suggests that the institutional arrangements and conventions created to mitigate potential misuse of accounting by managers are effective in providing assurance to investors. The research indicates that investors do not view earnings management as so pervasive as to make earnings data unreliable.

A number of research studies have examined whether superior accounting analysis is a valuable activity. By and large, this evidence indicates that there are opportunities for superior analysts to earn positive stock returns. Research findings indicate that companies criticized in the financial press for misleading financial reporting subsequently suffered an average stock price drop of 8 percent.[26] Firms where managers appeared to inflate reported earnings prior to an equity issue and subsequently reported poor earnings performance had more negative stock performance after the offer than firms with no apparent earnings management.[27] Finally, firms subject to SEC investigation for earnings management showed an average stock price decline of 9 percent when the earnings management was first announced and continued to have poor stock performance for up to two years.[28]

These findings imply that analysts who are able to identify firms with misleading accounting are able to create value for investors. The findings also indicate that the stock market ultimately sees through earnings management. For all of these cases, earnings management is eventually uncovered and the stock price responds negatively to evidence that firms have inflated prior earnings through misleading accounting.

SUMMARY

In summary, accounting analysis is an important step in the process of analyzing corporate financial reports. The purpose of accounting analysis is to evaluate the degree to which a firm's accounting captures the underlying business reality. Sound accounting analysis improves the reliability of conclusions from financial analysis, the next step in financial statement analysis.

There are six key steps in accounting analysis. The analyst begins by identifying the key accounting policies and estimates, given the firm's industry and its business strategy. The second step is to evaluate the degree of flexibility available to managers, given the accounting rules and conventions. Next, the analyst has to evaluate how managers exercise their accounting flexibility and the likely motivations behind managers' accounting strategy. The fourth step involves assessing the depth and quality of a firm's disclosures. The analyst should next identify any red flags needing further investigation. The final accounting analysis step is to restate accounting numbers to remove any noise and bias introduced by the accounting rules and management decisions.

The next chapter discusses how to implement these concepts and shows how to make some of the most common types of adjustments.

DISCUSSION QUESTIONS

1. A finance student states, "I don't understand why anyone pays any attention to accounting earnings numbers, given that a 'clean' number like cash from operations is readily available." Do you agree? Why or why not?

2. Fred argues, "The standards that I like most are the ones that eliminate all management discretion in reporting—that way I get uniform numbers across all companies and don't have to worry about doing accounting analysis." Do you agree? Why or why not?

3. Bill Simon says, "We should get rid of the FASB and SEC, since free market forces will make sure that companies report reliable information." Do you agree? Why or why not?

4. Many firms recognize revenues at the point of shipment. This provides an incentive to accelerate revenues by shipping goods at the end of the quarter. Consider two companies, one of which ships its product evenly throughout the quarter, and the second of which ships all its products in the last two weeks of the quarter. Each company's customers pay thirty days after receiving shipment. Using accounting ratios, how can you distinguish these companies?

5. a. If management reports truthfully, what economic events are likely to prompt the following accounting changes?
   • Increase in the estimated life of depreciable assets
   • Decrease in the uncollectibles allowance as a percentage of gross receivables
   • Recognition of revenues at the point of delivery rather than at the point cash is received
   • Capitalization of a higher proportion of software R&D costs
   b. What features of accounting, if any, would make it costly for dishonest managers to make the same changes without any corresponding economic changes?

6. The conservatism principle arises because of concerns about management's incentives to overstate the firm's performance. Joe Banks argues, "We could get rid of conservatism and make accounting numbers more useful if we delegated financial reporting to independent auditors rather than to corporate managers." Do you agree? Why or why not?

7. A fund manager states, "I refuse to buy any company that makes a voluntary accounting change, since it's certainly a case of management trying to hide bad news." Can you think of any alternative interpretation?

NOTES

1. Accounting analysis is sometimes also called quality of earnings analysis. We prefer to use the term accounting analysis since we are discussing a broader concept than merely a firm's earnings quality.

2. These definitions paraphrase those of the Financial Accounting Standards Board, Statement of Financial Accounting Concepts No. 6, "Elements of Financial Statements" (1985). Our intent is to present the definitions at a conceptual, not technical, level. For more complete discussion of these and related concepts, see the FASB's Statements of Financial Accounting Concepts.

3. Strictly speaking, the comprehensive net income of a firm also includes gains and losses from increases and decreases in equity from nonoperating activities or extraordinary items.

4. Thus, although accrual accounting is theoretically superior to cash accounting in measuring a firm's periodic performance, the distortions it introduces can make accounting data less valuable to

users. If these distortions are large enough, current cash flows may measure a firm's periodic performance better than accounting profits. The relative usefulness of cash flows and accounting profits in measuring performance, therefore, varies from firm to firm. For empirical evidence on this issue, see P. Dechow, "Accounting Earnings and Cash Flows as Measures of Firm Performance: The Role of Accounting Accruals," *Journal of Accounting and Economics* 18 (July 1994): 3–42.

5. For example, Abraham Briloff wrote a series of accounting analyses of public companies in *Barron's* over several years. On average, the stock prices of the analyzed companies changed by about 8 percent on the day these articles were published, indicating the potential value of performing such analysis. For a more complete discussion of this evidence, see G. Foster, "Briloff and the Capital Market," *Journal of Accounting Research* 17 (Spring 1979): 262–74.

6. For a complete discussion of these motivations, see *"Positive Accounting Theory,"* by R. Watts and J. Zimmerman, (Englewood Cliffs, NJ: Prentice-Hall, 1986). A summary of this research is provided by T. Fields, T. Lys, and L. Vincent in "Empirical Research on Accounting Choice," *Journal of Accounting & Economics* 31 (September 2001): 255–307.

7. The most convincing evidence supporting the covenant hypothesis is reported in a study of the accounting decisions by firms in financial distress: A. Sweeney, "Debt-Covenant Violations and Managers' Accounting Responses," *Journal of Accounting and Economics* 17 (May 1994): 281–308.

8. Studies that examine the bonus hypothesis generally report evidence supporting the view that managers' accounting decisions are influenced by compensation considerations. See, for example, P. Healy, "The Effect of Bonus Schemes on Accounting Decisions," *Journal of Accounting and Economics* 7 (April 1985): 85–107; R. Holthausen, D. Larcker, and R. Sloan, "Annual Bonus Schemes and the Manipulation of Earnings," *Journal of Accounting and Economics* 19 (February 1995): 29–74; and F. Guidry, A. Leone, and S. Rock, "Earnings-Based Bonus Plans and Earnings Management by Business Unit Managers," *Journal of Accounting and Economics*, 26 (January 1999): 113–42.

9. L. DeAngelo, "Managerial Competition, Information Costs, and Corporate Governance: The Use of Accounting Performance Measures in Proxy Contests," *Journal of Accounting and Economics* 10 (January 1988): 3–36.

10. The trade-off between taxes and financial reporting in the context of managers' accounting decisions is discussed in detail in *Taxes and Business Strategy* by M. Scholes and M. Wolfson (Englewood Cliffs, NJ: Prentice-Hall, 1992). Many empirical studies have examined firms' LIFO/FIFO choices.

11. Several researchers have documented that firms affected by such situations have a motivation to influence regulators' perceptions through accounting decisions. For example, J. Jones documents that firms seeking import protections make income-decreasing accounting decisions in "Earnings Management During Import Relief Investigations," *Journal of Accounting Research* 29, no. 2 (Autumn 1991): 193–228. A number of studies find that banks that are close to minimum capital requirements overstate loan loss provisions, understate loan write-offs, and recognize abnormal realized gains on securities portfolios (see S. Moyer, "Capital Adequacy Ratio Regulations and Accounting Choices in Commercial Banks," *Journal of Accounting and Economics* 12 (1990): 123–54; M. Scholes, G. P. Wilson, and M. Wolfson, "Tax Planning, Regulatory Capital Planning, and Financial Reporting Strategy for Commercial Banks," *Review of Financial Studies* 3 (1990): 625–50; A. Beatty, S. Chamberlain, and J. Magliolo, "Managing Financial Reports of Commercial Banks: The Influence of Taxes, Regulatory Capital and Earnings," *Journal of Accounting Research* 33, no. 2 (1995): 231–61; and J. Collins, D. Shackelford, and J. Wahlen, "Bank Differences in the Coordination of Regulatory Capital, Earnings and Taxes," *Journal of Accounting Research* 33, no. 2 (Autumn 1995): 263–91). Finally, Petroni finds that financially weak property-casualty insurers that risk regulatory attention understate claim loss reserves: K. Petroni, "Optimistic Reporting in the Property Casualty Insurance Industry," *Journal of Accounting and Economics* 15 (December 1992): 485–508.

12. P. Healy and K. Palepu "The Effect of Firms' Financial Disclosure Strategies on Stock Prices," *Accounting Horizons* 7 (March 1993): 1–11. For a summary of the empirical evidence, see P. Healy and J. Wahlen, "A Review of the Earnings Management Literature and Its Implications for Standard Setting," *Accounting Horizons* 13 (December 1999): 365–84.

13. Financial analysts pay close attention to managers' disclosure strategies; the Association for Investment Management and Research publishes an annual report evaluating them for U.S. firms.

For a discussion of these ratings, see M. Lang and R. Lundholm, "Cross-sectional Determinants of Analysts' Ratings of Corporate Disclosures," *Journal of Accounting Research* 31 (Autumn 1993): 246–71.

14. See P. Healy and K. Palepu, "The Fall of Enron," *Journal of Economic Perspectives* 17, no. 2 (Spring 2003): 3–26.

15. For a detailed analysis of a company that made such changes, see "Anatomy of an Accounting Change" by K. Palepu in *Accounting & Management: Field Study Perspectives*, edited by W. Bruns, Jr. and R. Kaplan (Boston: Harvard Business School Press, 1987).

16. An example of this type of behavior is documented by John Hand in his study, "Did Firms Undertake Debt-Equity Swaps for an Accounting Paper Profit or True Financial Gain?" *The Accounting Review* 64 (October 1989): 587–623.

17. For an empirical analysis of inventory build-ups, see V. Bernard and J. Noel, "Do Inventory Disclosures Predict Sales and Earnings?" *Journal of Accounting, Auditing, and Finance* (Fall 1991).

18. This is true by and large in the United States and in several other countries. However, in some countries, such as Germany and Japan, tax accounting and financial reporting are closely tied together and this particular red flag is not very meaningful.

19. For research on accounting and economic incentives in the formation of R&D partnerships, see A. Beatty, P. Berger, and J. Magliolo, "Motives for Forming Research and Development Financing Organizations" *Journal of Accounting & Economics* 19 (April 1995): 411–42. An overview of Enron's use of special purpose entities to manage earnings and window-dress its balance is provided by P. Healy and K. Palepu, "The Fall of Enron," *Journal of Economic Perspectives* 17, no. 2 (Spring 2003): 3–26.

20. For an empirical examination of asset write-offs, see J. Elliott and W. Shaw "Write-offs as Accounting Procedures to Manage Perceptions," *Journal of Accounting Research* 26, 1988: 91–119.

21. R. Mendenhall and W. Nichols report evidence consistent with managers taking advantage of their discretion to postpone reporting bad news until the fourth quarter. See R. Mendenhall and W. Nichols, "Bad News and Differential Market Reactions to Announcements of Earlier-Quarter versus Fourth-Quarter Earnings," *Journal of Accounting Research*, Supplement (1988): 63–86.

22. The role of insider transactions in the collapse of Enron are discussed by P. Healy and K. Palepu, "The Fall of Enron," *Journal of Economic Perspectives* 17, no. 2 (Spring 2003): 3–26.

23. This type of analysis is presented in the context of provisions for bad debts by M. McNichols and P. Wilson in their study, "Evidence of Earnings Management from the Provisions for Bad Debts," *Journal of Accounting Research*, Supplement (1988): 1–31.

24. This point has been made by several accounting researchers. For a summary of research on earnings management, see K. Schipper, "Earnings Management," *Accounting Horizons* (December 1989): 91–102.

25. See J. Chang, "The Decline in Value Relevance of Earnings and Book Values," unpublished dissertation, Harvard University, 1998. Evidence is also reported by J. Francis and K. Schipper, "Have Financial Statements Lost Their Relevance?" *Journal of Accounting Research* 37, no. 2 (Autumn 1999): 319–52; and W. E. Collins, E. Maydew, and I. Weiss, "Changes in the Value-Relevance of Earnings and Book Value over the Past Forty Years, *Journal of Accounting and Economics* 24 (1997): 39–67.

26. See G. Foster, "Briloff and the Capital Market," *Journal of Accounting Research* 17, no. 1 (Spring 1979): 262–74.

27. See S. H. Teoh, I. Welch, and T. J. Wong, "Earnings Management and the Long-Run Market Performance of Initial Public Offerings," *Journal of Finance* 53 (December 1998a): 1935–74; S. H. Teoh, I. Welch, and T. J. Wong, "Earnings Management and the Post-Issue Underperformance of Seasoned Equity Offerings," *Journal of Financial Economics* 50 (October 1998): 63–99; and S. Teoh, T. Wong, and G. Rao, "Are Accruals During Initial Public Offerings Opportunistic?" *Review of Accounting Studies* 3, no. 1-2 (1998): 175–208.

28. See P. Dechow, R. Sloan, and A. Sweeney, "Causes and Consequences of Earnings Manipulation: An Analysis of Firms Subject to Enforcement Actions by the SEC," *Contemporary Accounting Research* 13, no. 1 (1996): 1–36, and M. D. Beneish, "Detecting GAAP Violation: Implications for Assessing Earnings Management among Firms with Extreme Financial Performance," *Journal of Accounting and Public Policy* 16 (1997): 271–309.

Implementing Accounting Analysis

We learned in Chapter 3 that accounting analysis requires the analyst to adjust a firm's accounting numbers using cash flow and footnote information to "undo" any accounting distortions. This entails recasting a firm's financial statements using standard reporting nomenclature and formats. Firms frequently use somewhat different formats and terminology for presenting their financial results. Recasting the financial statements using a standard template, therefore, helps ensure that performance metrics used for financial analysis are calculated using comparable definitions across companies and over time.

Once the financial statements have been standardized, the analyst is ready to identify any distortions in financial statements. The analyst's primary focus should be on those accounting estimates and methods that the firm uses to measure its key success factors and risks. If there are differences in these estimates and/or methods between firms or for the same firm over time, the analyst's job is to assess whether they reflect legitimate business differences and therefore require no adjustment, or whether they reflect differences in managerial judgment or bias and require adjustment. In addition, even if accounting rules are adhered to consistently, accounting distortions can arise because accounting rules themselves do a poor job of capturing firm economics, creating opportunities for the analyst to adjust a firm's financials in a way that presents a more realistic picture of its performance.

This chapter shows how to recast the firm's financial statements into a template that uses standard terminology and classifications, discusses the most common types of accounting distortions that can arise, and shows how to make adjustments to the standardized financial statements to undo these distortions.

A balance sheet approach is used to identify whether there have been any distortions to assets, liabilities, or owners' equity. Once any asset and liability misstatements have been identified, the analyst can make adjustments to the balance sheet at the beginning and/or end of the current year, as well as any needed adjustments to revenues and expenses in the latest income statement. This approach ensures that the most recent financial ratios used to evaluate a firm's performance and forecast its future results are based on financial data that appropriately reflect its business economics.

In some instances, information taken from a firm's footnotes and cash flow statement enables the analyst to make a precise adjustment for an accounting distortion. However, for many types of accounting adjustments the company does not disclose all of the information needed to perfectly undo the distortion, requiring the analyst to make an approximate adjustment to the financial statements.

RECASTING FINANCIAL STATEMENTS

Firms sometimes use different nomenclature and formats to present their financial results. For example, the asset goodwill can be reported separately using such titles as Goodwill, "Excess of cost over net assets of acquired companies," and "Cost in excess of fair value," or it can be included in the line item Other Intangible Assets. Interest Income can be reported as a subcategory of Revenues, shown lower down the income statement as part of Other Income and Expenses, or it is sometimes reported as Interest Expense, Net of Interest Income.

These differences in financial statement terminology, classifications, and formats can make it difficult to compare performance across firms, and sometimes to compare performance for the same firm over time. The first task for the analyst in accounting analysis is, therefore, to recast the financial statements into a common format. This involves designing a template for the balance sheet, income statement, and cash flow statement that can be used to standardize financial statements for any company. Tables 4-1, 4-2, and 4-3 present the format used throughout the book to standardize the income statement, balance sheet, and cash flow statement, respectively.

Table 4-1 Standardized Income Statement Format

Standard Income Statement Accounts	Sample Line Items Classified in Account
Sales	Revenues Membership fees Commissions Licenses
Cost of Sales	Cost of merchandise sold Cost of products sold Cost of revenues Cost of services Depreciation on manufacturing facilities
SG&A	General and administrative Marketing & sales Salaries and benefits Servicing and maintenance Depreciation on selling and administrative facilities
Other Operating Expense	Amortization of intangibles Product development Research & development Provision for losses on credit sales Pre-opening costs Special charges

Net Interest Expense (Income)
   Interest Income
   Interest Expense	

Investment Income	Equity income from associates Dividend income Rental income
Other Income	Gains on sale of investments/long-term assets Foreign exchange gains Pre-tax gains from accounting changes
Other Expense	Losses on sale of investments/long-term assets Foreign exchange losses Pre-tax losses from accounting changes Restructuring charges Merger expenses Asset impairments
Minority Interest	
Tax Expense	Provision for taxes

Unusual Items (after tax)	Any gains or losses reported on an after tax-basis, such as:
	   Extraordinary items
	   Non-recurring charges
	   Effect of accounting changes

Table 4-2 Standardized Balance Sheet Format

Standard Balance Sheet Accounts	Sample Line Items Classified in Account
Assets	
Cash and Marketable Securities	Cash Short-term investments Time deposits
Accounts Receivable	Accounts/trade receivables Trade debtors
Inventory	Inventory Finished goods Raw materials Work-in-process Stocks
Deferred Taxes – Current Asset	
Other Current Assets	Prepaid expenses Taxes refundable Current assets of discontinued operations Due from affiliates Due from employees
Long-Term Tangible Assets	Plant, property & equipment Land Non-current assets of discontinued operations
Long-Term Intangible Assets	Goodwill Software development costs Deferred financing costs Deferred subscriber acquisition costs Deferred charges Trademarks License rights
Deferred Taxes – LT Asset	
Other Long-Term Assets	Long-term investments Long-term receivables Investment in sales-type or direct-financing leases

Standard Balance Sheet Accounts	Sample Line Items Classified in Account
Liabilities and Equity	
Short-Term Debt	Notes payable Current portion of long-term debt Current portion of capital lease obligation
Accounts Payable	Accounts/trade payables Trade creditors
Other Current Liabilities	Accrued expenses Accrued liabilities Taxes payable Dividends payable Deferred (unearned) revenue Customer advances
Deferred Taxes – Current Liability	
Long-Term Debt	Long-term debt Senior term notes Subordinated debt Capital lease obligations Convertible debt Pension/post-retirement benefit obligation
Deferred Taxes – Long-term Liability	
Other Long-Term Liabilities (non-interest bearing)	Non-current deferred (unearned) revenues Other non-current liabilities
Minority Interest	
Preferred Stock	Preferred stock Preferred convertible stock
Common Shareholders' Equity	Common stock Additional paid-in capital Capital in excess of par Treasury stock Retained earnings Cumulative foreign currency gains and losses Accumulated other comprehensive income

Table 4-3 Standardized Cash Flow Statement Format

Standard Cash Flow Statement Accounts	Sample Line Items Classified in Account
Net Income	
Non-operating Gains (Losses)	Gain (loss) on sale of investments/non-current assets Cumulative effect of accounting changes Gain (loss) on foreign exchange Extraordinary gains (losses)
Long-Term Operating Accruals	Depreciation and amortization Deferred revenues/costs Deferred income taxes Impairment of non-current assets Other non-cash charges to operations Equity earnings of affiliates/unconsolidated subs, net of cash received Minority interest Stock bonus awards

Net (Investments in) or Liquidation of Operating Working Capital	Changes in:
	    Trade accounts receivable
	    Other receivables
	    Prepaid expenses
	    Trade accounts payable
	    Accrued expenses (liabilities)
	    Due from affiliates
	    Accounts payable and accrued expenses
	    Refundable/payable income taxes
	    Inventories
	    Provision for doubtful accounts
	    Other current liabilities
	    Other current assets

Net (Investment in) or Liquidation of Operating Long-Term Assets	Purchase/sale of non-current assets Acquisition of research and development Acquisition/sale of business Capital expenditures Equity investments Acquisition of subsidiary stock Capitalization of computer software development costs Cost in excess of the fair value of net assets acquired Investment in sales-type and direct financing leases
Net Debt (Repayment) or Issuance	Principal payments on debt Borrowings (repayments) under credit facility Issuance (repayment) of long-term debt Net increase (decrease) in short-term borrowings Notes payable
Dividend (Payments)	Cash dividends paid on common stock Cash dividends paid on preferred stock Distributions
Net Stock (Repurchase) or Issuance	Proceeds from issuance of common stock Issue of common stock for services Issue (redemption) of preferred securities Issue of subsidiary equity Purchase (issue) of treasury stock

To create standardized financials for a particular company of interest, the analyst classifies each line item in that firm's financial statements using the appropriate account name from the above templates. This may require using information from the footnotes to ensure that accounts are classified appropriately. An example, applying the above template to standardize the 2002 financial statements for fashion retailer Nordstrom Inc., is shown in the appendix at the end of this chapter.

Once the financials have been standardized, the analyst can evaluate whether accounting adjustments are needed to correct for any distortions in assets, liabilities, or equity.

ASSET DISTORTIONS

Accountants define assets as resources that a firm owns or controls as a result of past business transactions, and which are expected to produce future economic benefits that can be measured with a reasonable degree of certainty. Assets can take a variety of forms, including cash, marketable securities, receivables from customers, inventory, fixed assets, long-term investments in other companies, and intangibles.

Distortions in asset values generally arise because there is ambiguity about whether

- The firm owns or controls the economic resources in question, or
- The economic resources are likely to provide future economic benefits that can be measured with reasonable certainty, or
- The fair value of assets fall below their book values.

Who owns or controls resources?

For most resources used by a firm, ownership or control is relatively straightforward: the firm using the resource owns the asset. However, some types of transactions make it difficult to assess who owns a resource. For example, who owns or controls a resource that has been leased? Is it the lessor or the lessee? Or consider a firm that discounts a customer receivable with a bank. If the bank has recourse against the firm should the customer default, is the real owner of the receivable the bank or the company?

Accountants frequently use mechanical rules to determine whether a company owns or controls an asset. While these rules make it easy for accountants to implement accounting standards, they also permit managers to "groom" transactions to satisfy their own financial reporting objectives. For example, U.S. rules on lease accounting permit two lease transactions with essentially the same terms to be structured so that one is reported as an asset by the lessee, and the other is shown as an asset by the lessor. Accounting analysis, therefore, involves assessing whether a firm's reported assets adequately reflect the key resources that are under its control, and whether adjustments are required to compare its performance with that of competitors.

Asset ownership issues also arise indirectly from the application of rules for revenue recognition. Firms are permitted to recognize revenues only when their product has been shipped or their service has been provided to the customer. Revenues are then considered "earned," and the customer has a legal commitment to pay for the product or service. As a result, for the seller, recognition of revenue frequently coincides with "ownership" of a receivable that is shown as an asset on its balance sheet. Accounting analysis that raises questions about whether or not revenues have been earned therefore often affects the valuation of assets.

Ambiguity over whether a company owns an asset creates a number of opportunities for accounting analysis:

- Despite management's best intentions, financial statements sometimes do a poor job of reflecting the firm's economic assets since it is difficult for accounting rules to capture all of the subtleties associated with ownership and control.

- Because accounting rules on ownership and control permit managers to groom transactions so that essentially similar transactions can be reported in very different ways, important assets may be omitted from the balance sheet even though the firm bears many of the economic risks of ownership.
- There may be legitimate differences in opinion between managers and analysts over residual ownership risks borne by the company, leading to differences in opinion over reporting for these assets.
- Aggressive revenue recognition, which boosts reported earnings, is also likely to affect asset values.

Can economic benefits be measured with reasonable certainty?

It is almost always difficult to accurately forecast the future benefits associated with capital outlays because the world is uncertain. A company does not know whether a competitor will offer a new product or service that makes its own obsolete. It does not know whether the products manufactured at a new plant will be the type that customers want to buy. A company does not know whether changes in oil prices will make the oil drilling equipment that it manufactures less valuable.

Accounting rules deal with these challenges by stipulating which types of resources can be recorded as assets and which cannot. For example, the economic benefits from research and development are generally considered highly uncertain: research projects may never deliver promised new products, the products they generate may not be economically viable, or products may be made obsolete by competitors' research. Accounting rules in most countries, therefore, require that R&D outlays be expensed.[1] In contrast, the economic benefits from plant acquisitions are considered less uncertain and are required to be capitalized.

Rules that require the immediate expensing of outlays for some key resources may be good accounting, but they create a challenge for the analyst—namely, they lead to less timely financial statements. For example, if all firms expense R&D, financial statements will reflect differences in R&D success only when new products are commercialized rather than during the development process. The analyst may attempt to correct for this distortion by capitalizing key R&D outlays and adjusting the value of the intangible asset based on R&D updates.[2]

Have fair values of assets declined below book value?

An asset is impaired when its fair value falls below its book value. In most countries accounting rules require that a loss be recorded for permanent asset impairments. U.S. rules (SFAS 144) specify that an impairment loss be recognized on a long-term asset when its book value exceeds the *undiscounted* cash flows expected to be generated from future use and sale. If this condition is satisfied, the firm is required to report a loss for the difference between the asset's fair value and its book value.

Of course markets for many long-term operating assets are illiquid and incomplete, making it highly subjective to infer their fair values. Consequently, considerable management judgement is involved in deciding whether an asset is impaired and determining the value of any impairment loss.

For the analyst, this raises the possibility that asset values are misstated. U.S. accounting rules themselves permit a certain amount of asset overstatement since the test for asset impairment compares the asset's book value to the expected value of *undiscounted* (rather than *discounted*) future cash flows associated with the asset. This can create situations where no financial statement loss is reported for an asset that is economically impaired.

In addition, the task of determining whether there has been an asset impairment and valuing the impairment is delegated to management, with oversight by the firm's auditors, potentially leaving opportunities for management bias in valuing assets and for legitimate differences in opinion between managers and analysts over asset valuations. In most cases, management bias will lead to overstated assets since managers will prefer not to recognize an impairment. However, managers can also bias asset values downward by "taking a bath," reducing future expenses and increasing future earnings.

In summary, distortions in assets are likely to arise when there is ambiguity about whether the firm owns or controls a resource, when there is a high degree of uncertainty about the value of the economic benefits to be derived from the resource, and when there are differences in opinion about the value of asset impairments. Opportunities for accounting adjustments can arise in these situations if

- Accounting rules do not do a good job of capturing the firm's economics, or
- Managers use their discretion to distort the firm's performance, or
- There are legitimate differences in opinion between managers and analysts about economic uncertainties facing the firm that are reflected in asset values.

OVERSTATED ASSETS

Asset overstatements are likely to arise when managers have incentives to increase reported earnings. Thus, adjustments to assets also typically require adjustments to the income statement in the form of either increased expenses or reduced revenues. The most common forms of asset (and earnings) overstatement are the following:

1. *Delays in writing down current assets.* If current assets become impaired, that is, their book values fall below their realizable values, accounting rules generally require that they be written down to their fair values. Current asset impairments also affect earnings since write-offs are charged directly to earnings. Deferring current asset write-downs is, therefore, one way for managers to boost reported profits.[3] Analysts that cover firms where management of inventories and receivables is a key success factor (e.g., the retail and manufacturing industries) need to be particularly cognizant of this form of earnings management. If managers over-buy or over-produce in the current period, they are likely to have to offer customers discounts to get rid of surplus inventories. In addition, providing customers with credit carries risks of default. Warning signs for delays in current asset write-downs include growing days' inventory and days' receivable, write-downs by competitors, and business downturns for a firm's major customers.

2. *Underestimated reserves (e.g., allowances for bad debts or loan losses).* Managers make estimates of expected customer defaults on accounts receivable and loans. If managers underestimate the value of these reserves, assets and earnings will be overstated. Warning signs of inadequate allowances include growing days receivable, business downturns for a firm's major clients, and growing loan delinquencies.

3. *Accelerated recognition of revenues (increasing receivables).* Managers typically have the best information on the uncertainties governing revenue recognition—whether a product or service has been provided to customers and whether cash collection is reasonably likely. However, managers may also have incentives to accelerate the recognition of revenues, boosting reported earnings for the period. Accounts

receivable and earnings will then be overstated. Aggressive revenue recognition is one of the most popular forms of earnings management cited by the SEC.

4. *Delayed write-downs of long-term assets.* Deteriorating industry or firm economic conditions can affect the value of long-term assets as well as current assets. Firms are required to recognize impairments in the values of long-term assets when they arise. However, since second-hand markets for long-term assets are typically illiquid and incomplete, estimates of asset valuations and impairment are inherently subjective. This is particularly true for intangible assets such as goodwill. As a result, managers can use their reporting judgment to delay write-downs on the balance sheet and avoid showing impairment charges in the income statement.[4] This issue is likely to be particularly critical for heavy asset-intensive firms in volatile markets (e.g., airlines) or for firms that follow a strategy of aggressive growth through acquisitions.[5] Warning signs of impairments in long-term assets include declining long-term asset turnover, declines in return on assets to levels lower than the weighted average cost of capital, write-downs by other firms in the same industry that have also suffered deteriorating asset use, and overpayment for or unsuccessful integration of key acquisitions.

5. *Overstated depreciation/amortization on long-term assets.* Managers make estimates of asset lives, salvage values, and amortization schedules for depreciable long-term assets. If these estimates are optimistic, long-term assets and earnings will be overstated. This issue is likely to be most pertinent for firms in heavy asset businesses (e.g., airlines, utilities).

Examples of How to Correct for Asset Overstatement

We illustrate some of the distortions that lead to overstated assets, and the types of corrections that the analyst can make to reduce bias in the financial statements.

Delaying Write-Downs of Current Assets   The dot-com stock market crash in April 2000 had a ripple effect on firms selling equipment to the telecommunications and Internet industries. One of the firms affected was Lucent Technologies. For Lucent the first sign of a downturn came in the June 2000 quarter, when earnings declined markedly over the same period one year earlier. This pattern persisted through the September and December 2000 quarters, when the company reported operating losses of $2.1 billion and $4.8 billion, respectively.

The decline in Lucent's performance and future prospects raised questions for analysts about whether the company's inventory was impaired. In December 2000 Lucent reported inventory valued at $6.9 billion, $1.5 billion higher than one year earlier. Yet sales for the December 2000 quarter ($5.8 billion) had declined precipitously relative to the same quarter in 1999 ($9.9 billion). As a result, Lucent's Day's Inventory increased from 58 days to 107 days. In the same period, the company's gross margins declined from 47 percent to 22 percent. Despite these significant declines in performance, Lucent recorded no inventory impairment charge for the December 2000 quarter.

Obviously it is difficult for an analyst to assess whether Lucent's inventory was impaired or to assess the severity of any impairment. By talking to Lucent's customers and by observing the performance of other firms in the industry, however, the analyst can judge whether the company's problems are likely to persist, whether there are serious technological risks for current inventory and, if so, the value of an appropriate impairment charge.

Having concluded that inventory was overstated, the analyst would have to revise the inventory level down, and show a decline in equity to reflect the after-tax cost of the impairment. In addition, the tax effect of the adjustment would be reflected in the company's Deferred Tax Liability, since the inventory write-down is assumed to only affect Lucent's financial reporting books. Its separate tax books are determined by IRS tax rules, which are assumed to be independent of financial reporting rules. For example, if an analyst concluded that Lucent's inventory was overstated by, say, $500 million, given the company's 35 percent marginal tax rate, the adjustment required to correct this overstatement in the December 31, 2000, financial statements would be as follows:

($ millions)	Adjustment	
	Assets	Liabilities & Equity
Balance Sheet		
Inventory	−500	
Deferred Tax Liability		−175
Common Shareholders' Equity		−325
Income Statement		
Cost of Sales		+500
Tax Expense		−175
Net Income		−325

In March 2001, following another quarter of deteriorating performance, Lucent announced that it would take a $536 million inventory write-down. This was followed by an additional write-down of $143 million at the end of June and $11 million in September.

Underestimating Reserves   Assets can also be overstated if reserve estimates are understated. For example, consider Lucent's accounts receivable allowances at the end of December 2000. As reported in its footnotes, allowances were increased from 5 percent in September 2000 to 7 percent in December of the same year. The challenge for the analyst is to assess whether this increase is adequate given the dramatic decline in the fortunes of Lucent's Internet and telecommunication customers. This requires a thorough review of the short-term cash generating potential of Lucent's major customers to judge how much of Lucent's receivables are likely to actually be collected.

If the analyst decides that receivable allowances are understated, adjustments have to be made to Accounts Receivable and to Equity for the after-tax cost of the incremental bad debt expense. For example, if the analyst decided that receivable allowances for Lucent should be 9 percent rather than 7 percent, Accounts Receivable would have to be reduced by $150 million. Given the company's marginal tax rate of 35 percent, this would reduce earnings and equity by $97.5 million, and reduce the Deferred Tax Liability by $52.5 million. The adjustment to the December 31, 2000, financial statements would, therefore, be as follows:

($ millions)	Adjustment	
	Assets	Liabilities & Equity
Balance Sheet		
Accounts Receivable	−150.0	
Deferred Tax Liability		−52.5
Common Shareholders' Equity		−97.5
Income Statement		
Cost of Sales		+150.0
Tax Expense		−52.5
Net Income		−97.5

Perhaps because it understated its receivables at the end of 2000, or perhaps because the problems facing the industry proved to be more serious than anyone could have anticipated, Lucent reported a steady increase in allowance estimates as a percent of gross receivables throughout 2001. Reported estimates were 8.7 percent in March, 11.2 percent in June, 12.5 percent in September, and 19.5 percent in December.

Accelerating Recognition of Revenues   In November 1999 and January 2000, analysts at the Center for Financial Research and Analysis (CFRA) raised questions about the propriety of revenue recognition for MicroStrategy, a software company. MicroStrategy recognized revenues from the sale of licenses "after execution of a licensing agreement and shipment of the product, provided that no significant Company obligations remain and the resulting receivable is deemed collectible by management."[6] CFRA analysts were concerned about MicroStrategy's booking two contracts worth $27 million as quarterly revenues when the contracts were not announced until several days after the quarter's end. If the analysts decided to adjust for these distortions, the following changes would have to be made to Micro-Strategy's financial reports:

1. In the quarter that the contracts were booked, Sales and Accounts Receivable would both decline by $27 million.
2. Cost of Sales would decline and Inventory would increase to reflect the reduction in sales. The value of the Cost of Sales/Inventory adjustment can be estimated by multiplying the sales adjustment by the ratio of cost of sales to sales. For MicroStrategy, cost of license revenues is only 3 percent of license revenues, indicating that the adjustment would be modest ($0.8m). Also, since MicroStrategy does not have any inventory, the balance sheet adjustment would be to prepaid expenses, which are included in Other Current Assets on the standardized balance sheet.
3. The decline in pretax income would result in a lower Tax Expense in the company's financial reporting books (but presumably not in its tax books). Consequently, the Deferred Tax Liability would have to be reduced. MicroStrategy's marginal tax rate was 35 percent, implying that the decline in the Tax Expense and Deferred Tax Liability was $9.2 million [($27 − 0.8) × .35].

The full effect of the adjustment on the quarterly financial statements would therefore be as follows:

($ millions)	Adjustment	
	Assets	Liabilities & Equity
Balance Sheet		
Accounts Receivable	−27.0	
Other Current Assets	+0.8	
Deferred Tax Liability		−9.2
Common Shareholders' Equity		−17.0
Income Statement		
Sales		−27.0
Cost of Sales		−0.8
Tax Expense		−9.2
Net Income		−17.0

Of course, provided the contracts were legitimate transactions, the above adjustments imply that forecasts of next quarter's revenues should include the $27 million worth of contracts.

In March 2000 MicroStrategy confirmed that the CFRA analysts' suspicions about aggressive revenue recognition were founded. The company announced that it had "recorded revenue on certain contracts in one reporting period where customer signature and delivery had been completed, but where the contract may not have been fully executed by the Company in that reporting period."[7] After reviewing all licensing contracts near the end of the prior three years, MicroStrategy was forced to restate its financial statements to correct for the improprieties. The outcome was that accounts receivable for 1999 were reduced from $61.1 million to $37.6 million, leading to a dramatic drop in the company's stock price.

Delaying Write-Downs of Long-Term Assets Consider the widely acclaimed merger between AOL and Time Warner. The combination of the two companies was justified as enabling AOL to cross-sell Time Warner's content (film, news, etc.) to its large subscriber base, a win for both companies. As evidence of the value created from the merger, in its first annual report after the merger, in December 2001, the new company reported goodwill valued at $128 billion. Careful strategic analysis, however, would raise some questions about the merits of the deal. Earlier combinations of content providers and distributors in the entertainment industry (e.g., Disney's acquisition of ABC) had faced difficulties in realizing their potential. Why would the outcome of an AOL and Time Warner merger be any different? Also, it was not clear why AOL had to buy Time Warner to access its content. Why couldn't AOL simply sign a long-term licensing agreement for content with Time Warner? Finally, the merger raised questions about AOL and Time Warner relations with existing customers and suppliers. For example, would Time Warner still be able to sell its content to AOL's competitors (e.g., Microsoft), or would its own market be narrowed? Would AOL still be able to negotiate content deals with Time Warner's competitors? If Time Warner's content became stale, would AOL be committed to continue supplying it to its subscribers, leading to a decline in the value of both firms?

The questions about the economic benefits from the merger were quickly answered when Internet sector stocks crashed in mid-2000. AOL subsequently struggled to retain and grow its subscriber base and encountered more difficulty than expected in developing a successful business model to take advantage of Time Warner's content. As a result, in its December 31, 2001, report, the new company was forced to recognize that goodwill recorded under the merger was impaired and would have to be written down by $54 billion at the end of the following quarter (March 2002).

This raises several issues for analyzing AOL Time Warner. First, given the questionable strategic rationale for the merger in the first place, did the initial $128 billion of goodwill ever represent a true economic asset? If not, when would it make sense to recognize the impairment of goodwill—prior to December 31, 2000, in the December 31 financials, or when the company subsequently reported the decline in value (March 2002)? Second, was the $54 billion write-down adequate given the magnitude of the Internet stock market crash, which indicated that investors as a whole had radically lowered their expectations for Internet stocks such as AOL.

If an analyst decided to record the $54 billion write-down in the December 2001 financials, it would be necessary to make the following balance sheet adjustments:

1. Reduce Long-term Intangible Assets by $54 billion.
2. Reduce the Deferred Tax Liability for the tax effect of the write-down. Assuming a 35 percent tax rate, this amounts to $19 billion.
3. Reduce Common Shareholders' Equity for the after-tax effect of the write-down ($35 billion).

	Adjustment	
($ billions)	Assets	Liabilities & Equity
Balance Sheet		
Long-Term Intangible Assets	−54	
Deferred Tax Liability		−19
Common Shareholders' Equity		−35
Income Statement		
Other Expenses		+54
Tax Expense		−19
Net Income		−35

Note that the write-down of depreciable assets at the beginning of the year will require the analyst to also estimate the write-down's impact on depreciation and amortization expense for the year. For AOL Time Warner, since the asset is goodwill, which is no longer amortized (see SFAS 142), no such expense adjustment is required.

At the end of 2002, AOL announced the write-down of a further $45.5 billion of goodwill, and many of the top AOL managers that had advocated the merger in the first place were no longer with the company.

UNDERSTATED ASSETS

Asset understatements typically arise when managers have incentives to deflate reported earnings. This may occur when the firm is performing exceptionally well and managers decide to store away some of the current strong earnings for a rainy day. Income smoothing, as it has come to be known, can be implemented by overstating current period expenses (and understating the value of assets) during good times. Asset (and expense) understatements can also arise in a particularly bad year, when managers decide to "take a bath" by understating current period earnings to create the appearance of a turnaround in following years. Accounting analysis involves judging whether managers have understated assets (and also income) and, if necessary, adjusting the balance sheet and income statement accordingly.

Accounting rules themselves can also lead to the understatement of assets. In many countries accounting standards require firms to expense outlays for R&D and advertising because, even though they may create future value for owners, their outcomes are highly uncertain. Also, until recently some U.S. acquisitions were accounted for using the pooling of interests method, whereby the acquirer recorded the target's assets at their book value rather than their actual (higher) purchase price. In these cases the analyst may want to make adjustments to the balance sheet and income statement to ensure that they reflect the economic reality of the transactions.

Finally, asset understatements can arise when managers have incentives to understate liabilities. For example, if a firm records lease transactions as operating leases or if it discounts receivables with recourse, neither the assets nor the accompanying obligations are shown on its balance sheet. Yet in some instances this accounting treatment does not reflect the underlying economics of the transactions—the lessee may effectively own the leased assets, and the firm that sells receivables may still bear all of the risks associated with ownership. The analyst may then want to adjust the balance sheet (and also the income statement) for these effects.

The most common forms of asset (and earnings) understatement arise when there are the following:

1. *Overstated write-downs of current assets.* Managers potentially have an incentive to overstate current asset write-downs during years of exceptionally strong performance, or when the firm is financially distressed. By overstating current asset impairments and overstating expenses in the current period, managers can show lower future expenses, boosting earnings in years of sub-par performance or when a turnaround is needed. Overstated current asset write-downs can also arise when managers are less optimistic about the firm's future prospects than the analyst.

2. *Overestimated reserves (e.g., allowances for bad debts or loan losses).* If managers overestimate reserves for bad debts or loan losses, accounts receivable and loans will be understated.

3. *Overstated write-downs of long-term assets.* Overly pessimistic management estimates of long-term asset impairments reduce current period earnings and boost earnings in future periods.

4. *Overstated depreciation/amortization on long-term assets.* Firms that use tax depreciation estimates of asset lives, salvage values, or amortization rates are likely to amortize assets more rapidly than justifiable given the assets' economic usefulness, leading to long-term asset understatements.

5. *Excluded goodwill assets through the use of pooling accounting.* Recent changes in U.S. rules for merger accounting (SFAS 141 and 142) require that firms report mergers using the purchase method. Under this method the cost of the merger for the acquirer is the actual value of the consideration paid for the target firm's shares. The identifiable assets and liabilities of the target are then recorded on the acquirer's books at their fair values. If the value of the consideration paid for the target exceeds the fair value of its identifiable assets and liabilities, the excess is reported

as goodwill on the acquirer's balance sheet. The new rules require goodwill assets to be written off only if they become impaired in the future. However, as recently as 2001 many large acquisitions were reported using the pooling of interests method. Under the pooling of interests method, the purchase of target firm's shares is recorded at their historical book value rather than at their market value, so that no goodwill is recorded. Consequently, pooling does not reflect the true economic cost of the acquisition on the acquirer's books, making it more difficult for shareholders to understand the economic performance of the new firm after the merger.[8] This is likely to be a consideration for the analyst in evaluating the performance of serial stock-for-stock acquirers.[9]

6. *Lease assets off balance sheet.* Assessing whether a lease arrangement should be considered a rental contract (and hence recorded using the operating method) or equivalent to a purchase (and hence shown as a capital lease) is subjective. It depends on whether the lessee has effectively accepted most of the risks of ownership, such as obsolescence and physical deterioration. To standardize the reporting of lease transactions, U.S. accounting standards have created clear criteria for distinguishing between the two types. Under SFAS 13, a lease transaction is equivalent to an asset purchase if any of the following conditions hold: (1) ownership of the asset is transferred to the lessee at the end of the lease term, (2) the lessee has the option to purchase the asset for a bargain price at the end of the lease term, (3) the lease term is 75 percent or more of the asset's expected useful life, and (4) the present value of the lease payments is 90 percent or more of the fair value of the asset. However, because the criteria for reporting leases are objective, they create opportunities for management to circumvent the spirit of the distinction between capital and operating leases, potentially leading to the understatement of lease assets.[10] This is likely to be an important issue for the analysis of heavy asset industries where there are options for leasing (e.g., airlines).[11]

7. *Discounted receivables off balance sheet even though the firm still retains considerable collection risk.* Under current U.S. accounting rules (SFAS 140), receivables that are discounted with a financial institution are considered "sold" if the "seller" cedes control over the receivables to the financier. Control is surrendered if the receivables are beyond the reach of the seller's creditors should the seller file for bankruptcy, if the financier has the right to pledge or sell the receivables, and if the seller has no commitment to repurchase the receivables. The seller can then record the discount transaction as an asset sale. Otherwise it is viewed as a financing transaction that generates a liability for the "seller." However, just because a firm has "sold" receivables for financial reporting purposes does not necessarily mean that it is off the hook for credit risks. Financial institutions that discount receivables often have recourse against the "seller," requiring the seller to continue to estimate bad debt losses. In this event, U.S. rules permit the transaction to be reported as an asset sale only when the seller satisfies the above conditions for surrendering control of the receivables and has experience in estimating the value of the recourse liability (i.e., allowances for credit and refinancing risks). In extreme cases, where there is significant uncertainty about the value of the recourse liability, the analyst has to decide whether to restate the firm's financial statements by returning the "sold" receivables to the balance sheet. As discussed later in this chapter, this will also increase the firm's liabilities, and it will affect its income statement since any gains and losses on the sale need to be excluded, and interest income on the notes receivables and interest expense on the loan need to be recorded each year.

8. *Key intangible assets, such as R&D and brands, not reported on the balance sheet.* Some firms' most important assets are excluded from the balance sheet. Examples include investments in R&D, software development outlays, and brands and membership bases that are created through advertising and promotions. Accounting rules in most countries specifically prohibit the capitalization of R&D outlays and membership acquisition costs, primarily because it is believed that the benefits associated with such outlays are too uncertain.[12] New products or software may never reach the market due to technological infeasibility or to the introduction of superior products by competitors; new members that sign up for a service as a result of a promotions campaign may subsequently quit. Expensing the cost of intangibles has two implications for analysts. First, the omission of intangible assets from the balance sheet inflates measured rates of return on capital (either return on assets or return on equity).[13] For firms with key omitted intangible assets, this has important implications for forecasting long-term performance; unlike firms with no intangibles, competitive forces will not cause their rates of return to fully revert to the cost of capital over time. For example, pharmaceutical firms have shown very high rates of return over many decades, in part because of the impact of R&D accounting. A second effect of expensing outlays for intangibles is that it makes it more difficult for the analyst to assess whether the firm's business model works. Under the matching concept, operating profit is a meaningful indicator of the success of a firm's business model since it compares revenues and the expenses required to generate them. Immediately expensing outlays for intangible assets runs counter to matching and, therefore, makes it more difficult to judge a firm's operating performance. Consistent with this, research shows that investors view R&D and advertising outlays as assets rather than expenses.[14] Understated intangible assets are likely to be important for firms in pharmaceutical, software, branded consumer products, and subscription businesses.

Examples of How to Correct for Asset Understatement

We illustrate some of the types of distortions that understate assets, and show corrections that the analyst can make to ensure that assets are reflected appropriately.

Overstated Depreciation for Long-Term Assets. In 2001 Lufthansa, the German national airline, reported that it depreciated its aircraft over 12 years on a straight-line basis, with an estimated residual value of 15 percent of initial cost. In contrast, British Airways (BA), the UK national carrier, reported that its aircraft depreciation was also estimated using the straight-line method but assuming an average life of 20 years and an 8 percent salvage value.[15]

For the analyst these differences raise several questions. Do Lufthansa and BA fly different types of routes, potentially explaining the differences in their depreciation policies? Alternatively, do they have different asset management strategies? For example, does Lufthansa use newer planes to attract more business travelers, to lower maintenance costs, or to lower fuel costs? If there do not appear to be operating differences that explain the differences in the two firms' depreciation rates, the analyst may well decide that it is necessary to adjust the depreciation rates for one or both firms to ensure that their performance is comparable.

The difference in depreciation assumptions for BA and Lufthansa appears to at least partially reflect Lufthansa's decision to use similar depreciation rates for financial and tax reporting purposes, whereas BA uses different rates for these purposes. To adjust for this effect, the analyst could decrease Lufthansa's depreciation rates to match those of BA's. The following financial statement adjustments would then be required in Lufthansa's financial statements:

1. Increase the book value of the fleet at the beginning of the year to adjust for the relatively low depreciation rates that had been used in the past. This will also require an offsetting increase in equity (retained earnings), and in the deferred tax liability.
2. Reduce the depreciation expense (and increase the book value of the fleet) to reflect the lower depreciation for the current year. There will also be an increase in the tax expense, and on the balance sheet an increase in equity and deferred tax liability. In 2001 Lufthansa's marginal tax rate was 35 percent.

Note that these changes are designed to show Lufthansa's results as if it had always used the same depreciation assumptions as BA rather than to reflect a change in the assumptions for the current year going forward. This enables the analyst to be able to compare ratios that use assets (e.g., return on assets) for the two companies.

At the beginning of 2001, Lufthansa reported in its footnotes that its fleet of aircraft had originally cost 13,579.6m Euros, and that accumulated depreciation was 6,679.9m Euros. This implies that the average life of Lufthansa's fleet was 6.9 years, calculated as follows:

€ (millions unless otherwise noted)		
Aircraft cost, 1/1/2001	13,579.6	Reported
Depreciable cost	11,542.7	Cost × (1 − .15)
Accumulated depreciation, 1/1/2001	6,679.6	Reported
Accumulated depreciation/Depreciable cost	57.87%	
Depreciable life	12 years	Reported
Average age of aircraft	6.944 years	12 × .5787 years

If Lufthansa used the same life and salvage estimates as BA, the depreciable cost of its fleet would have been €12,493.2 [13,579.6 · (1 − .08)]. The annual depreciation rate would have been 5 percent, implying that given the average age of its fleet, Accumulated Depreciation would have been €4,337.6 (6.944 · .05 · 12,493.2) versus the reported €6,679.6. Consequently, the company's Long-term Tangible Assets would have increased by €2,341.9. Given the 35% marginal tax rate, this adjustment to Long-Term Tangible Assets would have required offsetting adjustments of €819.7 (.35 · 2,341.9) to the Deferred Tax Liability and €1,522.2 (.65 · 2,341.9) to Common Shareholders' Equity.

Assuming that €1,021.5m net new aircraft purchased in 2001 were acquired throughout the year, the depreciation expense for 2001 (included in Cost of Sales) would have been €648.2m {.05 · [12,493.2 + (1,021.5 · .92)/2]} versus the €865m reported by the company.[16] Thus Cost of Sales would decline by €216.8m. Given the 35 percent tax rate for 2001, the Tax Expense for the year would increase by €75.9m. On the balance sheet, these changes would increase Long-Term Tangible Assets by €216.8m, increase Deferred Tax Liability by €75.9m, and increase Common Shareholders' Equity by €140.9m.

In summary, if Lufthansa were using the same depreciation method as BA, its financial statements for the years ended December 31, 2000 and 2001, would have to be modified as follows:

(€ millions)	Adjustment Dec. 31, 2000		Adjustment Dec. 31, 2001	
	Assets	Liabilities & Equity	Assets	Liabilities & Equity
Balance Sheet				
Long-Term Tangible Assets	+2,341.9		+2,341.9 +216.8	
Deferred Tax Liability		+819.7		+819.7 +75.9
Common Shareholders' Equity		+1,522.2		+1,522.2 +140.9
Income Statement				
Cost of Sales				−216.8
Tax Expense				+75.9
Net Income				+140.9

Goodwill Excluded Through Use of Pooling Accounting. In its June 2001 acquisition of ALZA, Johnson and Johnson (J&J) announced that it would use the pooling of interests method to record the transaction. Under the terms of the deal, J&J acquired ALZA's 234.3 million shares for 229.6 million J&J shares, valued at $12.2 billion. To adjust for the distortion from using pooling, the analyst can restate the acquirer's financial statements as follows:

1. Revalue the target's assets (and potentially its liabilities) to their fair values.
2. Recognize any goodwill from the transaction, computed as the difference between the purchase price and the fair value of the identifiable net assets of the target.
3. Record the consideration paid by the acquirer, usually acquirer shares, at its fair value.

For J&J's acquisition of ALZA, under pooling, the cost of acquiring ALZA's stock is shown at its book value of $1.6 billion, far below the actual purchase price of $12.2 billion. To record the acquisition under the purchase method, the analyst requires information on the fair value of ALZA's identifiable assets, which is not available. One solution is to assign the full $10.6 billion asset adjustment ($12.2 billion less $1.6 billion) to goodwill. This implicitly assumes that the book and fair values of ALZA's assets are roughly similar. The adjustment to the financial statements of the combined firm on July 31, 2001, immediately following the transaction, would therefore be as follows:

($ millions)	Adjustment	
	Assets	Liabilities & Equity
Balance Sheet		
Long-Term Intangible Assets	+10,600	
Common Shareholders' Equity		+10,600

Note that this adjustment includes in-process R&D as part of goodwill. While not in keeping with U.S. accounting standards, which require any in-process R&D to be expensed at the time of the acquisition, it does reflect the economics of the transaction—the price paid by J&J includes a premium for in-process R&D precisely because J&J expects that some of these projects will generate future benefits for shareholders.

Lease Assets Off Balance Sheet. Japan Airlines (JAL) rents part of its flight equipment and reports for these transactions using the operating method. These rented resources are therefore excluded from JAL's balance sheet, making it difficult for an analyst to compare JAL's financial performance to other airlines that either own their equipment or record leased resources using the capital method, and hence show their value on their balance sheet.

JAL notes that, even though it uses the operating method to report for leases, its leases actually qualify as capital leases. To correct this accounting, the analyst can use information on lease commitments presented in JAL's lease footnote to estimate the value of the assets and liabilities that are omitted from the balance sheet. The leased equipment is then depreciated over the life of the lease, and the lease payments are treated as interest and debt repayment. JAL estimates the present value of its future lease commitments for the years ended March 31, 2001 and 2002, as follows[17]:

(¥ millions)	March 31, 2002	March 31, 2001
Within 1 year	43,077	38,417
Over 1 year	148,777	212,871
	187,194	255,949

In addition, JAL indicates that its historical annual interest rate on outstanding interest-bearing debt is 3 percent, the lease life is 11 years, and the lease expense reported in 2002 is ¥48,816. Given this information, the analyst can make the following adjustments to JAL's beginning and ending balance sheets, and to its income statement for the year ended March 31, 2002:

1. Capitalize the present value of the lease commitments for March 31, 2001, increasing Long-Term Tangible Assets and Long-Term Debt by ¥255,949.
2. Calculate the value of any change in lease assets and lease liabilities during the year from new lease transactions or the return of leased equipment prior to the end of the contracted lease term. On March 31, 2001, JAL's liability for lease commitments in 2003 and beyond was ¥212,871. If there had been no changes in these commitments, one year later (on March 31, 2002), they would have been valued at ¥219,257 (¥212,871 · 1.03). Yet JAL's actual lease commitment on March 31, 2002, was only ¥187,194, indicating that the company reduced its leased aircraft equipment capacity following the economic downturn after September 11, 2001 by ¥32,063. JAL's Long-Term Tangible Assets and Long-Term Debt therefore declined by ¥32,063 during 2002 as a result of lease cancellations or sub-leases.
3. Reflect the change in lease asset value and expense from the depreciation during the year. The depreciation expense for 2002 (included in Cost of Sales) is the depreciation rate (1/11) multiplied by the beginning cost of leased equipment (¥255,949) less depreciation on the decline in leased equipment for 2002

(¥32,063), prorated throughout the year. The depreciation expense for 2002 is therefore ¥21,811 [¥255,949/11 − .5 · (¥32,063/11)].

4. Add back the lease expense in the income statement, included in Cost of Sales, and apportion the payment between Interest Expense and repayment of Long-Term Debt. As previously mentioned, the lease expense is ¥48,816. The portion of this that is shown as Interest Expense is calculated as follows:

Interest on beginning lease obligation (.03 · ¥255,949)	¥7,678
Less: interest on reduction in lease liability in 2002 from return on equipment, prorated throughout the year (.03 · .5 · ¥32,063)	(481)
Interest expense on lease debt	¥7,197

The Long-Term Debt repayment portion is then the remainder of the total lease payment, ¥41,619.

5. Make any needed changes to the Deferred Tax Liability to reflect differences in earnings under the capital and operating methods. JAL's expenses under the capital lease method are ¥29,008 (¥21,811 depreciation expense plus ¥7,197 interest expense) versus ¥48,816 under the operating method. JAL will not change its tax books, but for financial reporting purposes it will show higher earnings before tax and thus a higher Tax Expense through deferred taxes. Given its 33 percent tax rate, the Tax Expense will increase by ¥6,537 [.33 · (¥29,008 − ¥48,816)] and the Deferred Tax Liability will increase by the same amount.

In summary, the adjustments to JAL's financial statements on March 31, 2001 and 2002, are as follows:

(¥ millions)	Adjustment March 31, 2001		Adjustment March 31, 2002	
	Assets	Liabilities & Equity	Assets	Liabilities & Equity
Balance Sheet				
Long-Term Tangible Assets				
Beginning capitalization	+255,949		+255,949	
Lease cancellations			−32,063	
Annual depreciation			−21,811	
Long-Term Debt				
Beginning debt		+255,949		+255,949
Lease cancellations				−32,063
Debt repayment				−41,619
Deferred Tax Liability				+6,537
Common Shareholders' Equity				+13,271
Income Statement				
Cost of Sales:				
Lease expense				−48,816
Depreciation expense				+21,811
Interest Expense				+7,197
Tax Expense				+6,537
Net Income				+13,271

These adjustments increase JAL's fixed assets by 24 percent in 2001 and 20 percent in 2002, reducing the company's asset turnover (sales/assets) from the reported value of 147 percent to 121 percent in 2001, and from 136 percent to 117 percent in 2002. There is also a difference in earnings, since the lease expense is replaced with the depreciation and interest expenses. This leads to an increase in operating earnings (before interest). As a result, the company's return on operating assets for 2002 actually increases from the reported value of –0.7 percent to 2.5 percent.

Key Intangible Assets Off Balance Sheet. How should the analyst approach the omission of intangibles? One way is to leave the accounting as is, but to recognize that forecasts of long-term rates of return will have to reflect the inherent biases that arise from this accounting method. A second approach is to capitalize intangibles and amortize them over their expected lives.

For example, consider the case of Microsoft, the most valuable software company in the world. Microsoft does not capitalize any software R&D costs, even those arising after software products have passed the stage of technological feasibility. What adjustment would be required if the analyst decided to capitalize all of Microsoft's software R&D and to amortize the intangible asset using the straight-line method over the expected life of software (approximately three years)? Assume that R&D spending occurs evenly throughout the year, and that only half a year's amortization is taken on the latest year's spending. Given R&D outlays for the years 1999 to 2001, the R&D asset at the end of 2001 is $6.1 billion, calculated as follows:

Year	R&D Outlay	Proportion Capitalized 12/31/01	Asset 12/31/01	Proportion Capitalized 12/31/02	Asset 12/31/02
2002	$4.3b			$(1 - .33/2)$	$3.6b
2001	4.4	$(1 - .33/2)$	$3.7b	$(1 - .33/2 - .33)$	2.2
2000	3.8	$(1 - .33/2 - .33)$	1.9	$(1 - .33/2 - .67)$	0.6
1999	3.0	$(1 - .33/2 - .67)$	0.5		
Total			$6.1		$6.4

The R&D amortization expense (included in Other Operating Expenses) for 2001 and 2002 are $3.4 billion and $3.9 billion, respectively, and are calculated as follows:

Year	R&D Outlay	Proportion Amortized 12/31/01	Expense 12/31/01	Proportion Amortized 12/31/02	Expense 12/31/02
2002	$4.3b			.33/2	$0.7b
2001	4.4	.33/2	$0.7b	.33	1.5
2000	3.8	.33	1.2	.33	1.2
1999	3.0	.33	1.0	.33/2	0.5
1998	2.8	.33/2	0.5		
Total			$3.4		$3.9

Since Microsoft will continue to expense software R&D immediately for tax purposes, the change in reporting method will give rise to a Deferred Tax Liability. Given a marginal tax rate of 35 percent, this liability will equal 35 percent of the value of the Intangible Asset reported, with the balance increasing Common Shareholders' Equity.

In summary, the adjustments required to capitalize software R&D for Microsoft for the years 2001 and 2002 are as follows:

($ billions)	Adjustment Dec. 31, 2001		Adjustment Dec. 31, 2002	
	Assets	Liabilities & Equity	Assets	Liabilities & Equity
Balance Sheet				
Long-Term Intangible Assets	+6.1		+6.4	
Deferred Tax Liability		+2.2		+2.2
Common Shareholders' Equity		+3.9		+4.2
Income Statement				
Other Operating Expenses		−4.4 +3.4		−4.3 +3.9
Tax Expense		+0.3		+0.1
Net Income		+0.7		+0.3

LIABILITY DISTORTIONS

Liabilities are defined as economic obligations arising from benefits received in the past, and for which the amount and timing is known with reasonable certainty. Liabilities include obligations to customers that have paid in advance for products or services; commitments to public and private providers of debt financing; obligations to federal and local governments for taxes; commitments to employees for unpaid wages, pensions, and other retirement benefits; and obligations from court or government fines or environmental cleanup orders.

Distortions in liabilities generally arise because there is ambiguity about whether (1) an obligation has really been incurred and/or (2) the obligation can be measured.

Has an obligation been incurred?

For most liabilities there is little ambiguity about whether an obligation has been incurred. For example, when a firm buys supplies on credit, it has incurred an obligation to the supplier. However, for some transactions it is more difficult to decide whether there is any such obligation. For example, if a firm announces a plan to restructure its business by laying off employees, has it made a commitment that would justify recording a liability? Or, if a software firm receives cash from its customers for a five-year software license, should the firm report the full cash inflow as revenues, or should some of it represent the ongoing commitment to the customer for servicing and supporting the license agreement?

Can the obligation be measured?

Many liabilities specify the amount and timing of obligations precisely. For example, a 20-year $100 million bond issue with an 8 percent coupon payable semi-annually specifies that the issuer will pay the holders $100 million in twenty years, and it will pay out interest of $4 million every six months for the duration of the loan. However, for some liabilities it is difficult to estimate the amount of the obligation. For example, a firm that is responsible for an environmental cleanup clearly has incurred an obligation, but the amount is highly uncertain.[18] Similarly, firms that provide pension and post-retirement benefits for employees have incurred commitments that depend on uncertain future events, such as employee mortality rates, and on future inflation rates, making valuation of the obligation subjective. Future warranty and insurance claim obligations fall into the same category—the commitment is clear but the amount depends on uncertain future events.

Accounting rules frequently specify when a commitment has been incurred and how to measure the amount of the commitment. However, as discussed earlier, accounting rules are imperfect—they cannot cover all contractual possibilities and reflect all of the complexities of a firm's business relationships. They also require managers to make subjective estimates of future events to value the firm's commitments. Thus the analyst may decide that some important obligations are omitted from the financial statements or, if included, are understated, either because of management bias or because there are legitimate differences in opinion between managers and analysts over future risks and commitments. As a result, analysis of liabilities is usually with an eye to assessing whether the firm's financial commitments and risks are understated and/or its earnings overstated.

Understated Liabilities

Liabilities are likely to be understated when the firm has key commitments that are difficult to value and therefore not considered liabilities for financial reporting purposes. Understatements are also likely to occur when managers have strong incentives to overstate the soundness of the firm's financial position, or to boost reported earnings. By understating leverage, managers present investors with a rosy picture of the firm's financial risks. Earnings management also understates liabilities (namely deferred or unearned revenues) when revenues are recognized upon receipt of cash, even though not all services have been provided.

The most common forms of asset (and earnings) overstatement arise when the following conditions exist:

1. *Unearned revenues are understated through aggressive revenue recognition.* If cash has already been received but the product or service has yet to be provided, a liability (called unearned or deferred revenues) is created. This liability reflects the company's commitment to provide the service or product to the customer and is extinguished once that is accomplished. Firms that recognize revenues prematurely, after the receipt of cash but prior to fulfilling their product or service commitments to customers, understate deferred revenue liabilities and overstate earnings. Firms that bundle service contracts with the sale of a product are particularly prone to deferred revenue liability understatement since separating the price of the product from the price of the service is subjective.

2. *Loans from discounted receivables are off balance sheet.* As discussed earlier, receivables that are discounted with a financial institution are considered "sold" if the "seller" cedes control over the receivables to the financier. Yet if the sale permits the buyer to have recourse against the seller in the event of default, the seller continues to face collection risk. Given the management judgment involved in forecasting default and refinancing costs, as well as the incentives faced by managers to keep debt off the balance sheet, it will be important for the analyst to evaluate the firm's

estimates for default as well as the inherent commitments that it has for discounted receivables. Are the firm's estimates reasonable? Is it straightforward to forecast the costs of the default and prepayment risks? If not, does the analyst need to increase the value of the recourse liability? Or, in the extreme, does the analyst need to undo the sale and recognize a loan from the financial institution for the discounted value of the receivables.

3. *Long-term liabilities for leases are off balance sheet.* As discussed earlier in the chapter, key lease assets and liabilities can be excluded from the balance sheet if the company structures lease transactions to fit the accounting definition of an operating lease. Firms that groom transactions to avoid showing lease assets and obligations will have very different balance sheets from firms with virtually identical economics but which either use capital leases or borrow from the bank to actually purchase the equivalent resources. For firms that choose to structure lease transactions to fit the definition of an operating lease, the analyst can restate the leases as capital leases, as discussed in the Asset Understatement section. This will ensure that the firm's true financial commitments and risks will be reflected on its balance sheet, enabling comparison with peer firms.

4. *Pension and post-retirement obligations are not fully recorded.* Many firms make commitments to provide pension and retirement benefits to their employees. Accounting rules require managers to estimate and report the present value of the commitments that have been earned by employees over their years of working for the firm. This obligation is offset by any assets that the firm has committed to pension/retirement plans to fund future plan benefits. If the funds set aside in the retirement plan are greater (less) than the plan commitments, the plan is overfunded (underfunded). Several important issues arise for analyzing pension/post-retirement plan obligations. First, estimating the obligations themselves is subjective—managers have to make forecasts of future wage and benefit rates, worker attrition rates, the expected lives of retirees, and the discount rate.[19] If these forecasts are too low, the firm's benefit obligations (as well as the annual expenses for benefits reported in the income statement) will be understated.[20] Second, accounting rules require that incremental benefit commitments that arise from changes to a plan, and changes in plan funding status that arise from abnormal investment returns on plan assets, are smoothed over time rather than reflected immediately. As a result, for labor-intensive firms that offer attractive retirement benefits to employees, it is important that the analyst assess whether reported pension and retirement plan liabilities reflect the firms' true commitments.

Examples of How to Correct for Liability Understatement

We illustrate some of these types of liability understatements and the corrections that the analyst can make to reduce bias in the financial statements.

Unearned Revenues Understated Consider the case of MicroStrategy, the software company discussed earlier, which bundles customer support and software updates with its initial licensing agreements. This raises questions about how much of the contract price should be allocated to the initial license versus the company's future commitments. In March 2000 MicroStrategy conceded that it had incorrectly overstated revenues on contracts that involved significant future customization and consulting by $54.5 million. As a result, it would have to restate its financial statements for 1999 as well as for several earlier years. To undo the distortion to 1999 financials, the following adjustments would have to be made:

1. In the quarter that the contracts were booked by the company, Sales would decline and unearned revenues (included in Other Current Liabilities) would increase by $54.5 million.
2. Cost of Sales would decline and prepaid expenses (inventory for product companies) would increase to reflect the lower sales. As noted earlier, MicroStrategy's cost of license revenues is only 3 percent of license revenues, implying that the adjustment to prepaid expenses (included in Other Current Assets) and Cost of Sales is modest ($1.6m).
3. The decline in pretax income would result in a lower Tax Expense in the company's financial reporting books (but presumably not in its tax books). Given MicroStrategy's marginal tax rate of 35 percent, the decline in the Tax Expense as well as in the Deferred Tax Liability is $18.5 million [($54.5 − 1.6) · .35].

The full effect of the adjustment on the quarterly financial statements would, therefore, be as follows:

| ($ millions) | Adjustment | |
	Assets	Liabilities & Equity
Balance Sheet		
Other Current Assets	+1.6	
Other Current Liabilities		+54.5
Deferred Tax Liability		−18.5
Common Shareholders' Equity		−34.4
Income Statement		
Sales		−54.5
Cost of Sales		−1.6
Tax Expense		−18.5
Net Income		−34.4

MicroStrategy's March 10 announcement that it had overstated revenues prompted the SEC to investigate the company. In the period when it announced its overstatements, MicroStrategy's stock price plummeted 94 percent, compared to the 37 percent drop by the NASDAQ in the same period.

Discounted Receivables Off Balance Sheet. Prior to 2000 Computer Associates (CA) discounted notes receivable from its long-term licensing contracts. In 2002 it reported a contingent liability of $218 million for receivables that had been discounted with recourse. The company did not provide information on the value of the recourse liability for these notes receivable, making it difficult to judge the adequacy of the allowance for credit and refinancing losses that potentially could arise on the discounted receivables. One way for the analyst to assess the impact of the financing is to reverse the sale and include a liability for the full $218 million on CA's balance sheet. This would require the following adjustments:

1. CA's Other Long-Term Assets would be increased by the receivable commitment ($218 million). In turn, Long-Term Debt would be recorded to reflect the value of the cash advanced to CA under the discount transaction. CA appears to charge its customers an annual interest rate of roughly 9 percent. Assuming customers repay the receivables in equal monthly installments over the next four years, and the bank charges a 10 percent interest rate, the receivable loan would be valued at $214.1 million.

2. The after-tax difference between the face value of the receivables and the loan, which would have been shown as a loss on sale under the reported accounting, needs to be reversed, increasing equity. Given the above assumptions and CA's 35 percent marginal tax rate, the adjustment would increase Common Shareholders' Equity by $2.5 million [$3.9 \cdot (1 - .35)$].

3. The impact of the tax deduction from reporting a loss on sale, which would have reduced the Deferred Tax Liability, needs to be reversed. For CA, this amount would have resulted in a roughly $1.4 million ($3.9 \cdot .35$) increase in the Deferred Tax Liability.

4. During the year ended March 31, 2003, customers are scheduled to make monthly payments on the discounted receivables, reducing the value of notes receivable under the adjusted accounting. For CA, these amounted to $54.5 million ($218 million $\cdot$ .25). Notes receivable would increase if any additional notes were discounted during the year. For CA, no new receivable discounts were undertaken since the company changed its sales strategy.

5. For 2003, CA's income statement would include Interest Income from notes receivable for $18.7 million $\{(218.0 \cdot .09) - [(54.5 \cdot .09) \cdot .5]\}$ and Interest Expense from the loan for roughly $17.2 million $\{(214.0 \cdot .10) - [(54.5 \cdot .10) \cdot .5]\}$ along with any tax effects.[21] The loan would decline by a smaller amount, since $1.6 million of the receivable repayments are allocated to covering the higher interest charged on the loan (exactly offsetting the wedge between the Interest Income and the Interest Expense for the year).

6. The value of the loan increases by the amount of any additional discounts undertaken during the year ($0), and declines by the value of receivable repayments by customers ($54.5 million) net of the portion of the repayment that represents incremental interest charged by the bank relative to the rate CA charged its customers ($1.5 million, or $18.7 million – $17.2 million).

The overall effect of these adjustments on CA's financial statements would, therefore, be as follows:

($ millions)	Adjustment for March 31, 2002		Adjustment for March 31, 2003	
	Assets	Liabilities & Equity	Assets	Liabilities & Equity
Balance Sheet				
Other Long-Term Assets	+218.0		+218.0 −54.5	
Long-Term Debt		+214.1		+214.1 −54.5 +1.5

(continued)

($ millions)	Adjustment for March 31, 2002		Adjustment for March 31, 2003	
	Assets	Liabilities & Equity	Assets	Liabilities & Equity
Balance Sheet (continued)				
Deferred Tax Liability		+1.4		+1.4
				−0.5
Common Shareholders' Equity		+2.5		+2.5
				−1.0
Income Statement				
Interest Income				+17.2
Interest Expense				+18.7
Tax Expense				−0.5
Net Income				−1.0

Pension/Post-Retirement Obligations Not Fully Recorded   Accounting rules require that firms estimate the value of pension and post-retirement commitments as the present value of future expected payouts under the plans. The obligation under pension plans is referred to as the Projected Benefit Obligation, and is the present value of plan commitments factoring in the impact of future increases in wage rates and salary scales on projected payouts.[22] For post-retirement plans, the firm's obligation is called the Expected Post-Retirement Benefit Obligation, and is calculated as the present value of expected future benefits for employees and their beneficiaries.

Each year the firm's pension and post-retirement obligations are adjusted to reflect the following factors:

- *Service Cost:* Defined benefit plans typically provide higher benefits for each additional year of service with the company. For example, in their 1996 agreement with the United Auto Workers, the three major U.S. auto manufacturers increased pension benefits for new employees by $4.55 a month for every year worked. The value of incremental benefits earned from another year of service is called the service cost, and increases the firm's obligation each year.
- *Interest Cost:* The passage of time increases the present value of the firm's obligation. The interest cost recognizes this effect, and it is calculated by multiplying the obligation at the beginning of the year by the discount rate.
- *Actuarial Gains and Losses:* Each year the actuarial assumptions used to estimate the firm's commitments are reviewed and, if appropriate, changes are made. The effect of these changes is shown as Actuarial Gains and Losses.
- *Benefits Paid:* The plan commitments are reduced as the plan makes payments to retirees each year.

For example, in its financial statement footnotes, General Motors (GM) provided the following information on its Expected Post-Retirement Benefit Obligation for the years ended December 31, 2001 and 2000:

($ millions)	2001	2000
Benefit Obligations		
Benefit obligation at beginning of year	$49,889	$44,683
Service cost	480	448
Interest cost	3,733	3,346
Actuarial losses	1,582	4,392
Benefits paid	(3,173)	(2,805)
Other	(22)	(175)
Benefit obligation at end of year	$52,489	$49,889

GM's obligation at the end of 2001 was $52.5 billion, a 5 percent increase over the prior year.

To meet their commitments under pension and other post-retirement plans, firms make contributions to the plans. These contributions are then invested in equities, debt, and other assets. Plan assets, therefore, are increased each year by new company (and employee) contributions. They are also increased or decreased by the returns generated each year from plan investments. Finally, plan assets decline when the plan pays out benefits to retirees. For the years ended December 31, 2001 and 2000, GM reported the following assets for post-retirement plans:

($ millions)	2001	2000
Plan assets		
Fair value of plan assets at beginning of year	$6,724	$6,291
Actual return on plan assets	(479)	421
Employer contributions	—	743
Plan participants' contributions	—	—
Benefits paid	(1,300)	(731)
Fair value of plan assets at end of year	$4,945	$6,724

In 2001 GM's plan assets declined significantly because they generated a negative return during the year. The difference between GM's post-retirement plan obligations and the plan assets, $47.5 billion, represents the company's unfunded obligation to employees under the plan. The company also reports that it has a $12.6 billion gap between its obligations under pension plans ($86.3 billion in 2001) and pension plan assets ($73.7 billion).

Of course, estimating pension and post-retirement obligations is highly subjective. It requires managers to forecast the future payouts under the plans, which in turn involves making projections of employees' service with the firm, retirement ages, and life expectancies, as well as future wage rates and health insurance costs. It also requires managers to select an interest rate to estimate the present value of the future benefits. For example, GM projected that health care costs would grow at 6 percent per year in 2002, 7.3 percent in 2004, and decline linearly to a steady state rate of 5 percent in 2008. It also assumed that the appropriate discount rate was 7.3 percent. GM reports that a 1 percent increase in the rate of health care inflation would increase the post-retirement obligation by $5.4 billion. Given the management judgment involved in making these forecasts and assumptions, analysts should question whether reported obligations adequately reflect the firm's true commitments.

So, given GM's unfunded post-retirement benefit obligation of $47.5 billion, it seems reasonable to expect that the company will report a liability on its balance sheet for $47.5 billion. Unfortunately, pension and post-retirement accounting is more complex than this. Financial reporting rules require that firms smooth out shocks to plan obligations and assets. For example, if GM agrees to increase its post-retirement or pension benefits for current workers, it will have to increase the value of its obligation. SFAS 87 requires this "prior period service obligation" to be amortized over employees' average expected remaining years of service rather than right away. Also, if the value of plan assets increases or decreases unexpectedly in a given year, or there needs to be adjustment in the actuarial assumptions made to estimate the obligation, the financial statement impact is reflected gradually rather than immediately. Thus, even though the actual gap between GM's post-retirement obligation and plan assets is $47.5 billion, this is not the value of the liability recorded on its balance sheet. GM provides a separate disclosure that reconciles the actual and the reported obligation:

($ millions)	2001	2000
Funded status	$(47,544)	$(43,165)
Unrecognized actuarial loss	8,902	6,444
Unrecognized prior service cost	249	207
Net amount recognized	$(38,393)	$(36,514)

The unrecognized actuarial loss arises because GM's earlier actuarial assumptions about parameters such as future health care costs, retirement rates, and assumed rates of return on plan assets have proven to be optimistic. These effects are recognized over time rather than right away. Similarly, prior service costs represent additional commitments from post-retirement plan changes that are recognized over time. Consequently, GM's reported post-retirement liability understates its real commitment by $9.1 billion ($47.5 billion less $38.4 billion). The company reports that its pension liability also understates it actual commitment by $28.3 billion.[23]

What does pension and post-retirement accounting imply for financial analysis? It is reasonable for the analyst to raise several questions about a firm's pension and post-retirement obligations, particularly for firms in labor-intensive industries.

1. Are the assumptions made by the firm to estimate its pension and post-retirement obligations realistic? These include assumptions about the discount rate, which is supposed to represent the current market interest rate for benefits, as well as assumptions about increases in wage and benefit costs. If these assumptions are optimistic, the obligations recorded on the books understate the firm's real economic commitment. As discussed above, GM notes that a 1 percent increase in expected health care costs increases its obligation by $5.4 billion. The analyst can use this information to adjust for any optimism in management's assumptions. For example, if the analyst decided that GM's forecasts of future healthcare costs were too low and needed to increase by 1 percent, the post-retirement obligation would have to be increased by $5.4 billion, with offsetting declines to equity (for the after-tax effect) and to the deferred tax liability. The adjustment to GM's 2001 balance sheet, assuming a 35 percent tax rate, would be as follows:

($ millions)	Adjustment	
	Assets	Liabilities & Equity
Balance Sheet		
Long-Term Debt		+$5,400
Deferred Tax Liability		−1,890
Common Shareholders' Equity		−$3,510

2. The process of smoothing prior service costs and differences between actual and forecasted parameters for pension and other benefit plans understates any obligations for pensions and post-retirement benefits. For GM this understatement is substantial. As noted above, GM reports a liability for unfunded post-retirement benefits that is $9.1 billion less than the actual obligations. The analyst can adjust for this distortion by increasing the firm's Long-Term Debt, and making offsetting adjustments to the Deferred Tax Liability (since the change would not affect the company's taxable income) and Common Shareholders' Equity. Assuming a 35 percent tax rate, the adjustment to GM's 2001 balance sheet would be as follows:

($ millions)	Adjustment	
	Assets	Liabilities & Equity
Balance Sheet		
Long-Term Debt		+$9,151
Deferred Tax Liability		−3,203
Common Shareholders' Equity		−$5,948

3. What effect do pension assumptions play in the income statement? The pension cost each year comprises (a) Service cost, plus (b) Interest cost, plus (c) Amortization of any prior period service costs, plus or minus (d) Amortization of actuarial gains and losses, minus (e) Expected return on plan assets (the expected long-term return multiplied by beginning assets under management). For example, GM shows that its post-retirement expenses for 2001 and 2000 are as follows:

($ millions)	2001	2000
Service cost	$480	$448
Interest cost	3,733	3,346
Expected return on plan assets	−542	−650
Amortization of prior service cost	−45	−42
Recognized net actuarial loss/(gain)	96	70
Net expense	$3,722	$3,172

This expense reflects the effect of smoothing actual asset returns, prior period service costs, and revisions in actuarial assumptions discussed earlier. For example, in 2001 the actual return on post-retirement plan assets was −$497 million, whereas the expected return reflected in the expense was $542 million. If the analyst used the actual return to compute the pension expense, an additional $1,039 million in post-retirement expenses, included in SG&A Expense, would be required. Since this adjustment would not change the firm's tax books, it would lower the Tax Expense by $364 million (.35 · $1,039m). The full income statement adjustment would therefore be as follows:

($ millions)	Adjustment
Income Statement	
SG&A Expense	+$1,039
Tax Expense	−364
Net Income	−$675

If desired, similar adjustments can be made to undo the income effects of smoothing changes in actuarial assumptions and prior-period service costs.

EQUITY DISTORTIONS

Accounting treats stockholders' equity as a residual claim on the firm's assets, after paying off the other claimholders. Consequently, equity distortions arise primarily from distortions in assets and liabilities. For example, distortions in assets or liabilities that affect earnings also lead to distortions in equity. However, there are two forms of equity distortions that would not typically arise in asset and liability analyses:

1. *Effect of hybrid securities.* Hybrid securities include convertible debt and debt with warrants attached. These securities are partially pure debt and partially equity. Current accounting rules do not separate these components, typically implying that the balance sheet overstates firm debt and understates its equity. Without adjusting for this distortion, it can be difficult to understand the real financial risks and returns for firms with different types of hybrids. New accounting rules proposed by the FASB are likely to address this issue by requiring securities such as convertible debt to be separated into two components on the balance sheet, a debt component and an equity component. Each would be valued at its fair value at the date of issue. This approach could be adopted by the analyst.
2. *Stock option expenses.* A stock option gives the holder the right to purchase a certain number of shares of stock at a predetermined price, called the exercise or strike price, for a specified period of time, termed the exercise period. In the 1980s and 1990s, stock options became the most significant component of compensation for many corporate executives. As a result, top management owned or had a claim to 13.2 percent of their company's shares in 1997, almost double the 1989 ownership percentage. Proponents of options argue that they provide managers with incentives to maximize shareholder value and make it easier to attract talented managers. In addition, many managers view options as a low-cost form of compensation, since no expense is typically recorded either when they are issued or when they are exercised.

   U.S. rules permit firms to report stock options using either the intrinsic value method (outlined in Accounting Principles Board [APB] 25) or the fair value method (discussed in SFAS 123). Under the intrinsic value method, no compensation expense is reported at the grant date for the vast majority of stock options awarded, where the exercise price is equal to the firm's current stock price. If the options are subsequently exercised, there is also no expense recorded, and the new stock that is issued is valued at the exercise price rather than its higher market value. In contrast, the fair value method requires firms to record an expense for stock option compensation when the options are issued. The value of the options issued is estimated using a recognized valuation model, such as the Black-Scholes model, and is then expensed over the vesting period.[24]

FASB's initial proposal that all companies use the fair value method met with considerable opposition from practitioners, particularly in the high-tech sector where stock options were most popular. Opponents of the proposal argued that Black-Scholes valuations are imprecise and overvalue nonmarketable management options. Consequently FASB backed down on its proposal and permitted companies to choose either the intrinsic or the fair value method. However, those that chose the intrinsic value method—and most did—were required to report in the footnotes the earnings effect from using the fair value method.[25]

Following the demise of Enron, there has been increased recognition that overuse of stock options can encourage managers to manage earnings to boost short-term stock prices. There has also been increased shareholder and political pressure to recognize some form of cost for stock option compensation, leading companies such as Coca-Cola, The Washington Post, and Amazon.com to voluntarily begin using the fair value method for reporting stock option awards. FASB has decided to revisit stock options in the coming years, and it may well mandate some form of fair value method.

The net effect of the debate over stock option accounting is that many firms still show no expense for stock option awards. While Black-Scholes valuations are imperfect, there is no question that they present a more accurate reflection of the economic cost of stock option awards to the firm's shareholders than the zero cost reported under the intrinsic value method. Consequently, for firms that rely heavily on stock options, such as high-technology firms, it is important for the analyst to understand how the firm accounts for management stock options and whether an adjustment is required.

Examples of How to Correct for Equity Distortions

We illustrate these types of equity distortions and the corrections that the analyst can make to reduce bias in the financial statements.

Hybrid Securities   On February 3, 1999, Amazon.com completed an offering of $1.25 billion of 4.75 percent Convertible Subordinated Notes due in 2009. Several months earlier Amazon had issued senior notes with an annual interest rate of 10 percent. The conversion premium was therefore significant—if the notes had not included a conversion option, Amazon would probably have had to pay a coupon rate in excess of 10 percent. The value of the $1.25 billion convertible issue at a 10 percent discount rate is only $0.87 billion, implying that the convertibility premium was worth roughly $0.38 billion. One way to adjust for this effect is to record the debt component at $0.87 billion and to show the $0.38 conversion premium as part of Common Shareholders' Equity. Interest on the debt would then be based on the 10 percent coupon rate rather than the 4.75 percent (which reflects the conversion premium).

The effect of this adjustment on Amazon's financial statements at March 31, 2002, would be as follows:

($ billions)	Adjustment for March 31, 2002	
	Assets	Liabilities & Equity
Balance Sheet		
Long-Term Debt		−0.38
Common Shareholders Equity		+0.38

Stock Option Expenses To adjust for the effective cost to the company from providing stock option compensation, the analyst must first recognize the fair value of options earned in the period as an expense and as an increase in Common Shareholders' Equity (reflecting the option grants). The second step is to adjust the firm's tax expense to reflect the deferred tax impact of expensing the fair value of options awarded. Given the footnote disclosures required under SFAS 123, it is relatively easy to determine these effects.

For example, consider the case of Microsoft, which uses stock options extensively and reports using the intrinsic value method. In its June 30, 2001, financial statement footnotes, Microsoft noted that earnings before taxes using fair value accounting would have been $8.148 billion versus $11.525 billion reported earnings, a difference of $3.377 billion. Of this amount, $0.32 billion is allocated to Cost of Sales, $1.727 billion is allocated to R&D Expense, and the remaining $1.33 is reported as Selling and Administrative expenses. In addition, the lower fair value method earnings would have lowered the Tax Expense by $1.115 billion (indicating a 33 percent tax rate), with an offset on the balance sheet to Deferred Tax Liability. Finally, stock options, included in equity, would be reported at a value of $3.337 billion. The overall effect of the adjustment on Microsoft's financial statements would, therefore, be as follows:

($ billions)	Adjustment	
	Assets	Liabilities & Equity
Balance Sheet		
Deferred Tax Liability		−1.115
Common Shareholders Equity		−2.262
		+3.377
Income Statement		
Cost of Sales		+0.320
SG&A Expense		+1.330
Other Operating Expenses		+1.727
Tax Expense		−1.115
Net Income		−2.262

SUMMARY

To implement accounting analysis, the analyst must first recast the financial statements into a common format so that financial statement terminology and formatting is comparable between firms and across time. A standard template for recasting the financials, presented in this chapter, is used throughout the remainder of the book.

Once the financial statements are standardized, the analyst can determine what accounting distortions exist in the firm's assets, liabilities, and equity. Common distortions that overstate assets include delays in recognizing asset impairments, underestimated reserves, aggressive revenue recognition leading to overstated receivables, and optimistic assumptions on long-term asset depreciation. Asset understatements can arise if managers overstate asset write-offs, use operating leases to keep assets off the balance sheet, or make conservative assumptions for asset depreciation. They can also arise because accounting rules require outlays for key assets (e.g., R&D and brands) to be immediately expensed. For liabilities, the primary concern for the analyst is whether the firm understates its real commitments. This can arise from off-balance liabilities (e.g., operating lease obligations), from questionable management judgment and limitations in accounting rules for estimating pension and benefit plan liabilities, and from aggressive revenue recognition that understates unearned revenue obligations. Equity distortions frequently arise when there are distortions in assets and liabilities. However, they can also arise if no expense is reported for stock option compensation, or for firms that issue hybrid securities.

Adjustments for distortions can, therefore, arise because accounting standards, although applied appropriately, do not reflect a firm's economic reality. They can also arise if the analyst has a different point of view than management about the estimates and assumptions made in preparing the financial statements. Once distortions have been identified, the analyst can use footnote and cash flow statement information to make adjustments to the balance sheet at the beginning and/or end of the current year, as well as any needed adjustments to revenues and expenses in the latest income statement. This ensures that the most recent financial ratios used to evaluate a firm's performance and to forecast its future results are based on financial data that appropriately reflect its business economics.

Several points are worth remembering when doing accounting analysis. First, the bulk of the analyst's time and energy should be focused on evaluating and adjusting accounting policies and estimates that describe the firm's key strategic value drivers. Of course this does not mean that management bias is not reflected in other accounting estimates and policies, and the analyst should certainly examine these. But given the importance of evaluating how the firm is managing its key success factors and risks, the bulk of the accounting analysis should be spent examining those policies that describe these factors and risks.

It is also important to recognize that many accounting adjustments can only be approximations rather than precise calculations, since much of the information necessary for making precise adjustments is not disclosed. The analyst should, therefore, try to avoid worrying about being overly precise in making accounting adjustments. By making even crude adjustments, it is usually possible to mitigate some of the limitations of accounting standards and problems of management bias in financial reporting.

DISCUSSION QUESTIONS

1. Use the templates shown in Tables 4-1, 4-2, and 4-3 to recast the following financial statements for Amazon.com.

Amazon.com Inc. Consolidated Balance Sheet at December 31, 2002 ($ thousands)

	12/31/02	12/31/01
ASSETS		
Current assets:		
Cash and cash equivalents	$738,254	$540,282
Marketable securities	562,715	456,303
Inventories	202,425	143,722
Accounts receivable, net and other current assets	112,282	67,613
Total current assets	$1,615,676	$1,207,920
Fixed assets, net	239,398	271,751
Goodwill, net	70,811	45,367
Other intangibles, net	3,460	34,382
Other equity investments	15,442	28,359
Other assets	45,662	49,768
Total assets	$1,990,449	$1,637,547
LIABILITIES AND STOCKHOLDERS' DEFICIT		
Current liabilities:		
Accounts payable	618,128	444,748
Accrued expenses and other current liabilities	314,935	305,064
Unearned revenue	47,916	87,978
Interest payable	71,661	68,632
Current portion of long-term debt and other	13,318	14,992
Total current liabilities	$1,065,958	$921,414
Long-term debt and other	2,277,305	2,156,133
Shareholders' deficit:		
Common stock, $0.01 par value: Authorized shares 5,000,000 ; Issued and outstanding shares—387,906 and 373,218 shares, respectively	3,879	3,732
Additional paid-in capital	$1,649,946	$1,462,769
Deferred stock-based compensation	(6,591)	(9,853)
Accumulated other comprehensive income (loss)	9,662	(36,070)
Accumulated deficit	(3,009,710)	(2,860,578)
Total stockholders' deficit	$(1,352,814)	$(1,440,000)
Total liabilities and stockholders' deficit	1,990,449	1,637,547

Amazon.com Inc. Consolidated Income Statement for the Year Ended December 31, 2002 ($ thousands)

	12/31/02	12/31/01	12/31/00
Net sales	$3,932,936	$3,122,433	$2,761,983
Cost of sales	2,940,318	2,323,875	2,106,206
Gross profit	992,618	798,558	655,777

(continued)

	12/31/02	12/31/01	12/31/00
Operating expenses:			
Fulfillment	392,467	374,250	414,509
Marketing	125,383	138,283	179,980
Technology and content	215,617	241,165	269,326
General and administrative	79,049	89,862	108,962
Stock-based compensation	68,927	4,637	24,797
Amortization of goodwill and other intangibles	5,478	181,033	321,772
Restructuring-related and other	41,573	181,585	200,311
Total operating expenses	$928,494	$1,210,815	$1,519,657
Income (loss) from operations	64,124	(412,257)	(863,880)
Interest income	23,687	29,103	40,821
Interest expense	(142,925)	(139,232)	(130,921)
Other income (expense), net	5,623	(1,900)	(10,058)
Other gains (losses), net	(96,273)	(2,141)	(142,639)
Total non-operating expenses, net	$(209,888)	$(114,170)	$(242,797)
Loss before equity in losses of equity-method investees	(145,764)	(526,427)	(1,106,677)
Equity in losses of equity-method investees, net	(4,169)	(30,327)	(304,596)
Loss before change in accounting principle	$(149,933)	$(556,754)	$(1,411,273)
Cumulative effect of change in accounting principle	801	(10,523)	
Net loss	$(149,132)	$(567,277)	$(1,411,273)

Amazon.com Inc. Consolidated Cash Flow Statement for the Year Ended December 31, 2002 ($ thousands)

	12/31/02	12/31/01	12/31/00
OPERATING ACTIVITIES:			
Net loss	$(149,132)	$(567,277)	$(1,411,273)
Adjustments to reconcile net loss to net cash provided by (used in) operating activities:			
Depreciation of fixed assets and other amortization	82,274	84,709	84,460
Stock-based compensation	68,927	4,637	24,797
Equity in losses of equity-method investees, net	4,169	30,327	304,596
Amortization of goodwill and other intangibles	5,478	181,033	321,772
Non-cash restructuring-related and other	3,470	73,293	200,311
Gain on sale of marketable securities, net	(5,700)	(1,335)	(280)
Other losses (gains), net	96,273	2,141	142,639
Non-cash interest expense and other	29,586	26,629	24,766
Cumulative effect of change in accounting principle	(801)	10,523	
Changes in operating assets and liabilities:			
Inventories	(51,303)	30,628	46,083
Accounts receivable, net and other current assets	(32,948)	20,732	(8,585)
Accounts payable	156,542	(44,438)	22,357
Accrued expenses and other current liabilities	4,491	50,031	93,967
Unearned revenue	95,404	114,738	97,818
Amortization of previously unearned revenue	(135,466)	(135,808)	(108,211)
Interest payable	3,027	(345)	34,341
Net cash provided by (used in) operating activities	$174,291	$(119,782)	$(130,442)

(continued)

	12/31/02	12/31/01	12/31/00
INVESTING ACTIVITIES:			
Sales/maturities of marketable securities and investments	553,289	370,377	545,724
Purchases of marketable securities	(635,810)	(567,152)	(184,455)
Purchases of fixed assets, including internal-use software	(39,163	(50,321)	(134,758)
Investments (including equity-method investees)		(6,198)	(62,533)
Net cash provided by (used in) investing activities	$(121,684)	$(253,294)	$163,978
FINANCING ACTIVITIES:			
Proceeds from exercise of stock options and other	121,689	16,625	44,697
Proceeds from issuance of common stock, net of issue costs		99,831	
Proceeds from long-term debt and other		10,000	681,499
Repayment of capital lease obligations and other	(14,795)	(19,575)	(16,927)
Financing costs			(16,122)
Net cash provided by financing activities	$106,894	$106,881	$693,147
Effect of exchange-rate changes on cash and cash equivalents	38,471	(15,958)	(37,557)
Net increase (decrease) in cash and cash equivalents	$197,972	$(282,153)	$689,126

2. Refer to the Lucent example on delaying write-downs of current assets (page 4-9). How much excess inventory do you estimate Lucent is holding in December 2000 if the firm's optimal Days' Inventory is 58 days? Calculate the inventory impairment charge for Lucent if 50 percent of this excess inventory is deemed worthless? Record the changes to Lucent's financial statements from adjusting for this impairment.

3. Acceptance Insurance Companies Inc. underwrites and sells specialty property and casualty insurance. The company is the third largest writer of crop insurance products in the United States. In its 1998 10-K report to the SEC, it discloses the following information on the loss reserves created for claims originating in 1990:

Percentage of claim liability arising in 1990 paid as of:	
One year later	40.6%
Two years later	70.8
Three years later	88.5
Four years later	101.2
Five years later	107.5
Six years later	109.7
Seven years later	111.4
Eight years later	111.8
Net reserves for 1990 obligations reestimated as of:	
One year later	100.3%
Two years later	102.3
Three years later	107.4
Four years later	110.7
Five years later	112.7
Six years later	112.0
Seven years later	112.5
Eight years later	113.4
Net cumulative deficiency	–13.4

Was the initial estimate for loss reserves originating in 1990 too low or too high? How has the firm updated its estimate of this obligation over time? What percentage of the original liability remains outstanding for 1990 claims at the end of 1998? As a financial analyst, what questions would you have for the CFO on its 1990 liability?

4. AMR, the parent of American Airlines, provides the following footnote information on its capital and operating leases:

> AMR's subsidiaries lease various types of equipment and property, primarily aircraft and airport facilities. Lease terms vary but are generally 10 to 25 years for aircraft. The future minimum lease payments required under capital leases, together with the present value of such payments, and future minimum lease payments required under operating leases that have initial or remaining non-cancelable lease terms in excess of one year as of December 31, 2001, were (in millions):

Year Ending December 31,	Capital Leases	Operating Leases
2002	$326	$1,336
2003	243	1,276
2004	295	1,199
2005	229	1,138
2006	231	1,073
2007 and subsequent years	1,233	11,639
	2,557	$17,661
Less amount representing interest	817	
Present value of net minimum lease payments	$1,740	

What interest rate does AMR use to capitalize its capital leases? Use this rate to capitalize AMR's operating leases at December 31, 2001. Record the adjustment to AMR's balance sheet to reflect the capitalization of operating leases. How would this reporting change affect AMR's Income Statement in 2002?

5. What approaches would you use to estimate the value of brands? What assumptions underlie these approaches? As a financial analyst, what would you use to assess whether the brand value of £1.575 billion reported by Cadbury Schweppes in 1997 was a reasonable reflection of the future benefits from these brands? What questions would you raise with the firm's CFO about the firm's brand assets?

6. As the CFO of a company, what indicators would you look at to assess whether your firm's long-term assets were impaired? What approaches could be used, either by management or an independent valuation firm, to assess the dollar value of any asset impairment? As a financial analyst, what indicators would you look at to assess whether a firm's long-term assets were impaired? What questions would you raise with the firm's CFO about any charges taken for asset impairment?

7. The cigarette industry is subject to litigation for health hazards posed by its products. The industry has been negotiating a settlement of these claims with state and federal governments. As the CFO for Philip Morris, one of the larger firms in the industry, what information would you report to investors in the annual report on the firm's litigation risks? How would you assess whether the firm should record a liability for this risk, and if so, how would you assess the value of this liability? As a financial analyst following Philip Morris, what questions would you raise with the CEO over the firm's litigation liability?

8. Refer to the General Motors example on post-retirement benefits (page 4-27). Show the adjustments that would be required to record the full amount of the unfunded post-retirement benefit on December 31, 2000. What factors account for the difference between the adjustments to Common Shareholders' Equity on December 31, 2000 and 2001?

9. Intel reports the following information on its stock options incentive programs in its December 31, 2001, financial statement footnotes.

> The company's stock option plans are accounted for under the intrinsic value recognition and measurement principles of APB Opinion No. 25, "Accounting for Stock Issued to Employees," and related interpretations. As the exercise price of all options granted under these plans was equal to the market price of the underlying common stock on the grant date, no stock-based employee compensation cost, other than acquisition-related compensation, is recognized in net income. The following table illustrates the effect on net income and earnings per share if the company had applied the fair value recognition provisions of SFAS No. 123, "Accounting for Stock-Based Compensation," to employee stock benefits, including shares issued under the stock option plans and under the company's Stock Participation Plan, collectively called "options."

($ millions)	2002	2001	2000
Net income, as reported	$3,117	$1,291	$10,535
Less: Total stock-based employee compensation expense determined under the fair value method for all awards, net of tax	1,170	1,037	836
Pro-forma net income	$1,947	$ 254	$ 9,699

Record the adjustments to the financial statements required to show an expense for stock options under the fair value method for 2001 and 2002. Intel reports that its marginal tax rate is 35 percent.

10. Refer to the Lufthansa example on asset depreciation estimates (pages 4-16 and 4-17). What adjustments would be required if Lufthansa's aircraft depreciation were computed using an average life of 25 years and salvage value of 5 percent (instead of the reported values of 12 years and 15 percent)? Show the adjustments to the 2000 and 2001 balance sheets, and to the 2001 income statement.

11. In early 2003 Bristol-Myers Squibb announced that it would have to restate its financial statements as a result of stuffing as much as $3.35 billion worth of products into wholesalers' warehouses from 1999 through 2001. The company's sales and cost of sales during this period was as follows:

	2001	2000	1999
Net sales	$18,139	$17,695	$16,502
Cost of products sold	5,454	4,729	4,458

The company's marginal tax rate during the three years was 35 percent. What adjustments are required to correct Bristol-Myers Squibb's balance sheet for December 31, 2001? What assumptions underlie your adjustments? How would you expect the adjustments to affect Bristol-Myers Squibb's performance in the coming few years?

NOTES

1. A notable exception in the U.S. is the requirement that software development costs be capitalized once the software reaches the stage of technological feasibility (see SFAS 86).

2. See P. Healy, S. Myers, and C. Howe, "R&D Accounting and the Tradeoff Between Relevance and Objectivity," *Journal of Accounting Research* 40 (June 2002): 677–711, for analysis of the value of capitalizing R&D and then annually assessing impairment.

3. J. Elliott and D. Hanna find that the market anticipates large write-downs by about one quarter, consistent with managers being reluctant to take write-downs on a timely basis. See "Repeated Accounting Write-Offs and the Information Content of Earnings," *Journal of Accounting Research* 34, Supplement, 1996.

4. J. Francis, D. Hanna, and L. Vincent find that management is more likely to exercise judgment in its self-interest for goodwill write-offs and restructuring charges than for inventory or PP&E write-offs. See "Causes and Effects of Discretionary Asset Write-Offs," *Journal of Accounting Research* 34, Supplement, 1996.

5. P. Healy, K. Palepu, and R. Ruback find that acquisitions add value for only one third of the 50 largest acquisitions during the early 1980s, suggesting that acquirers frequently do not recover goodwill. See "Which Takeovers Are Profitable—Strategic or Financial?" *Sloan Management Review*, Summer 1997.

6. MicroStrategy 1998 10-K, Footnote 1.

7. Ibid.

8. Recent evidence indicates that there are negative stock price effects for acquirers that use pooling. See J. Weber, "Shareholder Wealth Effects of Pooling-of-Interests Accounting: Evidence from the SEC's Restriction on Share Repurchases Following Pooling Transactions," working paper, MIT Sloan School of Management, October 2000, and A. Martinez-Jarad, "Interaction Between Accounting and Corporate Governance: Evidence from Business Combinations," working paper, Harvard Business School, February 2003.

9. Several studies indicate that some firms are willing to go to considerable lengths, including paying an additional premium, to be able to use the pooling method for recording an acquisition. See J. Robinson and P. Shane, "Acquisition Accounting Method and Bid Premia for Target Firms," *The Accounting Review* 65 (January 1990): 25–49, and T. Lys and L. Vincent, "An Analysis of Value Destruction in AT&T's Acquisition of NCR," *Journal of Financial Economics* 39 (October/November 1995): 353–79.

10. Research indicates that some firms responded to the adoption of SFAS 13, which changed the rules for lease capitalization, by grooming transactions to avoid having to capitalize leases. See E. Imhoff and J. Thomas, "Economic Consequences of Accounting Standards: The Lease Disclosure Rule Change," *Journal of Accounting & Economics,* 10 (December 1988): 277–311, and S. El-Gazzar, S. Lilien, and V. Pastena, "Accounting for Leases by Lessees," *Journal of Accounting & Economics* 8 (October 1986): 217–38.

11. E. Imhoff, R. Lipe, and D. Wright show that adjustments to capitalize operating leases have a significant impact on leverage and other key financial ratios. See "Operating Leases: Impact of Constructive Capitalization," *Accounting Horizons* 5 (March 1991): 51–64.

12. Accounting rules in the U.S., the U.K., Canada, and Germany require expensing R&D outlays. Expensing is the norm in Japan and France, even though capitalization is permitted.

13. P. Healy, S. Myers, and C. Howe, "R&D Accounting and the Tradeoff Between Relevance and Objectivity," *Journal of Accounting Research* 40 (June 2002): 677–711, show that the magnitude of this bias is sizable.

14. See B. Bublitz and M. Ettredge, "The Information in Discretionary Outlays: Advertising, Research and Development," *The Accounting Review* 64 (1989): 108–124; S. Chan, J. Martin, and J. Kensinger, "Corporate Research and Development Expenditures and Share Value," *Journal of Financial Economics* 26 (1990): 255–76; R. Dukes, "An Investigation of the Effects of Expensing Research and Development Costs on Security Prices," in proceedings of the conference on topical research in accounting (New York University, 1976); J. Elliott, G. Richardson, T. Dyckman, and R. Dukes, "The Impact of SFAS No. 2 on Firm Expenditures on Research and Development:

Replications and Extensions," *Journal of Accounting* 22 (1984): 85–102; M. Hirschey and J. Weygandt, "Amortization Policy for Advertising and Research and Development Expenditures," *Journal of Accounting Research* 23 (1985): 326–35; C. Wasley and T. Linsmeier, "A Further Examination of the Economic Consequences of SFAS No. 2," *Journal of Accounting Research* 30 (1992): 156–64; E. Eccher, "The Value Relevance of Capitalized Software Development Costs," working paper, MIT Sloan School of Management, Cambridge, MA, 1997; B. Lev and T. Sougiannis, "The Capitalization, Amortization, and Value-Relevance of R&D," *Journal of Accounting and Economics* 21 (1996): 107–138; and D. Aboody and B. Lev, "The Value-Relevance of Intangibles: The Case of Software Capitalization," working paper, University of California, 1998.

15. See BA versus Lufthansa case, Lakshmanan Shivakumar, London Business School.

16. It is interesting to note that Lufthansa's depreciation expense for the year 2001 is significantly lower than expected given its 12 year life and 15 percent salvage estimates. The reported depreciation under these assumptions would have been 994m $(.083 \cdot \{11,542.7 + [(1,021.5 \cdot .85)/2]\})$. The company provides no explanation for the difference.

17. JAL actually shows the present value of its lease commitments. However, most companies report the value of future lease payments for the next five years and then show a lump sum value for all payments beyond five years. To estimate the value of the lease liability, the analyst must decide how to allocate this lump sum over year six and beyond, and estimate a suitable interest rate on the lease debt. It is then possible to compute the present value of the lease payments.

18. Mary E. Barth and Maureen McNichols discuss ways for investors to estimate the value of environmental liabilities. See "Estimation and Market Valuation of Environmental Liabilities Relating to Superfund Sites," *Journal of Accounting Research* 32, Supplement, 1994.

19. Defined contribution plans, where companies agree to contribute fixed amounts today to cover future benefits, require very little forecasting to estimate their annual cost since the firm's obligation is limited to its annual obligation to contribute to the employees' retirement funds.

20. E. Amir and E. Gordon show that firms with larger postretirement benefit obligations and more leverage tend to make more aggressive estimates of postretirement obligation parameters. See "A Firm's Choice of Estimation Parameters: Empirical Evidence from SFAS No. 106," *Journal of Accounting, Auditing & Finance* 11, no. 3, Summer 1996.

21. The interest expense is only a rough approximation of the amount that would be reported by CA, since it does not adjust for the portion of the customer payments that were effectively interest for the bank given the premium rate charged.

22. In their footnotes firms also report the Accumulated Benefit Obligation for the pension plan, which is the present value of plan commitments using current wage rates and salary scales.

23. M. Barth finds that investors regard these footnote disclosures as more useful than the liability reported in the financial statements. See "Relative Measurement Errors Among Alternative Pension Asset and Liability Measures," *The Accounting Review* 66, no. 3, 1991.

24. The Black-Scholes option-pricing model estimates the value of an option as a nonlinear function of the exercise price, the remaining time to expiration, the estimated variance of the underlying stock, and the risk-free interest rate. Studies of the valuation of executive stock options include T. Hemmer, S. Matsunaga, and T. Shevlin, "Optimal Exercise and the Cost of Granting Employee Stock Options with a Reload Provision," *Journal of Accounting Research* 36, no. 2, 1998; C. Cuny and P. Jorion, "Valuing Executive Stock Options with Endogenous Departure," *Journal of Accounting and Economics* 20 (September 1995): 193–206; and S. Huddart, "Employee Stock Options," *Journal of Accounting and Economics* 18 (September 1994): 207–32.

25. P. Dechow, A. Hutton, and R. Sloan find that lobbying against SFAS 123 was motivated by concerns about reporting higher levels of executive compensation. See "Economic Consequences of Accounting for Stock-Based Compensation," *Journal of Accounting Research*, Supplement, 1996.

APPENDIX: RECASTING FINANCIAL STATEMENTS INTO STANDARDIZED TEMPLATES

The following tables show the financial statements for Nordstrom, Inc. for the year ended December 31, 2002. The first column in each statement presents the recast financial statement classifications that are used for each line item. Note that the classifications are not applied to subtotal lines such as Total current assets or Net income. The recast financial statements for Nordstrom are prepared by simply totaling the balances of line-items with the same standard classifications. For example, on the recast balance sheet there are two line items classified as Other Current Assets: Prepaid expenses and Other current assets.

Nordstrom Reported Balance Sheet ($ 000's)

Classifications	Fiscal Year Ended December 31,	2002	2001
	ASSETS		
	Current assets:		
Cash and Marketable Securities	Cash and cash equivalents	$331,327	$25,259
Accounts Receivable	Accounts receivable, net	698,475	721,953
Inventory	Merchandise inventories	888,172	945,687
Other Current Assets	Prepaid expenses	34,375	28,760
Other Current Assets	Other current assets	102,249	91,323
	Total current assets	2,054,598	1,812,982
Long-Term Tangible Assets	Land, buildings and equipment, net	1,761,082	1,599,938
Long-Term Intangible Assets	Intangible assets, net	138,331	143,473
Other Long-Term Assets	Other assets	94,768	52,110
	TOTAL ASSETS	$4,048,779	$3,608,503
	LIABILITIES AND SHAREHOLDERS' EQUITY		
	Current liabilities:		
Short-Term Debt	Notes payable	$148	$83,060
Accounts Payable	Accounts payable	490,988	466,476
Other Current Liabilities	Accrued salaries, wages and related benefits	236,373	234,833
Other Current Liabilities	Income taxes and other accruals	142,002	153,613
Short-Term Debt	Current portion of long-term debt	78,227	12,586
	Total current liabilities	947,738	950,568
Long-Term Debt	Long-term debt	1,351,044	1,099,710
Other Long-Term Liabilities (non-interest-bearing)	Deferred lease credits	342,046	275,252
Other Long-Term Liabilities (non-interest-bearing)	Other liabilities	93,463	53,405
	Shareholders' equity:		
Common Shareholders' Equity	Common stock, no par: 250,000,000 shares authorized; 134,468,608 and 133,797,757 shares issued and outstanding	341,316	330,394
Common Shareholders' Equity	Unearned stock compensation	(2,680)	(3,740)
Common Shareholders' Equity	Retained earnings	975,203	900,090
Common Shareholders' Equity	Accumulated other comprehensive earnings	649	2,824
	Total shareholders' equity	1,314,488	1,229,568
	TOTAL LIABILITIES AND SHAREHOLDERS' EQUITY	$4,048,779	$3,608,503

Nordstrom Reported Income Statement ($ 000's)

Classifications	Fiscal-Year Ended December 31,	2002	2001	2000
Sales	Net sales	$5,634,130	$5,528,537	$5,149,266
Cost of Sales	Cost of sales and related buying and occupancy	(3,765,859)	(3,649,516)	(3,359,760)
	Gross profit	1,868,271	1,879,021	1,789,506
SG&A	Selling, general and administrative	(1,722,635)	(1,747,048)	(1,523,836)
	Operating income	145,636	131,973	265,670
Net Interest Expense (Income)	Interest expense, net	(75,038)	(62,698)	(50,396)
Other Expense	Write-down of investment	0	(32,857)	0
Other Income	Service charge income and other, net	133,890	130,600	116,783
	Earnings before income taxes	204,488	167,018	332,057
Tax Expense	Income taxes	−79,800	−65,100	−129,500
	NET EARNINGS	$124,688	$101,918	$202,557

Nordstrom Reported Cash Flow Statement ($ 000's)

Classifications	Fiscal-Year Ended December 31,	2002	2001	2000
	OPERATING ACTIVITIES			
Net Income	Net earnings	$124,688	$101,918	$202,557
	Adj. to reconcile net earnings to net cash provided by operating activities:			
Long-Term Operating Accruals	Depreciation and amortization of buildings and equipment	213,089	203,048	193,718
Long-Term Operating Accruals	Amortization of intangible assets	4,630	1,251	0
Long-Term Operating Accruals	Amortization of deferred lease credits and other, net	(8,538)	(12,349)	(6,387)
Long-Term Operating Accruals	Stock-based compensation expense	3,414	6,480	3,331
Long-Term Operating Accruals	Deferred income taxes, net	15,662	(3,716)	(22,859)
Long-Term Operating Accruals	Write-down of investment	0	32,857	0
	Change in operating assets and liabilities, net of effects from acquisition of business:			
Net (Investment) Liquidation of Oper. WC.	Accounts receivable, net	22,556	(102,945)	(29,854)
Net (Investment) Liquidation of Oper. WC.	Merchandise inventories	215,731	6,741	79,894
Net (Investment) Liquidation of Oper. WC.	Prepaid expenses	(1,684)	(173)	(6,976)
Net (Investment) Liquidation of Oper. WC.	Other assets	(16,770)	(3,821)	(8,880)
Net (Investment) Liquidation of Oper. WC.	Accounts payable	(159,636)	(67,924)	(76,417)
Net (Investment) Liquidation of Oper. WC.	Accrued salaries, wages and related benefits	(203)	17,850	14,942
Net (Investment) Liquidation of Oper. WC.	Income tax liabilities and other accruals	(11,310)	3,879	965
Net (Investment) Liquidation of Oper. WC.	Other liabilities	12,088	(7,184)	25,212
	Net cash provided by operating activities	413,717	175,912	369,246
	INVESTING ACTIVITIES			
Net (Investment) Liquidation of Oper. LT Assets	Capital expenditures	($390,138)	($321,454)	(305,052)
Net (Investment) Liquidation of Oper. LT Assets	Additions to deferred lease credits	$126,383	$92,361	114,910
Net (Investment) Liquidation of Oper. LT Assets	Payment for acquisition, net of cash acquired	$0	($83,828)	0
Net (Investment) Liquidation of Oper. LT Assets	Other, net	($3,309)	($1,781)	(452)
	Net cash used in investing activities	(267,064)	(314,702)	(190,594)

(continued)

	FINANCING ACTIVITIES			
Net Debt (Repayment) or Issuance	Proceeds (payments) from notes payable	(82,912)	12,126	(7,849)
Net Debt (Repayment) or Issuance	Proceeds from issuance of long-term debt	300,000	308,266	0
Net Debt (Repayment) or Issuance	Principal payments on long-term debt	(18,640)	(58,191)	(63,341)
Net Stock (Repurchase) or Issuance	Capital contribution to subsidiary from minority shareholders	0	0	16,000
Net Stock (Repurchase) or Issuance	Proceeds from issuance of common stock	10,542	6,250	9,577
Dividend (Payments)	Cash dividends paid	(48,265)	(45,935)	(44,463)
Net Stock (Repurchase) or Issuance	Purchase and retirement of common stock	(1,310)	(85,509)	(302,965)
	Net cash provided by (used in) financing activities	159,415	137,007	(393,041)
	Net increase (decrease) in cash and cash equivalents	306,068	(1,783)	(214,389)
	Cash and cash equivalents at beginning of year	25,259	27,042	241,431
	CASH AND CASH EQUIVALENTS AT END OF YEAR	$331,327	$25,259	$27,042

The standardized financial statements for Nordstrom Inc. are as follows:

Nordstrom Standardized Balance Sheet ($ 000's)

Fiscal Year Ending December 31,	2001	2002
Balance Sheet		
Assets		
Cash and Marketable Securities	25,259	331,327
Accounts Receivable	721,953	698,475
Inventory	945,687	888,172
Other Current Assets	120,083	136,624
Total Current Assets	**1,812,982**	**2,054,598**
Long-Term Tangible Assets	1,599,938	1,761,082
Long-Term Intangible Assets	143,473	138,331
Other Long-Term Assets	52,110	94,768
Total Long-Term Assets	**1,795,521**	**1,994,181**
Total Assets	**3,608,503**	**4,048,779**
Liabilities		
Accounts Payable	466,476	490,988
Short-Term Debt	95,646	78,375
Other Current Liabilities	388,446	378,375
Total Current Liabilities	**950,568**	**947,738**
Long-Term Debt	1,099,710	1,351,044
Deferred Taxes	0	0
Other Long-Term Liabilities (non-interest bearing)	328,657	435,509
Total Long-Term Liabilities	**1,428,367**	**1,786,553**
Total Liabilities	**2,378,935**	**2,734,291**
Minority Interest	0	0
Shareholders' Equity		
Preferred Stock	0	0
Common Shareholders' Equity	1,229,568	1,314,488
Total Shareholders' Equity	**1,229,568**	**1,314,488**
Total Liabilities and Shareholders' Equity	**3,608,503**	**4,048,779**

Nordstrom Standardized Income Statement ($ 000's)

Fiscal Year Ending December 31,	2000	2001	2002
Sales	5,149,266	5,528,537	5,634,130
Cost of Sales	3,359,760	3,649,516	3,765,859
Gross Profit	1,789,506	1,879,021	1,868,271
SG&A	1,523,836	1,747,048	1,722,635
Other Operating Expense	0	0	0
Operating Income	265,670	131,973	145,636
Investment Income	0	0	0
Other Income, net of Other Expense	116,783	97,743	133,890
Other Income	116,783	130,600	133,890
Other Expense	0	32,857	0
Net Interest Expense (Income)	−50,396	−62,698	−75,038
Interest Income	na	na	na
Interest Expense	na	na	na
Minority Interest	na	na	na
Pre-Tax Income	432,849	292,414	354,564
Tax Expense	129,500	65,100	79,800
Unusual Items (after tax)	0	0	0
Net Income	303,349	227,314	274,764
Preferred Dividends	0	0	0
Net Income to Common	303,349	227,314	274,764

Nordstrom Standardized Cash Flow Statement ($ 000's)

	2000	2001	2002
Net Income	202,557	101,918	124,688
After-tax net interest expense (income)	30,742	38,260	45,755
Non-operating losses (gains)	0	0	0
Long-term operating accruals	167,803	227,571	228,257
Operating cash flow before working capital investments	401,102	367,749	398,700
Net (investments in) or liquidation of operating working capital	(1,114)	(153,577)	60,772
Operating cash flow before investment in long-term assets	399,988	214,172	459,472
Net (investment in) or liquidation of operating long-term assets	(190,594)	(314,702	(267,064)
Free cash flow available to debt and equity	209,394	(100,530)	192,408
After-tax net interest expense (income)	30,742	38,260	45,755
Net debt (repayment) or issuance	(71,190)	262,201	198,448
Free cash flow available to equity	107,462	123,411	345,101
Dividend (payments)	(44,463)	(45,935)	(48,265)
Net stock (repurchase) or issuance	(277,388)	(79,259)	9,232
Net increase (decrease) in cash balance	(214,389)	(1,783)	306,068

Financial Analysis

The goal of financial analysis is to assess the performance of a firm in the context of its stated goals and strategy. There are two principal tools of financial analysis: ratio analysis and cash flow analysis. Ratio analysis involves assessing how various line items in a firm's financial statements relate to one another. Cash flow analysis allows the analyst to examine the firm's liquidity, and how the firm is managing its operating, investment, and financing cash flows.

Financial analysis is used in a variety of contexts. Ratio analysis of a company's present and past performance provides the foundation for making forecasts of future performance. As we will discuss in later chapters, financial forecasting is useful in company valuation, credit evaluation, financial distress prediction, security analysis, mergers and acquisitions analysis, and corporate financial policy analysis.

RATIO ANALYSIS

The value of a firm is determined by its profitability and growth. As shown in Figure 5-1, the firm's growth and profitability are influenced by its product market and financial market strategies. The product market strategy is implemented through the firm's competitive strategy, operating policies, and investment decisions. Financial market strategies are implemented through financing and dividend policies.

Thus the four levers managers can use to achieve their growth and profit targets are (1) operating management, (2) investment management, (3) financing strategy, and (4) dividend policies. The objective of ratio analysis is to evaluate the effectiveness of the firm's policies in each of these areas. Effective ratio analysis involves relating the financial numbers to the underlying business factors in as much detail as possible. While ratio analysis may not give all the answers to an analyst regarding the firm's performance, it will help the analyst frame questions for further probing.

In ratio analysis, the analyst can (1) compare ratios for a firm over several years (a time-series comparison), (2) compare ratios for the firm and other firms in the industry (cross-sectional comparison), and/or (3) compare ratios to some absolute benchmark. In a time-series comparison, the analyst can hold firm-specific factors constant and examine the effectiveness of a firm's strategy over time. Cross-sectional comparison facilitates examining the relative performance of a firm within its industry, holding industry-level factors constant. For most ratios there are no absolute benchmarks. The exceptions are measures of rates of return, which can be compared to the cost of the capital associated with the investment. For example, subject to distortions caused by accounting, the rate of return on equity (ROE) can be compared to the cost of equity capital.

In the discussion below, we will illustrate these approaches using the example of Nordstrom, Inc., a prominent U.S. retailer. We will compare Nordstrom's ratios for the fiscal year ending January 31, 2002, with its own ratios for the fiscal year ending January 31, 2001, and with the ratios for TJX Companies, Inc., another U.S. retailer, for the fiscal year ending January 31, 2002.[1]

Nordstrom is in the middle of implementing a restructuring and turnaround strategy, so analyzing its performance over time allows us to assess how well the strategy is working in terms of financial performance. Comparison of Nordstrom with TJX allows

Figure 5-1	Drivers of a Firm's Profitability and Growth

us to see the impact of different strategies on financial ratios. While pursuing different competitive strategies, Nordstrom and TJX also follow different investment and financing strategies. Nordstrom makes significant investment in its stores whereas TJX leases its stores. Nordstrom has a credit card operation whereas TJX does not. We will illustrate how these differences between the two companies affect their ratios. We will also try to see which strategy is delivering better performance for shareholders.

In order to facilitate replication of the ratio calculations presented below, we present financial statements of both these companies in the appendix to this chapter. Three versions of these companys' financials are presented in the appendix. The first version is the one reported by the two companies in their SEC filings. The second set of financial statements are presented in the standardized format described in Chapter 4. These "standardized financial statements" put both companies' financials in one standard format to facilitate direct comparison. We also present the two companies' financial statements in a third format in the appendix. These statements, labeled "Condensed Financial Statements," are essentially a recasting of the standardized financial statements to facilitate the calculation of several ratios discussed in the chapter. We will discuss later in the chapter how this recasting process works.

Background Information on Nordstrom and TJX

Nordstrom

Nordstrom is a leading fashion specialty retailer, offering a wide variety of high-end apparel, shoes, and accessories for men, women, and children. As of January 31, 2002, the company operated 156 stores, including 80 full-line Nordstrom stores, 45

Nordstrom Rack stores, two free-standing Nordstrom shoe stores, and one Last Chance clearance store. Following the acquisition of Faconnable, S.A. of Nice, France, in October 2000, Nordstrom also operated 24 Faconnable boutiques in Europe and 4 in the U.S.[*]

Dissatisfied with inconsistent earnings performance in recent years, Nordstrom introduced a new management team in August of 2000, which again put Nordstrom family members at the helm.[†] Shortly thereafter management announced a turn-around plan aimed at improving the company's profit performance. Central to the plan were several key promises including improving inventory control, expense control, and merchandising, as well as the implementation of new information systems.

Nordstrom management also had to contend with shifting consumers' perceptions of the brand. Since its founding as a single shoe store in 1901, Nordstrom's strategy consistently emphasized the breadth and depth of its quality offerings. In recent years an aggressive expansion plan that included opening bigger and more glamorous stores coupled with an unbalanced merchandising strategy that favored stocking the highest quality product, rather than matching the quality of offerings to key price points, resulted in an increase in Nordstrom's average price point and the erosion of the company's value proposition. In the process, Nordstrom alienated a portion of its core customer base as the brand became increasingly associated with premium pricing. The need to subdue the company's elitist image was recognized by management and securities analysts alike.

By 2002 management had begun to deliver on its promises. The rollout of a new perpetual inventory management system was on track to be fully implemented by the second quarter. Additionally, alterations to the company's merchandising strategy provided more price balance to the product mix.

Analysts were intrigued by management's accomplishments, yet a string of past disappointments engendered ample skepticism. Citing these improvements, a number of analysts issued buy ratings during the first half of 2002. Among them were Wayne Hood and Laura Macedo of Prudential Financial who believed that "Nordstrom is finally in the midst of a sustainable earnings recovery."[‡] Other analysts including Michael Exstein and Jennifer Justynski of Credit Suisse First Boston were less sanguine about the company's strategy. Though Exstein and Justynski upgraded their stock rating from Hold to Buy, in the company analysis section of their report the analysts profess "we are somewhat confused by the message Nordstrom is trying to convey to the customer . . . [asking, but not answering the question] Is Nordstrom a high-end retailer?"[§]

TJX

TJX Companies pursues a strategy quite different from Nordstrom's. TJX is the leading off-price apparel and home fashions retailer in the U.S. and worldwide.[**] As of

---

[*] *Facconable, S.A. is a designer, wholesaler and retailer of high quality women's and men's clothing and accessories.*

[†] *Nordstrom's management restructuring eliminated the company's copresidency structure adopted in 1995 when six fourth-generation members of the Nordstrom family were named copresidents. This restructuring also entailed replacing CEO John Whitacre with Bruce Nordstrom, after five years of retirement.*

[‡] *Wayne Hood and Laura Macedo, "Nordstrom Inc.," Prudential Financial, May 10, 2002.*

[§] *Michael Exstein and Jennifer Justynski, "Nordstrom Inc.," Credit Suisse First Boston, September 6, 2002.*

[**] *The TJX Companies, Inc., 2001 Annual Report.*

January 31, 2002, the company operated 1,665 retail outlets through its T.J. Maxx, T.K. Maxx (Europe), Marshall's, HomeGoods, HomeSense (Canada), A.J. Wright, and Winners stores. TJX's divisions are united by the same strategy: offer a rapidly changing assortment of quality, brand-name merchandise at 20–60 percent below department and specialty store regular prices. The company sought to accomplish this by buying opportunistically and by operating with a highly efficient distribution network and a low cost structure.

Regarding competitive advantage, TJX management asserted, "Among TJX's most valuable assets is the equity built into our brands . . . for our customers, these brands are synonymous with value . . . [B]ecause our brands are so strong, TJX is able to spend far less than the industry average on advertising specials or promotions. Instead, advertising campaigns keep stores at the top of customers' minds as places to find great bargains on quality merchandise."* TJX also benefits from its pursuit of continuous improvement in its approach to inventory management. Recent enhancements to TJX's distribution network allowed buyers to further delay purchase decisions, getting better deals in the process, while maintaining confidence that goods will arrive in stores in a timely manner.

During fiscal 2001 (ended January 31, 2002), TJX management reported solid results despite a challenging economic environment. In that year TJX expanded the store base for each of its concepts, launched a new business, and expanded its distribution network. Despite the financing requirements from this ambitious growth strategy, the company also pursued an aggressive share buyback program.

TJX analysts generally maintained a positive outlook. For example, early in 2002 UBS Warburg analysts Richard Jaffe and Corinna Freedman upgraded their stock rating from Buy to Strong Buy with the comment, "maintain[ing] an overall positive view, as we believe TJX is a long-term growth story with an attractive inventory and new business concepts that are expected to perform well."†

---

* Ibid.

† Richard Jaffe and Corinna Freedman, "The TJX Companies, Inc.," UBS Warburg, March 5, 2002.

Measuring Overall Profitability

The starting point for a systematic analysis of a firm's performance is its return on equity (ROE), defined as

$$\text{ROE} = \frac{\text{Net income}}{\text{Shareholder's equity}}$$

ROE is a comprehensive indicator of a firm's performance because it provides an indication of how well managers are employing the funds invested by the firm's shareholders to generate returns. On average over long periods, large publicly traded firms in the U.S. generate ROEs in the range of 11 to 13 percent.

In the long run, the value of the firm's equity is determined by the relationship between its ROE and its cost of equity capital.[2] That is, those firms that are expected over the long run to generate ROEs in excess of the cost of equity capital should have market values in excess of book value, and vice versa. (We will return to this point in more detail in the chapter on valuation.)

A comparison of ROE with the cost of capital is useful not only for contemplating the value of the firm but also in considering the path of future profitability. The generation of consistent supernormal profitability will, absent significant barriers to entry, attract competition. For that reason ROEs tend over time to be driven by competitive forces toward a "normal" level—the cost of equity capital. Thus one can think of the cost of equity capital as establishing a benchmark for the ROE that would be observed in a long-run competitive equilibrium. Deviations from this level arise for two general reasons. One is the industry conditions and competitive strategy that cause a firm to generate supernormal (or subnormal) economic profits, at least over the short run. The second is distortions due to accounting.

Table 5-1 shows the ROE based on reported earnings for Nordstrom and TJX.

Table 5-1 Return on Equity for Nordstrom and TJX

Ratio	Nordstrom 2001	Nordstrom 2000	TJX 2001
Return on equity	10.1%	8.6%	41.1%

Nordstrom's ROE showed an improvement, from 8.6 percent to 10.1 percent, between 2000 and 2001. This indicates that Nordstrom's strategy of focusing on profit improvement is beginning to show positive results. Compared to historical trends of ROE in the economy, Nordstrom's 2000 performance can be viewed as being below average. Further, its ROE in 2000 is not adequate to cover reasonable estimates of its equity cost of capital. The 1.5 percentage points increase in ROE in 2001 allowed Nordstrom to get closer to both these benchmarks.[3]

Despite the improvement in 2001, Nordstrom's performance was still far behind TJX's ROE of 41.1 percent. At that performance TJX was earning excess returns relative to both the historical trends in ROE in the U.S. economy, as well as to its own cost of equity.

TJX's superior performance relative to Nordstrom is reflected in the difference in the two companies' ratio of market value of equity to book value. As we will discuss in Chapter 7, ROE is a key determinant of a company's market to book ratio. As of January 31, 2002, Nordstrom's market value to book value ratio was 2.6, while the same ratio for TJX was 8.4.

Decomposing Profitability: Traditional Approach

A company's ROE is affected by two factors: how profitably it employs its assets and how big the firm's asset base is relative to shareholders' investment. To understand the effect of these two factors, ROE can be decomposed into return on assets (ROA) and a measure of financial leverage, as follows:

$$\text{ROE} = \text{ROA} \times \text{Financial leverage}$$

$$= \frac{\text{Net income}}{\text{Assets}} \times \frac{\text{Assets}}{\text{Shareholders' equity}}$$

ROA tells us how much profit a company is able to generate for each dollar of assets invested. Financial leverage indicates how many dollars of assets the firm is able to deploy for each dollar invested by its shareholders.

The return on assets itself can be decomposed as a product of two factors:

$$\text{ROA} = \frac{\text{Net income}}{\text{Sales}} \times \frac{\text{Sales}}{\text{Assets}}$$

The ratio of net income to sales is called net profit margin or return on sales (ROS); the ratio of sales to assets is known as asset turnover. The profit margin ratio indicates how much the company is able to keep as profits for each dollar of sales it makes. Asset turnover indicates how many sales dollars the firm is able to generate for each dollar of its assets.

Table 5-2 displays the three drivers of ROE for our retail firms: net profit margins, asset turnover, and financial leverage. In 2001 Nordstrom's ROE is largely driven by increases in its net profit margin and in its financial leverage. In fact, its return on equity in 2001 was hurt by a decline in its asset turnover. TJX's superior ROE seems to be driven by higher profit margins and better asset utilization; TJX was able to achieve higher ROE than Nordstrom even though it has a lower financial leverage ratio. In other words, TJX's superior performance is attributable to its superior operating performance, as indicated by its high ROA relative to Nordstrom's ROA. And Nordstrom's inferior operating performance is cushioned by its more aggressive financial management relative to TJX.

Table 5-2 Traditional Decomposition of ROE

Ratio	Nordstrom 2001	Nordstrom 2000	TJX 2001
Net profit margin (ROS)	2.2%	1.8%	4.67%
Asset turnover	1.56	1.81	3.71
= Return on assets (ROA)	3.4%	3.3%	17.3%
× Financial leverage	2.93	2.58	2.37
= Return on equity (ROE)	10.1%	8.6%	41.1%

Decomposing Profitability: Alternative Approach

Even though the above approach is popularly used to decompose a firm's ROE, it has several limitations. In the computation of ROA, the denominator includes the assets claimed by all providers of capital to the firm, but the numerator includes only the earnings available to equity holders. The assets themselves include both operating assets and financial assets such as cash and short-term investments. Further, net income includes income from operating activities, as well as interest income and expense, which are consequences of financing decisions. Often it is useful to distinguish between these two sources of performance. Finally, the financial leverage ratio used above does not recognize the fact that a firm's cash and short-term investments are in essence "negative debt" because they can be used to pay down the debt on the company's balance sheet.[4] These issues are addressed by an alternative approach to decomposing ROE discussed below.[5]

Before discussing this alternative ROE decomposition approach, we need to define some terminology used in this section as well as in the rest of this chapter. This terminology is given in Table 5-3.

Table 5-3 Definitions of Accounting Items Used in Ratio Analysis

Item	Definition
Net interest expense after tax	(Interest expense − Interest income) × (1 − Tax rate)[a]
Net operating profit after taxes (NOPAT)	Net income + Net interest expense after tax
Operating working capital	(Current assets − Cash and marketable securities) − (Current liabilities − Short-term debt and current portion of long-term debt)
Net long-term assets	Total long-term assets − Non-interest-bearing long-term liabilities
Net debt	Total interest bearing liabilities − Cash and marketable securities
Net assets	Operating working capital + Net long-term assets
Net capital	Net debt + Shareholders' equity

a. *The calculation of net interest expense treats interest expense and interest income as absolute values, independent of how these figures are reported in the income statement.*

We use the terms defined above to recast the financial statements of Nordstrom and TJX. These recasted financial statements, which are shown in the appendix, are used to decompose ROE in the following manner:

$$
\begin{aligned}
\text{ROE} &= \frac{\text{NOPAT}}{\text{Equity}} - \frac{(\text{Net interest expense after tax})}{\text{Equity}} \\[2mm]
&= \frac{\text{NOPAT}}{\text{Net assets}} \times \frac{\text{Net assets}}{\text{Equity}} - \frac{\text{Net interest expense after tax}}{\text{Net debt}} \times \frac{\text{Net debt}}{\text{Equity}} \\[2mm]
&= \frac{\text{NOPAT}}{\text{Net assets}} \times \left(1 + \frac{\text{Net debt}}{\text{Equity}}\right) - \frac{\text{Net interest expense after tax}}{\text{Net debt}} \times \frac{\text{Net debt}}{\text{Equity}} \\[2mm]
&= \text{Operating ROA} + (\text{Operating ROA} - \text{Effective interest rate after tax}) \\
&\quad \times \text{ Net financial leverage} \\[2mm]
&= \text{Operating ROA} + \text{Spread} \times \text{Net financial leverage}
\end{aligned}
$$

Operating ROA is a measure of how profitably a company is able to deploy its operating assets to generate operating profits. This would be a company's ROE if it were financed with all equity. Spread is the incremental economic effect from introducing debt into the capital structure. This economic effect of borrowing is positive as long as the return on operating assets is greater than the cost of borrowing. Firms that do not earn adequate operating returns to pay for interest cost reduce their ROE by borrowing. Both the positive and negative effect is magnified by the extent to which a firm borrows relative to its equity base. The ratio of net debt to equity provides a measure of this net financial leverage. A firm's spread times its net financial leverage, therefore, provides a measure of the financial leverage gain to the shareholders.

Operating ROA can be further decomposed into NOPAT margin and operating asset turnover as follows:

$$\text{Operating ROA} = \frac{\text{NOPAT}}{\text{Sales}} \times \frac{\text{Sales}}{\text{Net assets}}$$

NOPAT margin is a measure of how profitable a company's sales are from an operating perspective. Operating asset turnover measures the extent to which a company is able to use its operating assets to generate sales.

Table 5-4 presents the decomposition of ROE for Nordstrom and TJX. The ratios in this table show that there is a significant difference between Nordstrom's ROA and its operating ROA. In 2001, for example, Nordstrom's ROA was 3.4 percent, while its operating ROA was 7.1 percent.

This difference in ROA and operating ROA is even more remarkable for TJX: its ROA in 2001 was 17.3 percent whereas the operating ROA was 35.7 percent. Because TJX had a large amount of non-interest-bearing liabilities and short-term investments, its operating ROA is dramatically larger than its ROA. This shows that, for at least some firms, it is important to adjust the simple ROA to take into account interest expense, interest income, and financial assets.

Table 5-4 Distinguishing Operating and Financing Components in ROE Decomposition

Ratio	Nordstrom 2001	Nordstrom 2000	TJX 2001
Net operating profit margin	3.0%	2.5%	4.8%
× Net operating asset turnover	2.35	2.75	7.41
= Operating ROA	7.1%	7.0%	35.7%
Spread	3.2%	2.3%	28.7%
× Net financial leverage	0.95	0.69	0.19
= Financial leverage gain	3.0%	1.6%	5.3%
ROE = Operating ROA + Financial leverage gain	10.1%	8.6%	41.1%

The appropriate benchmark for evaluating operating ROA is the weighted average cost of debt and equity capital, or WACC. In the long run, the value of the firm's assets is determined by where operating ROA stands relative to this norm. Moreover, over the long run and absent some barrier to competitive forces, operating ROA will tend to be pushed toward the weighted average cost of capital. Since the WACC is lower than the cost of equity capital, operating ROA tends to be pushed to a level lower than that to which ROE tends.

The average operating ROA for large firms in the U.S., over long periods of time, is in the range of 9 to 11 percent. Nordstrom's operating ROA in 2000 and 2001 is beneath this range, indicating that its operating performance is below average. At 35.7 percent, TJX's operating ROA is far larger than Nordstrom's and also the U.S. industrial average and any reasonable estimates of TJX's weighted average cost of capital. This dramatic superior operating performance of TJX would have been obscured by using the simple ROA measure.[6]

TJX dominates Nordstrom in terms of both operating drivers of ROE—it has a better NOPAT margin and a dramatically higher operating asset turnover. TJX's higher operating asset turnover is primarily a result of its strategy of renting its stores, unlike Nordstrom, which owns many of its stores. What is surprising is discount retailer TJX's higher NOPAT margin, given that Nordstrom is supposed to be the firm with the premium pricing strategy. Nordstrom's inferior NOPAT margin suggests that the company is unable to price its merchandise high enough to recoup the cost of its high service strategy.

Nordstrom is able to create shareholder value through its financing strategy. In 2000 the spread between Nordstrom's operating ROA and its after-tax interest cost was 2.3 percent; its net debt as a percent of its equity was 69 percent. Both these factors contributed to a net increment of 1.6 percent to its ROE. Thus, while Nordstrom's operating ROA in 2000 was 7 percent, its ROE was 8.6 percent. In 2001 Nordstrom's spread increased to 3.2 percent, its net financial leverage went up to 95 percent, leading to a 3 percent net increment to ROE due to its debt policy. With an operating ROA of 7.1 percent in that year, its ROE went up to 10.1 percent.

TJX had a very high spread in 2001, to the tune of 28.7 percent. As a result, even though it had only a modest financial leverage of 18.5 percent, it had a high financial leverage gain of 5.3 percent. This financial leverage gain added to its already higher operating ROA to produce a high ROE of 41.1 percent. In fact, TJX appears not to have exploited its financial leverage potential fully. With a higher level of leverage, it could have exploited its spread to produce an even higher ROE.

Assessing Operating Management: Decomposing Net Profit Margins

A firm's net profit margin or return on sales (ROS) shows the profitability of the company's operating activities. Further decomposition of a firm's ROS allows an analyst to assess the efficiency of the firm's operating management. A popular tool used in this analysis is the common-sized income statement in which all the line items are expressed as a ratio of sales revenues.

Common-sized income statements make it possible to compare trends in income statement relationships over time for the firm, and trends across different firms in the industry. Income statement analysis allows the analyst to ask the following types of questions: (1) Are the company's margins consistent with its stated competitive strategy? For example, a differentiation strategy should usually lead to higher gross margins than a low-cost strategy. (2) Are the company's margins changing? Why? What are the underlying business causes—changes in competition, changes in input costs, or poor overhead cost management? (3) Is the company managing its overhead and administrative costs well? What are the business activities driving these costs? Are these activities necessary?

To illustrate how the income statement analysis can be used, common-sized income statements for Nordstrom and TJX are shown in Table 5-5. The table also shows some commonly used profitability ratios. We will use the information in Table 5-5 to investigate why Nordstrom had a net income margin (or return on sales) of 2.2 percent in 2001 and 1.8 percent in 2000, while TJX had a net margin of 4.7 percent in 2001.

Gross Profit Margins

The difference between a firm's sales and cost of sales is gross profit. Gross profit margin is an indication of the extent to which revenues exceed direct costs associated with sales, and it is computed as

$$\text{Gross profit margin} = \frac{\text{Sales} - \text{Cost of sales}}{\text{Sales}}$$

Gross margin is influenced by two factors: (1) the price premium that a firm's products or services command in the marketplace and (2) the efficiency of the firm's procurement

Table 5-5 Common-Sized Income Statement and Profitability Ratios

	Nordstrom 2001	Nordstrom 2000	TJX 2001
Line Items as a Percent of Sales			
Sales	100%	100%	100%
Cost of sales	(66.8)	(66.0)	(75.9)
Selling, general, and admin. expense	(30.6)	(31.6)	(15.7)
Other income/expense	2.4	2.4	0
Net interest expense/income	(1.3)	(1.1)	(.24)
Income taxes	(1.4)	(1.2)	(3.1)
Unusual gains/losses, net of taxes			(0.4)
Net income	2.2%	1.8%	4.7%
Key Profitability Ratios			
Gross profit margin	33.2%	34.0%	24.1%
EBITDA margin	5.0%	4.2%	8.4%
NOPAT margin	3.0%	2.5%	4.8%
Net Income Margin	2.2%	1.8%	4.7%

and production process. The price premium a firm's products or services can command is influenced by the degree of competition and the extent to which its products are unique. The firm's cost of sales can be low when it can purchase its inputs at a lower cost than competitors and/or run its production processes more efficiently. This is generally the case when a firm has a low-cost strategy.

Table 5-5 indicates that Nordstrom's gross margin in 2001 decreased slightly to 33.2 percent, reflecting pricing pressure as a result of increased competition and a weakened economy. This brings into question whether the new merchandising strategy of the company is indeed effective in shoring up its margins.

Consistent with Nordstrom's premium price strategy, its gross margins in both 2001 and 2000 were significantly higher than TJX's gross margin in 2001, which stood at 24.1 percent.

Selling, General, and Administrative Expenses

A company's selling, general, and administrative (SG&A) expenses are influenced by the operating activities it has to undertake to implement its competitive strategy. As discussed in Chapter 2, firms with differentiation strategies have to undertake activities to achieve differentiation. A company competing on the basis of quality and rapid introduction of new products is likely to have higher R&D costs relative to a company competing purely on a cost basis. Similarly, a company that attempts to build a brand image, distribute its products through full-service retailers, and provide significant customer service is likely to have higher selling and administration costs relative to a company that sells through warehouse retailers or direct mail and does not provide much customer support.

A company's SG&A expenses are also influenced by the efficiency with which it manages its overhead activities. The control of operating expenses is likely to be especially important for firms competing on the basis of low cost. However, even for differentiators, it is important to assess whether the cost of differentiation is commensurate with the price premium earned in the marketplace.

Several ratios in Table 5-5 allow us to evaluate the effectiveness with which Nordstrom and TJX were managing their SG&A expenses. First, the ratio of SG&A expense to sales shows how much a company is spending to generate each sales dollar. We see that Nordstrom has a significantly higher ratio of SG&A to sales than does TJX. This should not be surprising given that TJX pursues a low-cost off-price strategy whereas Nordstrom pursues a high service strategy. In accordance with its stated goal to manage its profitability better, Nordstrom improved its cost management: its SG&A expense as a percent of sales decreased from 31.6 percent in 2000 to 30.6 percent in 2001.

Given that Nordstrom and TJX are pursuing radically different pricing, merchandising, and service strategies, it is not surprising that they have very different cost structures. As a percent of sales, Nordstrom's cost of sales is lower, and its SG&A expense is higher. The question is, when both these costs are netted out, which company is performing better? Two ratios provide useful signals here: net operating profit margin (NOPAT margin) ratio and EBITDA margin:

$$\text{NOPAT margin} \quad = \quad \frac{\text{NOPAT}}{\text{Sales}}$$

$$\text{EBITDA margin} \quad = \quad \frac{\text{Earnings before interest, taxes, depreciation, and amortization}}{\text{Sales}}$$

NOPAT margin provides a comprehensive indication of the operating performance of a company because it reflects all operating policies and eliminates the effects of debt policy. EBITDA margin provides similar information, except that it excludes depreciation and amortization expense, a significant noncash operating expense. Some analysts prefer to use EBITDA margin because they believe that it focuses on "cash" operating items. While this is to some extent true, it can be potentially misleading for two reasons. EBITDA is not a strictly cash concept because sales, cost of sales, and SG&A expenses often include non-cash items. Also, depreciation is a real operating expense, and it reflects to some extent the consumption of resources. Therefore, ignoring it can be misleading.

From Table 5-5 we see that Nordstrom's NOPAT margin has improved between 2000 and 2001. Even with this improvement, in 2001 the company is able to retain only 3 cents in net operating profits for each dollar of sales, whereas TJX is able to retain 4.8 cents.

Recall that in Table 5-3 we define NOPAT as net income plus net interest expense. Therefore, NOPAT is influenced by any unusual or nonoperating income (expense) items included in net income. We can calculate a "recurring" NOPAT margin by eliminating these items. For Nordstrom, recurring NOPAT margin was 1.46 percent in 2000 and 1.53 percent in 2001. These numbers are significantly lower than the NOPAT margin numbers we discussed above, suggesting that a significant portion of the company's NOPAT is derived from sources other than its core retailing operations. These sources include a significant amount of investment income that Nordstrom reported in its financial statements. In contrast, the recurring NOPAT margin for TJX is 5.2 percent, which is higher than its NOPAT margin discussed above since the company reported a one-time loss due to discontinued operations. Recurring NOPAT may be a better benchmark to use when one is extrapolating current performance into the future since it reflects margins from the core business activities of a firm.

TJX also has a better EBITDA margin than Nordstrom. However, this comparison is potentially misleading because TJX leases most of its stores while Nordstrom owns its stores; TJX's leasing expense is included in the EBITDA calculation, but Nordstrom's store depreciation is excluded. This is an example of how EBITDA margin can sometimes be misleading.

Tax Expense

Taxes are an important element of firms' total expenses. Through a wide variety of tax planning techniques, firms can attempt to reduce their tax expenses.[7] There are two measures one can use to evaluate a firm's tax expense. One is the ratio of tax expense to sales, and the other is the ratio of tax expense to earnings before taxes (also known as the average tax rate). The firm's tax footnote provides a detailed account of why its average tax rate differs from the statutory tax rate.

When evaluating a firm's tax planning, the analyst should ask two questions: (1) Are the company's tax policies sustainable, or is the current tax rate influenced by one-time tax credits? (2) Do the firm's tax planning strategies lead to other business costs? For example, if the operations are located in tax havens, how does this affect the company's profit margins and asset utilization? Are the benefits of tax planning strategies (reduced taxes) greater than the increased business costs?

Table 5-5 shows that Nordstrom's tax rate did not change significantly between 2000 and 2001. Nordstrom's taxes as a percent of sales were somewhat lower than TJX's. An important reason for this is that TJX's pretax profits as a percent of sales were higher. In fact, the average tax rate (ratio of tax expense to pretax profits) for both Nordstrom and TJX were nearly the same, at 39 percent and 38 percent, respectively.

In summary, we conclude that Nordstrom's small improvement in return on sales is primarily driven by a reduction in its selling, general, and administrative costs. In all other areas, Nordstrom's performance either stayed the same or worsened a bit. TJX is able to earn a superior return on its sales despite following an off-price strategy because it is able to save significantly on its SG&A expenses.

Evaluating Investment Management: Decomposing Asset Turnover

Asset turnover is the second driver of a company's return on equity. Since firms invest considerable resources in their assets, using them productively is critical to overall profitability. A detailed analysis of asset turnover allows the analyst to evaluate the effectiveness of a firm's investment management.

There are two primary areas of asset management: (1) working capital management and (2) management of long-term assets. Working capital is defined as the difference between a firm's current assets and current liabilities. However, this definition does not distinguish between operating components (such as accounts receivable, inventory, and accounts payable) and the financing components (such as cash, marketable securities, and notes payable). An alternative measure that makes this distinction is operating working capital, as defined in Table 5-3:

Operating working capital = (Current assets – cash and marketable securities)
 – (Current liabilities – Short-term and current portion of long-term debt)

Working Capital Management

The components of operating working capital that analysts primarily focus on are accounts receivable, inventory, and accounts payable. A certain amount of investment in working capital is necessary for the firm to run its normal operations. For example, a firm's credit policies and distribution policies determine its optimal level of accounts receivable. The nature of the production process and the need for buffer stocks determine the optimal level of inventory. Finally, accounts payable is a routine source of financing for the firm's working capital, and payment practices in an industry determine the normal level of accounts payable.

The following ratios are useful in analyzing a firm's working capital management: operating working capital as a percent of sales, operating working capital turnover, accounts receivable turnover, inventory turnover, and accounts payable turnover. The turnover ratios can also be expressed in number of days of activity that the operating working capital (and its components) can support. The definitions of these ratios are given below.

$$\text{Operating working capital to sales ratio} = \frac{\text{Operating working capital}}{\text{Sales}}$$

$$\text{Operating working capital turnover} = \frac{\text{Sales}}{\text{Operating working capital}}$$

$$\text{Accounts receivable turnover} = \frac{\text{Sales}}{\text{Accounts receivable}}$$

$$\text{Inventory turnover} = \frac{\text{Cost of goods sold}}{\text{Inventory}}$$

$$\text{Accounts payable turnover} = \frac{\text{Purchases}}{\text{Accounts payable}} \ or \ \frac{\text{Cost of goods sold}}{\text{Accounts payable}}$$

$$\text{Days' receivables} = \frac{\text{Accounts receivable}}{\text{Average sales per day}}$$

$$\text{Days' inventory} = \frac{\text{Inventory}}{\text{Average cost of goods sold per day}}$$

$$\text{Days' payables} = \frac{\text{Accounts payable}}{\text{Average purchases (or cost of goods sold) per day}}$$

Operating working capital turnover indicates how many dollars of sales a firm is able to generate for each dollar invested in its operating working capital. Accounts receivable turnover, inventory turnover, and accounts payable turnover allow the analyst to examine how productively the three principal components of working capital are being used. Days' receivables, days' inventory, and days' payables are another way to evaluate the efficiency of a firm's working capital management.[8]

Long-Term Assets Management

Another area of investment management concerns the utilization of a firm's long-term assets. It is useful to define a firm's investment in long-term assets as follows:

Net long-term assets = (Total long-term assets
            − Non-interest-bearing long-term liabilities)

Long-term assets generally consist of net property, plant, and equipment (PP&E), intangible assets such as goodwill, and other assets. Non-interest-bearing long-term liabilities include such items as deferred taxes. We define net long-term assets and net working capital in such a way that their sum, net operating assets, is equal to the sum of net debt and equity, or net capital. This is consistent with the way we defined operating ROA earlier in the chapter.

The efficiency with which a firm uses its net long-term assets is measured by the following two ratios: net long-term assets as a percent of sales and net long-term asset turnover. Net long-term asset turnover is defined as

$$\text{Net long-term asset turnover} = \frac{\text{Sales}}{\text{Net long-term assets}}$$

Property plant and equipment (PP&E) is the most important long-term asset in a firm's balance sheet. The efficiency with which a firm's PP&E is used is measured by the ratio of PP&E to sales, or by the PP&E turnover ratio:

$$\text{PP\&E turnover} = \frac{\text{Sales}}{\text{Net property, plant, and equipment}}$$

The ratios listed above allow the analyst to explore a number of business questions in four general areas:

1. How well does the company manage its inventory? Does the company use modern manufacturing techniques? Does it have good vendor and logistics management systems? If inventory ratios are changing, what is the underlying business reason? Are new products being planned? Is there a mismatch between the demand forecasts and actual sales?
2. How well does the company manage its credit policies? Are these policies consistent with its marketing strategy? Is the company artificially increasing sales by loading the distribution channels?
3. Is the company taking advantage of trade credit? Is it relying too much on trade credit? If so, what are the implicit costs?
4. Are the company's investment in plant and equipment consistent with its competitive strategy? Does the company have a sound policy of acquisitions and divestitures?

Table 5-6 shows the asset turnover ratios for Nordstrom and TJX. Nordstrom experienced an erosion in its working capital management between 2000 and 2001, as can be seen from an increase of operating working capital as a percent of sales and a decrease in operating working capital turnover. This erosion is attributable to an increase in accounts receivable and a downturn in inventory management. There was also an extension in its accounts payable days, which favorably impacted the company's working capital management ratios. In addition, Nordstrom's long-term asset utilization did not improve in 2001: its net long-term asset turnover and PP&E turnover show declines. In its annual report, Nordstrom acknowledges that the sales from stores that it operated for more than a year

Table 5-6 Asset Management Ratios

Ratio	Nordstrom 2001	Nordstrom 2000	TJX 2001
Operating working capital/Sales	19.3%	16.5%	3.7%
Net long-term assets/Sales	23.3%	19.9%	9.8%
PP&E/Sales	28.6%	25.6%	8.5%
Operating working capital turnover	5.2	6.1	26.8
Net long-term assets turnover	4.3	5.0	10.2
PP&E turnover	3.5	3.9	11.8
Accounts receivable turnover	7.8	9.0	173.2
Inventory turnover	4.0	4.6	5.6
Accounts payable turnover	8.1	9.3	12.6
Days' accounts receivable	46.8	40.7	2.1
Days' inventory	91.7	79.8	65.3
Days' accounts payable	45.2	39.1	29.0

(also called same-store sales) showed a small decline in 2001 because management was focusing on controlling costs.

TJX achieved dramatically better asset utilization ratios in 2001 relative to Nordstrom. TJX was able to invest a negligible amount of money in its operating working capital by taking full advantage of trade credit from its vendors and by delaying payment of some of its operating expenses. Also, because TJX has no credit card operations of its own, it is able to collect its receivables in 2.1 days, in contrast to Nordstrom's 46.8 receivable days. TJX is also managing its inventory more efficiently, perhaps because of its more focused merchandising strategy. Finally, because TJX uses operating leases to rent its stores, it has significantly lower capital tied up in its stores. As a result, its PP&E turnover is more than three times as much as Nordstrom's. One should, however, be cautious in interpreting this difference between the two companies because, as TJX discloses in its footnotes, it owes a substantial amount of money in the coming years on noncancelable operating leases. TJX's financial statements do not fully recognize its investment in its stores through these non-cancelable leases, potentially inflating its operating asset turns.

Evaluating Financial Management: Financial Leverage

Financial leverage enables a firm to have an asset base larger than its equity. The firm can augment its equity through borrowing and the creation of other liabilities like accounts payable, accrued liabilities, and deferred taxes. Financial leverage increases a firm's ROE as long as the cost of the liabilities is less than the return from investing these funds. In this respect it is important to distinguish between interest-bearing liabilities such as notes payable, other forms of short-term debt and long-term debt that carry an explicit interest charge, and other forms of liabilities. Some of these other forms of liability, such as accounts payable or deferred taxes, do not carry any interest charge at all. Other liabilities, such as capital lease obligations or pension obligations, carry an implicit interest charge. Finally, some firms carry large cash balances or investments in marketable securities. These balances reduce a firm's net debt because conceptually the firm can pay down its debt using its cash and short-term investments.

While financial leverage can potentially benefit a firm's shareholders, it can also increase their risk. Unlike equity, liabilities have predefined payment terms, and the firm faces risk of financial distress if it fails to meet these commitments. There are a number of ratios to evaluate the degree of risk arising from a firm's financial leverage.

Current Liabilities and Short-Term Liquidity

The following ratios are useful in evaluating the risk related to a firm's current liabilities:

$$\text{Current ratio} = \frac{\text{Current assets}}{\text{Current liabilities}}$$

$$\text{Quick ratio} = \frac{\text{Cash} + \text{Short-term investments} + \text{Accounts receivable}}{\text{Current liabilities}}$$

$$\text{Cash ratio} = \frac{\text{Cash} + \text{Marketable securities}}{\text{Current liabilities}}$$

$$\text{Operating cash flow ratio} = \frac{\text{Cash flow from operations}}{\text{Current liabilities}}$$

All the above ratios attempt to measure the firm's ability to repay its current liabilities. The first three compare a firm's current liabilities with its short-term assets that can be used to repay those liabilities. The fourth ratio focuses on the ability of the firm's operations to generate the resources needed to repay its current liabilities.

Since both current assets and current liabilities have comparable duration, the current ratio is a key index of a firm's short-term liquidity. Analysts view a current ratio of more than one to be an indication that the firm can cover its current liabilities from the cash realized from its current assets. However, the firm can face a short-term liquidity problem even with a current ratio exceeding one when some of its current assets are not easy to liquidate. Quick ratio and cash ratio capture the firm's ability to cover its current liabilities from liquid assets. Quick ratio assumes that the firm's accounts receivable are liquid. This is true in industries where the credit-worthiness of the customers is beyond dispute, or when receivables are collected in a very short period. When these conditions do not prevail, cash ratio, which considers only cash and marketable securities, is a better indication of a firm's ability to cover its current liabilities in an emergency. Operating cash flow is another measure of the firm's ability to cover its current liabilities from cash generated from operations of the firm.

The liquidity ratios for Nordstrom and TJX are shown in Table 5-7. Nordstrom's liquidity situation in 2001 was comfortable when measured in terms of current ratio or quick ratio. Both these ratios improved in 2001. All this was good news for Nordstrom's short-term creditors. TJX also had a comfortable liquidity position, thanks to its large cash balance and a sound operating cash flow. Because of its tight management of operating working capital, however, TJX's current and quick ratios are smaller than Nordstrom's.

Table 5-7 Liquidity Ratios

Ratio	Nordstrom 2001	Nordstrom 2000	TJX 2001
Current ratio	2.28	2.14	1.40
Quick ratio	0.94	0.92	0.16
Cash ratio	0.03	0.07	0.11
Operating cash flow ratio	0.58	0.29	0.75

Debt and Long-Term Solvency

A company's financial leverage is also influenced by its debt financing policy. There are several potential benefits from debt financing. First, debt is typically cheaper than equity because the firm promises predefined payment terms to debt holders. Second, in most countries, interest on debt financing is tax deductible whereas dividends to shareholders are not tax deductible. Third, debt financing can impose discipline on the firm's management and motivate it to reduce wasteful expenditures. Fourth, it is often easier for management to communicate their proprietary information on the firm's strategies and prospects to private lenders than to public capital markets. Such communication can potentially reduce a firm's cost of capital. For all these reasons, it is optimal for firms to use at least some debt in their capital structure. Too much reliance on debt financing, however, is potentially costly to the firm's shareholders. The firm will face financial distress if it defaults on the interest and principal payments. Debt holders also impose covenants on the firm, restricting the firm's operating, investment, and financing decisions.

The optimal capital structure for a firm is determined primarily by its business risk. A firm's cash flows are highly predictable when there is little competition or there is little threat of technological changes. Such firms have low business risk and hence they can rely heavily on debt financing. In contrast, if a firm's operating cash flows are highly volatile and its capital expenditure needs are unpredictable, it may have to rely primarily on equity financing. Managers' attitude towards risk and financial flexibility also often determine a firm's debt policies.

There are a number of ratios which help the analyst in this area. To evaluate the mix of debt and equity in a firm's capital structure, the following ratios are useful:

$$\text{Liabilities-to-equity ratio} \quad = \quad \frac{\text{Total liabilities}}{\text{Shareholders' equity}}$$

$$\text{Debt-to-equity ratio} \quad = \quad \frac{\text{Short-term debt} + \text{Long-term debt}}{\text{Shareholders' equity}}$$

$$\text{Net-debt-to-equity ratio} \quad = \quad \frac{\text{Short-term debt} + \text{Long-term debt} - \text{Cash and marketable securities}}{\text{Shareholders' equity}}$$

$$\text{Debt-to-capital ratio} \quad = \quad \frac{\text{Short-term debt} + \text{Long-term debt}}{\text{Short-term debt} + \text{Long-term debt} + \text{Shareholders' equity}}$$

$$\text{Net-debt-to-net-capital ratio} \quad = \quad \frac{\text{Interest bearing liabilities} - \text{Cash and marketable securities}}{\text{Interest bearing liabilities} - \text{Cash and marketable securities} + \text{Shareholders' equity}}$$

The first ratio restates the assets-to-equity ratio (one of the three primary ratios underlying ROE) by subtracting one from it. The second ratio provides an indication of how many dollars of debt financing the firm is using for each dollar invested by its shareholders. The third ratio uses net debt, which is total debt minus cash and marketable securities, as the measure of a firm's borrowings. The fourth and fifth ratios measure debt as a proportion of total capital. In calculating all the above ratios, it is important to include all interest-bearing obligations, whether the interest charge is explicit or implicit. Recall that examples of line items which carry an implicit interest charge include capital lease obligations and pension obligations. Analysts sometimes include any potential off-balance-sheet obligations that a firm may have, such as noncancelable operating leases, in the definition of a firm's debt.

The ease with which a firm can meet its interest payments is an indication of the degree of risk associated with its debt policy. The interest coverage ratio provides a measure of this construct:

$$\text{Interest coverage (earnings basis)} \quad = \quad \frac{\text{Net income} + \text{Interest expense} + \text{Tax expense}}{\text{Interest expense}}$$

$$\text{Interest coverage (cash flow basis)} \quad = \quad \frac{\text{Cash flow from operations} + \text{Interest expense} + \text{Taxes paid}}{\text{Interest expense}}$$

One can also calculate coverage ratios that measure a firm's ability to measure all fixed financial obligations, such as interest payment, lease payments, and debt repayments, by appropriately redefining the numerator and denominator in the above ratios. In doing so it is important to remember that while some fixed charge payments, such as interest and lease rentals, are paid with pretax dollars while others, such as debt repayments, are made with after-tax dollars.

The earnings-based coverage ratio indicates the dollars of earnings available for each dollar of required interest payment; the cash-flow-based coverage ratio indicates the dollars of cash generated by operations for each dollar of required interest payment. In both these ratios, the denominator is the interest expense. In the numerator we add taxes back because taxes are computed only after interest expense is deducted. A coverage ratio of one implies that the firm is barely covering its interest expense through its operating activities, which is a very risky situation. The larger the coverage ratio, the greater the cushion the firm has to meet interest obligations.

Key Analysis Questions

Some of the business questions to ask when the analyst is examining a firm's debt policies follow:

- Does the company have enough debt? Is it exploiting the potential benefits of debt—interest tax shields, management discipline, and easier communication?
- Does the company have too much debt given its business risk? What type of debt covenant restrictions does the firm face? Is it bearing the costs of too much debt, risking potential financial distress and reduced business flexibility?
- What is the company doing with the borrowed funds? Investing in working capital? Investing in fixed assets? Are these investments profitable?
- Is the company borrowing money to pay dividends? If so, what is the justification?

We show debt and coverage ratios for Nordstrom and TJX in Table 5-8. Nordstrom recorded an increase in its liabilities-to-equity and debt-to-equity ratios. Nordstrom also increased its net financial leverage even after taking into account a significant increase in its cash balance in 2001. The company's interest coverage also remained at comfortable levels. All these ratios suggest that Nordstrom has been following a fairly conservative debt policy.

TJX's debt ratios confirm that it is primarily relying on non-interest-bearing liabilities such as accounts payable and accrued expenses to finance its operations. Its interest

Table 5-8 Debt and Coverage Ratios

Ratio	Nordstrom 2001	Nordstrom 2000	TJX 2001
Liabilities to equity	1.94	1.58	1.37
Debt to equity	0.97	0.74	0.29
Net debt to equity	0.95	0.69	.19
Debt to capital	0.49	0.43	0.23
Net debt to net capital	0.49	0.41	.16
Net debt to equity, including operating lease obligations	not available	not available	2.23
Interest coverage (earnings based)	3.35	3.33	21.54
Interest coverage (cash flow based)	7.02	5.26	31.04
Fixed charges coverage, including lease payments (earnings based)	2.44	2.40	2.71
Fixed charges coverage, including lease payments (cash flow based)	4.69	3.57	3.50

coverage ratios are extraordinarily high. But this picture changes when one considers the fact that TJX relies heavily on operating leases for its stores. If the present value of minimum lease rental obligations is added to TJX's net debt, its net-debt-to-equity ratio increases dramatically. Similarly, when one includes both interest and minimum rental payments in the coverage ratio, TJX's coverage drops dramatically relative to when only interest is included. This illustrates the importance of considering off-balance-sheet obligations in analyzing a company's financial management.

Ratios of Disaggregated Data

So far we have discussed how to compute ratios using information in the financial statements. Analysts often probe the above ratios further by using disaggregated financial and physical data. For example, for a multibusiness company, one could analyze the information by individual business segments. Such an analysis can reveal potential differences in the performance of each business unit, allowing the analyst to pinpoint areas where a company's strategy is working and where it is not. It is also possible to probe financial ratios further by computing ratios of physical data pertaining to a company's operations. The appropriate physical data to look at varies from industry to industry. As an example in retailing, one could compute productivity statistics such as sales per store, sales per square foot, customer transactions per store, and amount of sale per customer transactions; in the hotel industry, room occupancy rates provide important information; in the cellular telephone industry, acquisition cost per new subscriber and subscriber retention rate are important. These disaggregated ratios are particularly useful for young firms and young industries such as Internet firms, where accounting data may not fully capture the business economics due to conservative accounting rules.

Putting It All Together: Assessing Sustainable Growth Rate

Analysts often use the concept of sustainable growth as a way to evaluate a firm's ratios in a comprehensive manner. A firm's sustainable growth rate is defined as

$$\text{Sustainable growth rate} = \text{ROE} \times (1 - \text{Dividend payout ratio})$$

We already discussed the analysis of ROE in the previous four sections. The dividend payout ratio is defined as

$$\text{Dividend payout ratio} = \frac{\text{Cash dividends paid}}{\text{Net income}}$$

A firm's dividend payout ratio is a measure of its dividend policy. As we discuss in detail in Chapter 12, firms pay dividends for several reasons. Dividends are a way for the firm to return to its shareholders any cash generated in excess of its operating and investment needs. When there are information asymmetries between a firm's managers and its shareholders, dividend payments can serve as a signal to shareholders about managers' expectation of the firm's future prospects. Firms may also pay dividends to attract a certain type of shareholder base.

Sustainable growth rate is the rate at which a firm can grow while keeping its profitability and financial policies unchanged. A firm's return on equity and its dividend payout policy determine the pool of funds available for growth. Of course the firm can grow at a rate different from its sustainable growth rate if its profitability, payout policy, or financial leverage changes. Therefore, the sustainable growth rate provides a benchmark against which a firm's growth plans can be evaluated. Figure 5-2 shows how a firm's sustainable

Figure 5-2   Sustainable Growth Rate Framework for Financial Ratio Analysis

growth rate can be linked to all the ratios discussed in this chapter. These linkages allow an analyst to examine the drivers of a firm's current sustainable growth rate. If the firm intends to grow at a higher rate than its sustainable growth rate, one could assess which of the ratios are likely to change in the process. This analysis can lead to asking business questions such as these: Where is the change going to take place? Is management expecting profitability to increase? Or asset productivity to improve? Are these expectations realistic? Is the firm planning for these changes? If the profitability is not likely to go up, will the firm increase its financial leverage or cut dividends? What is the likely impact of these financial policy changes?

Table 5-9 shows the sustainable growth rate and its components for Nordstrom and TJX. Nordstrom had a lower ROE and a higher dividend payout ratio relative to TJX, leading to a significantly lower sustainable growth rate in both 2001 and 2000. However, Nordstrom improved its sustainable growth rate because of its improved ROE and a marginal decline in its payout ratio.

Table 5-9   Sustainable Growth Rate

Ratio	Nordstrom 2001	Nordstrom 2000	TJX 2001
ROE	10.1%	8.6%	41.1%
Dividend payout ratio	39%	45%	9.7%
Sustainable growth rate	6.2%	4.7%	37.1%

Nordstrom's actual growth rates in 2001 in sales, assets, and liabilities were different from its sustainable growth rate in 2000. In 2001 Nordstrom's sales declined by 7 percent, net operating assets increased by 18.7 percent, and its net debt grew by 42 percent. These differences in Nordstrom's sustainable growth rate and its actual growth rates in sales, net assets, and net debt are reconciled by the fact that Nordstrom reduced its equity base through significant stock repurchases. Nordstrom has the room to grow in future years at about 6 percent without altering its operating and financial policies. In contrast, TJX has a significantly higher sustainable growth rate of 37.1 percent, implying that it can grow at a much faster rate than Nordstrom without altering its operating and financial policies.

Historical Patterns of Ratios for U.S. Firms

To provide a benchmark for analysis, Table 5-10 reports historical values of the key ratios discussed in this chapter. These ratios are calculated using financial statement data for all publicly listed U.S. companies. The table shows the values of ROE, its key components, and the sustainable growth rate for each of the years 1983 to 2002, and the average for this twenty-year period. The data in the table show that the average ROE during this period has been 11.2 percent, average operating ROA has been 7.8 percent, and the average spread between operating ROA and net borrowing costs after tax has been 2.6 percent. Average

Table 5-10 Historical Values of Key Financial Ratios

Year	ROE	NOPAT Margin	Operating Asset Turnover	Operating ROA	Spread	Net Financial Leverage	Sustainable Growth Rate
1984	12.2%	6.1%	1.71	9.4%	3.8%	0.52	6.3%
1985	10.6%	5.7%	1.66	8.7%	1.9%	0.63	4.3%
1986	10.2%	5.9%	1.54	7.9%	1.6%	0.74	3.7%
1987	11.2%	6.9%	1.55	9.5%	2.7%	0.81	4.6%
1988	13.7%	7.0%	1.61	11.0%	6.9%	0.84	6.8%
1989	12.1%	6.9%	1.54	9.8%	4.6%	1.07	5.5%
1990	10.6%	6.7%	1.53	9.2%	2.4%	1.17	4.0%
1991	7.5%	6.4%	1.45	6.6%	−0.8%	1.19	1.1%
1992	5.1%	4.6%	1.47	5.4%	−1.7%	1.13	−1.5%
1993	9.6%	5.1%	1.48	5.7%	−0.2%	1.16	2.8%
1994	14.4%	7.0%	1.50	9.1%	2.7%	1.18	8.1%
1995	14.3%	5.8%	1.54	6.8%	6.3%	1.13	7.8%
1996	15.1%	6.5%	1.53	7.6%	6.3%	1.17	8.8%
1997	14.3%	7.1%	1.54	8.5%	3.7%	1.14	8.6%
1998	13.6%	7.5%	1.49	8.3%	3.1%	1.26	7.8%
1999	14.0%	7.5%	1.42	8.3%	4.0%	1.28	8.7%
2000	10.7%	6.5%	1.45	6.4%	2.4%	1.34	5.9%
2001	1.6%	3.7%	1.24	2.3%	−3.2%	1.29	−3.0%
2002	2.1%	3.4%	1.13	−1.0%	−5.7%	1.34	−2.4%
Average	11.2%	6.3%	1.51	7.8%	2.6%	1.06	5.0%

Because Table 5-10 ratios are based on beginning balance sheet data, the ratios for 1983 are not computed.

Source: Financial statement data for all companies publicly traded in the U.S. from 1983 to 2002, listed in the Compustat files.

sustainable growth rate for U.S. companies during this period has been 5.0 percent. Of course an individual company's ratios might depart from these economy-wide averages for a number of reasons, including industry effects, company strategies, and management effectiveness. Nonetheless, the average values in the table serve as useful benchmarks in financial analysis.

CASH FLOW ANALYSIS

The ratio analysis discussion focused on analyzing a firm's income statement (net profit margin analysis) or its balance sheet (asset turnover and financial leverage). The analyst can get further insights into the firm's operating, investing, and financing policies by examining its cash flows. Cash flow analysis also provides an indication of the quality of the information in the firm's income statement and balance sheet. As before, we will illustrate the concepts discussed in this section using Nordstrom's and TJX's cash flows.

Cash Flow and Funds Flow Statements

All U.S. companies are required to include a statement of cash flows in their financial statements under Statement of Financial Accounts Standard No. 95 (SFAS 95). In the reported cash flow statement, firms classify their cash flows into three categories: cash flow from operations, cash flow related to investments, and cash flow related to financing activities. Cash flow from operations is the cash generated by the firm from the sale of goods and services after paying for the cost of inputs and operations. Cash flow related to investment activities shows the cash paid for capital expenditures, intercorporate investments, acquisitions, and cash received from the sales of long-term assets. Cash flow related to financing activities shows the cash raised from (or paid to) the firm's stockholders and debt holders.

Firms use two cash flow statement formats: the direct format and the indirect format. The key difference between the two formats is the way they report cash flow from operating activities. In the direct cash flow format, which is used by only a small number of firms in practice, operating cash receipts and disbursements are reported directly. In the indirect format, firms derive their operating cash flows by making adjustments to net income. Because the indirect format links the cash flow statement with the firm's income statement and balance sheet, many analysts and managers find this format more useful. As a result, the FASB required firms using the direct format to report operating cash flows in the indirect format as well.

Recall from Chapter 3 that net income differs from operating cash flows because revenues and expenses are measured on an accrual basis. There are two types of accruals embedded in net income. First, there are current accruals like credit sales and unpaid expenses. Current accruals result in changes in a firm's current assets (such as accounts receivable, inventory, prepaid expenses) and current liabilities (such as accounts payable and accrued liabilities). The second type of accruals included in the income statement is noncurrent accruals such as depreciation, deferred taxes, and equity income from unconsolidated subsidiaries. To derive cash flow from operations from net income, adjustments have to be made for both these types of accruals. In addition, adjustments have to be made for nonoperating gains included in net income such as profits from asset sales.

Most firms outside the U.S. report a funds flow statement rather than a cash flow statement of the type described above. Prior to SFAS 95, U.S. firms also reported a similar statement. Funds flow statements show working capital flows, not cash flows. It is useful for analysts to know how to convert a funds flow statement into a cash flow statement.

Funds flow statements typically provide information on a firm's working capital from operations, defined as net income adjusted for noncurrent accruals, and gains from the sale of long-term assets. As discussed above, cash flow from operations essentially involves a third adjustment, the adjustment for current accruals. Thus it is relatively straightforward to convert working capital from operations to cash flow from operations by making the relevant adjustments for current accruals related to operations.

Information on current accruals can be obtained by examining changes in a firm's current assets and current liabilities Typically, operating accruals represent changes in all the current asset accounts other than cash and cash equivalents, and changes in all the current liabilities other than notes payable and the current portion of long-term debt.[9] Cash from operations can be calculated as follows:

Working capital from operations
− Increase (or + decrease) in accounts receivable
− Increase (or + decrease) in inventory
− Increase (or + decrease) in other current assets excluding cash and cash equivalents
+ Increase (or − decrease) in accounts payable
+ Increase (or − decrease) in other current liabilities excluding debt.

Funds flow statements also often do not classify investment and financing flows. In such a case, the analyst has to classify the line items in the funds flow statement into these two categories by evaluating the nature of the business transactions that give rise to the flow represented by the line items.

Analyzing Cash Flow Information

Cash flow analysis can be used to address a variety of questions regarding a firm's cash flow dynamics:

- How strong is the firm's internal cash flow generation? Is the cash flow from operations positive or negative? If it is negative, why? Is it because the company is growing? Is it because its operations are unprofitable? Or is it having difficulty managing its working capital properly?
- Does the company have the ability to meet its short-term financial obligations, such as interest payments, from its operating cash flow? Can it continue to meet these obligations without reducing its operating flexibility?
- How much cash did the company invest in growth? Are these investments consistent with its business strategy? Did the company use internal cash flow to finance growth, or did it rely on external financing?
- Did the company pay dividends from internal free cash flow, or did it have to rely on external financing? If the company had to fund its dividends from external sources, is the company's dividend policy sustainable?
- What type of external financing does the company rely on? Equity, short-term debt, or long-term debt? Is the financing consistent with the company's overall business risk?
- Does the company have excess cash flow after making capital investments? Is it a long-term trend? What plans does management have to deploy the free cash flow?

While the information in reported cash flow statements can be used to answer the above questions directly in the case of some firms, it may not be easy to do so always for a number of reasons. First, even though SFAS 95 provides broad guidelines on the format of a cash flow statement, there is still significant variation across firms in how cash flow data are disclosed. Therefore, to facilitate a systematic analysis and comparison across firms, analysts often recast the information in the cash flow statement using their own cash flow model. Second, firms include interest expense and interest income in computing their cash flow from operating activities. However, these two items are not strictly related to a firm's operations. Interest expense is a function of financial leverage, and interest income is derived from financial assets rather than operating assets. Therefore it is useful to restate the cash flow statement to take this into account.

Analysts use a number of different approaches to restate the cash flow data. One such model is shown in Table 5-11. This presents cash flow from operations in two stages. The first step computes cash flow from operations before operating working capital investments. In computing this cash flow, the model excludes interest expense and interest income. To compute this number starting with a firm's net income, an analyst adds back three types of items: (1) after-tax net interest expense because this is a financing item that will be considered later, (2) nonoperating gains or losses typically arising out of asset disposals or asset write-offs because these items are investment related and will be considered later, and (3) long-term operating accruals such as depreciation and deferred taxes because these are noncash operating charges.

Table 5-11 Cash Flow Analysis

Line Item	Nordstrom 2001	Nordstrom 2000	TJX 2001
Net income (dollars in millions)	124.7	101.9	500.4
After-tax net interest expense (income)	45.8	38.3	15.9
Nonoperating losses (gains)	0	32.9	70.6
Long-term operating accruals	228.3	194.7	239.3
Operating cash flow before working capital investments	**398.7**	**367.7**	**826.2**
Net (investments in) or liquidation of operating working capital	60.8	(153.6)	95.3
Operating cash flow before investment in long-term assets	**459.5**	**214.2**	**921.5**
Net (investment in) or liquidation of operating long-term assets	(267.1)	(314.7)	(442.6)
Free cash flow available to debt and equity	**192.4**	**(100.5)**	**478.9**
After-tax net interest (expense) or income	(45.8)	(38.3)	(15.9
Net debt (repayment) or issuance	198.5	262.2	302.1
Free cash flow available to equity	**345.1**	**123.4**	**765.1**
Dividend (payments)	(48.3)	(45.9)	(48.3)
Net stock (repurchase) or issuance	9.2	(79.3)	(359.0
Net increase (decrease) in cash balance	**306.1**	**(1.8)**	**357.9**

Several factors affect a firm's ability to generate positive cash flow from operations. Healthy firms that are in a steady state should generate more cash from their customers than they spend on operating expenses. In contrast, growing firms—especially those investing cash in research and development, advertising and marketing, or building an organization to sustain future growth—may experience negative operating cash flow. Firms' working capital management also affects whether they generate positive cash flow from operations. Firms in the growing stage typically invest some cash flow in operating working capital items like accounts receivable, inventories, and accounts payable. Net investments in working capital are a function of firms' credit policies (accounts receivable), payment policies (payables, prepaid expenses, and accrued liabilities), and expected growth in sales (inventories). Thus, in interpreting firms' cash flow from operations after working capital, it is important to keep in mind their growth strategy, industry characteristics, and credit policies.

The cash flow analysis model next focuses on cash flows related to long-term investments. These investments take the form of capital expenditures, intercorporate investments, and mergers and acquisitions. Any positive operating cash flow after making operating working capital investments allows the firm to pursue long-term growth opportunities. If the firm's operating cash flows after working capital investments are not sufficient to finance its long-term investments, it has to rely on external financing to fund its growth. Such firms have less flexibility to pursue long-term investments than those that can fund their growth internally. There are both costs and benefits from being able to fund growth internally. The cost is that managers can use the internally generated free cash flow to fund unprofitable investments. Such wasteful capital expenditures are less likely if managers are forced to rely on external capital suppliers. Reliance on external capital markets may make it difficult for managers to undertake long-term risky investments if it is not easy to communicate to the capital markets the benefits from such investments.

Any excess cash flow after these long-term investments is free cash flow that is available for both debt holders and equity holders. Payments to debt holders include interest payments and principal payments. Firms with negative free cash flow have to borrow additional funds to meet their interest and debt repayment obligations, or cut some of their investments in working capital or long-term investments, or issue additional equity. This situation is clearly financially risky for the firm.

Cash flow after payments to debt holders is free cash flow available to equity holders. Payments to equity holders consist of dividend payments and stock repurchases. If firms pay dividends despite negative free cash flow to equity holders, they are borrowing money to pay dividends. While this may be feasible in the short term, it is not prudent for a firm to pay dividends to equity holders unless it has a positive free cash flow on a sustained basis. On the other hand, firms that have a large free cash flow after debt payments run the risk of wasting that money on unproductive investments to pursue growth for its own sake. An analyst, therefore, should carefully examine the investment plans of such firms.

The model in Table 5-11 suggests that the analyst should focus on a number of cash flow measures: (1) cash flow from operations before investment in working capital and interest payments, to examine whether or not the firm is able to generate a cash surplus from its operations, (2) cash flow from operations after investment in working capital, to assess how the firm's working capital is being managed and whether or not it has the flexibility to invest in long-term assets for future growth, (3) free cash flow available to debt and equity holders, to assess a firm's ability to meet its interest and principal payments, and (4) free cash flow available to equity holders, to assess the firm's financial ability to sustain its dividend policy and to identify potential agency problems from excess free cash flow. These measures have to be evaluated in the context of the company's business, its growth strategy, and its financial policies. Further, changes in these measures from year to year provide valuable information on the stability of the cash flow dynamics of the firm.

Key Analysis Questions

The cash flow model in Table 5-11 can be also used to assess a firm's earnings quality, as discussed in Chapter 3. The reconciliation of a firm's net income with its cash flow from operations facilitates this exercise. Following are some of the questions an analyst can probe in this respect:

- Are there significant differences between a firm's net income and its operating cash flow? Is it possible to clearly identify the sources of this difference? Which accounting policies contribute to this difference? Are there any one-time events contributing to this difference?
- Is the relationship between cash flow and net income changing over time? Why? Is it because of changes in business conditions or because of changes in the firm's accounting policies and estimates?
- What is the time lag between the recognition of revenues and expenses and the receipt and disbursement of cash flows? What type of uncertainties need to be resolved in between?
- Are the changes in receivables, inventories, and payables normal? If not, is there adequate explanation for the changes?

Finally, as we will discuss in Chapter 7, free cash flow available to debt and equity and free cash flow available to equity are critical inputs into the cash-flow-based valuation of firms' assets and equity, respectively.

Analysis of Nordstrom's Cash Flow

Nordstrom and TJX reported their cash flows using the indirect cash flow statement. Table 5-11 recasts these statements using the approach discussed above so that we can analyze the two companies' cash flow dynamics.

Cash flow analysis presented in Table 5-11 shows Nordstrom had an operating cash flow before working capital investments of $398.7 million in 2001, an improvement from $367.7 million in 2000. The difference between earnings and these cash flows is primarily attributable to the depreciation and amortization charge included in the company's income statement.

In 2001 Nordstrom managed to squeeze an additional $60.8 million from its operating working capital, primarily by reducing its investment in accounts receivable and inventory. This contrasts with a net operating working capital investment of $153.6 million in 2000. As a result of this improvement in working capital management, the company had an operating cash flow before long-term investments to the tune of $459.5 million in 2001, a significant improvement over the 2000 figure of $214.2 million. As a result, unlike in 2000, Nordstrom generated more than adequate cash flow from operations in 2001 to meet its total investment in long-term assets. Nordstrom thus had $192.4 million of free cash flow available to debt and equity holders in 2001, compared to a deficit of $100.5 million in 2000.

Both in 2000 and 2001, Nordstrom was a net borrower. As a result, there was considerable free cash flow available to equity holders in both years. The company utilized this free cash flow to pay its regular dividends and also buy back stock in 2000. The difference between the two years, however, is that in 2001 Nordstrom had adequate internal cash flow to make distributions to shareholders, while in 2000 the company could not have made these payments to equity holders either without borrowing or without cutting its long-term investments. Clearly, Nordstrom's cash flow improved significantly in 2001.

TJX also had a very strong cash flow situation in 2001. It had $826.2 million in operating cash flow before working capital investments. TJX was also able to reduce its investments in operating working capital. There is, however, a significant difference between the way investments in working capital appear to have been managed by TJX and Nordstrom. While Nordstrom reduced its investments in inventory and accounts receivable, TJX stretched its payables and accrued expenses. Similar to Nordstrom, TJX was able to fund all its long-term investments in operating assets from its own operating cash flow. As a result, TJX had $478.9 million in free cash flow available to debt and equity holders. From this, the company paid out $15.9 million in interest (net of taxes). The company was a net borrower to the tune of $302.1 million, leaving it with a whopping $765.1 million in free cash flow available to equity holders. The company distributed close to half of it to its shareholders—$48.3 million in dividends and $359 million in stock repurchases—leaving a cash increase of about $357.9 million.

SUMMARY

This chapter presents two key tools of financial analysis: ratio analysis and cash flow analysis. Both these tools allow the analyst to examine a firm's performance and its financial condition, given its strategy and goals. Ratio analysis involves assessing the firm's income statement and balance sheet data. Cash flow analysis relies on the firm's cash flow statement.

The starting point for ratio analysis is the company's ROE. The next step is to evaluate the three drivers of ROE, which are net profit margin, asset turnover, and financial leverage. Net profit margin reflects a firm's operating management, asset turnover reflects its investment management, and financial leverage reflects its liability management. Each of these areas can be further probed by examining a number of ratios. For example, common-sized income statement analysis allows a detailed examination of a firm's net margins. Similarly, turnover of key working capital accounts like accounts receivable, inventory, and accounts payable, and turnover of the firm's fixed assets allow further examination of a firm's asset turnover. Finally, short-term liquidity ratios, debt policy ratios, and coverage ratios provide a means of examining a firm's financial leverage.

A firm's sustainable growth rate—the rate at which it can grow without altering its operating, investment, and financing policies—is determined by its ROE and its dividend policy. The concept of sustainable growth provides a way to integrate the ratio analysis and to evaluate whether or not a firm's growth strategy is sustainable. If a firm's plans call for growing at a rate above its current sustainable rate, then the analyst can examine which of the firm's ratios is likely to change in the future.

Cash flow analysis supplements ratio analysis in examining a firm's operating activities, investment management, and financial risks. Firms in the U.S. are currently required to report a cash flow statement summarizing their operating, investment, and financing cash flows. Firms in other countries typically report working capital flows, but it is possible to use this information to create a cash flow statement.

Since there are wide variations across firms in the way cash flow data are reported, analysts often use a standard format to recast cash flow data. We discussed in this chapter one such cash flow model. This model allows the analyst to assess whether a firm's operations generate cash flow before investments in operating working capital, and how much cash is being invested in the firm's working capital. It also enables the analyst to calculate the firm's free cash flow after making long-term investments, which is an indication of the firm's ability to meet its debt and dividend payments. Finally, the cash flow analysis shows how the firm is financing itself, and whether its financing patterns are too risky.

The insights gained from analyzing a firm's financial ratios and its cash flows are valuable in forecasts of the firm's future prospects.

DISCUSSION QUESTIONS

1. Which of the following types of firms do you expect to have particularly high or low asset turnover? Explain why.
   - a supermarket
   - a pharmaceutical company
   - a jewelry retailer
   - a steel company

2. Which of the following types of firms do you expect to have high or low sales margins? Why?
   - a supermarket
   - a pharmaceutical company
   - a jewelry retailer
   - a software company

3. James Broker, an analyst with an established brokerage firm, comments: "The critical number I look at for any company is operating cash flow. If cash flows are less than earnings, I consider a company to be a poor performer and a poor investment prospect." Do you agree with this assessment? Why or why not?

4. In 1995 Chrysler has a return on equity of 20 percent, whereas Ford's return is only 8 percent. Use the decomposed ROE framework to provide possible reasons for this difference.

5. Joe Investor asserts, "A company cannot grow faster than its sustainable growth rate." True or false? Explain why.

6. What are the reasons for a firm having lower cash from operations than working capital from operations? What are the possible interpretations of these reasons?

7. ABC Company recognizes revenue at the point of shipment. Management decides to increase sales for the current quarter by filling all customer orders. Explain what impact this decision will have on
   - Days' receivable for the current quarter
   - Days' receivable for the next quarter
   - Sales growth for the current quarter
   - Sales growth for the next quarter
   - Return on sales for the current quarter
   - Return on sales for the next quarter

8. What ratios would you use to evaluate operating leverage for a firm?

9. What are the potential benchmarks that you could use to compare a company's financial ratios? What are the pros and cons of these alternatives?

10. In a period of rising prices, how would the following ratios be affected by the accounting decision to select LIFO, rather than FIFO, for inventory valuation?
- Gross margin
- Current ratio
- Asset turnover
- Debt-to-equity ratio
- Average tax rate

NOTES

1. We will call the fiscal year ending January 2002 as the year 2001, and the fiscal year ending January 2001 as the year 2000.

2. In computing ROE, one can either use the beginning equity, ending equity, or an average of the two. Conceptually, the average equity is appropriate, particularly for rapidly growing companies. However, for most companies, this computational choice makes little difference as long as the analyst is consistent. Therefore, in practice most analysts use ending balances for simplicity. This comment applies to all ratios discussed in this chapter where one of the items in the ratio is a flow variable (items in the income statement or cash flow statement) and the other item is a stock variable (items in the balance sheet). Throughout this chapter we use the beginning balances of the stock variables.

3. We discuss in greater detail in Chapter 8 how to estimate a company's cost of equity capital. The equity beta for both Nordstrom and TJX was close to one in 1999, and the yield on long-term treasury bonds was approximately 6 percent. If one assumes a risk premium of 6 percent, the two firms' cost of equity is 12 percent; if the risk premium is assumed to be 8 percent, then their cost of equity is 14 percent. Lower assumed risk premium will, of course, lead to lower estimates of equity capital.

4. Strictly speaking, part of a cash balance is needed to run the firm's operations, so only the excess cash balance should be viewed as negative debt. However, firms do not provide information on excess cash, so we subtract all cash balance in our definitions and computations below. An alternative possibility is to subtract only short-term investments and ignore the cash balance completely.

5. See Doron Nissim and Stephen Penman, "Ratio Analysis and Valuation: From Research to Practice," *Review of Accounting Studies* 6 (2001): 109–154, for a more detailed description of this approach.

6. TJX has a small amount of debt and a cash balance larger than its debt. Therefore its weighted average cost of capital is likely to be similar to its cost of equity. We will discuss in Chapter 8 how to estimate a company's weighted average cost of capital.

7. See *Taxes and Business Strategy* by Myron Scholes and Mark Wolfson (Englewood Cliffs, NJ: Prentice-Hall, 1992).

8. There are a number of issues related to the calculation of these ratios in practice. First, in calculating all the turnover ratios, the assets used in the calculations can either be beginning of the year values, year-end values or an average of the beginning and ending balances in a year. We use the beginning of the year values in our calculations. Second, strictly speaking, one should use credit sales to calculate accounts receivable turnover and days' receivables. But since it is usually difficult to obtain data on credit sales, total sales are used instead. Similarly, in calculating accounts payable turnover or days' payables, cost of goods sold is substituted for purchases for data availability reasons.

9. Changes in cash and marketable securities are excluded because this is the amount being explained by the cash flow statement. Changes in short-term debt and the current portion of long-term debt are excluded because these accounts represent financing flows, not operating flows.

APPENDIX
PART A: NORDSTROM, INC. FINANCIAL STATEMENTS

CONSOLIDATED STATEMENTS OF EARNINGS ($ 000's)

Fiscal Year Ended January 31,	2000	2001	2002
Net sales	**5,149,266**	**5,528,537**	**5,634,130**
Cost of sales and related buying and occupancy	(3,359,760)	(3,649,516)	(3,765,859)
Gross profit	**1,789,506**	**1,879,021**	**1,868,271**
Selling, general, and administrative	(1,523,836)	(1,747,048)	(1,722,635)
Operating income	265,670	131,973	145,636
Interest expense, net	(50,396)	(62,698)	(75,038)
Write-down of investment	0	(32,857)	0
Service charge income and other, net	116,783	130,600	133,890
Earnings before income taxes	**332,057**	**167,018**	**204,488**
Income taxes	(129,500)	(65,100)	(79,800)
NET EARNINGS	**202,557**	**101,918**	**124,688**
Basic earnings per share	$1.47	$0.78	$0.93
Diluted earnings per share	$1.46	$0.78	$0.93
Cash dividends paid per share	$0.32	$0.35	$0.36

Source: Edgarscan.

CONSOLIDATED BALANCE SHEETS ($ 000's)

Fiscal Year Ended January 31,	2000	2001	2002
ASSETS			
Current assets:			
Cash and cash equivalents	52,569	25,259	331,327
Accounts receivable, net	616,989	721,953	698,475
Merchandise inventories	797,845	945,687	888,172
Prepaid expenses	97,245	28,760	34,375
Other current assets	0	91,323	102,249
Total current assets	1,564,648	1,812,982	2,054,598
Land, buildings, and equipment, net	1,429,492	1,599,938	1,761,082
Intangible assets, net	0	143,473	138,331
Other assets	67,941	52,110	94,768
TOTAL ASSETS	3,062,081	3,608,503	4,048,779
LIABILITIES AND SHAREHOLDERS' EQUITY			
Current liabilities:			
Notes payable	70,934	83,060	148
Accounts payable	390,688	466,476	490,988
Accrued salaries, wages, and related benefits	211,308	234,833	236,373
Income taxes and other accruals	135,388	153,613	142,002
Current portion of long-term debt	58,191	12,586	78,227
Total current liabilities	866,509	950,568	947,738

(continued)

Fiscal Year Ended January 31,	2000	2001	2002
Long-term debt	746,791	1,099,710	1,351,044
Deferred lease credits	194,995	275,252	342,046
Other liabilities	68,172	53,405	93,463
Shareholders' equity:			
Common stock, no par: 250,000,000 shares authorized; 134,468,608 and 133,797,757 shares issued and outstanding	247,559	330,394	341,316
Unearned stock compensation	(8,593)	(3,740)	(2,680)
Retained earnings	929,616	900,090	975,203
Accumulated other comprehensive earnings	17,032	2,824	649
Total shareholders' equity	1,185,614	1,229,568	1,314,488
TOTAL LIABILITIES & SHAREHOLDERS' EQUITY	3,062,081	3,608,503	4,048,779

Source: Edgarscan.

CONSOLIDATED STATEMENTS OF CASH FLOWS ($ 000's)

Fiscal Year Ended January 31,	2000	2001	2002
OPERATING ACTIVITIES			
Net earnings	202,557	101,918	124,688
Adjustments to reconcile net earnings to net cash provided by operating activities:			
Depreciation and amortization of buildings and equipment	193,718	203,048	213,089
Amortization of intangible assets	0	1,251	4,630
Amortization of deferred lease credits and other, net	(6,387)	(12,349)	(8,538)
Stock-based compensation expense	3,331	6,480	3,414
Deferred income taxes, net	(22,859)	(3,716)	15,662
Write-down of investment	0	32,857	0
Change in operating assets and liabilities, net of effects from acquisition of business:			
Accounts receivable, net	(29,854)	(102,945)	22,556
Merchandise inventories	79,894	6,741	215,731
Prepaid expenses	(6,976)	(173)	(1,684)
Other assets	(8,880)	(3,821)	(16,770)
Accounts payable	(76,417)	(67,924)	(159,636)
Accrued salaries, wages, and related benefits	14,942	17,850	(203)
Income tax liabilities and other accruals	965	3,879	(11,310)
Other liabilities	25,212	(7,184)	12,088
Net cash provided by operating activities	369,246	175,912	413,717
INVESTING ACTIVITIES			
Capital expenditures	(305,052)	(321,454)	(390,138)
Additions to deferred lease credits	114,910	92,361	126,383
Payment for acquisition, net of cash acquired	0	(83,828)	0
Other, net	(452)	(1,781)	(3,309)
Net cash used in investing activities	(190,594)	(314,702)	(267,064)

(continued)

CONSOLIDATED STATEMENTS OF CASH FLOWS (continued)

Fiscal Year Ended January 31,	2000	2001	2002
FINANCING ACTIVITIES	0	0	0
Proceeds (payments) from notes payable	(7,849)	12,126	(82,912)
Proceeds from issuance of long-term debt	0	308,266	300,000
Principal payments on long-term debt	(63,341)	(58,191)	(18,640)
Capital contribution to subsidiary from minority shareholders	16,000	0	0
Proceeds from issuance of common stock	9,577	6,250	10,542
Cash dividends paid	(44,463)	(45,935)	(48,265)
Purchase and retirement of common stock	(302,965)	(85,509)	(1,310)
Net cash provided by (used in) financing activities	(393,041)	137,007	159,415
Net increase (decrease) in cash and cash equivalents	(214,389)	(1,783)	306,068
Cash and cash equivalents at beginning of year	241,431	27,042	25,259
CASH AND CASH EQUIVALENTS AT END OF YEAR	27,042	25,259	331,327

Source: Edgarscan.

STANDARDIZED STATEMENTS OF EARNINGS ($ 000's)

Fiscal Year Ended January 31,	2000	2001	2002
Sales	5,149,266	5,528,537	5,634,130
Cost of goods sold	3,359,760	3,649,516	3,765,859
Gross Profit	1,789,506	1,879,021	1,868,271
SG&A	1,523,836	1,747,048	1,722,635
Depreciation & amortization	0	0	0
Other operating expense	0	32,857	0
Operating Income	265,670	99,116	145,636
Investment income	0	0	0
Other income, net of other expense	116,783	130,600	133,890
Other income	116,783	130,600	133,890
Other expense	0	0	0
Net interest expense (income)	50,396	62,698	75,038
Interest income	0	0	0
Interest expense	0	0	0
Minority interest	0	0	0
Pretax Income	332,057	167,018	204,488
Tax expense	129,500	65,100	79,800
Unusual items (after tax)	0	0	0
Net Income	202,557	101,918	124,688
Preferred dividends	0	0	0
Net Income to Common	202,557	101,918	124,688

Source: BAV Model (v.2.0).

STANDARDIZED BEGINNING BALANCE SHEETS ($ 000's)

Fiscal Year Beginning February 1,	2000	2001	2002
Assets			
Cash and marketable securities	52,569	25,259	331,327
Accounts receivable	616,989	721,953	698,475
Inventory	797,845	945,687	888,172
Other current assets	97,245	120,083	136,624
Total current assets	**1,564,648**	**1,812,982**	**2,054,598**
Long-term tangible assets	1,429,492	1,599,938	1,761,082
Long-term intangible assets	0	143,473	138,331
Other long-term assets	67,941	52,110	94,768
Total long-term assets	**1,497,433**	**1,795,521**	**1,994,181**
Total Assets	**3,062,081**	**3,608,503**	**4,048,779**
Liabilities			
Accounts payable	390,688	466,476	490,988
Short-term debt	129,125	95,646	78,375
Other current liabilities	211,308	234,833	236,373
Total current liabilities	**731,121**	**796,955**	**805,736**
Long-term debt	746,791	1,099,710	1,351,044
Deferred taxes	135,388	153,613	142,002
Other long-term liabilities (non-interest-bearing)	263,167	328,657	435,509
Total long-term liabilities	**1,145,346**	**1,581,980**	**1,928,555**
Total Liabilities	**1,876,467**	**2,378,935**	**2,734,291**
Minority interest	0	0	0
Shareholders' equity			
Preferred stock	0	0	0
Common shareholders' equity	1,185,614	1,229,568	1,314,488
Total shareholders' equity	**1,185,614**	**1,229,568**	**1,314,488**
Total Liabilities and Shareholders' Equity	**3,062,081**	**3,608,503**	**4,048,779**

Source: BAV Model (v.2.0).

STANDARDIZED STATEMENTS OF CASH FLOWS ($ 000's)

Fiscal Year Ended January 31,	2000	2001	2002
Net income	202,557	101,918	124,688
After-tax net interest expense (income)	30,742	38,260	45,755
Non-operating losses (gains)	0	32,857	0
Long-term operating accruals	167,803	194,714	228,257
Operating cash flow before working capital investments	401,102	367,749	398,700
Net (investments in) or liquidation of operating working capital	(1,114)	(153,577)	60,772
Operating cash flow before investment in long-term assets	399,988	214,172	459,472
Net (investment in) or liquidation of operating long-term assets	(190,594)	(314,702)	(267,064)
Free cash flow available to debt and equity	209,394	(100,530)	192,408
After-tax net interest expense (income)	30,742	38,260	45,755
Net debt (repayment) or issuance	(71,190)	262,201	198,448
Free cash flow available to equity	107,462	123,411	345,101
Dividend (payments)	(44,463)	(45,935)	(48,265)
Net stock (repurchase) or issuance	(277,388)	(79,259)	9,232
Net increase (decrease) in cash balance	(214,389)	(1,783)	306,068

Source: BAV Model (v.2.0).

CONDENSED STATEMENTS OF EARNINGS ($ 000's)

Fiscal Year Ended January 31,	2000	2001	2002
Sales	5,149,266	5,528,537	5,634,130
Net Operating Profit after Tax	233,299	140,178	170,443
Net income	202,557	101,918	124,688
+ Net interest expense after tax	30,742	38,260	45,755
= Net Operating Profit after Tax	233,299	140,178	170,443
− Net Interest Expense after Tax	30,742	38,260	45,755
Interest expense	0	0	0
− Interest income	0	0	0
= Net interest expense (income)	50,396	62,698	75,038
× (1 − Tax expense/pre-tax income)	.6098	.6102	.6100
= Net Interest Expense after Tax	30,742	38,260	45,755
= Net Income	202,557	101,918	124,688
− Preferred stock dividends	0	0	0
= Net Income to Common	202,557	101,918	124,688

Source: BAV Model (v.2.0).

CONDENSED BEGINNING BALANCE SHEETS ($ 000's)

Fiscal Year Beginning February 1,	**2000**	**2001**	**2002**
Beginning Net Working Capital	910,083	1,086,414	995,910
Accounts receivable	616,989	721,953	698,475
+ Inventory	797,845	945,687	888,172
+ Other current assets	97,245	120,083	136,624
− Accounts payable	390,688	466,476	490,988
− Other current liabilities	211,308	234,833	236,373
= **Beginning Net Working Capital**	**910,083**	**1,086,414**	**995,910**
+ **Beginning Net Long-Term Assets**	1,098,878	1,313,251	1,416,670
Long-term tangible assets	1,429,492	1,599,938	1,761,082
+ Long-term intangible assets	0	143,473	138,331
+ Other long-term assets	67,941	52,110	94,768
− Minority interest	0	0	0
− Deferred taxes	135,388	153,613	142,002
− Other long-term liabilities (non-interest-bearing)	263,167	328,657	435,509
= **Beginning Net Long-Term Assets**	**1,098,878**	**1,313,251**	**1,416,670**
= **Total Assets**	**2,008,961**	**2,399,665**	**2,412,580**
Beginning Net Debt	823,347	1,170,097	1,098,092
Short-term debt	129,125	95,646	78,375
+ Long-term debt	746,791	1,099,710	1,351,044
− Cash	52,569	25,259	331,327
= **Beginning Net Debt**	**823,347**	**1,170,097**	**1,098,092**
+ **Beginning Preferred Stock**	0	0	0
+ **Beginning Shareholders' Equity**	1,185,614	1,229,568	1,314,488
= **Total Net Capital**	**2,008,961**	**2,399,665**	**2,412,580**

Source: BAV Model (v.2.0).

APPENDIX
PART B: THE TJX COMPANIES, INC. FINANCIAL STATEMENTS

CONSOLIDATED STATEMENTS OF INCOME ($ 000's)

Fiscal Year Ended January 31,	2000	2001	2002
Net sales	8,795,347	9,579,006	10,708,998
Cost of sales, including buying and occupancy costs	6,579,400	7,188,124	8,122,922
Selling, general, and administrative expenses	1,354,665	1,503,036	1,686,389
Interest expense, net	7,345	22,904	25,643
Income from continuing operations before income taxes and cumulative effect of accounting change	853,937	864,942	874,044
Provision for income taxes	327,115	326,876	333,647
Income from continuing operations before cumulative effect of accounting change	526,822	538,066	540,397
(Loss) from discontinued operations, net of income taxes	0	0	(40,000)
Income before cumulative effect of accounting change	526,822	538,066	500,397
Cumulative effect of accounting change, net of income taxes	(5,154)	0	0
Net income	521,668	538,066	500,397
Basic earnings per share:			
Income from continuing operations before cumulative effect of accounting change	$1.67	$1.87	$1.96
Net income	$1.66	$1.87	$1.82
Weighted average common shares—basic	314,577,145	287,440,637	275,323,741
Diluted earnings per share:			
Income from continuing operations before cumulative effect of accounting change	$1.66	$1.86	$1.94
Net income	$1.64	$1.86	$1.80
Weighted average common shares—diluted	317,790,764	289,196,228	278,133,862
Cash dividends declared per share	$0.14	$0.16	$0.18

Source: Edgarscan.

CONSOLIDATED BALANCE SHEETS ($ 000's)

Fiscal Year Ended January 31,	2000	2001	2002
ASSETS			
Current assets:			
Cash and cash equivalents	371,759	132,535	492,776
Accounts receivable, net	55,461	61,845	69,209
Merchandise inventories	1,229,587	1,452,877	1,456,976
Prepaid expenses and other current assets	43,758	74,690	84,962
Current deferred income taxes, net	0	43,997	12,003
Total current assets	1,700,565	1,765,944	2,115,926
Property at cost:			
Land and buildings	116,005	133,714	144,958
Leasehold costs and improvements	622,962	704,011	880,791
Furniture, fixtures, and equipment	849,932	984,848	1,210,366
	1,588,899	1,822,573	2,236,115
Less accumulated depreciation and amortization	754,314	914,590	1,076,196
	834,585	907,983	1,159,919

(continued)

Fiscal Year Ended January 31,	2000	2001	2002
Property under capital lease net of accumulated amortization of $1,489	0	0	31,083
Other assets	55,826	69,976	83,139
Non-current deferred income taxes, net	23,143	3,394	26,575
Goodwill and trade name, net of amortization	190,844	184,986	179,101
Total Assets	**2,804,963**	**2,932,283**	**3,595,743**
LIABILITIES			
Current liabilities:			
Current installments of long-term debt	100,359	73	0
Obligation under capital lease due within one year	0	0	1,244
Short-term debt	0	39,000	0
Accounts payable	615,671	645,672	761,546
Accrued expenses and other current liabilities	471,159	544,014	552,220
Total current liabilities	**1,187,189**	**1,228,759**	**1,315,010**
Other long-term liabilities	179,179	165,440	237,656
Obligation under capital lease, less portion due within one year	0	0	30,336
Long-term debt, exclusive of current installments	319,367	319,372	672,043
Commitments and contingencies	0	0	0
Shareholders' Equity			
Common stock, authorized 1,200,000,000 shares, par value $1, issued and outstanding, 271,537,653 and 280,378,675 shares	299,979	280,379	271,538
Additional paid-in capital	0	0	0
Accumulated other comprehensive income (loss)	(1,433)	(3,288)	(6,755)
Retained earnings	820,682	941,621	1,075,915
Total shareholders' equity	**1,119,228**	**1,218,712**	**1,340,698**
Total Liabilities and Shareholders' Equity	**2,804,963**	**2,932,283**	**3,595,743**

Source: Edgarscan.

CONSOLIDATED STATEMENTS OF CASH FLOWS ($ 000's)

Fiscal Year Ended January 31,	2000	2001	2002
Cash flows from operating activities:			
Net income	521,668	538,066	500,397
Adjustments to reconcile net income to net cash provided by operating activities:			
Loss from discontinued operations, net of tax	0	0	40,000
Cumulative effect of accounting change	5,154	0	0
Depreciation and amortization	160,466	175,781	204,081
Property disposals and impairments	4,624	4,559	6,832
Tax benefit of employee stock options	11,736	15,941	30,644
Deferred income tax provision (benefit)	1,790	(24,235)	35,230
Changes in assets and liabilities:			
(Increase) in accounts receivable	(8,137)	(6,501)	(7,615)
(Increase) in merchandise inventories	(26,856)	(232,031)	(13,292)
(Increase) in prepaid expenses and other current assets	(15,519)	(12,083)	(1,273)
Increase (decrease) in accounts payable	(2,747)	34,158	120,770
Increase (decrease) in accrued expenses & other liabilities	(35,673)	69,134	16,054
Other, net	(21,282)	(6,026)	(19,382)
Net cash provided by operating activities	595,224	556,763	912,446

(continued)

CONSOLIDATED STATEMENTS OF CASH FLOWS *(continued)*

Fiscal Year Ended January 31,	2000	2001	2002
Cash flows from investing activities:			
Property additions	(238,569)	(257,005)	(449,444)
Issuance of note receivable	(5,848)	(23,100)	(5,402)
Proceeds from sale of other assets	0	9,183	0
Net cash (used in) investing activities	(244,417)	(270,922)	(454,846)
Cash flows from financing activities:			
Proceeds from borrowings of short-term debt, net	0	39,000	0
Proceeds from borrowings of long-term debt	198,060	0	347,579
Principal payments on long-term debt	(695)	(100,203)	(73)
Payments on short-term debt	0	0	(39,000)
Payments on capital lease obligation	0	0	(992)
Proceeds from sale and issuance of common stock, net	9,312	26,101	65,202
Cash payments for repurchase of common stock	(604,560)	(444,105)	(424,163)
Cash dividends paid	(42,739)	(44,693)	(48,290)
Net cash (used in) financing activities	(440,622)	(523,900)	(99,737)
Effect of exchange rate changes on cash	330	(1,165)	2,378
Net increase (decrease) in cash and cash equivalents	(89,485)	(239,224)	360,241
Cash and cash equivalents at beginning of year	461,244	371,759	132,535
Cash and cash equivalents at end of year	371,759	132,535	492,776

Source: Edgarscan.

STANDARDIZED STATEMENTS OF INCOME ($ 000's)

Fiscal Year Ended January 31,	2000	2001	2002
Sales	8,795,347	9,579,006	10,708,998
Cost of goods sold	6,579,400	7,188,124	8,122,922
Gross Profit	2,215,947	2,390,882	2,586,076
SG&A	1,354,665	1,503,036	1,686,389
Depreciation & amortization	0	0	0
Other operating expense	0	0	0
Operating Income	861,282	887,846	899,687
Investment income	0	0	0
Other income, net of other expense	0	0	0
Other income	0	0	0
Other expense	0	0	0
Net interest expense (income)	7,345	22,904	25,643
Interest income	0	0	0
Interest expense	0	0	0
Minority interest	0	0	0
Pretax Income	853,937	864,942	874,044
Tax expense	327,115	326,876	333,647
Unusual items (after tax)	(5,154)	0	(40,000)
Net Income	521,668	538,066	500,397
Preferred dividends	0	0	0
Net Income to Common	521,668	538,066	500,397

Source: BAV Model (v.2.0).

STANDARDIZED BEGINNING BALANCE SHEETS ($ 000's)

Fiscal Year Beginning February 1,	2000	2001	2002
ASSETS			
Cash and marketable securities	371,759	132,535	492,776
Accounts receivable	55,461	61,845	69,209
Inventory	1,229,587	1,452,877	1,456,976
Other current assets	43,758	74,690	84,962
Total current assets	**1,700,565**	**1,721,947**	**2,103,923**
Long-term tangible assets	834,585	907,983	1,191,002
Long-term intangible assets	190,844	184,986	179,101
Other long-term assets	55,826	69,976	83,139
Total long-term assets	**1,081,255**	**1,162,945**	**1,453,242**
Total Assets	**2,781,820**	**2,884,892**	**3,557,165**
LIABILITIES			
Accounts payable	615,671	645,672	761,546
Short-term debt	100,359	39,073	1,244
Other current liabilities	471,159	544,014	552,220
Total current liabilities	**1,187,189**	**1,228,759**	**1,315,010**
Long-term debt	319,367	319,372	702,379
Deferred taxes	−23,143	−47,391	−38,578
Other long-term liabilities (non-interest-bearing)	179,179	165,440	237,656
Total long-term liabilities	**475,403**	**437,421**	**901,457**
Total Liabilities	**1,662,592**	**1,666,180**	**2,216,467**
Minority interest	0	0	0
Shareholders' Equity			
Preferred stock	0	0	0
Common shareholders' equity	1,119,228	1,218,712	1,340,698
Total shareholders' equity	**1,119,228**	**1,218,712**	**1,340,698**
Total Liabilities and Shareholders' Equity	**2,781,820**	**2,884,892**	**3,557,165**

Source: BAV Model (v.2.0).

STANDARDIZED STATEMENTS OF CASH FLOWS ($ 000's)

Fiscal Year Ended January 31,	2000	2001	2002
Net Income	**521,668**	**538,066**	**500,397**
After-tax net interest expense (income)	4,531	14,248	15,854
Non-operating losses (gains)	16,890	15,941	70,644
Long-term operating accruals	162,256	151,546	239,311
Operating cash flow before working capital investments	**705,345**	**719,801**	**826,206**
Net (investments in) or liquidation of operating working capital	(110,214)	(153,349)	95,262
Operating cash flow before investment in long-term assets	**595,131**	**566,452**	**921,468**
Net (investment in) or liquidation of operating long-term assets	(233,945)	(243,263)	(442,612)
Free cash flow available to debt and equity	**361,186**	**323,189**	**478,856**
After-tax net interest expense (income)	4,531	14,248	15,854
Net debt (repayment) or issuance	191,517	(84,303)	302,112
Free cash flow available to equity	**548,172**	**224,638**	**765,114**
Dividend (payments)	(42,739)	(44,693)	(48,290)
Net stock (repurchase) or issuance	(595,248)	(418,004)	(358,961)
Net increase (decrease) in cash balance	**(89,815)**	**(238,059)**	**357,863**

Source: BAV Model (v.2.0).

CONDENSED STATEMENTS OF INCOME ($ 000's)

Fiscal Year Ended January 31,	2000	2001	2002
Sales	8,795,347	9,579,006	10,708,998
Net Operating Profit after Tax	526,199	552,314	516,251
Net income	521,668	538,066	500,397
+ Net interest expense after tax	4,531	14,248	15,854
= **Net Operating Profit after Tax**	526,199	552,314	516,251
− **Net Interest Expense after Tax**	4,531	14,248	15,854
Interest expense	0	0	0
− Interest income	0	0	0
= Net interest expense (income)	7,345	22,904	25,643
× (1 − Tax expense/pre-tax income)	.6098	.6102	.6100
= **Net Interest Expense after Tax**	4,531	14,248	15,854
= **Net Income**	521,668	538,066	500,397
− Preferred stock dividends	0	0	0
= **Net Income to Common**	521,668	538,066	500,397

Source: BAV Model (v.2.0).

CONDENSED BEGINNING BALANCE SHEET ($ 000's)

Fiscal Year Beginning February 1,	2000	2001	2002
Beginning Net Working Capital	241,976	399,726	297,381
Accounts receivable	55,461	61,845	69,209
+ Inventory	1,229,587	1,452,877	1,456,976
+ Other current assets	43,758	74,690	84,962
− Accounts payable	615,671	645,672	761,546
− Other current liabilities	471,159	544,014	552,220
= **Beginning Net Working Capital**	241,976	399,726	297,381
+ **Beginning Net Long-Term Assets**	925,219	1,044,896	1,254,164
Long-term tangible assets	834,585	907,983	1,191,002
+ Long-term intangible assets	190,844	184,986	179,101
+ Other long-term assets	55,826	69,976	83,139
− Minority interest	0	0	0
− Deferred taxes	−23,143	−47,391	−38,578
− Other long-term liabilities (non-interest-bearing)	179,179	165,440	237,656
= **Beginning Net Long-Term Assets**	925,219	1,044,896	1,254,164
= **Total Assets**	1,167,195	1,444,622	1,551,545
Beginning Net Debt	47,967	225,910	210,847
Short-term debt	100,359	39,073	1,244
+ Long-term debt	319,367	319,372	702,379
− Cash	371,759	132,535	492,776
= **Beginning Net Debt**	47,967	225,910	210,847
+ **Beginning Preferred Stock**	0	0	0
+ **Beginning Shareholders' Equity**	1,119,228	1,218,712	1,340,698
= **Total Net Capital**	1,167,195	1,444,622	1,551,545

Source: BAV Model (v.2.0).

Prospective Analysis: Forecasting

Most financial statement analysis tasks are undertaken with a forward-looking decision in mind—and much of the time, it is useful to summarize the view developed in the analysis with an explicit forecast. Managers need forecasts for planning and to provide performance targets; analysts need forecasts to help communicate their views of the firm's prospects to investors; bankers and debt market participants need forecasts to assess the likelihood of loan repayment. Moreover, there are a variety of contexts (including but not limited to security analysis) where the forecast is usefully summarized in the form of an estimate of the firm's value—an estimate that, after all, can be viewed as the best attempt to reflect in a single summary statistic the manager's or analyst's view of the firm's prospects.

Prospective analysis includes two tasks—forecasting and valuation—that together represent approaches to explicitly summarizing the analyst's forward-looking views. In this chapter we focus on forecasting; valuation is the topic of the next two chapters. The key concepts discussed in this chapter are again illustrated using analysts' forecasts for Nordstrom.

RELATION OF FORECASTING TO OTHER ANALYSES

Forecasting is not so much a separate analysis as it is a way of summarizing what has been learned through business strategy analysis, accounting analysis, and financial analysis. For example, a projection of the future performance of TJX as of early fiscal year 2002 must be grounded ultimately in an understanding of questions such as these:

- *From business strategy analysis:* How long will TJX's strategy and competitive advantage yield the type of spectacular performance it reported in prior years? At what rate can the company grow both in the short term and in the long term without sacrificing its superior margins? Will competition be able to replicate TJX's retailing model?
- *From accounting analysis:* Are there any aspects of TJX's accounting that suggest past earnings and assets are overstated, or expenses or liabilities are understated? If so, what are the implications for future accounting statements?
- *From financial analysis:* What are the sources of TJX's superior performance? Is it sustainable?

The upshot is that a forecast can be no better than the business strategy analysis, accounting analysis, and financial analysis underlying it. However, there are certain techniques and knowledge that can help a manager or analyst to structure the best possible forecast, conditional on what has been learned in the previous steps. Below we summarize an approach to structuring the forecast, offer information useful in getting started, and give detailed steps to forecast earnings, balance sheet data, and cash flows.

THE TECHNIQUES OF FORECASTING

The Overall Structure of the Forecast

The best way to forecast future performance is to do it comprehensively—producing not only an earnings forecast, but a forecast of cash flows and the balance sheet as well. A comprehensive approach is useful, even in cases where one might be interested primarily in a single facet of performance, because it guards against unrealistic implicit assumptions. For example, if an analyst forecasts growth in sales and earnings for several years without explicit consideration of the required increases in working capital and plant assets and the associated financing, the forecast might possibly imbed unreasonable assumptions about asset turnover, leverage, or equity capital infusions.

A comprehensive approach involves many forecasts, but in most cases they are all linked to the behavior of a few key "drivers." The drivers vary according to the type of business involved, but for businesses outside the financial services sector, the sales forecast is nearly always one of the key drivers; profit margin is another. When asset turnover is expected to remain stable—often a realistic assumption—working capital accounts and investment in plant should track the growth in sales closely. Most major expenses also track sales, subject to expected shifts in profit margins. By linking forecasts of such amounts to the sales forecast, one can avoid internal inconsistencies and unrealistic implicit assumptions.

In some contexts the manager or analyst is interested ultimately in a forecast of cash flows, not earnings per se. Nevertheless, even forecasts of cash flows tend to be grounded in practice on forecasts of accounting numbers, including sales, earnings, assets, and liabilities. Of course it would be possible in principle to move *directly* to forecasts of cash flows—inflows from customers, outflows to suppliers and laborers, and so forth—and in some businesses this is a convenient way to proceed. In most cases, however, the growth prospects, profitability, and investment and financing needs of the firm are more readily framed in terms of accrual-based sales, operating earnings, assets, and liabilities. These amounts can then be converted to cash flow measures by adjusting for the effects of non-cash expenses and expenditures for working capital and plant.

The most practical approach to forecasting a company's financial statements is to focus on projecting "condensed" financial statements, as used in the ratio analysis in Chapter 5, rather than attempting to project detailed financial statements that the company reports. There are several reasons for this recommendation. First, this approach involves making a relatively small set of assumptions about the future of the firm, so the analyst will have more ability to think about each of the assumptions carefully. A detailed line-item forecast is likely to be very tedious, and an analyst may not have a good basis to make all the assumptions necessary for such forecasts. Further, for most purposes condensed financial statements are all that are needed for analysis and decision making. We therefore approach the task of financial forecasting with this framework.

Recall that the condensed income statement that we used in Chapter 5 consists of the following elements: sales, net operating profits after tax (NOPAT), net interest expense after tax, taxes, and net income. The condensed balance sheet consists of: net operating working capital, net long-term assets, net debt, and equity. Also recall that we start with a balance sheet at the beginning of the forecasting period. Assumptions about how we use the beginning balance sheet and run the firm's operations will lead to the income statement for the forecasting period; assumptions about investment in working capital and long-term assets, and how we finance these assets, results in a balance sheet at the end of the forecasting period.

To forecast the condensed income statement, one needs to begin with an assumption about next period's sales. Beyond that, assumptions about NOPAT margin, interest rate on beginning debt, and tax rate are all that are needed to prepare the condensed income statement for the period.

To forecast the condensed balance sheet for the end of the period (or the equivalent, the beginning of the next period), we need to make the following additional assumptions: the ratio of operating working capital to the sales to estimate the level of working capital needed to support those sales, the ratio of net operating long-term assets to the following year's sales to calculate the expected level of net operating long-term assets, and the ratio of net debt to capital to estimate the levels of debt and equity needed to finance the estimated amount of assets in the balance sheet.

Once we have the condensed income statement and balance sheet, it is relatively straightforward to compute the condensed cash flow statement, including cash flow from operations before working capital investments, cash flow from operations after working capital investments, free cash flow available to debt and equity, and free cash flow available to equity.

Below we discuss how best to make the necessary assumptions to forecast the condensed income statement, balance sheet, and cash flow statements.

Getting Started: Points of Departure

Every forecast has, at least implicitly, an initial "benchmark" or point of departure—some notion of how a particular amount, such as sales or earnings, would be expected to behave in the absence of detailed information. For example, in beginning to contemplate fiscal 2002 profitability for TJX, one must start somewhere. A possibility is to begin with the 2001 performance. Another starting point might be 2001 performance adjusted for recent trends. A third possibility that might seem reasonable—but one that generally turns out not to be very useful—is the average performance over several prior years.

By the time one has completed a business strategy analysis, an accounting analysis, and a detailed financial analysis, the resulting forecast might differ significantly from the original point of departure. Nevertheless, simply for purposes of having a starting point that can help anchor the detailed analysis, it is useful to know how certain key financial statistics behave "on average."

In the case of some key statistics, such as earnings, a point of departure based only on prior behavior of the number is more powerful than one might expect. Research demonstrates that some such benchmarks for earnings are not much less accurate than the forecasts of professional security analysts, who have access to a rich information set. (We return to this point in more detail below.) Thus the benchmark is often not only a good starting point but also close to the amount forecast after detailed analysis. Large departures from the benchmark could be justified only in cases where the firm's situation is demonstrably unusual.

Reasonable points of departure for forecasts of key accounting numbers can be based on the evidence summarized below. Such evidence may also be useful for checking the reasonableness of a completed forecast.

The Behavior of Sales Growth

Sales growth rates tend to be "mean-reverting": firms with above-average or below-average rates of sales growth tend to revert over time to a "normal" level (historically in the range of 7 to 9 percent for U.S. firms) within three to ten years. Figure 6-1 documents this effect for 1984 through 2001 for all the publicly traded U.S. firms covered by the COMPSTAT database. All firms are ranked in terms of their sales growth in 1984 (year 1) and formed into five portfolios based on the relative ranking of their sales growth in that year. Firms in portfolio 1 have the top 20 percent of rankings in terms of their sales growth in 1984, and those in portfolio 2 fall into the next 20 percent; those in portfolio 5 have the bottom 20 percent sales growth ranks. The sales growth rates of firms in each of these five portfolios are traced from 1984 through the subsequent nine years (years 2 to 10). The same experiment is repeated with 1988 and then 1992 as the base year (year 1). The results are averaged over the three experiments and the resulting sales growth rates of each of the five portfolios for years 1 through 10 plotted in Figure 6-1.

The figure shows that the group of firms with the highest growth initially—sales growth rates of just over 60 percent—experience a decline to about 13 percent growth rate within two years and are never above 16 percent in the next seven years. Those with the lowest initial sales growth rates, minus 17 percent, experience an increase to about a 6 percent growth rate by year 5, and average about 8 percent annual growth in years 6 through 10. One explanation for the pattern of sales growth seen in Figure 6-1 is that as industries and companies mature, their growth rate slows down due to demand saturation and intra-industry competition. Therefore, even when a firm is growing rapidly at present, it is generally unrealistic to extrapolate the current high growth indefinitely. Of course, how quickly a firm's growth rate reverts to the average depends on the characteristics of its industry and its own competitive position within an industry.

Figure 6-1	Behavior of Sales Growth for U.S. Firms over Time, 1984–2001

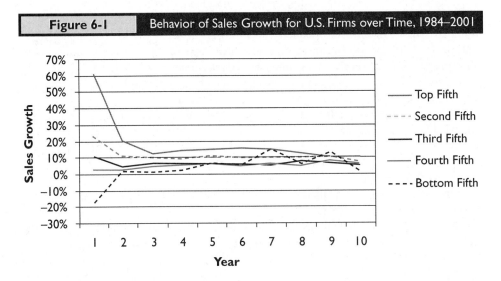

The Behavior of Earnings

Earnings have been shown on average to follow a process that can be approximated by a "random walk" or "random walk with drift." Thus the prior year's earnings is a good starting point in considering future earnings potential. As will be explained, it is reasonable to adjust this simple benchmark for the earnings changes of the most recent quarter (that is, changes relative to the comparable quarter of the prior year after controlling for the long-run trend in the series). Even a simple random walk forecast—one that predicts next year's earnings will be equal to last year's earnings—is surprisingly useful. One study documents that professional analysts' year-ahead forecasts are only 22 percent more accurate, on average, than a simple random walk forecast.[1] Thus a final earnings forecast will *usually* not differ dramatically from a random walk benchmark.

The implication of the evidence is that, in beginning to contemplate future earnings possibilities, a useful number to start with is last year's earnings; the average level of earnings over several prior years is not useful. Long-term trends in earnings tend to be sustained on average, and so they are also worthy of consideration. If quarterly data are also included, then some consideration should usually be given to any departures from the long-run trend that occurred in the most recent quarter. For most firms, these most recent changes tend to be partially repeated in subsequent quarters.[2]

The Behavior of Returns on Equity

Given that prior earnings serves as a useful benchmark for future earnings, one might expect the same to be true of rates of return on investment, like ROE. That, however, is not the case for two reasons. First, even though the *average* firm tends to sustain the current earnings level, this is not true of firms with unusual levels of ROE. Firms with abnormally high (low) ROE tend to experience earnings declines (increases).[3]

Second, firms with higher ROEs tend to expand their investment bases more quickly than others, which causes the denominator of the ROE to increase. Of course if firms could earn returns on the new investments that match the returns on the old ones, then the level of ROE would be maintained. However, firms have difficulty pulling that off. Firms with higher ROEs tend to find that, as time goes by, their earnings growth does not keep pace with growth in their investment base, and ROE ultimately falls.

The resulting behavior of ROE and other measures of return on investment is characterized as "mean-reverting": firms with above-average or below-average rates of return tend to revert over time to a "normal" level (for ROE, historically in the range of 10 to 15 percent for U.S. firms) within no more than ten years.[4] Figure 6-2 documents this effect for U.S. firms from 1984 through 2001. All firms are ranked in terms of their ROE in 1984 (year 1) and formed into five portfolios. Firms in portfolio 1 have the top 20 percent ROE rankings in 1984, those in portfolio 2 fall into the next 20 percent, and those in portfolio 5 have the bottom 20 percent. The average ROE of firms in each of these five portfolios is then traced through nine subsequent years (years 2 to 10). The same experiment is repeated with 1988 and 1992 as the base year (year 1), and the subsequent years as years +2 to +10. Figure 6-2 plots the average ROE of each of the five portfolios in years 1 to 10 averaged across these three experiments.

Though the five portfolios start out in year 1 with a wide range of ROEs (–49 percent to +29 percent), by year 10 the pattern of mean-reversion is clear. The most profitable group of firms initially—with average ROEs of 29 percent—experience a decline to 19.8 percent within three years. By year 10 this group of firms has an ROE of 16 percent. Those with the lowest initial ROEs (–49 percent) experience a dramatic increase in ROE and then level off at 7.5 percent in year 10.

| **Figure 6-2** | Behavior of ROE for U.S. Firms over Time, 1984–2001 |

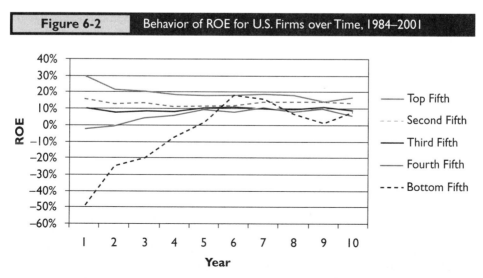

The pattern in Figure 6-2 is not a coincidence; it is exactly what the economics of competition would predict. The tendency of high ROEs to fall is a reflection of high profitability attracting competition; the tendency of low ROEs to rise reflects the mobility of capital away from unproductive ventures toward more profitable ones.

Despite the general tendencies documented in Figure 6-2, there are some firms whose ROEs may remain above or below normal levels for long periods of time. In some cases the phenomenon reflects the strength of a sustainable competitive advantage (e.g., Wal-Mart), but in other cases it is purely an artifact of conservative accounting methods. A good example of the latter phenomenon in the U.S. is pharmaceutical firms, whose major economic asset, the intangible value of research and development, is not recorded on the balance sheet and is therefore excluded from the denominator of ROE. For those firms, one could reasonably expect high ROEs—in excess of 20 percent—over the long run, even in the face of strong competitive forces.

The Behavior of Components of ROE

The behavior of rates of return on equity can be analyzed further by looking at the behavior of its key components. Recall from Chapter 5 that ROEs and profit margins are linked as follows:

$$
\begin{aligned}
\text{ROE} \ &= \ \text{Operating ROA} \ + \ (\text{Operating ROA} \ - \ \text{Net interest rate after tax}) \\
&\quad \times \ \text{Net financial leverage} \\
&= \ \text{NOPAT margin} \ \times \ \text{Operating asset turnover} \ + \ \text{Spread} \\
&\quad \times \ \text{Net financial leverage}
\end{aligned}
$$

The time-series behavior of the components of ROE for U.S. companies for 1984 through 2001 are shown in a series of figures in the appendix to this chapter. Some major conclusions can be drawn from these figures: (1) Operating asset turnover tends to be rather stable, in part because it is so much a function of the technology of the industry. The only exception to this is the set of firms with very high asset turnover, which tends to decline somewhat over time before stabilizing. (2) Net financial leverage also tends to be stable, simply because management policies on capital structure aren't often changed. (3) NOPAT margin and spread stand out as the most variable component of ROE; if the forces of competition drive abnormal ROEs toward more normal levels, the change is most likely to arrive in the form of changes in profit margins and the spread. The change in spread is itself driven by changes in NOPAT margin, since the cost of borrowing is likely to remain stable if leverage remains stable.

To summarize, profit margins, like ROEs, tend to be driven by competition to "normal" levels over time. What constitutes normal varies widely according to the technology employed within an industry and the corporate strategy pursued by the firm, both of which influence turnover and leverage.[5] In a fully competitive equilibrium, profit margins should remain high for firms that must operate with a low turnover, and vice versa.

The above discussion of rates of return and margins implies that a reasonable point of departure for forecasting such a statistic should consider more than just the most recent observation. One should also consider whether that rate or margin is above or below a normal level. If so, then absent detailed information to the contrary, one would expect some movement over time to that norm. Of course this central tendency might be overcome in some cases—for example, where the firm has erected barriers to competition that can protect margins, even for extended periods. The lesson from the evidence, however, is that such cases are unusual.

In contrast to rates of return and margins, it is reasonable to assume that asset turnover, financial leverage, and net interest rate remain relatively constant over time. Unless there is an explicit change in technology or financial policy being contemplated for future periods, a reasonable point of departure for assumptions for these variables is the current period level. The only exceptions to this appear to be firms with either very high asset turns that experience some decline in this ratio before stabilizing, or those firms with very low (usually negative) net debt to capital that appear to increase leverage before stabilizing.

As we proceed with the steps involved in producing a detailed forecast, the reader will note that we draw on the above knowledge of the behavior of accounting numbers to some extent. However, it is important to keep in mind that a knowledge of *average* behavior will not fit all firms well. The art of financial statements analysis requires not only knowing what the "normal" patterns are but also having expertise in identifying those firms that will *not* follow the norm.

MAKING FORECASTS

Here we summarize steps that could be followed in producing a comprehensive forecast. The discussion assumes that the firm being analyzed is among the vast majority for which the forecast would reasonably be anchored by a sales forecast. We use the example of TJX, the discount retailer discussed in Chapter 5, to illustrate the mechanics of forecasting. In Chapter 5 we analyzed the performance of TJX during the fiscal year ending January 31, 2002 (fiscal 2001). We begin our forecasting exercise using this as the point of departure.

Table 6-1 shows the forecasting assumptions for fiscal years 2002 to 2011. Table 6-2 shows the forecasted income statements for these same fiscal years, and beginning of the year balance sheets for fiscal years 2003 to 2011 (that for fiscal 2002 is the actual balance sheet reported by the company for the year ending January 31, 2002). We discuss below the logic behind the forecasting assumptions.

One Year Ahead Forecasts

As mentioned above, we have the actual balance sheet for the beginning of the year in fiscal 2002, so there is no need to forecast this. In general, making a short-term income statement forecast, such as a one year ahead forecast, is often a straightforward extrapolation of recent performance. This is a particularly valid approach for an established company such as TJX for several reasons. First, the company is unlikely to effect major changes in its operating and financing policies in the short term, unless it is in the middle of a restructuring program. Second, the beginning of the year balance sheet for any given year will put constraints on operating activities during that fiscal year. For example, inventories at the beginning of the year will determine to some extent the sales activities during the year; stores in operation at the beginning of the year also determine to some extent the level of sales achievable during the year. To put it another way, since our discussion above shows that asset turns for a company do not usually change significantly over time, sales in any period are to some extent constrained by the beginning of the period assets in place in the company's balance sheet. Of course it is possible to achieve some flexibility in this regard if there are explicit plans to either expand assets significantly during the year (for example, through new store openings in the case of TJX), or through a change in the asset utilization (for example, a change in the same-store sales in the case of TJX).

With this framework in mind, our assumptions for TJX for fiscal 2002 are the following: We assume that sales will grow at 12 percent. This sales growth rate is essentially the same as the actual growth rate achieved in fiscal year 2001, and it is based on the assumption that the company built up its assets during 2001 with an expectation of achieving a similar

Table 6-1 Forecasting Assumptions for TJX

For fiscal year	2002	2003	2004	2005	2006	2007	2008	2009	2010	2011	2012
Sales growth	12%	11.5%	11%	10.5%	10%	9.5%	9%	8.5%	8%	8%	8%
NOPAT margin	4.5%	4%	3.5%	3%	2.5%	2%	1.9%	1.8%	1.7%	1.6%	1.6%
After-tax net interest rate	7%	7%	7%	7%	7%	7%	7%	7%	7%	7%	7%
Beginning net working capital to sales ratio	2.5%	2.5%	2.5%	2.5%	2.5%	2.5%	2.5%	2.5%	2.5%	2.5%	2.5%
Beginning net long term assets to sales ratio	10.5%	10.5%	10.5%	10.5%	10.5%	10.5%	10.5%	10.5%	10.5%	10.5%	10.5%
Beginning net debt to capital ratio	13.6%	13.6%	13.6%	13.6%	13.6%	13.6%	13.6%	13.6%	13.6%	13.6%	13.6%

Note: In addition to these assumptions, we also assume that sales will continue to grow at 8 percent in 2012 and all the balance sheet ratios remain constant, to compute the beginning balance sheet for 2012 and cash flows for 2011.

growth rate as in the previous year. This growth rate leads to an expected sales level in fiscal 2002 of $11.994 billion. The implied ratio of beginning net working capital to sales is 2.5 percent, and beginning long-term assets to sales ratio is 10.5 percent, or a total of net operating assets to sales ratio of 13 percent. This is in line with the company's net operating assets to sales ratios for the two previous years, which were 12.2 percent and 13.5 percent, respectively.

Notice that a beginning of year balance sheet at the start of the forecasting horizon is a given. Therefore, we are starting with a given level of assets to work with. So we can either make an assumption about sales growth rate and check the implied ratio of beginning net assets to sales for reasonableness, or make an assumption of the beginning net assets to sales ratio for the year, and check for the reasonableness of the implied sales growth rate. In other words, we are free to make only one of the two assumptions—either sales growth or net asset turns. In subsequent years in the forecast horizon, we relax this constraint because we can build up both a desired beginning balance sheet and income statement for the following years.

Another assumption we make for TJX for fiscal 2002 is that its NOPAT margin will be 4.5 percent, slightly lower than the extraordinarily high margin the company achieved in the previous two years (5.8 percent and 4.8 percent, respectively). Notice that the time-series trends in NOPAT margins discussed earlier suggest that companies with very high margins tend to experience a gradual decline in margins over time. Our assumption for fiscal 2002 begins to reflect this trend.

The third assumption we make to forecast TJX's income statement for fiscal 2002 relates to the after-tax cost of debt. We know the company's beginning level of debt and its beginning debt to capital ratio for fiscal 2002, based on the company's actual balance sheet at that time. These ratios are somewhat similar to the ratios at the beginning of the previous fiscal year. Therefore, it is reasonable to assume that the company's interest rate on its debt will be somewhat similar to the effective interest during the previous year, which was about 10.8 percent. With an assumed tax rate of 35 percent, the after-tax interest rate is 7 percent.

These assumptions together lead to a projected $524.9 million net income in fiscal year 2002 compared with a reported net income of $500.4 million in fiscal 2001.

Forecasts for Years Two to Ten

In making longer-term forecasts, such as for years two to ten, we can rely on the time-series behavior of various performance ratios we discussed earlier in the chapter. We will assume that the relatively high sales growth rate of TJX will decline from 12 percent in 2002 gradually over time, by half a percentage point per year, reaching a level of 8 percent in year 2011. Beyond 2011, we assume that the sales growth rate will stabilize at 8 percent per year.

We assume a similar pattern of declining NOPAT margins over time, again consistent with the time-series trend we documented earlier in the chapter for firms with initially high NOPAT. While TJX clearly has a great deal of competitive advantage over its rivals, it is prudent to assume, given the history of U.S. firms, that this advantage will decline over time. So we assume that the company's NOPAT margin will decline by half a percentage point per year, from 4.5 percent in 2002 to 2.0 percent in 2007. Thereafter, we assume that the margin decline will be slower, by 0.1 percent per year, to reach a level of 1.6 percent in 2010. At that point we will assume that the NOPAT margin will have reached steady state and will remain at that level in subsequent years.

Since asset turns generally show a flat time series trend, and because TJX is known for its excellent asset utilization skills (inventory management and sales-per-store performance), we will assume that the ratio of beginning operating working capital to sales and beginning long-term assets to sales will remain unchanged during the entire forecasting period. Thus we assume that the beginning operating working capital to sales ratio will remain at 2.5 percent from 2003 to 2011 and beyond; we also assume that the beginning long-term assets to sales ratio will remain at 10.5 percent throughout this period.

We make a similar assumption for the company's capital structure policy. The company has a relatively conservative financing policy with 13.6 percent debt to net capital ratio at the beginning of 2002. We assume that it will remain at this level during the entire forecasting period. This assumption of a constant capital structure policy is consistent with the general pattern observed in historical data discussed earlier in the chapter. Since we hold the capital structure constant, we can assume that the company's borrowing rate also remains unchanged, at 10.8 percent before tax, or 7 percent after tax.

With these assumptions it is a straightforward task to derive the forecasted income statements for fiscal years 2002 to 2011, and beginning balance sheets for years 2003 to 2011, as shown in Table 6-2. Under these forecasts TJX's sales will grow to 27.3 billion dollars by 2011. By the beginning of 2011, TJX will have a net asset base of $3.54 billion. Its return on beginning equity will be at 34.5 percent in 2002. It will gradually decline from this high level to 13.1 percent in 2011, a level somewhat above its cost of equity.

Cash Flow Forecasts

Once we have forecasted income statements and balance sheets, deriving cash flows for the years 2002 to 2011 is straightforward. Note that we need to forecast the beginning balance sheet for 2012 to compute the cash flows for 2011. This balance sheet is not shown in Table 6-2. For the purpose of illustration, we assume that all the sales growth and all the balance sheet ratios remain the same in 2012 as in 2011. Based on this we project a beginning balance sheet for 2012 and compute the cash flows for 2011. Cash flow to capital is equal to NOPAT minus increases in net working capital and net long-term assets. Cash flow to equity is cash flow to capital minus net interest after tax plus increase in net debt. These two sets of forecasted cash flows are shown in Table 6-2.

Table 6-2 Forecasted Financial Statements for TJX

Fiscal Year	2002	2003	2004	2005	2006	2007	2008	2009	2010	2011	2012
Beginning Balance Sheet ($mm)											
Beg. Net Working Capital	297.4	334.3	371.1	410.1	451.1	493.9	538.4	584.2	630.9	681.4	735.9
+ Beg. Net Long-Term Assets	1,254.2	1,404.2	1,558.7	1,722.3	1,894.6	2,074.5	2,261.3	2,453.5	2,649.7	2,861.7	3,090.7
= **Net Operating Assets**	**1,551.5**	**1,738.5**	**1,929.8**	**2,132.4**	**2,345.6**	**2,568.5**	**2,799.6**	**3,037.6**	**3,280.6**	**3,543.1**	**3,826.5**
Net Debt	210.8	236.3	262.2	289.8	318.8	349.0	380.5	412.8	445.8	481.5	520.0
+ Preferred Stock	0.0	0.0	0.0	0.0	0.0	0.0	0.0	0.0	0.0	0.0	0.0
+ Shareholders' Equity	1,340.7	1,502.3	1,667.5	1,842.6	2,026.9	2,219.4	2,419.2	2,624.8	2,834.8	3,061.6	3,306.5
= **Net Capital**	**1,551.5**	**1,738.5**	**1,929.8**	**2,132.4**	**2,345.6**	**2,568.5**	**2,799.6**	**3,037.6**	**3,280.6**	**3,543.1**	**3,826.5**
Income Statement ($mm)											
Sales	11,994.1	13,373.4	14,844.5	16,403.1	18,043.5	19,757.6	21,535.8	23,366.3	25,235.6	27,254.5	29,434.8
Net Operating Profits After Tax	539.7	534.9	519.6	492.1	451.1	395.2	409.2	420.6	429.0	436.1	471.0
− Net Interest Expense After Tax	14.8	16.6	18.4	20.3	22.4	24.5	26.7	29.0	31.3	33.8	36.5
= **Net Income**	**524.9**	**518.4**	**501.1**	**471.8**	**428.7**	**370.6**	**382.5**	**391.6**	**397.7**	**402.3**	**434.5**
Operating ROA	34.8%	30.8%	26.9%	23.1%	19.2%	15.4%	14.6%	13.8%	13.1%	12.3%	12.3%
ROE	39.2%	34.5%	30.1%	25.6%	21.2%	16.7%	15.8%	14.9%	14.0%	13.1%	13.1%
BV of Assets Growth Rate	7.4%	12.1%	11.0%	10.5%	10.0%	9.5%	9.0%	8.5%	8.0%	8.0%	8.0%
BV of Equity Growth Rate	10.0%	12.1%	11.0%	10.5%	10.0%	9.5%	9.0%	8.5%	8.0%	8.0%	8.0%
Net Operating Asset Turnover	7.7	7.7	7.7	7.7	7.7	7.7	7.7	7.7	7.7	7.7	7.7
Free Cash Flow to Capital	352,737	343,696	316,929	278,853	228,250	163,988	171,209	177,584	166,555	152,625	164,835
Free Cash Flow to Equity	312,524	301,122	270,984	229,532	175,590	108,071	112,162	115,582	99,593	80,306	86,730

Note: We do not show the beginning balance sheet forecasted for 2012 here, but it is implicit in the calculation of cash flows for 2011. As stated in Table 6-1, we assume that sales continue to grow in 2012 and that all the balance sheet ratios continue to be the same, to derive the beginning balance sheet for 2012.

SENSITIVITY ANALYSIS

The projections discussed thus far represent nothing more than a "best guess." Managers and analysts are typically interested in a broader range of possibilities. For example, in considering the likelihood that short-term financing will be necessary, it would be wise to produce projections based on a more pessimistic view of profit margins and asset turnover. Alternatively, an analyst estimating the value of TJX should consider the sensitivity of the estimate to the key assumptions about sales growth, profit margins, and asset utilization. What if TJX is able to retain its competitive advantage better than assumed in the above forecasts? What if TJX is unable to maintain its high levels of asset utilization assumed?

There is no limit to the number of possible scenarios that can be considered. One systematic approach to sensitivity analysis is to start with the key assumptions underlying a set of forecasts and then examine the sensitivity to the assumptions with greatest uncertainty in a given situation. For example, if a company has experienced a variable pattern of gross margins in the past, it is important to make projections using a range of margins. Alternatively, if a company has announced a significant change in its expansion strategy, asset utilization assumptions might be more uncertain. In determining where to invest one's time in performing sensitivity analysis, it is therefore important to consider historical patterns of performance, changes in industry conditions, and changes in a company's competitive strategy.

Seasonality and Interim Forecasts

Thus far we have concerned ourselves with annual forecasts. However, especially for security analysts in the U.S., forecasting is very much a quarterly game. Forecasting quarter by quarter raises a new set of questions. How important is seasonality? What is a useful point of departure—the most recent quarter's performance? The comparable quarter of the prior year? Some combination of the two? How should quarterly data be used in producing an annual forecast? Does the item-by-item approach to forecasting used for annual data apply equally well to quarterly data? Full consideration of these questions lies outside the scope of this chapter, but we can begin to answer some of them.

Seasonality is a more important phenomenon in sales and earning behavior than one might guess. It is present for more than just the retail sector firms that benefit from holiday sales. Seasonality also results from weather-related phenomena (e.g., for electric and gas utilities, construction firms, and motorcycle manufacturers), new product introduction patterns (e.g., for the automobile industry), and other factors. Analysis of the time series behavior of earnings for U.S. firms suggests that at least some seasonality is present in nearly every major industry.

The implication for forecasting is that one cannot focus only on performance of the most recent quarter as a point of departure. In fact the evidence suggests that, in forecasting earnings, if one had to choose only one quarter's performance as a point of departure, it would be the comparable quarter of the prior year, not the most recent quarter. Note how this finding is consistent with the reports of analysts or the financial press; when they discuss a quarterly earnings announcement, it is nearly always evaluated relative to the performance of the comparable quarter of the prior year, not the most recent quarter.

Research has produced models that forecast sales, earnings, or EPS based solely on prior quarters' observations. Such models are not used by many analysts, since analysts have access to much more information than such simple models contain. However, the models are useful for helping those unfamiliar with the behavior earnings data to understand how it tends to evolve through time. Such an understanding can provide useful general background, a point of departure in forecasting that can be adjusted to reflect details not revealed in the history of earnings, or a "reasonableness" check on a detailed forecast.

Using Q_t to denote earnings (or EPS) for quarter t, and $E(Q_t)$ as its expected value, one model of the earnings process that fits well across a variety of industries is the so-called Foster model[7]:

$$E(Q_t) \;=\; Q_{t-4} + \delta + \phi(Q_{t-1} - Q_{t-5})$$

Foster shows that a model of the same form also works well with sales data.

The form of the Foster model confirms the importance of seasonality because it shows that the starting point for a forecast for quarter t is the earnings four quarters ago, Q_{t-4}. It states that, when constrained to using only prior earnings data, a reasonable forecast of earnings for quarter t includes the following elements:

the earnings of the comparable quarter of the prior year (Q_{t-4});

a long-run trend in year-to-year quarterly earnings increases (δ); and

a fraction (ϕ) of the year-to-year increase in quarterly earnings experienced most recently ($Q_{t-1} - Q_{t-5}$).

The parameters δ and ϕ can easily be estimated for a given firm with a simple linear regression model available in most spreadsheet software.[8] For most firms the parameter ϕ tends to be in the range of .25 to .50, indicating that 25 to 50 percent of an increase in quarterly earnings tends to persist in the form of another increase in the subsequent quarter. The parameter δ reflects in part the average year-to-year change in quarterly earnings over past years, and it varies considerably from firm to firm.

Research indicates that the Foster model produces one-quarter-ahead forecasts that are off, on average, by $.30 to $.35 per share. Such a degree of accuracy stacks up surprisingly well with that of security analysts, who obviously have access to much information ignored in the model. As one would expect, most of the evidence supports analysts' being more accurate, but the models are good enough to be "in the ball park" in most circumstances. While it would certainly be unwise to rely completely on such a naïve model, an understanding of the typical earnings behavior reflected by the model is useful.

SUMMARY

Forecasting represents the first step of prospective analysis and serves to summarize the forward-looking view that emanates from business strategy analysis, accounting analysis, and financial analysis. Although not every financial statement analysis is accompanied by such an explicit summarization of a view of the future, forecasting is still a key tool for managers, consultants, security analysts, investment bankers, commercial bankers and other credit analysts, and others.

The best approach to forecasting future performance is to do it comprehensively—producing not only an earnings forecast but a forecast of cash flows and the balance sheet as well. Such a comprehensive approach provides a guard against internal inconsistencies and unrealistic implicit assumptions. The approach described here involves line-by-line analysis, so as to recognize that different items on the income statement and balance sheet are influenced by different drivers. Nevertheless, it remains the case that a few key projections—such as sales growth and profit margin—usually drive most of the projected numbers.

The forecasting process should be embedded in an understanding of how various financial statistics tend to behave on average, and what might cause a firm to deviate from that average. Absent detailed information to the contrary, one would expect sales and earnings numbers to persist at their current levels, adjusted for overall trends of recent years. However, rates of return on investment (ROEs) tend, over several years, to move from abnormal to normal levels—close to the cost of equity capital—as the forces of competition come into play. Profit margins also tend to shift to normal levels, but for this statistic "normal" varies widely across firms and industries, depending on the levels of asset turnover and leverage. Some firms are capable of creating barriers to entry that enable them to fight these tendencies toward normal returns, even for many years, but such firms are the unusual cases.

For some purposes, including short-term planning and security analysis, forecasts for quarterly periods are desirable. One important feature of quarterly data is seasonality; at least some seasonality exists in the sales and earnings data of nearly every industry. An understanding of a firm's within-year peaks and valleys is a necessary ingredient of a good forecast of performance on a quarterly basis.

There are a variety of contexts (including but not limited to security analysis) where the forecast is usefully summarized in the form of an estimate of the firm's value—an estimate that, after all, can be viewed as the best attempt to reflect in a single summary statistic the manager's or analyst's view of the firm's prospects. That process of converting a forecast into a value estimate is labeled valuation. It is to that topic that we turn in the following chapter.

DISCUSSION QUESTIONS

1. Merck is one of the largest pharmaceutical firms in the world, and over an extended period of time in the recent past, it consistently earned higher ROEs than the pharmaceutical industry as a whole. As a pharmaceutical analyst, what factors would you consider to be important in making projections of future ROEs for Merck? In particular, what factors would lead you to expect Merck to continue to be a superior performer in its industry, and what factors would lead you to expect Merck's future performance to revert to that of the industry as a whole?

2. John Right, an analyst with Stock Pickers Inc., claims, "It is not worth my time to develop detailed forecasts of sales growth, profit margins, etcetera, to make earnings projections. I can be almost as accurate, at virtually no cost, using the random walk model to forecast earnings." What is the random walk model? Do you agree or disagree with John Right's forecast strategy? Why or why not?

3. Which of the following types of businesses do you expect to show a high degree of seasonality in quarterly earnings? Explain why.
   - a supermarket
   - a pharmaceutical company
   - a software company
   - an auto manufacturer
   - a clothing retailer

4. What factors are likely to drive a firm's outlays for new capital (such as plant, property, and equipment) and for working capital (such as receivables and inventory)? What ratios would you use to help generate forecasts of these outlays?

5. How would the following events (reported this year) affect your forecasts of a firm's future net income?
   - an asset write-down
   - a merger or acquisition
   - the sale of a major division
   - the initiation of dividend payments

6. Consider the following two earnings forecasting models:

   Model 1: $E_t(EPS_{t+1}) = EPS_t$

   Model 2: $E_t(EPS_{t+1}) = \frac{1}{5}\sum_{t=1}^{5} EPS_t$

   $E_t(EPS)$ is the expected forecast of earnings per share for year $t+1$, given information available at t. Model 1 is usually called a random walk model for earnings, whereas Model 2 is called a mean-reverting model. The earnings per share for Ford Motor Company for the period 1990 to 1994 are as follows:

Year	1	2	3	4	5
EPS	$0.93	$(2.40)	$(0.73)	$2.27	$4.97

   a. What would be the year 6 forecast for earnings per share for each model?
   b. Actual earnings per share for Ford in 6 were $3.58. Given this information, what would be the year 7 forecast for earnings per share for each model? Why do the two

models generate quite different forecasts? Which do you think would better describe earnings per share patterns? Why?

7. Joe Fatcat, an investment banker, states, "It is not worth my while to worry about detailed long-term forecasts. Instead, I use the following approach when forecasting cash flows beyond three years. I assume that sales grow at the rate of inflation, capital expenditures are equal to depreciation, and that net profit margins and working capital to sales ratios stay constant." What pattern of return on equity is implied by these assumptions? Is this reasonable?

NOTES

1. See Patricia O'Brien, "Analysts' Forecasts as Earnings Expectations," *Journal of Accounting and Economics* (January 1988): 53–83.

2. See George Foster, "Quarterly Accounting Data: Time Series Properties and Predictive Ability Results," *The Accounting Review* (January 1977): 1–21.

3. See Robert Freeman, James Ohlson, and Stephen Penman, "Book Rate-of-Return and Prediction of Earnings Changes: An Empirical Investigation," *Journal of Accounting Research* (Autumn 1982): 639–53.

4. See Stephen H. Penman, "An Evaluation of Accounting Rate-of-Return," *Journal of Accounting, Auditing, and Finance* (Spring 1991): 233–56; Eugene Fama and Kenneth French, "Size and Book-to-Market Factors in Earnings and Returns," *Journal of Finance* (March 1995): 131–56; and Victor Bernard, "Accounting-Based Valuation Methods: Evidence on the Market-to-Book Anomaly and Implications for Financial Statements Analysis," University of Michigan, working paper (1994). Ignoring the effects of accounting artifacts, ROEs should be driven in a competitive equilibrium to a level approximating the cost of equity capital.

5. A "normal" profit margin is that which, when multiplied by the turnover achievable within an industry and with a viable corporate strategy, yields a return on investment that just covers the cost of capital. However, as mentioned above, accounting artifacts can cause returns on investment to deviate from the cost of capital for long periods, even in a competitive equilibrium.

6. See Foster, op. cit. A somewhat more accurate model is furnished by Brown and Rozeff, but it requires interactive statistical techniques for estimation—Lawrence D. Brown and Michael Rozeff, "Univariate Time Series Models of Quarterly Accounting Earnings per Share," *Journal of Accounting Research* (Spring 1979): 179–89.

7. To estimate the model, we write in terms of realized earnings (as opposed to expected earnings) and move Q_{t-4} to the left-hand side:

$$Q_t - Q_{t-4} = \delta + \phi(Q_{t-1} - Q_{t-5}) + e_t$$

We now have a regression where $(Q_t - Q_{t-4})$ is the dependent variable, and its lagged value— $(Q_{t-1} - Q_{t-5})$—is the independent variable. Thus, to estimate the equation, prior earnings data must first be expressed in terms of year-to-year changes; the change for one quarter is then regressed against the change for the most recent quarter. The intercept provides an estimate of δ, and the slope is an estimate of ϕ. The equation is typically estimated using 24 to 40 quarters of prior earnings data.

8. See O'Brien, op. cit.

APPENDIX: THE BEHAVIOR OF COMPONENTS OF ROE

In Figure 6-2 we show that ROEs tend to be mean-reverting. In this appendix we show the behavior of the key components of ROE—operating ROA, operating margin, operating asset turnover, spread, and net financial leverage. These ratios are computed using the same portfolio approach described in the chapter, based on the data for all U.S. firms for the time period 1984 through 2001.

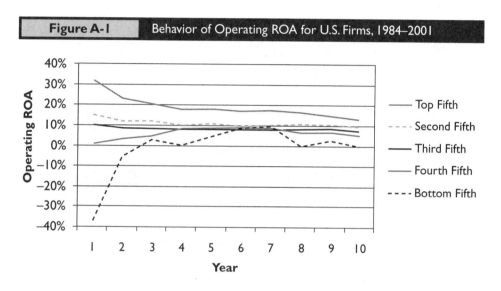

Figure A-1   Behavior of Operating ROA for U.S. Firms, 1984–2001

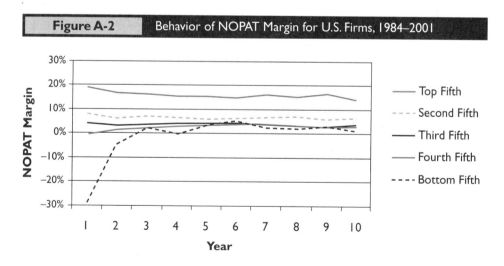

Figure A-2   Behavior of NOPAT Margin for U.S. Firms, 1984–2001

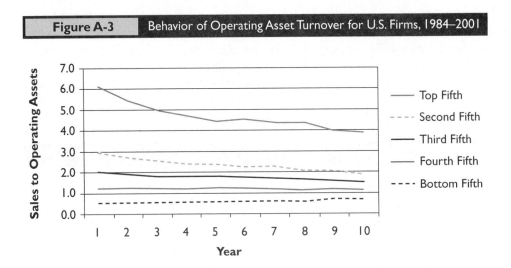

Figure A-3   Behavior of Operating Asset Turnover for U.S. Firms, 1984–2001

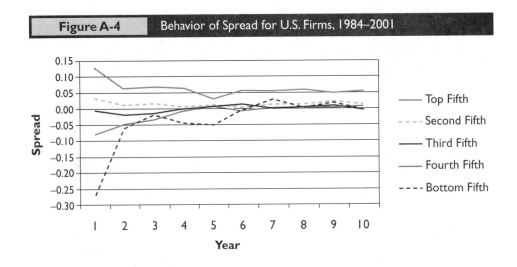

Figure A-4   Behavior of Spread for U.S. Firms, 1984–2001

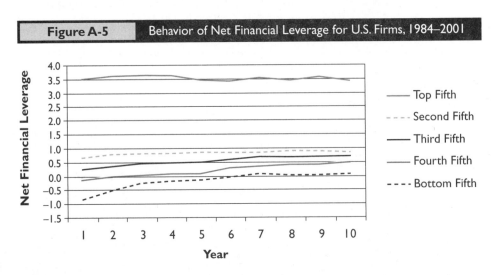

Figure A-5   Behavior of Net Financial Leverage for U.S. Firms, 1984–2001

Prospective Analysis:
Valuation Theory and Concepts

The previous chapter introduced forecasting, the first stage of prospective analysis. In this and the following chapter we describe the second and final stage of prospective analysis, valuation. This chapter focuses on valuation theory and concepts, and the following chapter discusses implementation issues.

Valuation is the process of converting a forecast into an estimate of the value of the firm or some component of the firm. At some level, nearly every business decision involves valuation (at least implicitly). Within the firm, capital budgeting involves consideration of how a particular project will affect firm value. Strategic planning focuses on how value is influenced by larger sets of actions. Outside the firm, security analysts conduct valuation to support their buy/sell decisions, and potential acquirers (often with the assistance of their investment bankers) estimate the value of target firms and the synergies they might offer. Valuation is necessary to price an initial public offering and to inform parties to sales, estate settlements, and divisions of property involving ongoing business concerns. Even credit analysts, who typically do not explicitly estimate firm value, must at least implicitly consider the value of the firm's equity "cushion" if they are to maintain a complete view of the risk associated with lending activity.

In practice, a wide variety of valuation approaches are employed. For example, in evaluating the fairness of a takeover bid, investment bankers commonly use five to ten different methods of valuation. Among the available methods are the following:

- *Discounted dividends.* This approach expresses the value of the firm's equity as the present value of forecasted future dividends.
- *Discounted abnormal earnings.* Under this approach the value of the firm's equity is expressed as the sum of its book value and discounted forecasts of abnormal earnings.
- *Valuation based on price multiples.* Under this approach a current measure of performance or single forecast of performance is converted into a value through application of some price multiple for other presumably comparable firms. For example, firm value can be estimated by applying a price-to-earnings ratio to a forecast of the firm's earnings for the coming year. Other commonly used multiples include price-to-book ratios and price-to-sales ratios.
- *Discounted cash flow (DCF) analysis.* This approach involves the production of detailed, multiple-year forecasts of cash flows. The forecasts are then discounted at the firm's estimated cost of capital to arrive at an estimated present value.

All of the above approaches can be structured in two ways. The first is to directly value the equity of the firm, since this is usually the variable the analyst is directly interested in estimating. The second is to value the assets of the firm, that is, the claims of equity and net debt, and then to deduct the value of net debt to arrive at the final equity estimate. Theoretically, both approaches should generate the same values. However, as we will see in the following chapter, there are implementation issues in reconciling the approaches. In this chapter we illustrate valuation using an all-equity firm to simplify the discussion. Where appropriate we discuss the theoretical issues in valuing the firm's assets.

From a theoretical perspective, shareholder value is the present value of future dividend payoffs. This definition can be implemented by forecasting and discounting future dividends directly. Alternatively, it can be framed by recasting dividends in terms of earnings and book values, or in terms of free cash flows to shareholders. These methods are developed throughout the chapter, and their pros and cons discussed.

Valuation using multiples is also discussed. Multiples are a popular method of valuation because, unlike the discounted dividend, discounted abnormal earnings, and discounted cash flow methods, they do not require analysts to make multiyear forecasts. However, the identification of comparable firms is a serious challenge in implementing the multiples approach. The chapter discusses how the discounted abnormal earnings valuation approach can be recast to generate firm-specific estimates of two popular multiples, value-to-book and value-earnings ratios. Value-to-book multiples are shown to be a function of future abnormal ROEs, book value growth, and the firm's cost of equity. Value-earnings multiples are driven by the same factors and also the current ROE.

DEFINING VALUE FOR SHAREHOLDERS

How should shareholders think about the value of their equity claims on a firm? Finance theory holds that the value of any financial claim is simply the present value of the cash payoffs that its claimholders receive. Since shareholders receive cash payoffs from a company in the form of dividends, the value of their equity is the present value of future dividends (including any liquidating dividend).

Equity value   =   PV of expected future dividends

If we denote the expected future dividend for a given year as DIV and r_e as the cost of equity capital (the relevant discount rate), the stock value is as follows:

$$\text{Equity value} \;=\; \frac{DIV_1}{(1 + r_e)} + \frac{DIV_2}{(1 + r_e)^2} + \frac{DIV_3}{(1 + r_e)^3} + \ldots$$

Notice that the valuation formula views a firm as having an indefinite life. But in reality firms can go bankrupt or get taken over. In these situations shareholders effectively receive a terminating dividend on their stock.

If a firm had a constant dividend growth rate (g^d) indefinitely, its value would simplify to the following formula:

$$\text{Equity value} \;=\; \frac{DIV_1}{r_e - g^d}$$

To better understand how the discounted dividend approach works, consider the following example. At the beginning of year 1, Down Under Company raises $60 million of equity and uses the proceeds to buy a fixed asset. Operating profits before depreciation (all received in cash) and dividends for the company are expected to be $40 million in year 1, $50 million in year 2, and $60 million in year 3, at which point the company terminates. The firm pays no taxes. If the cost of equity capital for this firm is 10 percent, the value of the firm's equity is computed as follows:

Year	Dividend	PV Factor	PV of Dividend
1	$40m	0.9091	$36.4m
2	50	0.8264	41.3
3	60	0.7513	45.1
Equity value			$122.8m

The above valuation formula is called the dividend discount model. It forms the basis for most of the popular theoretical approaches for stock valuation. The remainder of the chapter discusses how this model can be recast to generate the discounted abnormal earnings, discounted cash flow, and price multiple models of value.

THE DISCOUNTED ABNORMAL EARNINGS VALUATION METHOD

As discussed in Chapter 3, there is a link between dividends and earnings. If all equity effects (other than capital transactions) flow through the income statement,[1] the expected book value of equity for existing shareholders at the end of year 1 (BVE_1) is simply the book value at the beginning of the year (BVE_0) plus expected net income (NI_1) less expected dividends (DIV_1).[2] This relation can be rewritten as follows:

$$DIV_1 \ = \ NI_1 \ + \ BVE_0 \ - \ BVE_1$$

By substituting this identity for dividends into the dividend discount formula and rearranging the terms, stock value can be rewritten as follows[3]:

$$\text{Equity value} \ = \ \text{Book value of equity} \ + \ \text{PV of expected future abnormal earnings}$$

Abnormal earnings are net income adjusted for a capital charge computed as the discount rate multiplied by the beginning book value of equity. Abnormal earnings therefore make an adjustment to reflect the fact that accountants do not recognize any opportunity cost for equity funds used. Thus, the discounted abnormal earnings valuation formula is

$$\text{Equity value} \ = \ BVE_0 \ + \ \frac{NI_1 - r_e \cdot BVE_0}{(1 + r_e)} \ + \ \frac{NI_2 - r_e \cdot BVE_1}{(1 + r_e)^2} \ + \ \frac{NI_3 - r_e \cdot BVE_2}{(1 + r_e)^3} \ + \ \dots$$

As noted earlier, equity values can also be estimated by valuing the firm's assets and then deducting its net debt. Under the earnings-based approach, this implies that the value of the assets is

$$\text{Asset value} \ = \ BVA_0 \ + \ \frac{NOPAT_1 - WACC \cdot BVA_0}{(1 + WACC)} \ + \ \frac{NOPAT_2 - WACC \cdot BVA_1}{(1 + WACC)^2} \ + \ \dots$$

BVA is the book value of the firm's assets, NOPAT is net operating profit (before interest) after tax, and WACC is the firm's weighted-average cost of debt and equity. From this asset value the analyst can deduct the market value of net debt to generate an estimate of the value of equity.

The earnings-based formulation has intuitive appeal. It implies that if a firm can earn only a normal rate of return on its book value, then investors should be willing to pay no more than book value for the stock. Investors should pay more or less than book value if earnings are above or below this normal level. Thus the deviation of a firm's market value from book value depends on its ability to generate "abnormal earnings." The formulation also implies that a firm's stock value reflects the cost of its existing net assets (that is, its book equity) plus the net present value of future growth options (represented by cumulative abnormal earnings).

To illustrate the earnings-based valuation approach, let's return to the Down Under Company example. Since the company is an all-equity firm, the value of the firm's equity and its assets (debt plus equity) are the same. If the company depreciates its fixed assets using the straight-line method, its beginning book equity, earnings, abnormal earnings, and valuation will be as follows:

Year	Beginning Book Value	Earnings	Abnormal Earnings	PV Factor	PV of Abnormal Earnings
1	$60m	$20m	$14m	0.9091	$12.7m
2	40	30	26	0.8264	21.5
3	20	40	38	0.7513	28.6
Cumulative PV of abnormal earnings					62.8
+ Beginning book value					60.0
= Equity value					$122.8m

This stock valuation of $122.8 million is identical to the value estimated when the expected future dividends are discounted directly.

Key Analysis Questions

Valuation of equity (debt plus equity) under the discounted abnormal earnings method requires the analyst to answer the following questions:

- What are expected future net income (NOPAT) and book values of equity (assets) over a finite forecast horizon (usually 5 to 10 years)?
- What are expected future abnormal earnings (NOPAT), after deducting a capital charge from forecasts of net income (NOPAT)? The capital charge is the firm's cost of equity (WACC) multiplied by beginning book equity (assets).
- What is expected future abnormal net income (NOPAT) beyond the final year of the forecast horizon (called the "terminal year") based on some simplifying assumption?
- What is the present value of abnormal earnings (NOPAT) discounted at the cost of equity capital (WACC)?
- What is the estimated value of equity, computed by adding the current book value of equity (assets) to the cumulated present value of future abnormal earnings (NOPAT)? Are there nonoperating assets held by the firm that have been ignored in the previous abnormal earnings (NOPAT) forecasts (e.g., marketable securities or real estate held for sale)? If so, their values should be included in the equity estimate.

Recent research shows that abnormal earnings estimates of value outperform traditional multiples, such as price-earnings ratios, price-to-book ratios, and dividend yields, for predicting future stock movements.[4] Firms with high abnormal earnings model estimates of value relative to current price show positive abnormal future stock returns, whereas firms with low estimated value-to-price ratios have negative abnormal stock performance.

Accounting Methods and Discounted Abnormal Earnings

It may seem odd that firm value can be expressed as a function of accounting numbers. After all, accounting methods per se should have no influence on firm value (except as those choices influence the analyst's view of future real performance). Yet the valuation approach used here is based on numbers—earnings and book value—that vary with accounting method choices. How then can the valuation approach deliver correct estimates?

It turns out that because accounting choices affect *both* earnings *and* book value, and because of the self-correcting nature of double-entry bookkeeping (all "distortions" of accounting must ultimately reverse), estimated values based on the discounted abnormal earnings method will not be affected by accounting choices per se. For example, assume that Down Under Company's managers choose to be conservative and expense some unusual costs that could have been capitalized as inventory at year 1, causing earnings and ending book value to be lower by $10 million. This inventory is then sold in year 2. For the time being, let's say the accounting choice has no influence on the analyst's view of the firm's real performance.

Managers' choice reduces abnormal earnings in year 1 and book value at the beginning of year 2 by $10 million. However, future earnings will be higher, for two reasons. First, future earnings will be higher (by $10 million) when the inventory is sold in year 2 at a lower cost of sales. Second, the benchmark for normal earnings (based on book value of equity) will be lower by $10 million. The $10 million decline in abnormal earnings in year 1 is perfectly offset (on a present value basis) by the $11 million higher abnormal earnings in year 2. As a result, the value of Down Under Company under conservative reporting is identical to the value under the earlier accounting method ($122.8 million).

Year	Beginning Book Value	Earnings	Abnormal Earnings	PV Factor	PV of Abnormal Earnings
1	$60m	$10m	$4m	0.9091	$3.6m
2	30	40	37	0.8264	30.6
3	20	40	38	0.7513	28.6
Cumulative PV of abnormal earnings					62.8
+ Beginning book value					60.0
= Equity value					$122.8m

Provided the analyst is aware of biases in accounting data as a result of the use of aggressive or conservative accounting choices by management, abnormal earnings-based valuations are unaffected by the variation in accounting decisions. This implies that strategic and accounting analyses are critical precursors to abnormal earnings valuation. The strategic and accounting analysis tools help the analyst to identify whether abnormal earnings arise from sustainable competitive advantage or from unsustainable accounting manipulations. For example, consider the implications of failing to understand the reasons for a decline in earnings from a change in inventory policy for Down Under Company. If the analyst mistakenly interpreted the decline as indicating that the firm was having difficulty moving its inventory, rather than that it had used conservative accounting, she might reduce expectations of future earnings. The estimated value of the firm would then be lower than that reported in our example.

VALUATION USING PRICE MULTIPLES

Valuations based on price multiples are widely used by analysts. The primary reason for their popularity is their simplicity. Unlike the discounted abnormal earnings, discounted dividend, and discounted cash flow methods, they do not require detailed multiple-year forecasts about a variety of parameters, including growth, profitability, and cost of capital.

Valuation using multiples involves the following steps:

Step 1: Select a measure of performance or value (e.g., earnings, sales, cash flows, book equity, book assets) as the basis for multiple calculations.

Step 2: Estimate price multiples for comparable firms using the measure of performance or value.

Step 3: Apply the comparable firm multiple to the performance or value measure of the firm being analyzed.

Under this approach, the analyst relies on the market to undertake the difficult task of considering the short- and long-term prospects for growth and profitability and their implications for the values of the comparable firms. Then the analyst *assumes* that the pricing of those other firms is applicable to the firm at hand.

On the surface, using multiples seems straightforward. Unfortunately, in practice it is not as simple as it would appear. Identification of "comparable" firms is often quite difficult. There are also some choices to be made concerning how multiples will be calculated. Finally, explaining why multiples vary across firms, and how applicable another firm's multiple is to the one at hand, requires a sound understanding of the determinants of each multiple.

Selecting Comparable Firms

Ideally, price multiples used in a comparable firm analysis are those for firms with similar operating and financial characteristics. Firms within the same industry are the most obvious candidates. But even within narrowly defined industries, it is often difficult to find multiples for similar firms. Many firms are in multiple industries, making it difficult to identify representative benchmarks. In addition, firms within the same industry frequently have different strategies, growth opportunities, and profitability, creating comparability problems.

One way of dealing with these issues is to average across *all* firms in the industry. The analyst implicitly hopes that the various sources of noncomparability cancel each other out, so that the firm being valued is comparable to a "typical" industry member. Another approach is to focus on only those firms within the industry that are most similar.

For example, consider using multiples to value Nordstrom. OneSource classifies the company in the Retail: Apparel industry. OneSource reported that Nordstrom's competitors could be narrowed to the following firms: Ann Taylor, Charming Shoppes, Dayton Hudson (now Target), Dillard's, Federated Department Stores, The Gap, The Limited, May Department Stores, Neiman Marcus, J C Penney, Saks, and TJX Companies. The average price-earnings ratio for these direct competitors was 223.76 and the average price-to-book ratio was 2.64.

Multiples for Firms with Poor Performance

Price multiples can be affected when the denominator variable is performing poorly. This is especially common when the denominator is a flow measure, such as earnings or cash flows. For example, Sak's Inc., one of Nordstrom's competitors, had earnings of only 0.3 million in 2001 and a price-earnings ratio of 4,443.4. Similarly, the Gap had negative earnings in 2001, making the price-earnings ratio negative.

What are analysts' options for handling the problems for multiples created by transitory shocks to the denominator? One option is to simply exclude firms with large transitory effects from the set of comparable firms. If Sak's Inc. and the Gap are excluded from Nordstrom's peer set, the average industry price-earnings ratio declines from 223.76 to

6.32. This dramatic change in the industry average shows the sensitivity of price-earnings multiples to transitory shocks.

As an alternative to excluding some firms from the industry comparison group, if the poor performance is due to a transitory shock such as a write-off or special item, the effect can be excluded from computation of the multiple. Finally, the analyst can use a denominator that is a forecast of future performance rather than a past measure. Multiples based on forecasts are termed *leading* multiples, whereas those based on historical data are called *trailing* multiples. Leading multiples are less likely to include one-time gains and losses in the denominator, simply because such items are difficult to anticipate.

Adjusting Multiples for Leverage

Price multiples should be calculated in a way that preserves consistency between the numerator and denominator. Consistency is an issue for those ratios where the denominator reflects performance *before* servicing debt. Examples include the price-to-sales multiple and any multiple of operating earnings or operating cash flows. When calculating these multiples, the numerator should include not just the market value of equity but the value of debt as well.

Determinants of Value-to-Book and Value-Earnings Multiples

Even across relatively closely related firms, price multiples can vary considerably. Careful analysis of this variation requires consideration of factors that might explain why one firm's multiples should be higher than those of benchmark firms. We therefore return to the abnormal earnings valuation method and show how it provides insights into differences in value-to-book and value-to-earnings multiples across firms

If the abnormal earnings formula is scaled by book value, the left-hand side becomes the equity value-to-book ratio as opposed to the equity value itself. The right-hand side variables are now earnings deflated by book value, or our old friend return on equity (ROE), discussed in Chapter 5.[5] The valuation formula becomes

$$\text{Equity value-to-book ratio} = 1 + \frac{ROE_1 - r_e}{(1 + r_e)} + \frac{(ROE_2 - r_e)(1 + gbve_1)}{(1 + r_e)^2}$$

$$+ \frac{(ROE_3 - r_e)(1 + gbve_1)(1 + gbve_2)}{(1 + r_e)^3} + \ldots$$

where $gbve_t$ = growth in book value (*BVE*) from year t-1 to year t or

$$\frac{BVE_t - BVE_{t-1}}{BVE_{t-1}}$$

The formulation implies that a firm's equity value-to-book ratio is a function of three factors: its future abnormal ROEs, its growth in book equity, and its cost of equity capital. Abnormal ROE is defined as ROE less the cost of equity capital (ROE $- r_e$). Firms with positive abnormal ROE are able to invest their net assets to create value for shareholders and have price-to-book ratios greater than one. Firms that are unable to generate returns greater than the cost of capital have ratios below one.

The magnitude of a firm's value-to-book multiple also depends on the amount of growth in book value. Firms can grow their equity base by issuing new equity or by reinvesting profits. If this new equity is invested in positive valued projects for shareholders, that is, projects with ROEs that exceed the cost of capital, the firm will boost its equity value-to-book multiple. Of course for firms with ROEs that are less than the cost of capital, equity growth further lowers the multiple.

The valuation task can now be framed in terms of two key questions about the firm's "value drivers":

- How much greater (or smaller) than normal will the firm's ROE be?
- How quickly will the firm's investment base (book value) grow?

If desired, the equation can be rewritten so that future ROEs are expressed as the product of their components: profit margins, sales turnover, and leverage. Thus the approach permits us to build directly on projections of the same accounting numbers utilized in financial analysis (see Chapter 9) without the need to convert projections of those numbers into cash flows. Yet in the end, the estimate of value should be the same as that from the dividend discount model.[6]

It is also possible to structure the multiple valuation as the debt plus equity value-to-book assets ratio by scaling the abnormal NOPAT formula by book value of net operating assets. The valuation formula then becomes

$$\text{Debt plus equity value-to-book ratio} = 1 + \frac{ROA_1 - WACC}{(1 + WACC)} + \frac{(ROA_2 - WACC)(1 + gbva)}{(1 + WACC)^2}$$

$$+ \frac{(ROA_3 - WACC)(1 + gbva_1)(1 + gbva_2)}{(1 + WACC)^3} + \ldots$$

where ROA = operating return on assets = NOPAT/(Operating working capital + Net long-term assets)

$WACC$ = weighted average cost of debt and equity

$gbva_n$ = growth in book value of assets (BVA) from year t-1 to year t or

$$\frac{BVA_t - BVA_{t-1}}{BVA_{t-1}}$$

The value of a firm's debt and equity to net operating assets multiple therefore depends on its ability to generate asset returns that exceed its WACC, and on its ability to grow its asset base. The value of equity under this approach is then the estimated multiple times the current book value of assets less the market value of debt.

Returning to the Down Under Company example, the implied equity value-to-book multiple can be estimated as follows:

	Year 1	Year 2	Year 3
Beginning book value	$60m	$40m	$20m
Earnings	$20m	$30m	$40m
ROE	0.33	0.75	2.00
− Cost of capital	0.10	0.10	0.10
= Abnormal ROE	0.23	0.65	1.90
× (1+ cumulative book value growth)	1.00	0.67	0.33
= Abnormal ROE scaled by book value growth	0.23	0.43	0.63
× PV factor	0.9091	0.8264	0.7513
= PV of abnormal ROE scaled by book value growth	0.212%	0.358%	0.476%

	Year 1	Year 2	Year 3
Cumulative PV of abnormal ROE scaled by book value growth	1.046		
+ 1.00	1.000		
= Equity value-to-book multiple	2.046		

The equity value-to-book multiple for Down Under is therefore 2.046, and the implied stock value is $122.8 ($60 times 2.046), once again identical to the dividend discount model value. Recall that Down Under is an all-equity firm, so that the abnormal ROE and abnormal ROA structures for valuing the firm are the same.

The equity value-to-book formulation can also be used to construct the equity value-earnings multiple as follows:

$$\text{Equity value-to-earnings multiple} = \text{Equity value-to-book multiple} \times \frac{\text{Book value of equity}}{\text{Earnings}}$$

$$= \frac{\text{Equity value-to-book multiple}}{\text{ROE}}$$

In other words, the same factors that drive a firm's equity value-to-book multiple also explain its equity value-earnings multiple. The key difference between the two multiples is that the value-earnings multiple is affected by the firm's current level of ROE performance, whereas the value-to-book multiple is not. Firms with low current ROEs therefore have very high value-earnings multiples and vice versa. If a firm has a zero or negative ROE, its PE multiple is not defined. Value-earnings multiples are therefore more volatile than value-to-book multiples.

The following data for a subset of firms in the Retail: Apparel industry illustrate the relation between ROE, equity growth, the price-to-book ratio, and the price-earnings ratio:

Company	ROE	Book Value Growth	Price-to-Book Ratio	Price-Earnings Ratio
Dillard's	2.73%	1.47%	0.43	15.96
J C Penney	1.67%	−1.60%	1.14	66.95
Target	20.98%	20.57%	5.10	29.31
TJX	41.06%	10.01%	8.41	22.53

Both the price-to-book and price-earnings ratios are high for Target. Investors therefore expect that in the future Target will generate even higher ROEs than its current high level (21 percent). In contrast, TJX has a high price-to-book ratio (8.41) but a low price-earnings ratio (22.53). This indicates that investors expect that TJX will continue to generate positive abnormal ROEs but that the current level of ROE (41 percent) is not sustainable. J C Penney has a price-to-book ratio of 1.14, indicating that investors expect it to earn about normal ROEs. However it has a high price-earnings multiple (66.95), suggesting that the current low ROE (1.67) is considered temporary. Finally, Dillard's has a relatively low price-to-book ratio, 0.43, and a low price-earnings multiple. Investors apparently do not expect Dillard's to significantly improve its poor performance.

Key Analysis Questions

To value a firm using multiples, an analyst has to assess the quality of the variable used as the multiple basis, and to determine the appropriate peer firms to include in the benchmark multiple. Analysts are therefore likely to be interested in answering the following questions:

- What is the expected future growth in the variable to be used as the basis for the multiple? For example, if the variable is earnings, has the firm made conservative or aggressive accounting choices that are likely to unwind in the coming years? If the multiple is book value, what is the sustainability of the firm's growth and ROE? What is the dynamics of the firm's industry and product market? Is it a market leader in a high growth industry, or is it in a mature industry with fewer growth prospects? How is the firm's future performance likely to be affected by competition or potential new entry in the industry?
- Which are the most suitable peer companies to include in the benchmark multiple computation? Have these firms had comparable growth (earnings or book values), profitability, and quality of earnings as the firm being analyzed? Do they have the same risk characteristics?

SHORTCUT FORMS OF EARNINGS-BASED VALUATION

The discounted abnormal earnings valuation formula can be simplified by making assumptions about the relation between a firm's current and future abnormal earnings. Similarly, the equity value-to-book formula can be simplified by making assumptions about long-term ROEs and growth.

1. Relation Between Current and Future Abnormal Earnings

Several assumptions about the relation between current and future net income are popular for simplifying the abnormal earnings model. First, abnormal earnings are assumed to follow a random walk. The random walk model for abnormal earnings implies that an analyst's best guess about future expected abnormal earnings are current abnormal earnings. The model assumes that past shocks to abnormal earnings persist forever, but that future shocks are random or unpredictable. The random walk model can be written as follows:

$$\text{Forecasted } AE_1 \ = \ AE_0$$

Forecasted AE_1 is the forecast of next year's abnormal earnings and AE_0 is current period abnormal earnings. Under the model, forecasted abnormal earnings for two years ahead are simply abnormal earnings in year one, or once again current abnormal earnings. In other words, the best guess of abnormal earnings in any future year is just current abnormal earnings.[7]

How does the above assumption about future abnormal earnings simplify the discounted abnormal earnings valuation model? If abnormal earnings follow a random walk, all future forecasts of abnormal earnings are simply current abnormal earnings. It is then possible to rewrite value as follows:

$$\text{Stock value} \ = \ BVE_0 + \frac{AE_0}{r_e}$$

The stock value is the book value of equity at the end of the year plus current abnormal earnings divided by the cost of capital.

In reality of course, shocks to abnormal earnings are unlikely to persist forever. Firms that have positive shocks are likely to attract competitors that will reduce opportunities for future abnormal performance. Firms with negative abnormal earnings shocks are likely to fail or to be acquired by other firms that can manage their resources more effectively. The persistence of abnormal performance will therefore depend on strategic factors such as barriers to entry and switching costs, discussed in Chapter 2. To reflect this, analysts frequently assume that current shocks to abnormal earnings decay over time. Under this assumption, abnormal earnings are said to follow an autoregressive model. Forecasted abnormal earnings are then

$$\text{Forecasted } AE_1 = \beta AE_0$$

β is a parameter that captures the speed with which abnormal earnings decay over time. If there is no decay, β is one and abnormal earnings follow a random walk. If β is zero, abnormal earnings decay completely within one year. Estimates of β using actual company data indicate that for a typical U.S. firm, β is approximately 0.6. However, it varies by industry, and is smaller for firms with large accruals and one-time accounting charges.[8]

The autoregressive model implies that stock values can again be written as a function of current abnormal earnings and book values[9]:

$$\text{Stock value} = BVE_0 + \frac{\beta AE_0}{1 + r_e - \beta}$$

This formulation implies that stock values are simply the sum of current book value plus current abnormal earnings weighted by the cost of equity capital and persistence in abnormal earnings.

2. ROE and Growth Simplifications

It is also possible to make simplifications about long-term ROEs and equity growth to reduce forecast horizons for estimating the equity value-to-book multiple. Firms' long-term ROEs are affected by such factors as barriers to entry in their industries, change in production or delivery technologies, and quality of management. As discussed in Chapter 6, these factors tend to force abnormal ROEs to decay over time. One way to model this decay is to assume that ROEs follow a mean reverting process. Forecasted ROE in one period's time then takes the following form:

$$\text{Forecasted } ROE_1 = ROE_0 + \beta(ROE_0 - \overline{ROE})$$

$\overline{ROE}$ is the steady state ROE (either the firm's cost of capital or the long-term industry ROE) and β is a "speed of adjustment factor" that reflects how quickly it takes the ROE to revert to its steady state.[10]

Growth rates are affected by several factors. First, the size of the firm is important. Small firms can sustain very high growth rates for an extended period, whereas large firms find it more difficult to do so. Second, firms with high rates of growth are likely to attract competitors, which reduces their growth rates. As discussed in Chapter 10, book value growth rates for real firms exhibit considerable reversion to the mean.

The long-term patterns in ROE and book equity growth rates imply that for most companies there is limited value in making forecasts for valuation beyond a relatively short horizon, three to five years. Powerful economic forces tend to lead firms with superior or inferior performance early in the forecast horizon to revert to a level that is comparable to that of other firms in the industry or the economy. For a firm in steady state, that is, expected to have a stable ROE and book equity growth rate (*gbve*), the value-to-book multiple formula simplifies to the following:

$$\text{Equity value-to-book multiple} \;=\; 1 \;+\; \frac{ROE_0 \;-\; r_e}{r_e \;-\; gbve}$$

Consistent with this simplified model, there is a strong relation between price-to-book ratios and current ROEs. Figure 7-1 shows the relation between these variables for firms in the Retail: Apparel industry we discussed earlier.

Figure 7-I	Relation Between ROE and Price-to-Book Multiples

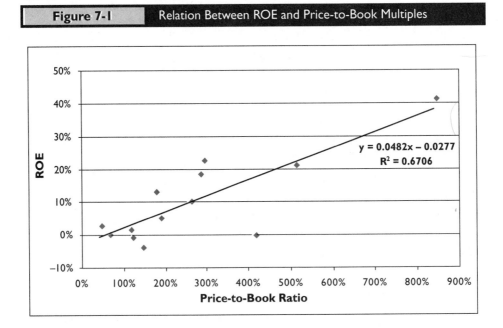

The correlation between the two variables is 0.82.

Of course, analysts can make a variety of simplifying assumptions about a firm's ROE and growth. For example, they can assume that they decay slowly or rapidly to the cost of capital and the growth rate for the economy. They can assume that the rates decay to the industry or economy average ROEs and book value growth rates. The valuation formula can easily be modified to accommodate these assumptions

THE DISCOUNTED CASH FLOW MODEL

The final valuation method discussed here is the discounted cash flow approach. This is the valuation method taught in most finance classes. Like the abnormal earnings approach, it is derived from the dividend discount model. It is based on the insight that dividends can be recast as free cash flows,[11] that is

$$\text{Dividends} \;=\; \text{Operating cash flow} \;-\; \text{Capital outlays} \;+\; \text{Net cash flows from debt owners}$$

As discussed in Chapter 5, operating cash flows to equity holders are simply net income plus depreciation less changes in working capital accruals. Capital outlays are capital expenditures less asset sales. Finally, net cash flows from debt owners are issues of new debt less retirements less the after-tax cost of interest. By rearranging these terms, the free cash flows to equity can be written as follows:

$$\text{Dividends} \quad = \quad \text{Free cash flows to equity} \quad = \quad NI - \Delta BVA + \Delta BVND$$

where NI is net income, ΔBVA is the change in book value of operating net assets (including changes in working capital plus capital expenditures less depreciation expense), and $\Delta BVND$ is the change in book value of net debt (interest-bearing debt less excess cash).

The dividend discount model can therefore be written as the present value of free cash flows to equity. Under this formulation firm value is estimated as follows:

$$\text{Equity value} \quad = \quad \text{PV of free cash flows to equity claim holders}$$

$$= \quad \frac{NI_1 - \Delta BVA_1 + \Delta BVND_1}{(1 + r_e)} + \frac{NI_2 - \Delta BVA_2 + \Delta BVND_2}{(1 + r_e)^2} + \ldots$$

Alternatively, the free cash flow formulation can be structured by estimating the value of claims to net debt and equity and then deducting the market value of net debt. This approach is more widely used in practice because it does not require explicit forecasts of changes in debt balances.[12] The value of debt plus equity is then

$$\text{Debt plus equity value} \quad = \quad \text{PV of free cash flows to net debt and equity claim holders}$$

$$= \quad \frac{NOPAT_1 - \Delta BVA_1}{(1 + WACC)} + \frac{NOPAT_2 - \Delta BVA_2}{(1 + WACC)^2} + \ldots$$

Valuation under the discounted cash flow method therefore involves the following steps:

Step 1: Forecast free cash flows available to equity holders (or to debt and equity holders) over a finite forecast horizon (usually 5 to 10 years).

Step 2: Forecast free cash flows beyond the terminal year based on some simplifying assumption.

Step 3: Discount free cash flows to equity holders (debt plus equity holders) at the cost of equity (weighted average cost of capital). The discounted amount represents the estimated value of free cash flows available to equity (debt and equity holders as a group).

Returning to the Down Under Company example, there is no debt, so that the free cash flows to owners are simply the operating profits before depreciation. Since Down Under is an all-equity firm, its WACC is the cost of equity (10 percent), and the present value of the free cash flows is as follows:

Year	Free Cash Flows	PV Factor	PV of Free Cash Flows
1	$40m	0.9091	$36.4m
2	50	0.8264	41.3
3	60	0.7513	45.1
Equity value			$122.8m

COMPARING VALUATION METHODS

We have discussed three methods of valuation derived from the dividend discount model: discounted dividends, discounted abnormal earnings (or abnormal ROEs), and discounted cash flows. What are the pluses and minuses of these approaches? Since the methods are all derived from the same underlying model, no one version can be considered superior to the others. As long as analysts make the same assumptions about firm fundamentals, value estimates under all four methods will be identical.

However, there are several important differences between the models that are worth noting:

- they focus the analyst's task on different issues;
- they require different levels of structure for valuation analysis; and
- they have different implications for the estimation of terminal values.

Focus on Different Issues

The methods frame the valuation task differently and can in practice focus the analyst's attention on different issues. The earnings-based approaches frame the issues in terms of accounting data such as earnings and book values. Analysts spend considerable time analyzing historical income statements and balance sheets, and their primary forecasts are typically for these variables.

Defining values in terms of ROEs has the added advantage that it focuses analysts' attention on ROE, the same key measure of performance that is decomposed in a standard financial analysis. Further, because ROEs control for firm scale, it is likely to be easier for analysts to evaluate the reasonableness of their forecasts by benchmarking them with ROEs of other firms in the industry and the economy. This type of benchmarking is more challenging for free cash flows and abnormal earnings.

Differences in Required Structure

The methods differ in the amount of analysis and structure required for valuation. The discounted abnormal earnings and ROE methods require analysts to construct both pro forma income statements and balance sheets to forecast future earnings and book values. In contrast, the discounted cash flow method requires analysts to forecast income statements and changes in working capital and long-term assets to generate free cash flows. Finally, the discounted dividend method requires analysts to forecast dividends.

The discounted abnormal earnings, ROE, and free cash flow models all require more structure for analysis than the discounted dividend approach. They therefore help analysts to avoid structural inconsistencies in their forecasts of future dividends by specifically allowing for firms' future performance and investment opportunities. Similarly, the discounted abnormal earnings/ROE method requires more structure and work than the discounted cash flow method to build full pro forma balance sheets. This permits analysts to avoid inconsistencies in the firm's financial structure.

Differences in Terminal Value Implications

A third difference between the methods is in the effort required for estimating terminal values. Terminal value estimates for the abnormal earnings and ROE methods tend to represent a much smaller fraction of total value than under the discounted cash flow or dividend methods. On the surface, this would appear to mitigate concerns about the aspect of valuation that leaves the analyst most uncomfortable. Is this apparent advantage real? As explained below, the answer turns on how well value is already reflected in the accountant's book value.

The abnormal earnings valuation does not eliminate the discounted cash flow terminal value problem, but it does reframe it. Discounted cash flow terminal values include the present value of *all* expected cash flows beyond the forecast horizon. Under abnormal earnings valuation, that value is broken into two parts: the present values of *normal* earnings and *abnormal* earnings beyond the terminal year. The terminal value in the abnormal earnings technique includes only the *abnormal* earnings. The present value of *normal* earnings is already reflected in the original book value or growth in book value over the forecast horizon.

The abnormal earnings approach, then, recognizes that current book value and earnings over the forecast horizon already reflect many of the cash flows expected to arrive after the forecast horizon. The approach builds directly on accrual accounting. For example, under accrual accounting book equity can be thought of as the minimum recoverable future benefits attributable to the firm's net assets. In addition, revenues are typically realized when earned, not when cash is received. The discounted cash flow approach, on the other hand, "unravels" all of the accruals, spreads the resulting cash flows over longer horizons, and then reconstructs its own "accruals" in the form of discounted expectations of future cash flows. The essential difference between the two approaches is that abnormal earnings valuation recognizes that the accrual process may already have performed a portion of the valuation task, whereas the discounted cash flow approach ultimately moves back to the primitive cash flows underlying the accruals.

The usefulness of the accounting-based perspective thus hinges on how well the accrual process reflects future cash flows. The approach is most convenient when the accrual process is "unbiased," so that earnings can be abnormal only as the result of economic rents and not as a product of accounting itself.[13] The forecast horizon then extends to the point where the firm is expected to approach a competitive equilibrium and earn only normal earnings on its projects. Subsequent abnormal earnings would be zero, and the terminal value at that point would be zero. In this extreme case, *all* of the firm's value is reflected in the book value and earnings projected over the forecast horizon.

Of course accounting rarely works so well. For example, in most countries research and development costs are expensed, and book values fail to reflect any research and development assets. As a result, firms that spend heavily on research and development—such as pharmaceuticals—tend on average to generate abnormally high earnings even in the face of stiff competition. Purely as an artifact of research and development accounting, abnormal earnings would be expected to remain positive indefinitely for such firms, and the terminal value could represent a substantial fraction of total value.

If desired, the analyst can alter the accounting approach used by the firm in his or her own projections. "Better" accounting would be viewed as that which reflects a larger fraction of the firm's value in book values and earnings over the forecast horizon.[14] This same view underlies analysts' attempts to "normalize" earnings; the adjusted numbers are intended to provide better indications of value, even though they reflect performance only over a short horizon.

Recent research has focused on the performance of earnings-based valuation relative to discounted cash flow and discounted dividend methods. The findings indicate that over relatively short forecast horizons, ten years or less, valuation estimates using the abnormal earnings approach generate more precise estimates of value than either the discounted dividend or discounted cash flow models. This advantage for the earnings-based approach persists for firms with conservative or aggressive accounting, indicating that accrual accounting in the U.S. does a reasonably good job of reflecting future cash flows.[15]

Key Analysis Questions

The above discussion on the trade-offs between different methods of valuing a company raises several questions for analysts about how to compare methods and to consider which is likely to be most reliable for their analysis:

- What are the key performance parameters that the analyst forecasts? Is more attention given to forecasting accounting variables, such as earnings and book values, or to forecasting cash flow variables?
- Has the analyst linked forecasted income statements and balance sheets? If not, is there any inconsistency between the two statements, or in the implications of the assumptions for future performance? If so, what is the source of this inconsistency and does it affect discounted earnings-based and discounted cash flow methods similarly?
- How well does the firm's accounting capture its underlying assets and obligations? Does it do a good enough job that we can rely on book values as the basis for long-term forecasts? Alternatively, does the firm rely heavily on off-balance-sheet assets, such as R&D, which make book values a poor lower bound on long-term performance?
- Has the analyst made very different assumptions about long-term performance in the terminal value computations under the different valuation methods? If so, which set of assumptions is more plausible given the firm's industry and its competitive positioning?

SUMMARY

Valuation is the process by which forecasts of performance are converted into estimates of price. A variety of valuation techniques are employed in practice, and there is no single method that clearly dominates others. In fact, since each technique involves different advantages and disadvantages, there are gains to considering several approaches simultaneously.

For shareholders, a stock's value is the present value of future dividends. This chapter described three valuation techniques directly based on this dividend discount definition of value: discounted dividends, discounted abnormal earnings/ROEs, and discounted free cash flows. The discounted dividend method attempts to forecast dividends directly. The abnormal earnings approach expresses the value of a firm's equity as book value plus discounted expectations of future abnormal earnings. Finally, the discounted cash flow method represents a firm's stock value by expected future free cash flows discounted at the cost of capital.

Although these three methods were derived from the same dividend discount model, they frame the valuation task differently. In practice they focus the analyst's attention on different issues and require different levels of structure in developing forecasts of the underlying primitive, future dividends.

Price multiple valuation methods were also discussed. Under these approaches, analysts estimate ratios of current price to historical or forecasted measures of performance for comparable firms. The benchmarks are then used to value the performance of the firm being analyzed. Multiples have traditionally been popular, primarily because they do not require analysts to make multiyear forecasts of performance. However it can be difficult to identify comparable firms to use as benchmarks. Even across highly related firms, there are differences in performance that are likely to affect their multiples.

The chapter discussed the relation between two popular multiples, value-to-book and value-earnings ratios, and the discounted abnormal earnings valuation. The resulting formulations indicate that value-to-book multiples are a function of future abnormal ROEs, book value growth, and the firm's cost of equity. The value-earnings multiple is a function of the same factors and also the current ROE.

DISCUSSION QUESTIONS

1. Joe Watts, an analyst at EMH Securities, states: "I don't know why anyone would ever try to value earnings. Obviously, the market knows that earnings can be manipulated and only values cash flows." Discuss.

2. Explain why terminal values in accounting-based valuation are significantly less than those for DCF valuation.

3. Manufactured Earnings is a "darling" of Wall Street analysts. Its current market price is $15 per share, and its book value is $5 per share. Analysts forecast that the firm's book value will grow by 10 percent per year indefinitely, and the cost of equity is 15 percent. Given these facts, what is the market's expectation of the firm's long-term average ROE?

4. Given the information in question 3, what will be Manufactured Earnings' stock price if the market revises its expectations of long-term average ROE to 20 percent?

5. Analysts reassess Manufactured Earnings' future performance as follows: growth in book value increases to 12 percent per year, but the ROE of the incremental book value is only 15 percent. What is the impact on the market-to-book ratio?

6. How can a company with a high ROE have a low PE ratio?

7. What types of companies have
   a. a high PE and a low market-to-book ratio?
   b. a high PE ratio and a high market-to-book ratio?
   c. a low PE and a high market-to-book ratio?
   d. a low PE and a low market-to-book ratio?

8. Free cash flows (FCF) used in DCF valuations discussed in the chapter are defined as follows:

   FCF to debt and equity = Earnings before interest and taxes × (1 − tax rate)
            + Depreciation and deferred taxes − Capital
            expenditures −/+ Increase/decrease in working capital

   FCF to equity = Net income + Depreciation and deferred taxes − Capital
            expenditures −/+ Increase/decrease in working capital
            +/− Increase/decrease in debt

   Which of the following items affect free cash flows to debt and equity holders? Which affect free cash flows to equity alone? Explain why and how.
   • An increase in accounts receivable
   • A decrease in gross margins
   • An increase in property, plant, and equipment

- An increase in inventory
- Interest expense
- An increase in prepaid expenses
- An increase in notes payable to the bank

9. Starite Company is valued at $20 per share. Analysts expect that it will generate free cash flows to equity of $4 per share for the foreseeable future. What is the firm's implied cost of equity capital?

10. Janet Stringer argues that "the DCF valuation method has increased managers' focus on short-term rather than long-term performance, since the discounting process places much heavier weight on short-term cash flows than long-term ones." Comment.

NOTES

1. The incorporation of all noncapital equity transactions into income is called clean surplus accounting. It is analogous to comprehensive income, the concept defined in FAS 130.

2. Changes in book value also include new capital contributions. However the dividend discount model assumes that new capital is issued at fair value. As a result, any incremental book value from capital issues is exactly offset by the discounted value of future dividends to new shareholders. Capital transactions therefore do not affect firm valuation.

3. The appendix to this chapter provides a simple proof of the earnings-based valuation formula.

4. See C. Lee and J. Myers, "What is the Intrinsic Value of the Dow?" Cornell University, working paper, 1997.

5. There is an important difference between the way ROE is defined in the value-to-book formulation and the way it is defined in Chapter 9. The valuation formula defines ROE as return on beginning equity, whereas in our ratio discussion we used return on ending or return on average equity.

6. It may seem surprising that one can estimate value with no explicit attention to two of the cash flow streams considered in DCF analysis, investments in working capital and capital expenditures. The accounting-based technique recognizes that these investments cannot possibly contribute to value without impacting abnormal earnings, and that therefore only their earnings impacts need be considered. For example, the benefit of an increase in inventory turnover surfaces in terms of its impact on ROE (and thus, abnormal earnings), without the need to consider explicitly the cash flow impacts involved.

7. It is also possible to include a drift term in the model, allowing earnings to grow by a constant amount, or at a constant rate each period.

8. See P. M. Dechow, A. P. Hutton, and R. G. Sloan, "An empirical assessment of the residual income valuation model," *Journal of Accounting and Economics* 23, January 1999.

9. This formulation is a variant of a model proposed by James Ohlson, "Earnings, book values, and dividends in security valuation," *Contemporary Accounting Research* 11, Spring 1995. Ohlson includes in his forecasts of future abnormal earnings a variable that reflects relevant information other than current abnormal earnings. This variable then also appears in the stock valuation formula. Empirical research by Dechow, Hutton, and Sloan, "An empirical assessment of the residual income valuation model," *Journal of Accounting and Economics* 23, January 1999, indicates that financial analysts' forecasts of abnormal earnings do reflect considerable information other than current abnormal earnings, and that this information is useful for valuation.

10. This specification is similar to the model for dividends developed by J. Lintner, "Distribution of incomes of corporations among dividends, retained earnings, and taxes," *American Economic Review* 46 (May 1956): 97–113.

11. In practice, firms do not have to pay out all of their free cash flows as dividends; they can retain surplus cash in the business. The conditions under which a firm's dividend decision affects its

value are discussed by M. H. Miller and F. Modigliani in "Dividend Policy, Growth and the Valuation of Shares," *Journal of Business* 34 (October 1961): 411–33.

12. A good forecast, however, would be grounded in an understanding of these changes as well as all other key elements of the firm's financial picture. The changes in financing cash flows are particularly critical for firms that anticipate changing their capital structure.

13. Unbiased accounting is that which, in a competitive equilibrium, produces an expected ROE equal to the cost of capital. The actual ROE thus reveals the presence of economic rents. Market-value accounting is a special case of unbiased accounting that produces an expected ROE equal to the cost of capital, even when the firm is *not* in a competitive equilibrium. That is, market-value accounting reflects the present value of future economic rents in book value, driving the expected ROEs to a normal level. For a discussion of unbiased and biased accounting, see G. Feltham and J. Ohlson, "Valuation and Clean Surplus Accounting for Operating and Financial Activities," *Contemporary Accounting Research* 11, No. 2 (Spring 1995): 689–731.

14. In Bennett Stewart's book on EVA valuation, *The Quest for Value* (New York: HarperBusiness, 1999), he recommends a number of accounting adjustments, including the capitalization of research and development.

15. S. Penman and T. Sougiannis, "A Comparison of Dividend, Cash Flow, and Earnings Approaches to Equity Valuation," *Contemporary Accounting Research* (Fall 1998): 343–83, compares the valuation methods using actual realizations of earnings, cash flows, and dividends to estimate prices. J. Francis, P. Olsson, and D. Oswald, "Comparing Accuracy and Explainability of Dividend, Free Cash Flow and Abnormal Earnings Equity Valuation Models," *Journal of Accounting Research* 38 (Spring 2000): 45–70, estimates values using *Value Line* forecasts.

APPENDIX: RECONCILING THE DISCOUNTED DIVIDENDS AND DISCOUNTED ABNORMAL EARNINGS MODELS

To derive the earnings-based valuation from the dividend discount model consider the following two-period valuation:

$$\text{Equity value} = \frac{DIV_1}{(1 + r_e)} + \frac{DIV_2}{(1 + r_e)^2}$$

With clean surplus accounting, dividends (DIV) can be expressed as a function of net income (NI) and the book value of equity (BVE):

$$DIV_t = NI_t + BVE_{t-1} - BVE_t$$

Substituting this expression into the dividend discount model yields the following:

$$\text{Equity value} = \frac{NI_1 + BVE_0 - BVE_1}{(1 + r_e)} + \frac{NI_2 + BVE_1 - BVE_2}{(1 + r_e)^2}$$

This can be rewritten as follows:

$$\text{Equity value} = \frac{NI_1 - r_e BVE_0 + BVE_0(1 + r_e) - BVE_1}{(1 + r_e)}$$

$$+ \frac{NI_2 - r_e BVE_1 + BVE_1(1 + r_e) - BVE_2}{(1 + r_e)^2}$$

$$= BVE_0 + \frac{NI_1 - r_e BVE_0}{(1 + r_e)} + \frac{NI_2 - r_e BVE_1}{(1 + r_e)^2} - \frac{BVE_2}{(1 + r_e)^2}$$

The value of equity is therefore the current book value plus the present value of future abnormal earnings. As the forecast horizon expands, the final term (the present value of liquidating book value) becomes inconsequential.

Prospective Analysis: Valuation Implementation

To move from the valuation theory discussed in the previous chapter to the actual task of valuing a company, one has to deal with a number of issues. First, the analyst needs to make forecasts of financial performance stated in terms of abnormal earnings and book values, or free cash flows over the life of the firm. As a practical matter, the forecasting task is often divided into two subcomponents—detailed forecasts over a finite number of years and a forecast of "terminal value," which represents a summary forecast of performance beyond the period of detailed forecasts. Second, the analyst needs to estimate the cost of capital to discount these forecasts. We discuss these issues in this chapter, and provide guidance on how to deal with them.

DETAILED FORECASTS OF PERFORMANCE

The horizon over which detailed forecasts are to be made is itself a choice variable. We will discuss later in this chapter how the analyst might make this choice. Once it is made, the next step is to consider the set of assumptions regarding a firm's performance that are needed to arrive at the forecasts. We described in Chapter 6 the general framework of financial forecasting. Since valuation involves forecasting over a long time horizon, it is not practical to forecast all the line items in a company's financial statements. Instead, the analyst has to focus on the key elements of a firm's performance.

The key to sound forecasts, of course, is that the underlying assumptions are grounded in a company's business reality. Strategy analysis provides a critical understanding of a company's value proposition, and whether current performance is likely to be sustainable in future. Accounting analysis and ratio analysis provide a deep understanding of a company's current performance, and whether the ratios themselves are reliable indicators of performance. It is, therefore, important to see the valuation forecasts as a continuation of the earlier steps in business analysis rather than as a discreet and unconnected exercise from the rest of the analysis.

Recall that we used the discount retailer TJX to illustrate ratio analysis and financial forecasting in Chapters 5 and 6. Specifically, we forecasted in Chapter 6 TJX's condensed income statement, beginning balance sheet, and free cash flows for a period of ten years starting in fiscal year 2002 (year beginning in February 2002). We will use these same forecasting assumptions and financial forecasts, which are shown in Tables 6-1 and 6-2, as a starting point to value TJX as of February 1, 2002.

The key forecasts required to use the formulas discussed in Chapter 7 for valuing a firm's equity are: abnormal earnings, abnormal ROE, and free cash flows to equity. If one is valuing a firm's assets, the corresponding variables of interest are abnormal NOPAT, abnormal operating ROA, and free cash flows to debt and equity. To calculate abnormal earnings and abnormal returns, we can begin with the forecasts in Table 6-2 for TJX, but we also need estimates of its cost of capital. So let us begin our discussion with a framework for estimating a firm's cost of capital. Then we will try to convert the financial forecasts in Table 6-2 into estimates of value.

COMPUTING A DISCOUNT RATE

To value a company's assets, the analyst discounts abnormal NOPAT, abnormal operating ROA, or cash flows available to both debt and equity holders. The proper discount rate to use is therefore the weighted average cost of capital (WACC). The WACC is calculated by weighting the costs of debt and equity capital according to their respective market values:

$$\text{WACC} = \frac{V_d}{V_d + V_e} r_d (1 - T) + \frac{V_e}{V_d + V_e} r_e$$

where V_d = the market value of debt and V_e = the market value of equity
r_d = the cost of debt capital
r_e = the cost of equity capital
T = the tax rate reflecting the marginal tax benefit of interest

Weighting the Costs of Debt and Equity

The weights assigned to debt and equity represent their respective fractions of total capital provided, measured in terms of market values. Computing a market value for debt should not be difficult. It is reasonable to use book values if interest rates have not changed significantly since the time the debt was issued. Otherwise, the value of the debt can be estimated by discounting the future payouts at current market rates of interest applicable to the firm.

What is included in debt? Should short-term as well as long-term debt be included? Should payables and accruals be included? The answer is revealed by considering how we calculated free cash flows. Free cash flows are the returns to the providers of the capital to which the WACC applies. The cash flows are those available *before* servicing short-term and long-term debt—indicating that both short-term and long-term debt should be considered a part of capital when computing the WACC. Servicing of other liabilities, such as accounts payable or accruals, should already have been considered as we computed free cash flows. Thus internal consistency requires that operating liabilities not be considered a part of capital when computing the WACC.

The tricky problem we face is assigning a market value to equity. That is the very amount we are trying to estimate in the first place! How can the analyst possibly assign a market value to equity at this intermediate stage, given that the estimate will not be known until all steps in the DCF analysis are completed?

One common approach to the problem is to insert at this point "target" ratios of debt to capital $[V_d/(V_d + V_e)]$ and equity to capital $[V_e/(V_d + V_e)]$. For example, one might expect that a firm will, over the long run, maintain a capital structure that is 40 percent debt and 60 percent equity. The long-run focus is reasonable because we are discounting cash flows over a long horizon.

Another way around the problem is to start with book value of equity as a weight for purposes of calculating an initial estimate of the WACC, which in turn can be used in the discounting process to generate an initial estimate of the value of equity. That initial estimate can then be used in place of the guess to arrive at a new WACC, and a second estimate of the value of equity can be produced. This process can be repeated until the value used to calculate the WACC and the final estimated value converge.

Estimating the Cost of Debt

The cost of debt (r_d) is the interest rate on the debt. If the assumed capital structure in future periods is the same as the historical structure, then current interest rate on debt will be a good proxy for this. However, if the analyst assumes a change in capital structure, then it is important to estimate the expected interest rate given the new level of debt ratio. One approach to this would be to estimate the expected credit rating of the company at the new level of debt and use the appropriate interest rates for that credit category.

The cost of debt should be expressed on a net-of-tax basis because it is after-tax cash flows that are being discounted. In most settings the market rate of interest can be converted to a net-of-tax basis by multiplying it by one minus the marginal corporate tax rate.

Estimating the Cost of Equity

Estimating the cost of equity (r_e) can be difficult, and a full discussion of the topic lies beyond the scope of this chapter. At any rate, even an extended discussion would not supply answers to all the questions that might be raised in this area because the field of finance is in a state of flux over what constitutes an appropriate measure of the cost of equity.

One possibility is to use the capital asset pricing model (CAPM), which expresses the cost of equity as the sum of a required return on riskless assets plus a premium for systematic risk:

$$r_e = r_f + \beta[E(r_m) - r_f]$$

where r_f is the riskless rate;

$[E(r_m) - r_f]$ is the risk premium expected for the market as a whole, expressed as the excess of the expected return on the market index over the riskless rate;

and β is the systematic risk of the equity.

To compute r_e, one must estimate three parameters: the riskless rate, r_f, the market risk premium $[E(r_m) - r_f]$, and systematic risk, β. For r_f, analysts often use the rate on intermediate-term treasury bonds, based on the observation that it is cash flows beyond the short term that are being discounted.[1] When r_f is measured in that way, then average common stock returns (based on the returns to the Standard and Poor's 500 index) have exceeded that rate by 7.0 percent over the 1926–2002 period.[2] This excess return constitutes an estimate of the market risk premium $[E(r_m) - r_f]$. Finally, systematic risk (β) reflects the sensitivity of the firm's value to economy-wide market movements.[3]

Although the above CAPM is often used to estimate the cost of capital, the evidence indicates that the model is incomplete. Assuming stocks are priced competitively, stock returns should be expected just to compensate investors for the cost of their capital. Thus long run average returns should be close to the cost of capital and should (according to the CAPM) vary across stocks according to their systematic risk. However, factors beyond just systematic risk seem to play some role in explaining variation in long-run average returns. The most important such factor is labeled the "size effect": smaller firms (as measured by market capitalization) tend to generate higher returns in subsequent periods. Why this is so is unclear. It could mean either that smaller firms are riskier than indicated by the CAPM or that they are underpriced at the point their market capitalization is measured, or some combination of both. Average stock returns for U.S. firms (including NYSE, AMEX, and NASDAQ firms) varied across size deciles from 1926 to 2002 as shown in Table 8-1.

The table shows that, historically, investors in firms in the top two deciles of the size distribution have realized returns of only 11.2 to 12.9 percent. In contrast, firms in the smallest two size deciles have realized significantly higher returns, ranging from 17.1 to 20.8 percent. Note, however, that if we use firm size as an indicator of the cost of capital, we are implicitly assuming that large size is indicative of lower risk. Yet finance theorists have not developed a well-accepted explanation for why that should be the case.

One method for combining the cost of capital estimates is based on the CAPM and the "size effect." The approach calls for adjustment of the CAPM-based cost of capital, based

Table 8-1   Stock Returns and Firm Size

Size decile	Market value of largest company in decile, in 2002 (millions of dollars)	Average annual stock return, 1926–2002 (%)	Fraction of total NYSE value represented by decile (in 2002, %)
1-small	141.5	20.8	0.89
2	314.0	17.1	1.28
3	521.3	16.2	1.48
4	791.3	15.2	1.91
5	1,143.8	14.9	2.24
6	1,691.2	14.5	3.07
7	2,680.6	14.0	3.74
8	5,012.7	13.5	6.35
9	11,628.7	12.9	12.76
10-large	293,137.3	11.2	66.27

Source: Ibbotson and Associates, *Stocks, Bonds, Bills, and Inflation* (2003).

on the difference between the average return on the market index used in the CAPM (the Standard and Poor's 500) and the average return on firms of size comparable to the firm being evaluated. The resulting cost of capital is

$$r_e \ = \ r_f \ + \ \beta[E(r_m) \ - \ r_f] \ + \ r_{\text{size}}$$

In light of the continuing debate on how to measure the cost of capital, it is not surprising that managers and analysts often consider a range of estimates. In particular, there has been considerable debate in recent times about whether or not the historical risk premium of 7 percent is valid today. Many analysts argue that a variety of changes in the U.S. economy make the historical risk premium an invalid basis for forecasting expected risk premium going forward. Some recent academic research has provided evidence that suggests that the expected risk premium in the market in recent years has declined substantially, to the range of 3 to 4 percent.[4] Since this debate is still unresolved, it is prudent for analysts to use a range of risk premium estimates in computing a firm's cost of capital.

Adjusting Cost of Equity for Changes in Leverage

Both cost of debt and cost of equity change as a function of a firm's leverage. As the leverage increases, debt and equity become more risky so they become more costly. If an analyst is contemplating changing capital structure during the forecasting time period relative to the historical capital structure of the firm, or changing the capital structure over time during the forecasting period, it is important to reestimate the cost of debt and equity to take these changes into account. We describe below a simple approach to this task.

We begin with the observation that the beta of a firm's assets is equal to the weighted average of its debt and equity betas, weighted by the proportion of debt and equity in its capital structure. A firm's equity beta can be estimated directly using its stock returns and the capital asset pricing model. Its debt beta can be inferred from the capital asset pricing model if we have information on the current interest rate and risk-free rate. From these estimated equity and debt betas at the current capital structure, we can infer the firm's asset beta.

When the firm's capital structure changes, its equity and debt betas will change, but its asset beta remains the same. We can take advantage of this fact to estimate the expected equity beta for the new capital structure. We first have to get an estimate of the interest rate on debt at the new capital structure level. Once we have this information, we can estimate the implied debt beta using the capital asset pricing model and the risk-free rate. Now we can estimate the equity beta for the new capital structure using the identity that the new equity beta and the new debt beta, weighted by the new capital structure weights, have to add up to the asset beta estimated earlier.

Estimating TJX's Cost of Capital

To estimate the cost of capital for TJX, we start with the assumption that its after-tax cost of debt is 7 percent, based on the ratio of the net interest expense after tax to beginning net debt in fiscal 2001 (with an assumed tax rate of 35 percent, this translates into a pre-tax cost of debt of 10.8 percent). The company's equity beta estimated in February 2002 was 0.90. The ten-year treasury bond rate at that time was 5.04 percent. Using the historical risk premium for equities of 7 percent, we can calculate its cost of equity to be 11.3 percent. Clearly this estimate is only a starting point, and the analyst can change the estimate by changing the assumed market risk premium or by adjusting for the size effect.

TJX's equity market value in February 2002 was $11,275 million; its net book debt was $210.8 million. Using these numbers we can calculate the "market value" weights of debt and equity in the company's capital structure as 2 percent and 98 percent respectively. Based on these weights and the above estimates of costs equity and debt, our estimate of TJX's weighted average cost of capital (WACC) in February 2002 is 11.3 percent (which is essentially the same as cost of equity since the company uses so little debt).

Since we keep the capital structure of TJX constant throughout the forecasting period, we will use these estimates of cost of equity and cost of capital.

Making Performance Forecasts for Valuing TJX

Recall that we made income statement, balance sheet, and cash flow forecasts for TJX for fiscal years 2002 to 2011 in Chapter 6 (Tables 6-1 and 6-2). Tables 8-2 and 8-3 present these same forecasts. Table 8-4 shows the performance forecasts implied by these financial statement forecasts for the ten-year period 2002 to 2011. Six performance forecasts, which can be used as input into the valuation exercise, are shown in the table. Abnormal earnings, abnormal ROE, and free cash flows to equity are inputs to value TJX's equity. Abnormal NOPAT, abnormal operating ROA, and free cash flows to debt and equity holders are three alternative inputs to value TJX's assets.

Table 8-2 Forecasting Assumptions for TJX

Fiscal year	2002	2003	2004	2005	2006	2007	2008	2009	2010	2011
Sales growth	12%	11.5%	11%	10.5%	10%	9.5%	9%	8.5%	8%	8%
NOPAT margin	4.5%	4%	3.5%	3%	2.5%	2%	1.9%	1.8%	1.7%	1.6%
After-tax net interest rate	7%	7%	7%	7%	7%	7%	7%	7%	7%	7%
Beginning net working capital to sales ratio	2.5%	2.5%	2.5%	2.5%	2.5%	2.5%	2.5%	2.5%	2.5%	2.5%
Beginning net long-term assets to sales ratio	10.5%	10.5%	10.5%	10.5%	10.5%	10.5%	10.5%	10.5%	10.5%	10.5%
Beginning net debt to capital ratio	13.6%	13.6%	13.6%	13.6%	13.6%	13.6%	13.6%	13.6%	13.6%	13.6%

Table 8-3 Forecasted Financial Statements for TJX

Fiscal year	2002	2003	2004	2005	2006	2007	2008	2009	2010	2011
Beginning Balance Sheet ($mm)										
Beg. Net Working Capital	297.4	334.3	371.1	410.1	451.1	493.9	538.4	584.2	630.9	681.4
+ Beg. Net Long-Term Assets	1,254.2	1,404.2	1,558.7	1,722.3	1,894.6	2,074.5	2,261.3	2,453.5	2,649.7	2,861.7
= **Net Operating Assets**	**1,551.5**	**1,738.5**	**1,929.8**	**2,132.4**	**2,345.6**	**2,568.5**	**2,799.6**	**3,037.6**	**3,280.6**	**3,543.1**
Net Debt	210.8	236.3	262.2	289.8	318.8	349.0	380.5	412.8	445.8	481.5
+ Preferred Stock	0.0	0.0	0.0	0.0	0.0	0.0	0.0	0.0	0.0	0.0
+ Shareholders' Equity	1,340.7	1,502.3	1,667.5	1,842.6	2,026.9	2,219.4	2,419.2	2,624.8	2,834.8	3,061.6
= **Net Capital**	**1,551.5**	**1,738.5**	**1,929.8**	**2,132.4**	**2,345.6**	**2,568.5**	**2,799.6**	**3,037.6**	**3,280.6**	**3,543.1**
Income Statement ($mm)										
Sales	11,994.1	13,373.4	14,844.5	16,403.1	18,043.5	19,757.6	21,535.8	23,366.3	25,235.6	27,254.5
Net operating profits after tax	539.7	534.9	519.6	492.1	451.1	395.2	409.2	420.6	429.0	436.1
− Net interest expense after tax	14.8	16.6	18.4	20.3	22.4	24.5	26.7	29.0	31.3	33.8
= **Net income**	**524.9**	**518.4**	**501.1**	**471.8**	**428.7**	**370.6**	**382.5**	**391.6**	**397.7**	**402.3**
Operating ROA	34.8%	30.8%	26.9%	23.1%	19.2%	15.4%	14.6%	13.8%	13.1%	12.3%
ROE	39.2%	34.5%	30.1%	25.6%	21.2%	16.7%	15.8%	14.9%	14.0%	13.1%
BV of Assets Growth Rate	7.4%	12.1%	11.0%	10.5%	10.0%	9.5%	9.0%	8.5%	8.0%	8.0%
BV of Equity Growth Rate	10.0%	12.1%	11.0%	10.5%	10.0%	9.5%	9.0%	8.5%	8.0%	8.0%
Net Operating Asset Turnover	7.7	7.7	7.7	7.7	7.7	7.7	7.7	7.7	7.7	7.7
Free Cash Flow to Capital	352,737	343,696	316,929	278,853	228,250	163,988	171,209	177,584	166,555	152,625
Free Cash Flow to Equity	312,524	301,122	270,984	229,532	175,590	108,071	112,162	115,582	99,593	80,306

The cash flows in 2011 are based on a forecasted beginning balance sheet for 2012, not shown here. To make this forecast, we assume that sales growth and all the beginning balance sheet ratios in 2012 remain at the same level as in 2011.

The calculations of performance forecasts in Table 8-4 use the following definitions: (1) abnormal earnings is net income less shareholders' equity at the beginning of the year times cost of equity; (2) abnormal ROE is the difference between ROE and cost of equity; (3) free cash flow to equity is net income less the increase in operating working capital less the increase in net long-term assets plus the increase in net debt; (4) abnormal NOPAT is NOPAT less total net capital at the beginning of the year times the weighted average cost of capital; (5) abnormal operating ROA is the difference between operating ROA and the weighted average cost of capital (WACC); and (6) free cash flow to capital is NOPAT less the increase in operating working capital less the increase in net long-term assets.

As discussed earlier, to derive cash flows in 2011, we need to make assumptions about sales growth rate and balance sheet ratios in 2012. We discuss below three different sets of assumptions in this regard. The cash flow forecasts shown in Table 8-4 are based on the simple assumption that the sales growth and beginning balance sheet ratios in 2012 remain the same as in 2011. We relax this assumption later.

Table 8-4 Performance Forecasts for TJX for the fiscal years 2002 to 2011

Fiscal year	2002	2003	2004	2005	2006	2007	2008	2009	2010	2011
Equity Valuation ($000's)										
Abnormal Earnings	372,897	347,992	312,048	262,798	198,860	118,964	108,135	93,960	76,242	55,086
Abnormal ROE	27.8%	23.2%	18.7%	14.3%	9.8%	5.4%	4.5%	3.6%	2.7%	1.8%
Free Cash Flow to Equity	363,347	353,099	326,056	287,489	236,155	170,899	176,840	181,629	170,924	157,344
Asset Valuation ($000's)										
Abnormal NOPAT	365,129	339,287	302,387	252,122	187,116	106,105	94,118	78,752	59,817	37,347
Abnormal Operating ROA	23.5%	19.5%	15.7%	11.8%	8.0%	4.1%	3.4%	2.6%	1.8%	1.1%
Free Cash Flow to Capital	352,737	343,696	316,929	278,853	228,250	163,988	171,209	177,584	166,555	152,625
Discount rates:										
Equity	0.898	0.807	0.725	0.651	0.584	0.525	0.471	0.423	0.380	0.342
Assets	0.899	0.808	0.726	0.653	0.587	0.527	0.474	0.426	0.383	0.344
Growth factors*:										
Equity	1.000	1.121	1.244	1.374	1.512	1.655	1.804	1.958	2.114	2.284
Assets	1.000	1.121	1.244	1.374	1.512	1.655	1.804	1.958	2.114	2.284

*The growth factor is relevant only for calculating the present value for abnormal ROA and ROE.

TERMINAL VALUES

The forecasts in Tables 8-3 and 8-4 extend only through the year 2011, and thus we label 2011 the "terminal year." (Selection of an appropriate terminal year is discussed later.) Terminal value is essentially the present value of either abnormal earnings or free cash flows occurring beyond the terminal year. Since this involves forecasting performance over the remainder of the firm's life, the analyst must adopt some assumption that simplifies the process of forecasting. Below we discuss a variety of alternative approaches to this task.

Terminal Values with the Competitive Equilibrium Assumption

Table 8-2 projects a sales growth rate and return on equity declining gradually over time during the period 2002 to 2011 before stabilizing sometime during that period. What should we assume beyond 2011? Is it reasonable to assume a continuation of the same stable 2011 performance in 2012 and beyond? Is some other pattern more reasonable?

One thing that seems clear is that continuation of a sales growth that is significantly greater than the average growth rate of the economy is unrealistic over a very long horizon. That rate would likely outstrip inflation in the dollar and the real growth rate of the world economy. Over many years, it would imply that TJX would grow to a size greater than that of all other firms in the world combined. But what would be a suitable alternative assumption? Should we expect the firm's sales growth rate to ultimately settle down to the rate of inflation? Or to a higher rate, such as the nominal GDP growth rate? Or to something else?

Ultimately, to answer these questions, one must consider how much longer the rate of growth in industry sales can outstrip the general growth in the world economy, and how long TJX's competitive advantages can enable it to grow faster than the overall industry. Clearly, looking eleven or more years into the future, any forecasts of sales growth rates are likely to be subject to considerable error.

Fortunately, in many if not most situations, how we deal with the seemingly imponderable questions about long-range growth in sales simply *does not matter very much!* In fact, under plausible economic assumptions, there is no practical need to consider sales growth beyond the terminal year. Such growth may be *irrelevant*, so far as the firm's current value is concerned!

How can long-range growth in sales *not* matter? The reasoning revolves around the forces of competition. Competition tends to constrain a firm's ability to identify, on a consistent basis, growth opportunities that generate supernormal profits. (Recall the evidence in Chapter 6 concerning the reversion of ROEs to normal levels over horizons of five to ten years.) Certainly a firm may at a point in time maintain a competitive advantage that permits it to achieve returns in excess of the cost of capital. When that advantage is protected with patents or a strong brand name, the firm may even be able to maintain it for many years, perhaps indefinitely. With hindsight, we know that some such firms—like Coca-Cola and Wal-Mart—were able not only to maintain their competitive edge but to expand it across dramatically increasing investment bases. But in the face of competition, one would typically not expect a firm to extend its supernormal profitability to new *additional* projects *year after year*. Ultimately, we would expect high profits to attract enough competition to drive the firm's return down to a normal level. Each new project would generate cash flows with a present value no greater than the cost of the investment—the investment would be a "zero net present value" project. Since the benefits of the project are offset by its costs, it does nothing to enhance the current value of the firm, and the associated growth can be ignored.

Of course, terminal value estimation does not necessarily *require* this "competitive equilibrium assumption." If the analyst expects that supernormal margins can be extended to new markets for many years, it can be accommodated within the context of a valuation analysis. At a minimum, as we will discuss in the next section, the analyst may expect that supernormal margins can be maintained on the existing sales base, or on markets that grow at the rate of inflation. However, the important lesson here is that the rate of growth in *sales* beyond the forecast horizon is *not* a relevant consideration *unless* the analyst believes that the growth can be achieved while generating supernormal margins—and competition may make that a difficult trick to pull off.

Assumption Only on Incremental Sales

An alternative version of the competitive equilibrium assumption is to assume that TJX will continue to earn abnormal earnings forever on the sales it had in 2011, but there will be no abnormal earnings on any incremental sales beyond that level. If we invoke the competitive equilibrium assumption on incremental sales for years beyond 2011, then it does not matter what sales growth rate we use beyond that year, and we may as well simplify our arithmetic by treating sales *as if* they will be constant at the year 2011 level. Then operating ROA, ROE, NOPAT, net income, free cash flow to debt and equity, and free cash flow to equity will all remain constant at the year 2011 level.

Under this scenario, it is simple to estimate the terminal value by dividing the 2011 level of each of the variables by the appropriate discount rate. As one would expect, terminal values in this scenario will be higher than those with no abnormal returns on all sales in years 2012 and beyond. This is entirely due to the fact that we are now assuming that TJX can retain its superior performance on its existing base of sales indefinitely.

Terminal Value with Persistent Abnormal Performance and Growth

Each of the approaches described above appeals in some way to the "competitive equilibrium assumption." However, there are circumstances where the analyst is willing to assume that the firm may defy competitive forces and earn abnormal rates of return on new projects for many years. If the analyst believes supernormal profitability can be extended to larger markets for many years, one possibility is to project earnings and cash flows over a longer horizon, until the competitive equilibrium assumption can reasonably be invoked. In the case of TJX, for example, we could assume that the supernormal profitability will continue for five years beyond 2011 (for a total forecasting horizon of 15 years from the beginning of the forecasting period), but after that period, the firm's ROE and Operating ROA will be equal to its cost of equity and its weighted average cost of capital.

Another possibility is to project growth in abnormal earnings or cash flows at some constant rate. Consider the following. By treating TJX as if its competitive advantage can be maintained only on the *nominal* sales level achieved in the year 2011, we will be assuming that in *real* terms its competitive advantage will shrink. Let's say that the analyst expects TJX to maintain its advantage (through supplies of new and more advanced products to a similar customer base) on a sales base that remains constant in *real* terms—that grows beyond the year 2011 at the expected long-run inflation rate of 3.5 percent. The computations implied by these assumptions are described below. The approach is more aggressive than the one described earlier, but it may be more realistic. After all, there is no obvious reason why the *real* size of the investment base on which TJX earns abnormal returns should depend on inflation rates.

The approach just described still relies to some extent on the competitive equilibrium assumption. The assumption is now invoked to suggest that supernormal profitability can be extended only to an investment base that remains constant in real terms. However, there is nothing about the valuation method that requires *any* reliance on the competitive equilibrium assumption. The calculations described below could be used with *any* rate of growth in sales. The question is not whether the arithmetic is available to handle such an approach, but rather how realistic it is.

Let's stay with the approach that assumes TJX will extend its supernormal margins to sales that grow beyond 2011 at the rate of inflation. How would abnormal earnings and free cash flows beyond 2011 behave?

Beyond our terminal year, 2011, as the sales growth rate remains constant at 3.5 percent, abnormal earnings, free cash flows, and book values of assets and equity also grow at a constant rate of 3.5 percent. This is simply because we held all other performance ratios constant in this period. As a result, abnormal operating ROA and abnormal ROE remain constant at the same rate as in the terminal year.

The above exercise shows that, when we assume that the abnormal performance persists at the same level as in the terminal year, projecting abnormal earnings and free cash flows is a simple matter of growing them at the assumed sales growth rate. Since the rate of abnormal earnings and cash flows growth is constant starting in 2012, it is also straightforward to discount those flows. For a given discount rate r, any flow stream growing at the constant rate g can be discounted by dividing the flows in the first year by the amount $(r-g)$.

Terminal Value Based on a Price Multiple

A popular approach to terminal value calculation is to apply a multiple to abnormal earnings, cash flows, or book values of the terminal period. The approach is not as ad hoc as it might at first appear. Note that under the assumption of no sales growth, abnormal earnings or cash flows beyond 2011 remain constant. Capitalizing these flows in perpetuity by dividing by the cost of capital is equivalent to multiplying them by the inverse of the cost of capital. For example, capitalizing free cash flows to equity at 11.3 percent is equivalent to assuming a terminal cash flow multiple of 8.84. Thus applying a multiple in this range is similar to discounting all free cash flows beyond 2011 while invoking the competitive equilibrium assumption on incremental sales.

The mistake to avoid here is to capitalize the future abnormal earnings or cash flows using a multiple that is too high. The earnings or cash flow multiples might be high currently because the market anticipates abnormally profitable growth. However, once that growth is realized, the PE multiple should fall to a normal level. It is that normal PE, applicable to a stable firm or one that can grow only through zero net present value projects, that should be used in the terminal value calculation. Thus multiples in the range of 7 to 10—close to the reciprocal of cost of equity and WACC—should be used here. Higher multiples are justifiable only when the terminal year is closer and there are still abnormally profitable growth opportunities beyond that point. A similar logic applies to the estimation of terminal values using book value multiples.

Selecting the Terminal Year

A question begged by the above discussion is how long to make the detailed forecast horizon. When the competitive equilibrium assumption is used, the answer is whatever time is required for the firm's returns on incremental investment projects to reach that equilibrium—an issue that turns on the sustainability of the firm's competitive advantage. As indicated in Chapter 6, historical evidence indicates that most firms in the U.S. should expect ROEs to revert to normal levels within five to ten years. But for the typical firm, we can justify ending the forecast horizon even earlier—note that the return on *incremental* investment can be normal even while the return on *total* investment (and therefore ROE) remains abnormal. Thus a five- to ten-year forecast horizon should be more than sufficient for most firms. Exceptions would include firms so well insulated from competition (perhaps due to the power of a brand name) that they can extend their investment base to new markets for many years and still expect to generate supernormal returns. In 1999 the Wrigley Company, producer of chewing gum, was still extending its brand name to untapped markets in other nations, and appears to be such a firm.

Estimates of TJX's Terminal Value

Choosing Terminal Year In the case of TJX, the terminal year used is ten years beyond the current one. Table 8-3 shows that the ROE (and operating ROA) is forecasted to decline only gradually over these ten years, from the unusually high 39.2 percent in 2002 to 13.1 percent by 2011. At this level the company will earn an abnormal return on equity of 1.8 percent, since its cost of equity is estimated to be 11.3 percent.

If NOPAT margins could be maintained at the projected 1.6 percent on ever-increasing sales, this abnormal ROE could be achieved even on new investment in 2012 and beyond. But even a slight decline in the NOPAT margin to about 1.5 percent would, in the face of continued sales growth, be enough to cause the return on the *incremental* investment to be very close to the cost of capital. Thus the performance we have already projected for the terminal year 2011 is not far removed from a competitive equilibrium, and extending the forecast horizon by a few more years would have little impact on the calculated value. Even if we project continuation of the 1.6 percent NOPAT margin through 2017 with 8 percent annual sales increases (and with the competitive equilibrium assumption invoked thereafter), the final estimated firm value would increase only marginally. Large changes in the value estimate would arise only if the analyst is willing to assume abnormal rates of return on investments well into the twenty-first century. In light of historical patterns for corporate performance, such an assumption would have to be based on a strong belief in TJX's continued competitive advantage. The upshot is that an analyst could argue that the terminal year used for TJX should be extended from the tenth year to, say, the fifteenth year, depending on the perceived sustainability of its competitive advantage. However, this becomes more of a significant issue only if the analyst assumes that TJX will have a significantly large competitive advantage in 2011 relative to what was assumed in the forecasts in Table 8-3. Based on this logic, we will fix the terminal year for TJX as 2011 and attempt to estimate its terminal value at that time.

Terminal Value Under Varying Assumptions   Table 8-5 shows TJX's terminal value under the three scenarios we discussed above. Scenario one of this table shows the terminal value if we assume that TJX will continue to grow its sales at 8 percent beyond fiscal year 2011, and that it will continue to earn the same level of abnormal returns as in 2011 (that is, we assume that all the other forecasting assumptions will be the same as in 2011). Scenario 2 shows the terminal value if we assume that TJX will grow at a lower rate, closer to the historical growth rate of U.S. GDP, at 4 percent in 2012 and beyond, but will maintain its competitive advantage and therefore its level of abnormal returns in 2011 forever. Scenario 3 shows the terminal value if we assume that the company will grow at 4 percent and will not have any significant abnormal returns in 2012 and beyond. In this scenario we are assuming that NOPAT margins will decline to 1.5 percent in 2012 and will remain at that level; all the remaining assumptions except sales level and NOPAT margins will remain unchanged from 2011.

COMPUTING ESTIMATED VALUES

Table 8-5 shows the estimated value of TJX's assets and equity, each using three different methods. Value of assets is estimated using abnormal operating ROA, abnormal NOPAT, and free cash flows to debt and equity. Value of equity is estimated using operating ROE, abnormal NOPAT, and free cash flow to equity. These values are computed using the financial forecasts in Table 8-4 and the terminal value forecasts under different scenarios we discussed earlier.

Note that the cash flow forecasts in Table 8-4 are based on scenario 1 for 2012. When we change these assumptions, the cash flow forecasts for 2011 change. Therefore the present values of cash flows for years 2002 to 2011 also vary across the three scenarios.

In Table 8-5, present values of abnormal NOPAT and free cash flow to capital are computed using a WACC of 11.3 percent; present values of abnormal earnings and free cash flow to equity are computed using a cost of equity of 11.3 percent. To calculate the present values of abnormal operating ROA and abnormal ROE, the values for each year are first multiplied by the corresponding growth factor, as shown in the formulae in Chapter 7, and then they are discounted using a WACC of 11.3 percent and cost of equity of 11.3 percent.

Value estimates presented in each scenario show that the abnormal returns method, abnormal earnings method, and the free cash flow method result in the same value, as

Table 8-5 Valuation Summary for TJX Under Varying Scenarios*

Scenario 1	Beginning Book Value	Value from Forecasts for 2002–2011	Value from Forecasts Beyond 2011 (Terminal Value)	Total Value	Value per Share ($)
Equity Value ($000s)					
Abnormal Earnings	1,340,698	1,329,973	608,428	3,279,098	11.91
Abnormal ROE	1,340,698	1,329,973	608,428	3,279,098	11.91
Free Cash Flows to Equity	N/A	1,541,241	1,737,857	3,279,098	11.91
Asset Value ($000s)					
Abnormal NOPAT	1,551,545	1,266,154	426,755	3,244,454	N/A
Abnormal ROA	1,551,545	1,266,154	426,755	3,244,454	N/A
Free Cash Flows to Capital	N/A	1,500,462	1,743,992	3,244,454	N/A

Scenario 2	Beginning Book Value	Value from Forecasts for 2002–2011	Value from Forecasts Beyond 2011 (Terminal Value)	Total Value	Value per Share ($)
Equity Value ($000s)					
Abnormal Earnings	1,340,698	1,329,973	266,605	2,937,276	10.67
Abnormal ROE	1,340,698	1,329,973	266,605	2,937,276	10.67
Free Cash Flows to Equity	N/A	1,583,072	1,354,204	2,937,276	10.67
Asset Value ($000s)					
Abnormal NOPAT	1,551,545	1,266,154	184,331	3,002,030	N/A
Abnormal ROA	1,551,545	1,266,154	184,331	3,002,030	N/A
Free Cash Flows to Capital	N/A	1,549,248	1,452,782	3,002,030	N/A

Scenario 3	Beginning Book Value	Value from Forecasts for 2002–2011	Value from Forecasts Beyond 2011 (Terminal Value)	Total Value	Value per Share ($)
Equity Value ($000s)					
Abnormal Earnings	1,340,698	1,329,973	134,700	2,805,371	10.19
Abnormal ROE	1,340,698	1,329,973	134,700	2,805,371	10.19
Free Cash Flows to Equity	N/A	1,583,072	1,222,299	2,805,371	10.19
Asset Value ($000s)					
Abnormal NOPAT	1,551,545	1,266,154	49,814	2,867,513	N/A
Abnormal ROA	1,551,545	1,266,154	49,814	2,867,513	N/A
Free Cash Flows to Capital	N/A	1,549,248	1,318,265	2,867,513	N/A

*Scenario 1: Sales growth and NOPAT/Sales of 8% and 1.6%, respectively.
Scenario 2: Sales growth and NOPAT/Sales of 4% and 1.6%, respectively.
Scenario 3: Sales growth and NOPAT/Sales of 4% and 1.5%, respectively.

claimed in Chapter 7. Note also that TJX's terminal value represents a significantly larger fraction of the total value of assets and equity under the free cash flow method relative to the other methods. As discussed in Chapter 7, this is due to the fact that the abnormal returns and earnings methods rely on a company's book value of assets and equity, so the terminal value estimates are estimates of incremental values over book values. In contrast, the free cash flow approach ignores the book values, so the terminal value forecasts are estimates of total value during this period.

The primary calculations in the above estimates treat all flows as if they arrive at the end of the year. Of course, they are likely to arrive throughout the year. If we assume for the sake of simplicity that cash flows will arrive mid-year, then we should adjust our value estimates upward by the amount $\left[1 + \left(\frac{r}{2}\right)\right]$, where r is the discount rate.

Value Estimates Versus Market Values

As the discussion above shows, valuation involves a substantial number of assumptions by analysts. Therefore the estimates of value will vary from one analyst to the other. The only way to ensure that one's estimates are reliable is to make sure that the assumptions are grounded in the economics of the business being valued. It is also useful to check the assumptions against the time-series trends for performance ratios discussed in Chapter 6. While it is quite legitimate for an analyst to make assumptions that differ markedly from these trends in any given case, it is important for the analyst to be able to articulate the business and strategy reasons for making such assumptions.

When a company being valued is publicly traded, it is possible to compare one's own estimated value with the market value of a company. When an estimated value differs substantially from a company's market value, it is useful for the analyst to understand why such differences arise. A way to do this is to redo the valuation exercise and figure out what valuation assumptions are needed to arrive at the observed stock price. One can then examine whether the market's assumptions are more or less valid relative to one's own assumptions. As we discuss in the next chapter, such an analysis can be invaluable in using valuation to make buy or sell decisions in the security analysis context.

For example in the case of TJX, our estimated value of the firm's equity is significantly smaller than the observed value at the beginning of fiscal 2002. Our estimated value per share under the most optimistic terminal value assumptions was about $12 per share, while the company's stock price at that time was $20.67. Clearly the market was making more optimistic assumptions than our own. The differences in the two sets of assumptions might be related either to growth rates, NOPAT margins, asset turns, or discount rates (primarily due to differences in assumed equity risk premium or capital structure). One could run different scenarios regarding each of these variables and test the sensitivity of the estimated value to these assumptions.

Other Practical Issues in Valuation

The above discussion provides a blueprint for doing valuation. In practice, the analyst has to deal with a number of other issues that have an important effect on the valuation task. We discuss below three frequently encountered complications—accounting distortions, negative book values, and excess cash.

Dealing with Accounting Distortions

We know from the discussion in Chapter 7 that accounting methods per se should have no influence on firm value (except as those choices influence the analyst's view of future real performance). Yet the abnormal returns and earnings valuation approaches used here are based on numbers—earnings and book value—that vary with accounting method choices. How, then, can the valuation approach deliver correct estimates?

Because accounting choices must affect both earnings *and* book value, and because of the self-correcting nature of double-entry bookkeeping (all "distortions" of accounting must ultimately reverse), estimated values will not be affected by accounting choices, *as long as the analyst recognizes the accounting distortions.*[5] As an example, let's assume that managers are aggressive in their accounting choices, choosing to provide for a lower allowance for uncollected receivables even though they have information to the contrary, thus causing the current period's abnormal earnings and the ending book value to be higher by $100. For the time being, let's say the accounting choice has no influence on the analyst's view of the firm's real performance. That is, the analyst is assumed to recognize that management's current estimate of future customer defaults is artificially lower and can make accurate forecasts of future defaults.

Our accounting-based valuation approach starts with the current period's abnormal earnings, which are $100 higher as a result of the accounting choice. However, the choice also causes future abnormal earnings to be lower for two reasons. First, future earnings will be lower (by $100) in a later period, when the customer actually defaults on the payments and receivables will have to be written off. Second, in the meantime the benchmark for normal earnings, the book value of equity, will be higher by $100. Let's say the accounts receivables are not written off until two years after the current period. Then assuming a discount rate of 13 percent and the impact of the current aggressive accounting, the subsequent write-down on our calculation of value is as follows:

	Dollar Impact	Present Value
Increase in current abnormal earnings (and book value)	$100	$100.00
Decrease in abnormal earnings of year 1, due to higher book value ($.13 \times \$100$)	−13	$\div 1.13 = -11.50$
Decrease in abnormal earnings of year 2, due to higher book value ($.13 \times \$100$)	−13	
due to lower earnings from accounts receivable write-off	−100	
	−113	$\div 1.13^2 = -88.50$
Impact of accounting choice on present value		$0.00

The impact of the higher current abnormal earnings and the lower future abnormal earnings offset exactly, leaving no impact of the current underestimation of the allowance for uncollected receivables on estimated firm value.

The above discussion makes it appear as if the analyst would be indifferent to the accounting methods used. There is an important reason why this is not necessarily true. When a company uses "biased" accounting—either conservative or aggressive—the analyst is forced to expend resources doing accounting analyses of the sort described in Chapter 3. These additional analysis costs are avoided for firms with unbiased accounting.

If a thorough analysis is not performed, a firm's accounting choices can, in general, influence analysts' perceptions of the real performance of the firm and hence the forecasts of future performance. In the above example, the managers' allowance and receivables estimates, if taken at face value, will influence the analyst's forecasts of future earnings and cash flows. If so, the accounting choice per se would affect expectations of future earnings and cash flows in ways beyond those considered above. The estimated value of the firm would presumably be higher—but it would still be the same regardless of whether the valuation is based on DCF or discounted abnormal earnings.[6]

An analyst who encounters biased accounting has two choices—either to adjust current earnings and book values to eliminate managers' accounting biases, or to recognize these biases and adjust future forecasts accordingly. Both approaches lead to the same estimated firm value. For example, in the above illustration a simple way to deal with managers' underestimation of current default allowance is to increase the allowance and to decrease the current period's abnormal earnings by $100. Alternatively, as shown above, the analyst could forecast the write-off two periods from now. Which of the two approaches is followed will have an important impact on what fraction of the firm's value is captured within the forecast horizon, and what remains in the terminal value.

Holding forecasting horizon and future growth opportunities constant, higher accounting quality allows a higher fraction of a firm's value to be captured by the current book value and the abnormal earnings within the forecasting horizon. Accounting can be of low quality either because it is unreliable or because it is extremely conservative. If accounting reliability is a concern, the analyst has to expend resources on "accounting adjustments." If accounting is conservative, the analyst is forced to increase the forecasting horizon to capture a given fraction of a firm's value, or to rely on relatively more uncertain terminal values estimates for a large fraction of the estimated value.

Dealing with Negative Book Values

A number of firms have negative earnings and book values of book equity. Firms in the start-up phase have negative equity, as do those in high technology industries. These firms incur large investments whose payoff is uncertain. Accountants write off these investments as a matter of conservatism, leading to negative book equity. Examples of firms in this situation include biotechnology firms, Internet firms, telecommunication firms, and other high technology firms. A second category of firms with negative book equity are those that are performing poorly, resulting in cumulative losses exceeding the original investment by the shareholders.

Negative book equity makes it difficult to use the accounting-based approach to value a firm's equity. There are several possible ways to get around this problem. The first approach is to value the firm's assets (using, for example, abnormal operating ROA or abnormal NOPAT) rather than equity. Then, based on an estimate of the value of the firm's debt, one can estimate the equity value. Another alternative is to "undo" accountants' conservatism by capitalizing the investment expenditures written off. This is possible if the analyst is able to establish that these expenditures are value creating. A third alternative, feasible for publicly traded firms, is to start from the observed stock and work backwards. Using reasonable estimates of cost of equity and steady-state growth rate, the analyst can calculate the average long-term level of abnormal earnings needed to justify the observed stock price. Then the analytical task can be framed in terms of examining the feasibility of achieving this abnormal earnings "target."

It is important to note that the value of firms with negative book equity often consists of a significant option value. For example, the value of high-tech firms is not only driven by the expected earnings from their current technologies but also the payoff from technology options embedded in their research and development efforts. Similarly, the value of troubled companies is driven to some extent by the "abandonment option"—shareholders with limited liability can put the firm to debt holders and creditors. One can use the options theory framework to estimate the value of these "real options."

Dealing with Excess Cash and Excess Cash Flow

Firms with excess cash balances, or large free cash flows, also pose a valuation challenge. In our projections in Table 8-2, we implicitly assumed that cash beyond the level required to finance a company's operations will be paid out to the firm's shareholders. Excess cash flows are assumed to be paid out to shareholders either in the form of dividends or stock repurchases. Notice that these cash flows are already incorporated into the valuation process when they are earned, so there is no need to take them into account when they are paid out.

It is important to recognize that both the accounting-based valuation and the discounted cash flow valuation assume a dividend payout that can potentially vary from period to period. This dividend policy assumption is required as long as one wishes to assume a constant level of financial leverage, a constant cost of equity, and a constant level of weighted average cost of capital used in the valuation calculations. As discussed in a later chapter, firms rarely have such a variable dividend policy in practice. However, this in itself does not make the valuation approaches invalid, as long as a firm's dividend policy does not affect its value. That is, the valuation approaches assume that the well known Modigliani-Miller theorem regarding the irrelevance of dividends holds.

A firm's dividend policy can affect its value if managers do not invest free cash flows optimally. For example, if a firm's managers are likely to use excess cash to undertake value-destroying acquisitions, then our approach overestimates the firm's value. If the analyst has these types of concerns about a firm, one approach is to first estimate the firm according to the approach described earlier and then adjust the estimated value for whatever agency costs the firm's managers may impose on its investors. One approach to evaluating whether or not a firm suffers from severe agency costs is to examine how effective its corporate governance processes are.

SUMMARY

We illustrate in this chapter how to apply the valuation theory discussed in Chapter 7. The chapter explains the set of business and financial assumptions one needs to make to conduct the valuation exercise. It also illustrates the mechanics of making detailed valuation forecasts and terminal values of earnings, free cash flows, and accounting rates of return. We also discuss how to compute cost of equity and the weighted average cost of capital. Using a detailed example, we show how a firm's equity values and asset values can be computed using earnings, cash flows, and rates of return. Finally, we offer ways to deal with some commonly encountered practical issues, including accounting distortions, negative book values, and excess cash balances.

DISCUSSION QUESTIONS

1. How will the forecasts in Table 8-3 for TJX change if the assumed growth rate in sales from 2002 to 2011 remains at 12 percent (and all the other assumptions are kept unchanged)?

2. Recalculate the forecasts in Table 8-3 assuming that the NOPAT profit margin declines by 0.1 percentage points per year between fiscal 2002 and 2011 (keeping all the other assumptions unchanged).

3. Recalculate the forecasts in Table 8-4 assuming that the ratio of net operating working capital to sales is 3 percent, and the ratio of net long-term assets to sales is 15 percent for all the years from fiscal 2003 to fiscal 2011. Keep all the other assumptions unchanged.

4. Calculate TJX's cash payouts to its shareholders in the years 2002–2011 that are implicitly assumed in the projections in Table 8-3.

5. How will the abnormal earnings calculations in Table 8-4 change if the cost of equity assumption is changed to 15 percent?

6. How will the terminal values in Table 8-5 change if the sales growth in years 2012 and beyond is 12 percent, and the company keeps forever its abnormal returns at the same level as in fiscal 2011 (keeping all the other assumptions in the table unchanged)?

7. Calculate the proportion of terminal values to total estimated values of equity under the abnormal earnings method and the discounted cash flow method. Why are these proportions different?

8. What will be TJX's cost of equity if the equity market risk premium is 5 percent?

9. Assume that TJX changes its capital structure so that its market value weight of debt to capital increases to 30 percent, and its after-tax interest rate on debt at this new leverage level is 8 percent. Assume that the equity market risk premium is 7 percent. What will be the cost of equity at the new debt level? What will be the weighted average cost of capital?

10. Nancy Smith says she is uncomfortable making the assumption that TJX's dividend payout will vary from year to year. If she makes a constant dividend payout assumption, what changes does she have to make in her other valuation assumptions to make them internally consistent with each other?

NOTES

1. See T. Copeland, T. Koller, and J. Murrin, *Valuation: Measuring and Managing the Value of Companies*, 2nd edition (New York: John Wiley & Sons, 1994). Theory calls for the use of a short-term rate, but if that rate is used here, a difficult practical question rises: how does one reflect the premium required for expected inflation over long horizons? While the premium could, in principle, be treated as a portion of the term $[E(r_m) - r_f]$, it is probably easier to use an intermediate- or long-term riskless rate that presumably reflects expected inflation.

2. The average return reported here is the arithmetic mean as opposed to the geometric mean. Ibbotson and Associates explain why this estimate is appropriate in this context (see *Stocks, Bonds, Bills, and Inflation*, 2002 Yearbook, Chicago).

3. One way to estimate systematic risk is to regress the firm's stock returns over some recent time period against the returns on the market index. The slope coefficient represents an estimate of β. More fundamentally, systematic risk depends on how sensitive the firm's operating profits are to shifts in economy-wide activity, and the firm's degree of leverage. Financial analysis that assesses these operating and financial risks should be useful in arriving at reasonable estimates of β.

4. See "Toward an Implied Cost of Capital" by William R. Gebhardt, Charles M. C. Lee, and Bhaskaran Swaminathan, Cornell University, working paper, 1999; and "The Equity Premium Is Much Lower Than You Think It Is: Empirical Estimates from a New Approach" by James Claus and Jacob Thomas, Columbia University, working paper, 1999.

5. Valuation based on discounted abnormal earnings does require one property of the forecasts: that they be consistent with "clean surplus accounting." Such accounting requires the

following relation:

End-of-period book value =

Beginning book value + earnings − dividends ± capital contributions/withdrawals

Clean surplus accounting rules out situations where some gain or loss is excluded from earnings but is still used to adjust the book value of equity. For example, under U.S. GAAP, gains and losses on foreign currency translations are handled this way. In applying the valuation technique described here, the analyst would need to deviate from GAAP in producing forecasts and treat such gains/losses as a part of earnings. However, the technique does *not* require that clean surplus accounting has been applied *in the past*—so the existing book value, based on U.S. GAAP or any other set of principles, can still serve as the starting point. All the analyst needs to do is apply clean surplus accounting in his/her forecasts. That much is not only easy but is usually the natural thing to do anyway.

6. It is important to recognize that when the analyst uses the "indirect" cash flow forecasting method, undetected accounting biases can influence not only future earnings forecasts but also future free cash flow forecasts. In the current example, since accounts receivables are overstated, the analyst will assume that they will be collected as cash in some future period, leading to a higher future cash flow estimate.

PART 3

Business Analysis and Valuation Applications

Chapter 9
Equity Security Analysis
Chapter 10
Credit Analysis and Distress Prediction
Chapter 11
Mergers and Acquisitions
Chapter 12
Corporate Financing Policies
Chapter 13
Communication and Governance

Equity Security Analysis

Equity security analysis is the evaluation of a firm and its prospects from the perspective of a current or potential investor in the firm's stock. Security analysis is one step in a larger investment process that involves (1) establishing the objectives of the investor, (2) forming expectations about the future returns and risks of individual securities, and then (3) combining individual securities into portfolios to maximize progress toward the investment objectives.

Security analysis is the foundation for the second step, projecting future returns and assessing risk. Security analysis is typically conducted with an eye toward identification of mispriced securities in hopes of generating returns that more than compensate the investor for risk. However, that need not be the case. For analysts who do not have a comparative advantage in identifying mispriced securities, the focus should be on gaining an appreciation for how a security would affect the risk of a given portfolio, and whether it fits the profile that the portfolio is designed to maintain.

Security analysis is undertaken by individual investors, by analysts at brokerage houses (sell-side analysts), and by analysts that work at the direction of funds managers for various institutions (buy-side analysts). The institutions employing buy-side analysts include mutual funds, pension funds, insurance companies, universities, and others.

A variety of questions are dealt with in security analysis:

- A sell-side analyst asks: How do my forecasts compare to those of the analysts' consensus? Is the observed market price consistent with that consensus? Given my expectations for the firm, does this stock appear to be mispriced? Should I recommend this stock as a buy, a sell, or a hold?
- A buy-side analyst for a "value stock fund" asks: Does this stock possess the characteristics we seek in our fund? That is, does it have a relatively low ratio of price to earnings, low price-to-book value, and other fundamental indicators? Do its prospects for earnings improvement suggest good potential for high future returns on the stock?
- An individual investor asks: Does this stock offer the risk profile that suits my investment objectives? Does it enhance my ability to diversify the risk of my portfolio? Is the firm's dividend payout rate low enough to help shield me from taxes while I continue to hold the stock?

As the above questions underscore, there is more to security analysis than estimating the value of stocks. Nevertheless, for most sell-side and buy-side analysts, the key goal remains the identification of mispriced stocks.

INVESTOR OBJECTIVES

The investment objectives of individual savers in the economy are highly idiosyncratic. For any given saver they depend on such factors as income, age, wealth, tolerance for risk, and tax status. For example, savers with many years until retirement are likely to prefer to have a relatively large share of their portfolio invested in equities, which offer a higher expected return but high short-term variability. Investors in high tax brackets are likely to prefer to have a large share of their portfolio in stocks that generate tax-deferred capital gains rather than stocks that pay dividends or interest-bearing securities.

Mutual funds (or unit trusts as they are termed in some countries) have become popular investment vehicles for savers to achieve their investment objectives. Mutual funds sell shares in professionally managed portfolios that invest in specific types of stocks and/or fixed income securities. They therefore provide a low-cost way for savers to invest in a portfolio of securities that reflects their particular appetite for risk.

The major classes of mutual funds include (1) money market funds that invest in CDs and treasury bills, (2) bond funds that invest in debt instruments, (3) equity funds that invest in equity securities, (4) balanced funds that hold money market, bond, and equity securities, and (5) real estate funds that invest in commercial real estate. Within the bond and equities classes of funds, however, there are wide ranges of fund types. For example, bond funds include:

- *Corporate bond funds* that invest in investment-grade rated corporate debt instruments
- *High yield funds* that invest in non-investment-grade rated corporate debt
- *Mortgage funds* that invest in mortgage-backed securities
- *Municipal funds* that invest in municipal debt instruments and which generate income that can be nontaxable

Equity funds include:

- *Income funds* that invest in stocks that are expected to generate dividend income
- *Growth funds* that invest in stocks expected to generate long-term capital gains
- *Income and growth funds* that invest in stocks that provide a balance of dividend income and capital gains
- *Value funds* that invest in equities that are considered to be undervalued
- *Short funds* that sell short equity securities that are considered to be overvalued
- *Index funds* that invest in stocks that track a particular market index, such as the S&P 500
- *Sector funds* that invest in stocks in a particular industry segment, such as the technology or health sciences sectors
- *Regional funds* that invest in equities from a particular country or geographic region, such as Japan, Europe, or the Asia-Pacific region

The focus of this chapter is on analysis for equity securities.

EQUITY SECURITY ANALYSIS AND MARKET EFFICIENCY

How a security analyst should invest his or her time depends on how quickly and efficiently information flows through markets and becomes reflected in security prices. In the extreme, information would be reflected in security prices fully and immediately upon its release. This is essentially the condition posited by the *efficient markets hypothesis*. This hypothesis states that security prices reflect all available information, as if such information could be costlessly digested and translated immediately into demands for buys or sells without regard to frictions imposed by transactions costs. Under such conditions, it would be impossible to identify mispriced securities on the basis of public information.

In a world of efficient markets, the expected return on any equity security is just enough to compensate investors for the unavoidable risk the security involves. Unavoidable risk is that which cannot be "diversified away" simply by holding a portfolio of many securities. Given efficient markets, the investor's strategy shifts away from the search for mispriced securities and focuses instead on maintaining a well diversified portfolio. Aside from this, the investor must arrive at the desired balance between risky securities and short-term government bonds. The desired balance depends on how much risk the investor is willing to bear for a given increase in expected returns.

The above discussion implies that investors who accept that stock prices already reflect available information have no need for analysis involving a search for mispriced securities. If all investors adopted this attitude, of course no such analysis would be conducted, mispricing would go uncorrected, and markets would no longer be efficient![1] This is why the efficient markets hypothesis cannot represent an equilibrium in a strict sense. In equilibrium there must be just enough mispricing to provide incentives for the investment of resources in security analysis.

The existence of some mispricing, even in equilibrium, does not imply that it is sensible for just anyone to engage in security analysis. Instead, it suggests that securities analysis is subject to the same laws of supply and demand faced in all other competitive industries: it will be rewarding only for those with the strongest comparative advantage. How many analysts are in that category depends on a number of factors, including the liquidity of a firm's stock and investor interest in the company.[2] For example, there are about 40 sell-side professional analysts who follow IBM, a company with a highly liquid stock and considerable investor interest. There are many other buy-side analysts who track the firm on their own account without issuing any formal reports to outsiders. For the smallest publicly traded firms in the U.S., there is typically no formal following by analysts, and would-be investors and their advisors are left to themselves to conduct securities analysis.

Market Efficiency and the Role of Financial Statement Analysis

The degree of market efficiency that arises from competition among analysts and other market agents is an empirical issue addressed by a large body of research spanning the last three decades. Such research has important implications for the role of financial statements in security analysis. Consider for example the implications of an extremely efficient market, where information is fully impounded in prices within minutes of its revelation. In such a market, agents could profit from digesting financial statement information in two ways. First, the information would be useful to the select few who receive newly announced financial data, interpret it quickly, and trade on it within minutes. Second, and probably more important, the information would be useful for gaining an understanding of the firm, so as to place the analyst in a better position to interpret other news (from financial statements as well as other sources) as it arrives.

On the other hand, if securities prices fail to reflect financial statement data fully, even days or months after its public revelation, there is a third way in which market agents could profit from such data. That is to create trading strategies designed to exploit any systematic ways in which the publicly available data are ignored or discounted in the price-setting process.

Market Efficiency and Managers' Financial Reporting Strategies

The degree to which markets are efficient also has implications for managers' approaches to communicating with their investment communities. The issue becomes most important when the firm pursues an unusual strategy, or when the usual interpretation of financial statements would be misleading in the firm's context. In such a case, the communication avenues managers can successfully pursue depend not only on management's credibility, but also on the degree of understanding present in the investment community. We will return to the issue of management communications in more detail in Chapter 13.

Evidence of Market Efficiency

There is an abundance of evidence consistent with a high degree of efficiency in the primary U.S. securities markets.[3] In fact, during the 1960s and 1970s, the evidence was so one-sided that the efficient markets hypothesis gained widespread acceptance within the academic community and had a major impact on the practicing community as well.

Evidence pointing to very efficient securities markets comes in several forms:

- When information is announced publicly, the markets react *very* quickly.
- It is difficult to identify specific funds or analysts who have consistently generated abnormally high returns.
- A number of studies suggest that stock prices reflect a rather sophisticated level of fundamental analysis.

While a large body of evidence consistent with efficiency exists, recent years have witnessed a re-examination of the once widely accepted thinking. A sampling of the research includes the following:

- On the issue of the speed of stock price response to news, a number of studies suggest that even though prices react quickly, the initial reaction tends to be incomplete.[4]
- A number of studies point to trading strategies that could have been used to outperform market averages.[5]
- Some related evidence—still subject to ongoing debate about its proper interpretation—suggests that, even though market prices reflect some relatively sophisticated analyses, prices still do not fully reflect all the information that could be garnered from publicly available financial statements.[6]

The controversy over the efficiency of securities markets is unlikely to end soon. However, there are some lessons that are accepted by most researchers. First, securities markets not only reflect publicly available information, they also anticipate much of it before it is released. The open question is what fraction of the response remains to be impounded in price once the day of the public release comes to a close. Second, even in most studies that suggest inefficiency, the degree of mispricing is relatively small for large stocks.

Finally, even if some of the evidence is currently difficult to align with the efficient markets hypothesis, it remains a useful benchmark (at a minimum) for thinking about the behavior of security prices. The hypothesis will continue to play that role unless it can be replaced by a more complete theory. Some researchers are developing theories that encompass the existence of market agents who are forced to trade for unpredictable "liquidity" reasons, and prices that differ from so-called "fundamental values," even in equilibrium. Also, behavioral finance models recognize that cognitive biases can affect investor behavior.[7]

APPROACHES TO FUND MANAGEMENT AND SECURITIES ANALYSIS

Approaches used in practice to manage funds and analyze securities are quite varied. One dimension of variation is the extent to which the investments are actively or passively managed. Another variation is whether a quantitative or a traditional fundamental approach is used. Security analysts also vary considerably in terms of whether they produce formal or informal valuations of the firm.

Active Versus Passive Management

Active portfolio management relies heavily on security analysis to identify mispriced securities. The passive portfolio manager serves as a price taker, avoiding the costs of security analysis and turnover while typically seeking to hold a portfolio designed to match some overall market index or sector performance. Combined approaches are also possible. For example, one may actively manage 20 percent of a fund balance while passively managing the remainder. The widespread growth of passively managed funds in the U.S. over the past twenty years serves as testimony to many fund managers' belief that earning superior returns is a difficult thing to do.

Quantitative Versus Traditional Fundamental Analysis

Actively managed funds must depend on some form of security analysis. Some funds employ "technical analysis," which attempts to predict stock price movements on the basis of market indicators (prior stock price movements, volume, etc.). In contrast, "fundamental analysis," the primary approach to security analysis, attempts to evaluate the current market price relative to projections of the firm's future earnings and cash-flow generating potential. Fundamental analysis involves all the steps described in the previous chapters of this book: business strategy analysis, accounting analysis, financial analysis, and prospective analysis (forecasting and valuation).

In recent years, some analysts have supplemented traditional fundamental analysis, which involves a substantial amount of subjective judgment, with more quantitative approaches. The quantitative approaches themselves are quite varied. Some involve simply "screening" stocks on the basis of some set of factors, such as trends in analysts' earnings revisions, price-earnings ratios, price-book ratios, and so on. Whether such approaches are useful depends on the degree of market efficiency relative to the screens.

Quantitative approaches can also involve implementation of some formal model to predict future stock returns. Longstanding statistical techniques such as regression analysis and probit analysis can be used, as can more recently developed, computer-intensive techniques such as neural network analysis. Again, the success of these approaches depends on the degree of market efficiency and whether the analysis can exploit information in ways not otherwise available to market agents as a group.

Quantitative approaches play a more important role in security analysis today than they did a decade or two ago. However, by and large, analysts still rely primarily on the kind of fundamental analysis involving complex human judgments, as outlined in our earlier chapters.

Formal Versus Informal Valuation

Full-scale, formal valuations based on the methods described in Chapter 7 have become more common, especially in recent years. However, less formal approaches are also possible. For example, an analyst can compare his or her long-term earnings projection with the consensus forecast to generate a buy or sell recommendation. Alternatively, an analyst might recommend a stock because his or her earnings forecast appears relatively high in comparison to the current price. Another possible approach might be labeled "marginalist." This approach involves no attempt to value the firm. The analyst simply assumes that if he or she has unearthed favorable (or unfavorable) information believed not to be recognized by others, the stock should be bought (or sold).

Unlike many security analysts, investment bankers produce formal valuations as a matter of course. Investment bankers, who estimate values for purposes of bringing a private firm to the public market, for evaluating a merger or buyout proposal, or for purposes of periodic managerial review, must document their valuation in a way that can readily be communicated to management and, if necessary, to the courts.

THE PROCESS OF A COMPREHENSIVE SECURITY ANALYSIS

Given the variety of approaches practiced in security analysis, it is impossible to summarize all of them here. Instead, we briefly outline steps to be included in a comprehensive security analysis. The amount of attention focused on any given step varies among analysts.

Selection of Candidates for Analysis

No analyst can effectively investigate more than a small fraction of the securities on a major exchange, and thus some approach to narrowing the focus must be employed. Sell-side analysts are often organized within an investment house by industry or sector. Thus they tend to be constrained in their choices of firms to follow. However, from the perspective of a fund manager or an investment firm as a whole, there is usually the freedom to focus on any firm or sector.

As noted earlier, funds typically specialize in investing in stocks with certain risk profiles or characteristics (e.g., growth stocks, "value" stocks, technology stocks, cyclical stocks). Managers of these types of funds seek to focus the energies of their analysts on identifying stocks that fit their fund objective In addition, individual investors who seek to maintain a well diversified portfolio without holding many stocks also need information about the nature of a firm's risks.

An alternative approach to stock selection is to screen firms on the basis of some hypothesis about mispricing—perhaps with follow-up detailed analysis of stocks that meet the specified criteria. For example, one fund managed by a large U.S. insurance company screens stocks on the basis of recent "earnings momentum," as reflected in revisions in the earnings projections of sell-side and buy-side analysts. Upward revisions trigger investigations for possible purchase. The fund operates on the belief that earnings momentum is a positive signal of future price movements. Another fund complements the earnings momentum screen with one based on recent short-term stock price movements, in the hopes of identifying earnings revisions not yet reflected in stock prices.

Key Analysis Questions

Depending on whether fund managers follow a strategy of targeting stocks with specific types of characteristics, or of screening stocks that appear to be mispriced, the following types of questions are likely to be useful:

- What is the risk profile of a firm? How volatile is its earnings stream and stock price? What are the key possible bad outcomes in the future? What is the upside potential? How closely linked are the firm's risks to the health of the overall economy? Are the risks largely diversifiable, or are they systematic?

- Does the firm possess the characteristics of a growth stock? What is the expected pattern of sales and earnings growth for the coming years? Is the firm reinvesting most or all of its earnings?
- Does the firm match the characteristics desired by "income funds"? Is it a mature or maturing company, prepared to "harvest" profits and distribute them in the form of high dividends?
- Is the firm a candidate for a "value fund"? Does it offer measures of earnings, cash flow, and book value that are high relative to the price? What specific screening rules can be implemented to identify misvalued stocks?

Inferring Market Expectations

If the security analysis is conducted with an eye toward the identification of mispricing, it must ultimately involve a comparison of the analyst's expectations with those of "the market." One possibility is to view the observed stock price as the reflection of market expectations and to compare the analyst's own estimate of value with that price. However, a stock price is only a "summary statistic." It is useful to have a more detailed idea of the market's expectations about a firm's future performance, expressed in terms of sales, earnings, and other measures. For example, assume that an analyst has developed new insights about a firm's near-term sales. Whether those insights represent new information for the stock market, and whether they indicate that a "buy" recommendation is appropriate, can be easily determined if the analyst knows the market consensus sales forecast.

Around the world a number of agencies summarize analysts' forecasts of sales and earnings. Forecasts for the next year or two are commonly available, and for many firms, a "long-run" earnings growth projection is also available—typically for three to five years. Some agencies in the U.S provide continuous on-line updates to such data, so if an analyst revises a forecast, that can be made known to fund managers and other analysts within seconds.

As useful as analysts' forecasts of sales and earnings are, they do not represent a complete description of expectations about future performance, and there is no guarantee that consensus analyst forecasts are the same as those reflected in market prices. Further, financial analysts typically forecast performance for only a few years, so that even if these do reflect market expectations, it is helpful to understand what types of long-term forecasts are reflected in stock prices. Armed with the model in Chapters 7 and 8 that expresses price as a function of future cash flows or earnings, an analyst can draw some educated inferences about the expectations embedded in stock prices.

For example, consider the valuation of IBM. On March 19, 2003, IBM's stock price was $81.50. For the year ended December 31, 2002, the company reported that earnings per share declined from $4.58 the prior year to $2.10, reflecting losses on discontinued operations and an economic downturn that hit the IT sector particularly severely. By mid-March analysts were forecasting that IBM would show a turnaround in 2003, with earnings projected to grow by 105 percent to $4.31. More modest growth was projected for following years: 14 percent in 2004 ($4.92) and 9.7 percent per year for 2004 to 2007.[8]

How do consensus forecasts by analysts reconcile with the market valuation of IBM? What are the market's implicit assumptions about the short-term and long-term earnings growth for the company? By altering the amounts for key value drivers and arriving at combinations that generate an estimated value equal to the observed market price, the analyst can infer what the market might have been expecting for IBM in mid-March 2003. Table 9-1 summarizes the combinations of earnings growth, book value growth, and cost of capital that generate prices comparable to the market price of $81.50.

IBM has an equity beta of 1.5. Given long-term government bond rates of 5 percent and a market risk premium of 3–4 percent, IBM's cost of equity capital probably lies between 10 and 11 percent. In addition, the company's growth in book value has been stable at 4 percent for the last three years, which is close to the historical long-term book value growth rate for the economy. Critical questions for judging the market valuation of IBM are (1) how quickly will the company's earnings return to the level reported in 2002, and (2) how quickly will earnings growth revert to the same level as average firms in the economy, historically around 4 percent. The analysis reported in Table 9-1 assumes that IBM's superior earnings growth persists for five years, through 2007, and then reverts to the economy average.

Table 9-1 Alternative Assumptions About Value Drivers for IBM Consistent with Observed Market Price of $81.50

Assumed equity cost of capital of 10%:	2003	2004	2005	2006	2007	Implied earnings per share in 2007
Earnings growth: Scenario 1	100%	12%	12%	12%	12%	$6.48
Scenario 2	50%	21.5%	21.5%	21.5%	21.5%	$6.73
Scenario 3	25%	28%	28%	28%	28%	$6.91
Assumed equity cost of capital of 11%:						
Earnings growth: Scenario 1	100%	17%	17%	17%	17%	$7.72
Scenario 2	50%	27%	27%	27%	27%	$8.04
Scenario 3	25%	33.5%	33.5%	33.5%	33.5%	$8.18

Table 9-1 shows the implications for IBM's earnings growth if the economic turnaround is slower than analysts anticipate. This analysis indicates that with a 10 percent cost of equity and a rapid return to pre-2002 performance (i.e., 100 percent growth in 2003), earnings need to grow by 12 percent per year between 2004 and 2007 to justify the $81.50 stock price. However, if 2003 growth is 50 percent, earnings have to increase by 21.5 percent per year for the next four years, and if 2003 growth is only 25 percent (due to, say, a longer downturn in the IT sector than expected), earnings growth from 2004 to 2007 will have to be 28 percent per year. The impact of a slow turnaround in 2003 is even more pronounced if IBM's cost of equity is 11 percent. In this case earnings growth from 2004 to 2007 needs to be 27 percent per year if there is a 50 percent recovery in 2003, and 33.5 percent per year if the recovery is only 25 percent. This type of scenario analysis provides the analyst with insights about investors' expectations for IBM, and is useful for judging whether the stock is correctly valued.

Security analysis need not involve such a detailed attempt to infer market expectations. However, whether the analysis is made explicit or not, a good analyst understands what economic scenarios could plausibly be reflected in the observed price.

Key Analysis Questions

By using the discounted abnormal earnings/ROE valuation model, analysts can infer the market's expectations for a firm's future performance. This permits analysts to ask whether the market is over- or undervaluing a company. Typical questions that analysts might ask from this analysis include the following:

- What are the market's assumptions about long-term ROE and growth? For example, is the market forecasting that the company can grow its earnings without a corresponding level of expansion in its asset base (and hence equity)? If so, how long can this persist?
- How do changes in the cost of capital affect the market's assessment of the firm's future performance? If the market's expectations seem to be unexpectedly high or low, has the market reassessed the company's risk? If so, is this change plausible?

Developing the Analyst's Expectations

Ultimately, a security analyst must compare his or her own view of a stock with the view embedded in the market price. The analyst's own view is generated using the same tools discussed in Chapters 2 through 8: business strategy analysis, accounting analysis, financial analysis, and prospective analysis. The final product of this work is, of course, a forecast of the firm's future earnings and cash flows and an estimate of the firm's value. However, that final product is less important than the understanding of the business and its industry that the analysis provides. It is such understanding that enables the analyst to interpret new information as it arrives and to infer its implications.

Key Analysis Questions

In developing expectations about the firm's future performance using the financial analysis tools discussed throughout this book, the analyst is likely to ask the following types of questions:

- How profitable is the firm? In light of industry conditions, the firm's corporate strategy, and its barriers to competition, how sustainable is that rate of profitability?
- What are the opportunities for growth for this firm?
- How risky is this firm? How vulnerable are operations to general economic downturns? How highly levered is the firm? What does the riskiness of the firm imply about its cost of capital?
- How do answers to the above questions compare to the expectations embedded in the observed stock price?

The Final Product of Security Analysis

For financial analysts, the final product of security analysis is a recommendation to buy, sell, or hold the stock (or some more refined ranking). The recommendation is supported by a set of forecasts and a report summarizing the foundation for the recommendation.

Analysts' reports often delve into significant detail and include an assessment of a firm's business as well as a line-by-line income statement, balance sheet, and cash flow forecasts for one or more years.

In making a recommendation to buy or sell a stock, the analyst has to consider the investment time horizon required to capitalize on the recommendation. Are anticipated improvements in performance likely to be confirmed in the near-term, allowing investors to capitalize quickly on the recommendation? Or do expected performance improvements reflect long-term fundamentals that will take several years to play out? Longer investment horizons impose greater risk on investors that the company's performance will be affected by changes in economic conditions that cannot be anticipated by the analyst, reducing the value of the recommendation. Consequently, thorough analysis requires not merely being able to recognize whether a stock is misvalued, but being able to anticipate when a price correction is likely to take place.

Because there are additional investment risks from following recommendations that require long-term commitments, security analysts tend to focus on making recommendations that are likely to pay off in the short-term. This potentially explains why so few analysts recommended selling dot-com and technology stocks during the late 1990s when their prices would be difficult to justify on the basis of long-term fundamentals. It also explains why analysts recommended Enron's stock at its peak, even though the kind of analysis performed in this chapter would have shown that the future growth and ROE performance implied by this price would be extremely difficult to achieve. It also implies that to take advantage of long-term fundamental analysis can often require access to patient, long-term capital.

PERFORMANCE OF SECURITY ANALYSTS AND FUND MANAGERS

There has been extensive research on the performance of security analysts and fund managers during the last two decades. We summarize a few of the key findings.

Performance of Security Analysts

Despite the recent failure of security analysts to foresee the dramatic price declines for dot-com and telecommunications stocks, and to detect the financial shenanigans and overvaluation of companies such as Enron and Worldcom, research shows that analysts generally add value in the capital market. Analyst earnings forecasts are more accurate than those produced by time series models that use past earnings to predict future earnings.[9] Of course this should not be too surprising since analysts can update their earnings forecasts between quarters to incorporate new firm and economy information, whereas time-series models cannot. In addition, stock prices tend to respond positively to upward revisions in analysts' earnings forecasts and recommendations, and negatively to downward revisions.[10] Finally, recent research finds that analysts play a valuable role in improving market efficiency. For example, stock prices for firms with higher analyst following more rapidly incorporate information on accruals and cash flows than prices of less followed firms.[11]

Several factors seem to be important in explaining analysts' earnings forecast accuracy. Not surprisingly, forecasts of near-term earnings are much more accurate than those of long-term performance.[12] This probably explains why analysts typically make detailed forecasts for only one or two years ahead. Studies of differences in earnings forecast accuracy across analysts find that analysts that are more accurate tend to specialize by industry and work for large well-funded firms that employ other analysts who follow the same industry.[13]

Although analysts perform a valuable function in the capital market, research shows that their forecasts and recommendations tend to be biased. Early evidence on bias indicated that analyst earnings forecasts tended to be optimistic and that their recommendations were almost exclusively for buys.[14] Several factors potentially explain this finding. First, security analysts at brokerage houses are typically compensated on the basis of the trading volume that their reports generate. Given the costs of short selling and the restrictions on short selling by many institutions, brokerage analysts have incentives to issue optimistic reports that encourage investors to buy stocks rather than to issue negative reports that create selling pressure. Second, analysts that work for investment banks are rewarded for promoting public issues by current clients and for attracting new banking clients, creating incentives for optimistic forecasts and recommendations. Studies show that analysts that work for lead underwriters make more optimistic long-term earnings forecasts and recommendations for firms raising equity capital than unaffiliated analysts.[15]

More recent evidence indicates that during the late 1990s there was a marked decline in analyst optimism for forecasts of near-term earnings.[16] One explanation offered for this change is that during the late 1990s analysts relied heavily on private discussions with top management to make their earnings forecasts. Management allegedly used these personal connections to manage analysts' short-term expectations downward so that the firm could subsequently report earnings that beat analysts' expectations. In response to concerns about this practice, in October 2000 the SEC approved Regulation Fair Disclosure, which prohibits management from making selective disclosures of non-public information.

Performance of Fund Managers

Measuring whether mutual and pension fund managers earn superior returns is a difficult task for several reasons. First, there is no agreement about how to estimate benchmark performance for a fund. Studies have used a number of approaches—some have used the Capital Asset Pricing Model (CAPM) as a benchmark, others have used multi-factor pricing models. For studies using the CAPM, there are questions about what type of market index to use. For example, should it be an equal- or value weighted index, a NYSE index or a broader market index? Second, many of the traditional measures of fund performance abstract from market-wide performance, which understates fund abnormal performance if fund managers can time the market by reducing portfolio risk prior to market declines and increasing risks before a market run-up. Third, given the overall volatility of stock returns, statistical power is an issue for measuring fund performance. Finally, tests of fund performance are likely to be highly sensitive to the time period examined. Value or momentum investing could therefore appear to be profitable depending on when the tests are conducted.

Perhaps because of these challenges, there is no consistent evidence that actively managed mutual funds generate superior returns for investors. While some studies find evidence of positive abnormal returns for the industry, others conclude that returns are generally negative.[17] Of course even if mutual fund managers on average can only generate "normal" returns for investors, it is still possible for the best managers to show consistently strong performance. Some studies do in fact document that funds earning positive abnormal returns in one period continue to outperform in subsequent periods. However, more recent evidence suggests that these findings are caused by general momentum in stock returns and fund expenses rather than superior fund manager ability.[18] Researchers have also examined which, if any, investment strategies are most successful. However, no clear consensus appears—several studies have found that momentum and high turnover strategies generate superior returns, whereas others conclude that value strategies are better.[19]

Finally, recent research has examined whether fund managers tend to buy and sell many of the same stocks at the same time. They conclude that there is evidence of "herding" behavior, particularly by momentum fund managers.[20] This could arise because managers have access to common information, because they are affected by similar cognitive biases, or because they have incentives to follow the crowd.[21] For example, consider the calculus of a fund manager who holds a stock but who, through long-term fundamental analysis, estimates that it is misvalued. If the manager changes the fund's holdings accordingly and the stock price returns to its intrinsic value in the next quarter, the fund will show superior relative portfolio performance and will attract new capital. However, if the stock continues to be misvalued for several quarters, the informed fund manager will underperform the benchmark and capital will flow to other funds. In contrast, a risk-averse manager who simply follows the crowd will not be rewarded for detecting the misvaluation, but neither will this manager be blamed for a poor investment decision when the stock price ultimately corrects, since other funds made the same mistake.

There has been considerably less research on the performance of pension fund managers. Overall, the findings show little consistent evidence that pension fund managers either over- or under-perform traditional benchmarks.[22]

SUMMARY

Equity security analysis is the evaluation of a firm and its prospects from the perspective of a current or potential investor in the firm's stock. Security analysis is one component of a larger investment process that involves (1) establishing the objectives of the investor or fund, (2) forming expectations about the future returns and risks of individual securities, and then (3) combining individual securities into portfolios to maximize progress toward the investment objectives.

Some security analysis is devoted primarily to assuring that a stock possesses the proper risk profile and other desired characteristics prior to inclusion in an investor's portfolio. However, especially for many professional buy-side and sell-side security analysts, the analysis is also directed toward the identification of mispriced securities. In equilibrium, such activity will be rewarding for those with the strongest comparative advantage. They will be the ones able to identify any mispricing at the lowest cost and exert pressure on the price to correct the mispricing. What kinds of efforts are productive in this domain depends on the degree of market efficiency. A large body of evidence exists that is supportive of a high degree of efficiency in the U.S. market, but recent evidence has reopened the debate on this issue.

In practice, a wide variety of approaches to fund management and security analysis are employed. However, at the core of the analyses are the same steps outlined in Chapters 2 through 8 of this book: business strategy analysis, accounting analysis, financial analysis, and prospective analysis (forecasting and valuation). For the professional analyst, the final product of the work is, of course, a forecast of the firm's future earnings and cash flows, and an estimate of the firm's value. But that final product is less important than the understanding of the business and its industry, which the analysis provides. It is such understanding that positions the analyst to interpret new information as it arrives and infer its implications.

DISCUSSION QUESTIONS

1. Despite many years of research, the evidence on market efficiency described in this chapter appears to be inconclusive. Some argue that this is because researchers have been unable to link company fundamentals to stock prices precisely. Comment.

2. Geoffrey Henley, a professor of finance, states: "The capital market is efficient. I don't know why anyone would bother devoting their time to following individual stocks and doing fundamental analysis. The best approach is to buy and hold a well-diversified portfolio of stocks." Do you agree? Why or why not?

3. What is the difference between fundamental and technical analysis? Can you think of any trading strategies that use technical analysis? What are the underlying assumptions made by these strategies?

4. Investment funds follow many different types of investment strategies. Income funds focus on stocks with high dividend yields, growth funds invest in stocks that are expected to have high capital appreciation, value funds follow stocks that are considered to be undervalued, and short funds bet against stocks they consider to be overvalued. What types of investors are likely to be attracted to each of these types of funds? Why?

5. Intergalactic Software Company went public three months ago. You are a sophisticated investor who devotes time to fundamental analysis as a way of identifying mispriced stocks. Which of the following characteristics would you focus on in deciding whether to follow this stock?
   - The market capitalization
   - The average number of shares traded per day
   - The bid–ask spread for the stock
   - Whether the underwriter that brought the firm public is a Top Five investment banking firm
   - Whether its audit company is a Big Four firm
   - Whether there are analysts from major brokerage firms following the company
   - Whether the stock is held mostly by retail or institutional investors

6. There are two major types of financial analysts: buy-side and sell-side. Buy-side analysts work for investment firms and make stock recommendations that are available only to the management of funds within that firm. Sell-side analysts work for brokerage firms and make recommendations that are used to sell stock to the brokerage firms' clients, which include individual investors and managers of investment funds. What would be the differences in tasks and motivations of these two types of analysts?

7. Many market participants believe that sell-side analysts are too optimistic in their recommendations to buy stocks and too slow to recommend sells. What factors might explain this bias?

8. Joe Klein is an analyst for an investment banking firm that offers both underwriting and brokerage services. Joe sends you a highly favorable report on a stock that his firm recently helped go public and for which it currently makes the market. What are the potential advantages and disadvantages in relying on Joe's report in deciding whether to buy the stock?

9. Intergalactic Software Company's stock has a market price of $20 per share and a book value of $12 per share. If its cost of equity capital is 15 percent and its book value is expected to grow at 5 percent per year indefinitely, what is the market's assessment of

its steady state return on equity? If the stock price increases to $35 and the market does not expect the firm's growth rate to change, what is the revised steady state ROE? If instead the price increase was due to an increase in the market's assessments about long-term book value growth rather than long-term ROE, what would the price revision imply for the steady state growth rate?

10. Joe states, "I can see how ratio analysis and valuation help me do fundamental analysis, but I don't see the value of doing strategy analysis." Can you explain to him how strategy analysis could be potentially useful?

NOTES

1. P. Healy and K. Palepu, "The Fall of Enron," *Journal of Economic Perspectives* 17, no. 2 (Spring 2003): 3–26, discuss how weak money manager incentives and long-term analysis contributed to the stock price run-up and subsequent collapse for Enron. A similar discussion on factors affecting the rise and fall of dot-com stocks is provided in "The Role of Capital Market Intermediaries in the Dot-Com Crash of 2000," Harvard Business School Case 9-101-110, 2001.

2. See R. Bhushan, "Firm characteristics and analyst following," *Journal of Accounting and Economics* 11 (2/5), July 1989: 255–75, and P. O'Brien and R. Bhushan, "Analyst following and institutional ownership," *Journal of Accounting Research* 28, Supplement (1990): 55–76.

3. Recent reviews of evidence on market efficiency are provided by E. Fama, "Efficient Capital Markets: II," *Journal of Finance* 46 (December 1991): 1575–1617; S. Kothari, "Capital Markets Research in Accounting," *Journal of Accounting and Economics* 31 (September 2001):105–231; and C. Lee, "Market Efficiency in Accounting Research," *Journal of Accounting and Economics* 31 (September 2001): 233–53.

4. For example, see V. Bernard and J. Thomas, "Evidence That Stock Prices Do Not Fully Reflect the Implications of Current Earnings for Future Earnings," *Journal of Accounting and Economics* 13 (December 1990): 305–41.

5. Examples of studies that examine a "value stock" strategy include J. Lakonishok, A. Shleifer, and R. Vishny, "Contrarian Investment, Extrapolation, and Risk," *Journal of Finance* 49 (December 1994): 1541–78, and R. Frankel and C. Lee, "Accounting Valuation, Market Expectation, and Cross-Sectional Stock Returns," *Journal of Accounting & Economics* 25 (June 1998): 283–319.

6. For example, see J. Ou and S. Penman, "Financial Statement Analysis and the Prediction of Stock Returns," *Journal of Accounting and Economics* 11 (November 1989): 295–330; R. Holthausen and D. Larcker, "The Prediction of Stock Returns Using Financial Statement Information," *Journal of Accounting and Economics* 15 (June/September 1992): 373–412; and R. Sloan, "Do Stock Prices Fully Reflect Information in Accruals and Cash Flows about Future Earnings?" *The Accounting Review* 71 (July 1996): 298–325.

7. For an overview of research in behavioral finance, see R. Thaler, *Advances in Behavioral Finance* (New York: Russell Sage Foundation, 1993), and A. Shleifer, *Inefficient Markets: An Introduction to Behavioral Finance* (Oxford: Oxford University Press, 2000).

8. These forecasts were taken from multexinvestor.com.

9. Time series model forecasts of future annual earnings are the most recent annual earnings (with or without some form of annual growth), and forecasts of future quarterly earnings are a function of growth in earnings for the latest quarter relative to both the last quarter and the same quarter one year ago. See L. Brown and M. Rozeff "The Superiority of Analyst Forecasts as Measures of Expectations: Evidence from Earnings," *Journal of Finance* 33 (1978): 1–16; L. Brown, P. Griffin, R. Hagerman, and M. Zmijewski, "Security Analyst Superiority Relative to Univariate Time-Series Models in Forecasting Quarterly Earnings," *Journal of Accounting and Economics* 9 (1987): 61–87; and D. Givoly, "Financial Analysts' Forecasts of Earnings: A Better Surrogate for Market Expectations," *Journal of Accounting and Economics* 4, no. 2 (1982): 85–108.

10. See D. Givoly and J. Lakonishok, "The Information Content of Financial Analysts' Forecasts of Earnings: Some Evidence on Semi-Strong Efficiency," *Journal of Accounting and Economics* 2 (1979): 165–86; T. Lys and S. Sohn, "The Association Between Revisions of Financial Analysts' Earnings

Forecasts and Security Price Changes," *Journal of Accounting & Economics* 13 (1990): 341–64; and J. Francis and L. Soffer, "The Relative Informativeness of Analysts' Stock Recommendations and Earnings Forecast Revisions," *Journal of Accounting Research* 35, no. 2 (1997): 193–212.

11. See M. Barth and A. Hutton, "Information Intermediaries and the Pricing of Accruals," working paper, Stanford University, 2000.

12. See P. O'Brien, "Forecasts Accuracy of Individual Analysts in Nine Industries." *Journal of Accounting Research* 28 (1990): 286–304.

13. See M. Clement, "Analyst Forecast Accuracy: Do Ability, Resources, and Portfolio Complexity Matter?" *Journal of Accounting and Economics* 27 (1999): 285–304; J. Jacob, T. Lys, and M. Neale, "Experience in Forecasting Performance of Security Analysts." *Journal of Accounting and Economics* 28 (1999): 51–82; and S. Gilson, P. Healy, C. Noe, and K. Palepu, "Analyst Specialization and Conglomerate Stock Breakups," *Journal of Accounting Research* 39 (December 2001): 565–73.

14. See L. Brown, G. Foster, and E. Noreen, "Security Analyst Multi-Year Earnings Forecasts and the Capital Market," Studies in Accounting Research, No. 23, American Accounting Association (Sarasota, FL), 1985. M. McNichols and P. O'Brien, in "Self-Selection and Analyst Coverage," *Journal of Accounting Research,* Supplement (1997): 167–208, find that analyst bias arises primarily because analysts issue recommendations on firms for which they have favorable information and withhold recommending firms with unfavorable information.

15. See H. Lin and M. McNichols, "Underwriting Relationships, Analysts' Earnings Forecasts and Investment Recommendations," *Journal of Accounting and Economics* 25, no. 1 (1998): 101–28; R. Michaely and K. Womack, "Conflict of Interest and the Credibility of Underwriter Analyst Recommendations," *Review of Financial Studies* 12, no. 4 (1999): 653–86; and P. Dechow, A. Hutton, and R. Sloan, "The Relation Between Analysts' Forecasts of Long-Term Earnings Growth and Stock Price Performance Following Equity Offerings," *Contemporary Accounting Research* 17, no. 1 (2000):1–32.

16. See L. Brown, "Analyst Forecasting Errors: Additional Evidence," *Financial Analysts' Journal* (November/December 1997): 81–88, and D. Matsumoto, "Management's Incentives to Avoid Negative Earnings Surprises," *The Accounting Review* 77 (July 2002): 483–515.

17. For example, evidence of superior fund performance is reported by M. Grinblatt and S. Titman, "Mutual Fund Performance: An Analysis of Quarterly Holdings, *Journal of Business* 62 (1994), and by D. Hendricks, J. Patel, and R. Zeckhauser, "Hot Hands in Mutual Funds: Short-Run Persistence of Relative Performance," *The Journal of Finance* 48 (1993): 93–130. In contrast, negative fund performance is shown by M. Jensen, "The Performance of Mutual Funds in the Period 1945–64," *The Journal of Finance* 23 (May 1968): 389–416, and B. Malkiel, "Returns from Investing in Equity Mutual Funds from 1971 to 1991," *Journal of Finance* 50 (June 1995): 549–73.

18. M. Grinblatt and S. Titman, "The Persistence of Mutual Fund Performance," *Journal of Finance* 47 (December 1992): 1977–86, and D. Hendricks, J. Patel, and R. Zeckhauser, "Hot Hands in Mutual Funds: Short-Run Persistence of Relative Performance," *Journal of Finance* 48 (March 1993): 93–130, find evidence of persistence in mutual fund returns. However, M. Carhart, "On Persistence in Mutual Fund Performance," *The Journal of Finance* 52 (March 1997): 57–83, shows that much of this is attributable to momentum in stock returns and to fund expenses; B. Malkiel, "Returns from Investing in Equity Mutual Funds from 1971 to 1991," *The Journal of Finance* 50 (June 1995): 549–73, shows that survivorship bias is also an important consideration.

19. See M. Grinblatt, S. Titman, and R. Wermers, "Momentum Investment Strategies, Portfolio Performance, and Herding: A Study of Mutual Fund Behavior," *The American Economic Review* 85 (December 1995): 1088–1105.

20. For example, J. Lakonishok, A. Shleifer, and R. Vishny, "Contrarian Investment, Extrapolation, and Risk," *Journal of Finance* 49 (December 1994): 1541–79, find that value funds show superior performance, whereas M. Grinblatt, S. Titman, and R. Wermers, "Momentum Investment Strategies, Portfolio Performance, and Herding: A Study of Mutual Fund Behavior," *The American Economic Review* 85 (December 1995): 1088–1105, find that momentum investing is profitable.

21. See D. Scharfstein and J. Stein, "Herd Behavior and Investment," *The American Economic Review* 80 (June 1990): 465–80, and P. Healy and K. Palepu, "The Fall of Enron," *Journal of Economic Perspectives* 17, no. 2 (Spring 2003): 3–26.

22. For evidence on performance by pension fund managers, see J. Lakonishok, A. Shleifer, and R. Vishny, "The Structure and Performance of the Money Management Industry," Brookings Papers on Economic Activity, Washington, DC (1992): 339–92; T. Coggin, F. Fabozzi, and S. Rahman, "The Investment Performance of U.S. Equity Pension Fund Managers: An Empirical Investigation," *The Journal of Finance* 48 (July 1993): 1039–56; and W. Ferson and K. Khang, "Conditional Performance Measurement Using Portfolio Weights: Evidence for Pension Funds," *Journal of Financial Economics* 65 (August 2002): 249–282.

Credit Analysis and Distress Prediction

Credit analysis is the evaluation of a firm from the perspective of a holder or potential holder of its debt, including trade payables, loans, and public debt securities. A key element of credit analysis is the prediction of the likelihood a firm will face financial distress.

Credit analysis is involved in a wide variety of decision contexts:

- A potential supplier asks: Should I sell products or services to this firm? The associated credit will be extended only for a short period, but the amount is large and I should have some assurance that collection risks are manageable.
- A commercial banker asks: Should we extend a loan to this firm? If so, how should it be structured? How should it be priced?
- If the loan is granted, the banker must later ask: Are we still providing the services, including credit, that this firm needs? Is the firm still in compliance with the loan terms? If not, is there a need to restructure the loan, and if so, how? Is the situation serious enough to call for accelerating the repayment of the loan?
- A pension fund manager, insurance company, or other investor asks: Are these debt securities a sound investment? What is the probability that the firm will face distress and default on the debt? Does the yield provide adequate compensation for the default risk involved?
- An investor contemplating purchase of debt securities in default asks: How likely is it that this firm can be turned around? In light of the high yield on this debt relative to its current price, can I accept the risk that the debt will not be repaid in full?

Although credit analysis is typically viewed from the perspective of the financier, it is obviously important to the borrower as well:

- A manager of a small firm asks: What are our options for credit financing? Would the firm qualify for bank financing? If so, what type of financing would be possible? How costly would it be? Would the terms of the financing constrain our flexibility?
- A manager of a large firm asks: What are our options for credit financing? Is the firm strong enough to raise funds in the public market? If so, what is our debt rating likely to be? What required yield would that rating imply?

Finally, there are third parties—those other than borrowers and lenders—who are interested in the general issue of how likely it is that a firm will avoid financial distress:

- An auditor asks: How likely is it that this firm will survive beyond the short run? In evaluating the firm's financials, should I consider it a going concern?
- An actual or potential employee asks: How confident can I be that this firm will be able to offer employment over the long term?
- A potential customer asks: What assurance is there that this firm will survive to provide warranty services, replacement parts, product updates, and other services?
- A competitor asks: Will this firm survive the current industry shakeout? What are the implications of potential financial distress at this firm for my pricing and market share?

THE MARKET FOR CREDIT

An understanding of credit analysis requires an appreciation for the various players in the market for credit. We describe those players briefly here.

Suppliers of Credit

The major suppliers in the market for credit are described below.

Commercial Banks

Commercial banks are very important players in the market for credit. Since banks tend to provide a range of services to a client, and have intimate knowledge of the client and its operations, they have a comparative advantage in extending credit in settings where (1) knowledge gained through close contact with management reduces the perceived riskiness of the credit and (2) credit risk can be contained through careful monitoring of the firm.

A constraint on bank lending operations is that the credit risk be relatively low so that the bank's loan portfolio will be of acceptably high quality to bank regulators. Because of the importance of maintaining public confidence in the banking sector and the desire to shield government deposit insurance from risk, governments have incentives to constrain banks' exposure to credit risk. Banks also tend to shield themselves from the risk of shifts in interest rates by avoiding fixed-rate loans with long maturities. Since banks' capital mostly comes from short-term deposits, such long-term loans leave them exposed to increases in interest rates, unless the risk can be hedged with derivatives. Thus, banks are less likely to play a role when a firm requires a very long-term commitment to financing. However, in some such cases they assist in providing a placement of the debt with, say, an insurance company, a pension fund, or a group of private investors.

Other Financial Institutions

Banks face competition in the commercial lending market from a variety of sources. In the U.S., there is competition from savings and loans, even though the latter are relatively more involved in financing mortgages. Finance companies compete with banks in the market for asset-based lending (i.e., the secured financing of specific assets such as receivables, inventory, or equipment). Insurance companies are involved in a variety of lending activities. Since life insurance companies face obligations of a long-term nature, they often seek investments of long duration (e.g., long-term bonds or loans to support large, long-term commercial real estate and development projects). Investment bankers are prepared to place debt securities with private investors or in the public markets (discussed below). Various government agencies are another source of credit.

Public Debt Markets

Some firms have the size, strength, and credibility necessary to bypass the banking sector and seek financing directly from investors, either through sales of commercial paper or through the issuance of bonds. Such debt issues are facilitated by the assignment of a debt rating. In the U.S., Moody's and Standard and Poor's are the two largest rating agencies. A firm's debt rating influences the yield that must be offered to sell the debt instruments. After the debt issue, the rating agencies continue to monitor the firm's financial condition. Changes in the rating are associated with fluctuation in the price of the securities.

Banks often provide financing in tandem with a public debt issue or other source of financing. In highly levered transactions, such as leveraged buyouts, banks commonly provide financing along with public debt that has a lower priority in case of bankruptcy. The bank's "senior financing" would typically be scheduled for earlier retirement than the public debt, and it would carry a lower yield. For smaller or startup firms, banks often provide credit in conjunction with equity financing from venture capitalists. Note that in the case of both the leveraged buyout and the startup company, the bank helps provide the cash needed to make the deal happen, but it does so in a way that shields it from risks that would be unacceptably high in the banking sector.

Sellers Who Provide Financing

Another sector of the market for credit are manufacturers and other suppliers of goods and services. As a matter of course, such firms tend to finance their customers' purchases on an unsecured basis for periods of 30 to 60 days. Suppliers will, on occasion, also agree to provide more extended financing, usually with the support of a secured note. A supplier may be willing to grant such a loan in the expectation that the creditor will survive a cash shortage and remain an important customer in the future. However the customer would typically seek such an arrangement only if bank financing is unavailable because it could constrain flexibility in selecting among and/or negotiating with suppliers.

THE CREDIT ANALYSIS PROCESS

At first blush, credit analysis might appear less difficult than the valuation task discussed in Chapters 7 and 8. After all, a potential creditor ultimately cares only about whether the firm is strong enough to pay its debts at the scheduled times. The firm's exact value, its upside potential, or its distance from the threshold of credit-worthiness may not appear so important. Viewed in that way, credit analysis may seem more like a "zero-one" decision: either the credit is extended, or it is not.

It turns out, however, that credit analysis involves more than just establishing credit-worthiness. First, there are ranges of credit-worthiness, and it is important to understand where a firm lies within that range for purposes of pricing and structuring a loan. Moreover, if the creditor is a bank or other financial institution with an expected continuing relationship with the borrower, the borrower's upside potential is important, even though downside risk must be the primary consideration in credit analysis. A firm that offers growth potential also offers opportunities for future income-generating financial services.

Given this broader view of credit analysis, it should not be surprising that it involves most of the same issues already discussed in the prior chapters on business strategy analysis, accounting analysis, financial analysis, and prospective analysis. Perhaps the greatest difference is that credit analysis rarely involves any explicit attempt to estimate the value of the firm's equity. However, the determinants of that value are relevant in credit analysis because a larger equity cushion translates into lower risk for the creditor.

Below we describe one series of steps that is used by commercial lenders in credit analysis. Of course not all commercial lenders follow the same process, but the steps are representative of typical approaches. The approach used by commercial lenders is of interest in its own right and illustrates a comprehensive credit analysis. However, analysis by others who grant credit often differs. For example, even when a manufacturer conducts some credit analysis prior to granting credit to a customer, it is typically much less extensive than the analysis conducted by a banker because the credit is very short-term and the manufacturer is willing to bear some credit risk in the interest of generating a profit on the sale.

We present the steps in a particular order, but they are in fact all interdependent. Thus, analysis at one step may need to be rethought depending on the analysis at some later step.

Step 1: Consider the Nature and Purpose of the Loan

Understanding the purpose of a loan is important not just for deciding whether it should be granted but also for structuring the loan. Loans might be required for only a few months, for several years, or even as a permanent part of a firm's capital structure. Loans might be used for replacement of other financing, to support working capital needs, or to finance the acquisition of long-term assets or another firm.

The required amount of the loan must also be established. In the case of small and medium-sized companies, a banker would typically prefer to be the sole financier of the business, in which case the loan would have to be large enough to retire existing debt. The preference for serving as the sole financier is not just to gain an advantage in providing a menu of financial services to the firm. It also reflects the desirability of not permitting another creditor to maintain a superior interest that would give it a higher priority in case of bankruptcy. If other creditors are willing to subordinate their positions to the bank, that would of course be acceptable so far as the bank is concerned.

Often the commercial lender deals with firms that may have parent-subsidiary relations. The question of to whom one should lend then arises. The answer is usually the entity that owns the assets that will serve as collateral (or that could serve as such if needed in the future). If this entity is the subsidiary and the parent presents some financial strength independent of the subsidiary, a guarantee of the parent could be considered.

Step 2: Consider the Type of Loan and Available Security

The type of loan considered is a function of not only its purpose but also the financial strength of the borrower. Thus, to some extent, the loan type will be dictated by the financial analysis described in the following step in the process. Some of the possibilities follow:

- *Open line of credit.* An open line of credit permits the borrower to receive cash up to some specified maximum on an as-needed basis for a specified term, such as one year. To maintain this option, the borrower pays a fee (e.g., ⅜ of 1 percent) on the unused balance in addition to the interest on any used amount. An open line of credit is useful in cases where the borrower's cash needs are difficult to anticipate.
- *Revolving line of credit.* When it is clear that a firm will need credit beyond the short run, financing may be provided in the form of a "revolver." Sometimes used to support working capital needs, the borrower makes scheduled payments as the operating cycle proceeds and inventory and receivables are converted to cash. It is also expected that cash will continue to be advanced so long as the borrower remains in good standing. In addition to interest on amounts outstanding, a fee is charged on the unused line.
- *Working capital loan.* Such a loan is used to finance inventory and receivables, and it is usually secured. The maximum loan balance may be tied to the balance of the working capital accounts. For example, the loan may be allowed to rise to no more than 80 percent of receivables less than 60 days old.
- *Term loan.* Term loans are used for long-term needs and are often secured with long-term assets such as plant or equipment. Typically, the loan will be amortized, requiring periodic payments to reduce the loan balance.
- *Mortgage loan.* Mortgages support the financing of real estate, have long terms, and require periodic amortization of the loan balance.
- *Lease financing.* Lease financing can be used to facilitate the acquisition of any asset but is most commonly used for equipment, including vehicles. Leases may be structured over periods of 1 to 15 years, depending on the life of the underlying asset.

Much bank lending is done on a secured basis, especially with smaller and more highly levered companies. Security will be required unless the loan is short-term and the borrower exposes the bank to minimal default risk. When security is required, one consideration is whether the amount of available security is sufficient to support the loan. The amount that a bank will lend on given security involves business judgment, and it depends on a variety of factors that affect the liquidity of the security in the context of a situation where the firm is distressed. The following are some rules of thumb often applied in commercial lending to various categories of security:

- *Receivables.* Accounts receivable are usually considered the most desirable form of security because they are the most liquid. One large regional bank allows loans of 50 to 80 percent of the balance of nondelinquent accounts. The percentage applied is lower when (1) there are many small accounts that would be costly to collect in the case the firm is distressed; (2) there are a few very large accounts, such that problems with a single customer could be serious; and/or (3) the customer's financial health is closely related to that of the borrower, so that collectibility is endangered just when the borrower is in default. On the latter score, banks often refuse to accept receivables from affiliates as effective security.
- *Inventory.* The desirability of inventory as security varies widely. The best-case scenario is inventory consisting of a common commodity that can easily be sold to other parties if the borrower defaults. More specialized inventory, with appeal to only a limited set of buyers, or inventory that is costly to store or transport is less desirable. The large regional bank mentioned above lends up to 60 percent on raw materials, 50 percent on finished goods, and 20 percent on work in process.
- *Machinery and equipment.* Machinery and equipment is less desirable as collateral. It is likely to be used, and it must be stored, insured, and marketed. Keeping the costs of these activities in mind, banks typically will lend only up to 50 percent of the estimated value of such assets in a forced sale such as an auction.
- *Real estate.* The value of real estate as collateral varies considerably. Banks will often lend up to 80 percent of the appraised value of readily salable real estate. On the other hand, a factory designed for a unique purpose would be much less desirable.

When security is required to make a loan viable, a commercial lender will estimate the amounts that could be lent on each of the assets available as security. Unless the amount exceeds the required loan balance, the loan would not be extended.

Even when a loan is not secured initially, a bank can require a "negative pledge" on the firm's assets—a pledge that the firm will not use the assets as security for any other creditor. In that case, if the borrower begins to experience difficulty and defaults on the loan, and if there are no other creditors in the picture, the bank can demand the loan become secured if it is to remain outstanding.

Step 3: Analyze the Potential Borrower's Financial Status

This portion of the analysis involves all the steps discussed in our chapters on business strategy analysis, accounting analysis, and financial analysis. The emphasis, however, is on the firm's ability to service the debt at the scheduled rate. The focus of the analysis depends on the type of financing under consideration. For example, if a short-term loan is considered to support seasonal fluctuations in inventory, the emphasis would be on the ability of the firm to convert the inventory into cash on a timely basis. In contrast, a term loan to support plant and equipment must be made with confidence in the long-run earnings prospects of the firm.

Key Analysis Questions

Some of the questions to be addressed in analyzing a potential borrower's financial status include the following:

- *Business strategy analysis*: How does this business work? Why is it valuable? What is its strategy for sustaining or enhancing that value? How well qualified is the management to carry out that strategy effectively? Is the viability of the business highly dependent on the talents of the existing management team?
- *Accounting analysis*: How well do the firm's financial statements reflect its underlying economic reality? Are there reasons to believe that the firm's performance is stronger or weaker than reported profitability would suggest? Are there sizable off-balance-sheet liabilities (e.g., operating leases) that would affect the potential borrower's ability to repay the loan?
- *Financial analysis*: Is the firm's level of profitability unusually high or low? What are the sources of any unusual degree of profitability? How sustainable are they? What risks are associated with the operating profit stream? How highly levered is the firm? What is the firm's funds flow picture? What are its major sources and uses of funds? Are funds required to finance expected growth? How great are fund flows expected to be relative to the debt service required? Given the possible volatility in those fund flows, how likely is it that they could fall to a level insufficient to service debt and meet other commitments?

Ultimately, the key question in the financial analysis is how likely it is that cash flows will be sufficient to repay the loan. With that question in mind, lenders focus much attention on solvency ratios: the magnitude of various measures of profits and cash flows relative to debt service and other requirements. To the extent such a ratio exceeds 1, it indicates the "margin of safety" the lender faces. When such a ratio is combined with an assessment of the variance in its numerator, it provides an indication of the probability of nonpayment.

Ratio analysis from the perspective of a creditor differs somewhat from that of an owner. For example, there is greater emphasis on cash flows and earnings available to *all* claimants (not just owners) *before* taxes (since interest is tax-deductible and paid out of pretax dollars). To illustrate, the creditor's perspective is apparent in the following solvency ratio, called the "funds flow coverage ratio":

$$\text{Funds flow coverage} = \frac{\text{EBIT} + \text{Depreciation}}{\text{Interest} + \dfrac{\text{Debt repayment}}{(1 - \text{tax rate})} + \dfrac{\text{Preferred dividends}}{(1 - \text{tax rate})}}$$

We see earnings before both interest and taxes in the numerator. This measures the numerator in a way that can be compared directly to the interest expense in the denominator, because interest expense is paid out of pretax dollars. In contrast, any payment of principal scheduled for a given year is nondeductible and must be made out of after-tax profits. In essence, with a 50 percent tax rate, one dollar of principal payment is "twice as expensive" as a one-dollar interest payment. Scaling the payment of principal by (1 – tax rate) accounts for this. The same idea applies to preferred dividends, which are not tax deductible.

The funds flow coverage ratio provides an indication of how comfortably the funds flow can cover unavoidable expenditures. The ratio excludes payments such as common dividends and capital expenditures on the premise that they could be reduced to zero to make debt payments if necessary.[1] Clearly, however, if the firm is to survive in the long run, funds flow must be sufficient to not only service debt but also maintain plant assets. Thus, long-run survival requires a funds flow coverage ratio well in excess of 1.[2]

It would be overly simplistic to establish any particular threshold above which a ratio indicates a loan is justified. However, a creditor clearly wants to be in a position to be repaid on schedule, even when the borrower faces a reasonably foreseeable difficulty. That argues for lending only when the funds flow coverage is expected to exceed 1, even in a recession scenario—and higher if some allowance for capital expenditures is prudent.

The financial analysis should produce more than an assessment of the risk of nonpayment. It should also identify the nature of significant risks. At many commercial banks it is standard operating procedure to summarize the analysis of the firm by listing the key risks that could lead to default and factors that could be used to control those risks if the loan were made. That information can be used in structuring the detailed terms of the loan so as to trigger default when problems arise, at a stage early enough to permit corrective action.

Step 4: Utilize Forecasts to Assess Payment Prospects

Already implicit in some of the above discussion is a forward-looking view of the firm's ability to service the loan. Good credit analysis should also be supported by explicit forecasts. The basis for such forecasts is usually management, but, not surprisingly, lenders do not accept such forecasts without question.

In forecasting, a variety of scenarios should be considered—including not just a "best guess" but also a "pessimistic" scenario. Ideally, the firm should be strong enough to repay the loan even in the latter scenario. Ironically, it is not necessarily a decline in sales that presents the greatest risk to the lender. If managers can respond quickly to a sales dropoff, it should be accompanied by a liquidation of receivables and inventory, which enhances cash flow for a given level of earnings. The nightmare scenario is one that involves large negative profit margins, perhaps because managers are caught by surprise by a downturn in demand and are forced to liquidate inventory at substantially reduced prices.

At times it is possible to reconsider the structure of a loan so as to permit it to "cash flow." That is, the term of the loan might be extended or the amortization pattern changed. Often a bank will grant a loan with the expectation that it will be continually renewed, thus becoming a permanent part of the firm's financial structure. (Such a loan is labeled an "evergreen.") In that case the loan will still be written as if it is due within the short term, and the bank must assure itself of a viable "exit strategy." However, the firm would be expected to service the loan by simply covering interest payments.

Step 5: Assemble the Detailed Loan Structure, Including Loan Covenants

If the analysis thus far indicates that a loan is in order, it is then time to pull together the detailed structure: type of loan, repayment schedule, loan covenants, and pricing. The first two items were discussed above. Here we discuss loan covenants and pricing.

Writing Loan Covenants

Loan covenants specify mutual expectations of the borrower and lender by specifying actions the borrower will and will not take. Some covenants require certain actions (such as regular provision of financial statements); others preclude certain actions (such as undertaking an acquisition without the permission of the lender); still others require maintenance of certain financial ratios. Violation of a covenant represents a default event that could cause immediate acceleration of the debt payment, but in most cases the lender uses it as an opportunity to re-examine the situation and either waive the violation or renegotiate the loan.

Loan covenants must strike a balance between protecting the interests of the lender and providing the flexibility management needs to run the business. The covenants represent a mechanism for ensuring that the business will remain as strong as the two parties anticipated at the time the loan was granted. Thus, required financial ratios are typically based on the levels that existed at that time, perhaps with some allowance for deterioration but often with some expected improvement over time.

The particular covenants included in the agreement should contain the significant risks identified in the financial analysis, or to at least provide early warning that such risks are surfacing. Some commonly used financial covenants include:

- *Maintenance of minimum net worth.* This covenant assures that the firm will maintain an "equity cushion" to protect the lender. Covenants typically require a level of net worth rather than a particular level of income. In the final analysis, the lender may not care whether that net worth is maintained by generating income, cutting dividends, or issuing new equity. Tying the covenant to net worth offers the firm the flexibility to use any of these avenues to avoid default.
- *Minimum coverage ratio.* Especially in the case of a long-term loan, such as a term loan, the lender may want to supplement a net worth covenant with one based on coverage of interest or total debt service. The funds flow coverage ratio presented above would be an example. Maintenance of some minimum coverage helps assure that the ability of the firm to generate funds internally is strong enough to justify the long-term nature of the loan.
- *Maximum ratio of total liabilities to net worth.* This ratio constrains the risk of high leverage and prevents growth without either retaining earnings or infusing equity.
- *Minimum net working capital balance or current ratio.* Constraints on this ratio force a firm to maintain its liquidity by using cash generated from operations to retire current liabilities (as opposed to acquiring long-lived assets).
- *Maximum ratio of capital expenditures to earnings before depreciation.* Constraints on this ratio help prevent the firm from investing in growth (including the illiquid assets necessary to support growth) unless such growth can be financed internally, with some margin remaining for debt service.

In addition to such financial covenants, loans sometimes place restrictions on other borrowing activity, pledging of assets to other lenders, selling of substantial parts of assets, engaging in mergers or acquisitions, and payment of dividends.

Covenants are included not only in private lending agreements with banks, insurance companies, and others, but also in public debt agreements. However, public debt agreements tend to have less restrictive covenants for two reasons. First, negotiations resulting from a violation of public debt covenants are costly (possibly involving not just the trustee, but also bondholders), and so they are written to be triggered only in serious circumstances. Second, public debt is usually issued by stronger, more credit-worthy firms. (The primary exception would be high-yield debt issued in conjunction with leveraged buyouts.) For the most financially healthy firms with strong debt ratings, very few covenants will be used—only those necessary to limit dramatic changes in the firm's operations, such as a major merger or acquisition.

Loan Pricing

A detailed discussion of loan pricing falls outside the scope of this text. The essence of pricing is to assure that the yield on the loan is sufficient to cover (1) the lender's cost of borrowed funds; (2) the lender's costs of administering and servicing the loan; (3) a premium for exposure to default risk; and (4) at least a normal return on the equity capital necessary to support the lending operation. The price is often stated in terms of a deviation from a bank's prime rate—the rate charged to stronger borrowers. For example, a loan might be granted at prime plus 1½ percent. An alternative base is LIBOR, or the London Interbank Offer Rate, the rate at which large banks from various nations lend large blocks of funds to each other.

Banks compete actively for commercial lending business, and it is rare that a yield includes more than 2 percentage points to cover the cost of default risk. If the spread to cover default risk is, say, 1 percent, and the bank recovers only 50 percent of amounts due on loans that turn out bad, then the bank can afford only 2 percent of their loans to fall into that category. This underscores how important it is for banks to conduct a thorough analysis and to contain the riskiness of their loan portfolio.

FINANCIAL STATEMENT ANALYSIS AND PUBLIC DEBT

Fundamentally, the issues involved in analysis of public debt are no different from those of bank loans and other private debt issues. Institutionally, however, the contexts are different. Bankers can maintain very close relations with clients so as to form an initial assessment of their credit risk and monitor their activities during the loan period. In the case of public debt, the investors are distanced from the issuer. To a large extent, they must depend on professional debt analysts, including debt raters, to assess the riskiness of the debt and monitor the firm's ongoing activities. Such analysts and debt raters thus serve an important function in closing the information gap between issuers and investors.

The Meaning of Debt Ratings

The two major debt rating agencies in the U.S. are Moody's and Standard and Poor's. Using the Standard and Poor's labeling system, the highest possible rating is AAA. Proceeding downward from AAA, the ratings are AA, A, BBB, BB, B, CCC, CC, C, and D, where "D" indicates debt in default. Table 10-1 presents examples of firms in rating categories AAA through CCC, as well as average yields across all firms in each category. Only about 1 percent of the public industrial companies rated by Standard & Poor's have the financial strength to merit an AAA rating. Among the few are General Electric, Johnson & Johnson, Merck, and Nestlé—all among the largest, most profitable firms in the world. AA firms are also very strong and include Microsoft and Wal-Mart. Firms rated AAA and AA have the lowest costs of debt financing; in January 2002 their average yields were roughly 3.5 percent over the 12 month LIBOR rate.

To be considered investment grade, a firm must achieve a rating of BBB or higher. Many funds are precluded by their charters from investing in any bonds below that grade. Even to achieve a grade of BBB is difficult. AT&T, the largest long-distance telephone carrier in the U.S., was rated as "only" BBB—barely investment grade—in 2003. Apple Computer and Delta Air Lines were in the BB category. Delta was the third largest airline carrier in the U.S. However, it had suffered from the dramatic decline in demand following September 11, 2001. The B category includes Continental Airlines, Lucent Technologies, and Northwest Airlines, all of which were facing financial difficulty. An example of a CCC rated firm is AMR, the parent of American Airlines, which was close to bankruptcy following the massive financial problems faced by the industry. UAL, the parent of United Airlines, was rated as D, since it had filed for bankruptcy in 2003.

Table 10-1 shows that the cost of debt financing rises markedly once firms' debt falls below investment grade. For example, in January 2002 yields for BBB rated debt issues were 4.4 percent over the 12 month LIBOR rate; yields for B rated issues were 7.3 percent above LIBOR rates; and yields for firms with CCC rated debt, which were close to bankruptcy, were 20.5 percent over LIBOR.

Table 10-1 Debt Ratings: Example Firms and Average Yields by Category

S&P debt rating	Example firms in 2003	Percentage of public industrials given same rating by S&P	Average yield, January 2002	Average spread over 12 month LIBOR rate
AAA	General Electric Johnson & Johnson Merck and Co. Nestlé S.A.	0.9%	5.95%	3.51%
AA	Microsoft GlaxoSmithKline Wal-Mart Stores, Inc.	3.6	5.98	3.54
A	American Express Coca-Cola Enterprises McDonald's Corp. Sony Corp.	20.0	6.23	3.79
BBB	AT&T British Airways Ford Motor Company General Motors Sears Roebuck & Co.	29.0	6.80	4.36
BB	Apple Computer Delta Air Lines	22.6	8.53	6.09
B	Continental Airlines Lucent Technologies Northwest Airlines	20.9	9.75	7.31
CCC	American Airlines (AMR)	3.0	22.90	20.46
D	United Air Lines (UAL)			

Source: Standard and Poor's 2003, and Standard and Poor's Compustat 2002.

Table 10-2 shows median financial ratios for firms by debt rating category. Firms with AAA and AA ratings have very strong earnings and cash flow performance as well as minimal leverage. Firms in the BBB class are only moderately leveraged, with about 37 percent of long- term capitalization coming in the form of debt. Earnings tend to be relatively strong, as indicated by a pretax interest coverage (EBIT/interest) of 2.8 and a cash flow debt coverage (cash flow from operations/total debt) of nearly 27 percent. Firms with B and CCC ratings, however, face significant risks: they typically report losses, have high leverage, and have interest coverage ratios less than 1.

Table 10-2 Debt Ratings: Median Financial Ratios by Category

Median ratios for overall category in January 2002
(industrials only)

S&P debt rating	Pretax return on long-term capital	Pretax interest coverage	Cash flow from operations to total debt	Long-term debt to total capital
AAA	27.6%	21.9 times	45.1%	8%
AA	17.4	7.4	52.1	20
A	10.9	4.2	29.2	34
BBB	7.1	2.8	26.7	37
BB	3.6	1.7	18.4	48
B	–3.9	0.5	8.1	64
CCC	–16.0	–0.9	1.4	59

Source: Standard and Poor's Compustat, 2002.

Factors That Drive Debt Ratings

Research demonstrates that some of the variation in debt ratings can be explained as a function of selected financial statement ratios, even as used within a quantitative model that incorporates no subjective human judgment. Some debt rating agencies rely heavily on quantitative models, and such models are commonly used by insurance companies, banks, and others to assist in the evaluation of the riskiness of debt issues for which a public rating is not available.

Table 10-3 lists the factors used by three different firms in their quantitative debt-rating models. The firms include one insurance company and one bank, which use the

Table 10-3 Factors Used in Quantitative Models of Debt Ratings

	Firm 1	Firm 2	Firm 3
Profitability measures	Return on long-term capital	Return on long-term capital	Return on long-term capital
Leverage measures	Long-term debt to capitalization	Long-term debt to capitalization Total debt to total capital	Long-term debt to capitalization
Profitability and leverage	Interest coverage Cash flow to long-term debt	Interest coverage Cash flow to long-term debt	Fixed charge coverage Coverage of short-term debt and fixed charges
Firm size	Sales	Total assets	
Other		Standard deviation of return Subordination status	

models in their private placement activities, and an investment research firm, which employs the model in evaluating its own debt purchases and holdings. In each case profitability and leverage play an important role in the rating. One firm also uses firm size as an indicator, with larger size associated with higher ratings.

Several researchers have estimated quantitative models used for debt ratings. Two of these models, developed by Kaplan and Urwitz and shown in Table 10-4, highlight the relative importance of the factors.[3] Model 1 has the greater ability to explain variation in bond ratings. However, it includes some factors based on stock market data, which are not available for all firms. Model 2 is based solely on financial statement data.

The factors in Table 10-4 are listed in the order of their statistical significance in Model 1. An interesting feature is that the most important factor explaining debt ratings is not a financial ratio at all—it is simply firm size! Large firms tend to get better ratings than small firms. Whether the debt is subordinated or unsubordinated is next most important, followed by a leverage indicator. Profitability appears less important, but in part that reflects the presence in the model of multiple factors (ROA and interest coverage) that capture profitability. It is only the explanatory power that is *unique* to a given variable that is indicated by the ranking in Table 10-4. Explanatory power common to the two variables is not considered.

Table 10-4 Kaplan-Urwitz Models of Debt Ratings

Firm or debt characteristic	Variable reflecting characteristic	Coefficients Model 1	Model 2
	Model intercept	5.67	4.41
Firm size	Total assets[a]	.0011	.0014
Subordination status of debt	1 = subordinated; 0 = unsubordinated	−2.36	−2.56
Leverage	Long-term debt to total assets	−2.85	−2.72
Systematic risk	Market model beta, indicating sensitivity of stock price to market-wide movements (1 = average)[b]	−.87	—
Profitability	Net income to total assets	5.13	6.40
Unsystematic risk	Standard deviation of residual from market model (average = .10)[b]	−2.90	—
Riskiness of profit stream	Coefficient of variation in net income over 5 years (standard deviation/mean)	—	−.53
Interest coverage	Pretax funds flow before interest to interest expense	.007	.006

The score from the model is converted to a bond rating as follows:
If score > 6.76, predict AAA
   score > 5.19, predict AA
   score > 3.28, predict A
   score > 1.57, predict BBB
   score < 0.00, predict BB

a. The coefficient in the Kaplan-Urwitz model was estimated at .005 (Model 1) and .006 (Model 2). Its scale has been adjusted to reflect that the estimates were based on assets measured in dollars from the early 1970s. Given that $1 from 1972 is approximately equivalent to $4.40 in 2003, the original coefficient estimate has been divided by 4.4

b. Market model is estimated by regressing stock returns on the market index, using monthly data for the prior 5 years.

When applied to a sample of bonds that were not used in the estimation process, the Kaplan-Urwitz Model 1 predicted the rating category correctly in 44 of 64 cases, or 63 percent of the time. Where it erred, the model was never off by more than one category, and in about half of those cases its prediction was more consistent with the market yield on the debt than was the actual debt rating. The discrepancies between actual ratings and those estimated using the Kaplan-Urwitz model indicate that rating agencies incorporate factors other than financial ratios in their analysis. These are likely to include the types of strategic, accounting, and prospective analyses discussed throughout this book.

Given that debt ratings can be explained reasonably well in terms of a handful of financial ratios, one might question whether ratings convey any *news* to investors—anything that could not already have been garnered from publicly available financial data. The answer to the question is yes, at least in the case of debt rating downgrades. That is, downgrades are greeted with drops in both bond and stock prices.[4] To be sure, the capital markets anticipate much of the information reflected in rating changes. But that is not surprising, given that the changes often represent reactions to recent known events and that the rating agencies typically indicate in advance that a change is being considered.

PREDICTION OF DISTRESS AND TURNAROUND

The key task in credit analysis is assessing the probability that a firm will face financial distress and fail to repay a loan. A related analysis, relevant once a firm begins to face distress, involves considering whether it can be turned around. In this section we consider evidence on the predictability of these states.

The prediction of either distress or turnaround is a complex, difficult, and subjective task that involves all of the steps of analysis discussed throughout this book: business strategy analysis, accounting analysis, financial analysis, and prospective analysis. Purely quantitative models of the process can rarely serve as substitutes for the hard work the analysis involves. However, research on such models does offer some insight into which financial indicators are most useful in the task. Moreover, there are some settings where extensive credit checks are too costly to justify, and where quantitative distress prediction models are useful. For example, the commercially available "Zeta" model is used by some manufacturers and other firms to assess the credit-worthiness of their customers.[5]

Several distress prediction models have been developed over the years.[6] They are similar to the debt rating models, but instead of predicting ratings, they predict whether a firm will face some state of distress within one year, typically defined as bankruptcy. One study suggests that the factors most useful (on a stand-alone basis) in predicting bankruptcy one year in advance are[7]:

1. Profitability $= \left[\dfrac{\text{Net income}}{\text{Net worth}} \right]$

2. Volatility $= \left[\text{Standard deviation of} \left(\dfrac{\text{Net income}}{\text{Net worth}} \right) \right]$

3. Financial leverage $= \left[\dfrac{\text{Market value of equity}}{(\text{Market value of equity} + \text{Book value of debt})} \right]$

The evidence indicates that the key to whether a firm will face distress is its level of profitability, the volatility of that profitability, and how much leverage it faces. Interestingly, liquidity measures turn out to be much less important. Current liquidity won't save an unhealthy firm if it is losing money at a fast pace.

Of course if one were interested in predicting distress, there would be no need to restrict attention to one variable at a time. A number of multi-factor models have been designed to predict financial distress. One such model, the Altman Z-score model, weights five variables to compute a bankruptcy score.[8] For public companies the model is as follows [9]:

$$Z = 1.2(X_1) + 1.4(X_2) + 3.3(X_3) + 0.6(X_4) + 1.0(X_5)$$

where X_1 = net working capital/total assets
   X_2 = retained earnings/total assets
   X_3 = EBIT/total assets
   X_4 = market value of equity/book value of total liabilities
   X_5 = sales/total assets

The model predicts bankruptcy when $Z < 1.81$. The range between 1.81 and 2.67 is labeled the "gray area."

The following table presents calculations for two companies, Lucent Technologies and Merck:

	Model Coefficient	Lucent Technologies		Merck	
		Ratios	Score	Ratios	Score
Net working capital/assets	0.717	0.16	0.19	0.05	0.06
Retained earnings/Total assets	0.847	−1.24	−1.73	0.75	1.04
EBIT/Total assets	3.11	−0.38	−1.24	0.21	0.71
Market value of equity/Book value of total liabilities	0.42	0.26	0.16	4.37	2.62
Sales/Total assets	0.998	0.69	0.69	1.09	1.09
			−1.93		5.53

With the fall of the dot-com sector in 2000, Lucent Technologies experienced a dramatic decline in revenues and profits that persisted for the next two years. In the year ended December 31, 2002, Lucent earned a loss before interest and taxes, its retained earnings were negative, and its market value of equity was only $5.9 billion. It is not surprising to see that the model rates Lucent's likelihood of failure as high. Merck, an AAA rated company, has much stronger financial performance and a much higher market valuation ($128.4 billion) than Lucent. Merck's score indicates that it has a very low likelihood of failure.

Such models have some ability to predict failing and surviving firms. Altman reports that when the model was applied to a holdout sample containing 33 failed and 33 non-failed firms (the same proportion used to estimate the model), it correctly predicted the outcome in 63 of 66 cases. However, the performance of the model would degrade substantially if applied to a holdout sample where the proportion of failed and nonfailed firms was not forced to be the same as that used to estimate the model.

Simple distress prediction models like the Altman model cannot serve as a replacement for in-depth analysis of the kind discussed throughout this book. But they do provide a useful reminder of the power of financial statement data to summarize important dimensions of the firm's performance. In addition, they can be useful for screening large numbers of firms prior to more in-depth analysis of corporate strategy, management expertise, market position, and financial ratio performance.

SUMMARY

Credit analysis is the evaluation of a firm from the perspective of a holder or potential holder of its debt. Credit analysis is important to a wide variety of economic agents—not just bankers and other financial intermediaries but also public debt analysts, industrial companies, service companies, and others.

At the heart of credit analysis lie the same techniques described in Chapters 2 through 8: business strategy analysis, accounting analysis, financial analysis, and portions of prospective analysis. The purpose of the analysis is not just to assess the likelihood that a potential borrower will fail to repay the loan. It is also important to identify the nature of the key risks involved, and how the loan might be structured to mitigate or control those risks. A well structured loan provides the lender with a viable "exit strategy," even in the case of default. A key to this structure is properly designed accounting-based covenants.

Fundamentally, the issues involved in analysis of public debt are no different from those involved in evaluating bank loans or other private debt. Institutionally, however, the contexts are different. Investors in public debt are usually not close to the borrower and must rely on other agents, including debt raters and other analysts, to assess credit-worthiness. Debt ratings, which depend heavily on firm size and financial measures of performance, have an important influence on the market yields that must be offered to issue debt.

The key task in credit analysis is the assessment of the probability of default. The task is complex, difficult, and to some extent, subjective. A small number of key financial ratios can help predict financial distress with some accuracy. The most important financial indicators for this purpose are profitability, volatility of profits, and leverage. However, the models cannot replace the in-depth forms of analysis discussed in this book.

DISCUSSION QUESTIONS

1. What are the critical performance dimensions for (a) a retailer and (b) a financial services company that should be considered in credit analysis? What ratios would you suggest looking at for each of these dimensions?

2. Why would a company pay to have its public debt rated by a major rating agency (such as Moody's or Standard and Poor's)? Why might a firm decide not to have its debt rated?

3. Some have argued that the market for original-issue junk bonds developed in the late 1970s as a result of a failure in the rating process. Proponents of this argument suggest that rating agencies rated companies too harshly at the low end of the rating scale, denying investment grade status to some deserving companies. What are proponents of this argument effectively assuming were the incentives of rating agencies? What economic forces could give rise to this incentive?

4. Many debt agreements require borrowers to obtain the permission of the lender before undertaking a major acquisition or asset sale. Why would the lender want to include this type of restriction?

5. Betty Li, the CFO of a company applying for a new loan, states, "I will never agree to a debt covenant that restricts my ability to pay dividends to my shareholders because it reduces shareholder wealth." Do you agree with this argument?

6. Cambridge Construction Company follows the percentage-of-completion method for reporting long-term contract revenues. The percentage of completion is based on the cost of materials shipped to the project site as a percentage of total expected

material costs. Cambridge's major debt agreement includes restrictions on net worth, interest coverage, and minimum working capital requirements. A leading analyst claims that "the company is buying its way out of these covenants by spending cash and buying materials, even when they are not needed." Explain how this may be possible.

7. Can Cambridge improve its Z score by behaving as the analyst claims in Question 6? Is this change consistent with economic reality?

8. A banker asserts, "I avoid lending to companies with negative cash from operations because they are too risky." Is this a sensible lending policy?

9. A leading retailer finds itself in a financial bind. It doesn't have sufficient cash flow from operations to finance its growth, and it is close to violating the maximum debt-to-assets ratio allowed by its covenants. The Vice-President for Marketing suggests: "We can raise cash for our growth by selling the existing stores and leasing them back. This source of financing is cheap since it avoids violating either the debt-to-assets or interest coverage ratios in our covenants." Do you agree with his analysis? Why or why not? As the firm's banker, how would you view this arrangement?

NOTES

1. The same is true of preferred dividends. However, when preferred stock is cumulative, any dividends missed must be paid later, when and if the firm returns to profitability.
2. Other relevant coverage ratios are discussed in Chapter 5.
3. Robert Kaplan and G. Urwitz, "Statistical Models of Bond Ratings: A Methodological Inquiry," *Journal of Business* (April 1979): 231–61.
4. See Robert Holthausen and Richard Leftwich, "The Effect of Bond Rating Changes on Common Stock Prices," *Journal of Financial Economics* (September 1986): 57–90; and John Hand, Robert Holthausen, and Richard Leftwich, "The Effect of Bond Rating Announcements on Bond and Stock Prices," *Journal of Finance* (June 1992): 733–52.
5. See Edward Altman, *Corporate Financial Distress* (New York: John Wiley, 1993).
6. See Edward Altman, "Financial Ratios, Discriminant Analysis, and the Prediction of Corporate Bankruptcy," *Journal of Finance* (September 1968): 589–609; Altman, *Corporate Financial Distress,* op. cit.; William Beaver, "Financial Ratios as Predictors of Distress," *Journal of Accounting Research,* Supplement (1966): 71–111; James Ohlson, "Financial Ratios and the Probabilistic Prediction of Bankruptcy," *Journal of Accounting Research* (Spring 1980): 109–131; and Mark Zmijewski, "Predicting Corporate Bankruptcy: An Empirical Comparison of the Extant Financial Distress Models," working paper, SUNY at Buffalo, 1983.
7. Zmijewski, op. cit.
8. Altman, *Corporate Financial Distress,* op. cit.
9. For private firms, Altman, ibid., adjusts the public model by changing the numerator for the variable X_4 from the market value of equity to the book value. The revised model follows:

$$Z = .717(X_1) + .847(X_2) + 3.11(X_3) + 0.420(X_4) + .998(X_5)$$

where X_1 = net working capital/total assets
X_2 = retained earnings/total assets
X_3 = EBIT/total assets
X_4 = book value of equity/book value of total liabilities
X_5 = sales/total assets

The model predicts bankruptcy when Z < 1.20. The range between 1.20 and 2.90 is labeled the "gray area."

Mergers and Acquisitions

Mergers and acquisitions have long been a popular form of corporate investment, particularly in countries with Anglo-American forms of capital markets. There is no question that these transactions provide a healthy return to target stockholders. However, their value to acquiring shareholders is less understood. Many skeptics point out that given the hefty premiums paid to target stockholders, acquisitions tend to be negative-valued investments for acquiring stockholders.[1]

A number of questions can be examined using financial analysis for mergers and acquisitions:

- Securities analysts can ask: Does a proposed acquisition create value for the acquiring firm's stockholders?
- Risk arbitrageurs can ask: What is the likelihood that a hostile takeover offer will ultimately succeed, and are there other potential acquirers likely to enter the bidding?
- Acquiring management can ask: Does this target fit our business strategy? If so, what is it worth to us, and how can we make an offer that can be successful?
- Target management can ask: Is the acquirer's offer a reasonable one for our stockholders? Are there other potential acquirers that would value our company more than the current bidder?
- Investment bankers can ask: How can we identify potential targets that are likely to be a good match for our clients? And how should we value target firms when we are asked to issue fairness opinions?

In this chapter we focus primarily on the use of financial statement data and analysis directed at evaluating whether a merger creates value for the acquiring firm's stockholders. However, our discussion can also be applied to these other merger contexts. The topic of whether acquisitions create value for acquirers focuses on evaluating motivations for acquisitions, the pricing of offers, and the methods of financing, as well as assessing the likelihood that an offer will be successful. Throughout the chapter we use Exxon's merger with Mobil in 1999 to illustrate how financial analysis can be used in a merger context.[2]

MOTIVATION FOR MERGER OR ACQUISITION

There are a variety of reasons that firms merge or acquire other firms. Some acquiring managers may want to increase their own power and prestige. Others, however, realize that business combinations provide an opportunity to create new economic value for their stockholders. New value can be created in the following ways:

1. *Taking advantage of economies of scale.* Mergers are often justified as a means of providing the two participating firms with increased economies of scale. Economies of scale arise when one firm can perform a function more efficiently than two. For example, Exxon and Mobil are both major oil firms with considerable overlap in production and administrative facilities. The merger was expected to provide operating synergies from eliminating duplicate facilities and excess capacity, and from reducing general and administrative costs. At the time of the merger, management estimated that it would save $730 million by cutting roughly 9,000 jobs and closing offices,

an additional $1.15 billion by trimming business overlap, and that sharing exploration, procurement budgets, and technology could save another $780 million. All told, the management stated that it could realize cost savings of about $2.8 billion per year through the merger.

2. *Improving target management.* Another common motivation for acquisition is to improve target management. A firm is likely to be a target if it has systematically underperformed its industry. Historical poor performance could be due to bad luck, but it could also be due to the firm's managers making poor investment and operating decisions, or deliberately pursuing goals which increase their personal power but cost stockholders.

3. *Combining complementary resources.* Firms may decide that a merger will create value by combining complementary resources of the two partners. For example, a firm with a strong research and development unit could benefit from merging with a firm that has a strong distribution unit. In the Exxon-Mobil merger, the two firms appeared to have complementary capabilities and resources. Exxon had a reputation for conservative financial management, reflected in successful cost-cutting efforts and modest financial leverage. However, its oil reserves had been growing only modestly, with an average five-year reserve replacement ratio of only 102 percent. In contrast, Mobil was touted as one of the leading exploration firms, with a five-year reserve replacement ratio of 147 percent, a 25 percent stake in the important Tengiz oil field, and extensive reserves elsewhere in the world.

4. *Capturing tax benefits.* In the U.S. the 1986 Tax Reform Act eliminated many of the tax benefits from mergers and acquisitions. However, several merger tax benefits remain. The major benefit is the acquisition of operating tax losses. If a firm does not expect to earn sufficient profits to fully utilize operating loss carryforward benefits, it may decide to buy another firm which is earning profits. The operating losses and loss carryforwards of the acquirer can then be offset against the target's taxable income.[3] A second tax benefit often attributed to mergers is the tax shield that comes from increasing leverage for the target firm. This was particularly relevant for leveraged buyouts in the 1980s.[4]

5. *Providing low-cost financing to a financially constrained target.* If capital markets are imperfect, perhaps because of information asymmetries between management and outside investors, firms can face capital constraints. Information problems are likely to be especially severe for newly formed, high-growth firms. These firms can be difficult for outside investors to value since they have short track records, and their financial statements provide little insight into the value of their growth opportunities. Further, since they typically have to rely on external funds to finance their growth, capital market constraints for high-growth firms are likely to affect their ability to undertake profitable new projects. Public capital markets are therefore likely to be costly sources of funds for these types of firms. An acquirer that understands the business and is willing to provide a steady source of finance may therefore be able to add value.[5]

6. *Increasing product-market rents.* Firms also can have incentives to merge to increase product-market rents. By merging and becoming a dominant firm in the industry, two smaller firms can collude to restrict their output and raise prices, thereby increasing their profits. This circumvents problems that arise in cartels of independent firms, where firms have incentives to cheat on the cartel and increase their output.

While product-market rents make sense for firms as a motive for merging, the two partners are unlikely to announce their intentions when they explain the merger to their investors, since most countries have antitrust laws which regulate mergers between two firms in the same industry. For example, in the U.S. there are three major antitrust statutes—The Sherman Act of 1890, The Clayton Act of 1914, and The Hart Scott Rodino Act of 1976.

Anti-competitive concerns were significant for the Exxon-Mobil merger since Exxon and Mobil were the largest and second-largest U.S. oil producers, respectively. Merger approval was required by both the U.S. Federal Trade Commission (FTC) and the European Commission. Both did eventually approve the merger but required the new firm to sell assets in certain businesses and regions to preserve competition.

While many of the motivations for acquisitions are likely to create new economic value for shareholders, some are not. Firms that are flush with cash but have few new profitable investment opportunities are particularly prone to using their surplus cash to make acquisitions. Stockholders of these firms would probably prefer that managers pay out any surplus or "free" cash flows as dividends, or use the funds to repurchase their firm's stock. However, these options reduce the size of the firm and the assets under management's control. Management may therefore prefer to invest the free cash flows to buy new companies, even if they are not valued by stockholders. Of course managers will never announce that they are buying a firm because they are reluctant to pay out funds to stockholders. They may explain the merger using one of the motivations discussed above, or they may argue that they are buying the target at a bargain price.

Another motivation for mergers that is valued by managers but not stockholders is diversification. Diversification was a popular motivation for acquisitions in the 1960s and early 1970s. Acquirers sought to dampen their earnings volatility by buying firms in unrelated businesses. Diversification as a motive for acquisitions has since been widely discredited. Modern finance theorists point out that in a well functioning capital market, investors can diversify for themselves and do not need managers to do so for them. In addition, diversification has been criticized for leading firms to lose sight of their major competitive strengths and to expand into businesses where they do not have expertise.[6]

Key Analysis Questions

In evaluating a proposed merger, analysts are interested in determining whether the merger creates new wealth for acquiring and target stockholders, or whether it is motivated by managers' desires to increase their own power and prestige. Key questions for financial analysis are likely to include:

- *What is the motivation(s) for an acquisition and any anticipated benefits disclosed by acquirers or targets?*
- *What are the industries of the target and acquirer?* Are the firms related horizontally or vertically? How close are the business relations between them? If the businesses are unrelated, is the acquirer cash-rich and reluctant to return free cash flows to stockholders?
- *What are the key operational strengths of the target and the acquirer?* Are these strengths complementary? For example, does one firm have a renowned research group and the other a strong distribution network?
- *Is the acquisition a friendly one, supported by target management, or hostile?* A hostile takeover is more likely to occur for targets with poor-performing management who oppose the acquisition to preserve its job. However, as discussed below, this typically reduces acquirer management's access to information about the target, increasing risk of overpayment.

> - *What is the premerger performance of the two firms?* Performance metrics are likely to include ROE, gross margins, general and administrative expenses to sales, and working capital management ratios. On the basis of these measures, is the target a poor performer in its industry, implying that there are opportunities for improved management? Is the acquirer in a declining industry and searching for new directions?
> - *What is the tax position of both firms?* What are the average and marginal current tax rates for the target and the acquirer? Does the acquirer have operating loss carryforwards and the target taxable profits?
>
> This analysis should help the analyst understand what specific benefits, if any, the merger is likely to generate.

Motivation for the Exxon-Mobil Merger

Several industry factors influenced Exxon and Mobil to merge. Since the OPEC oil embargo of 1973, the oil industry had been subjected to wide price fluctuations that increased exploration risks. For example, real prices per barrel increased from $11.83 in 1973 to $50.94 in 1981 and then declined precipitously to $16.61 per barrel in 1986. Between 1987 and 1998, prices continued to fluctuate wildly, with a low of $10.53 in 1998 and a high of $23.15 in 1990. In addition to pricing risks, oil companies faced significant political risks in exploration since much of their reserves were located in politically volatile countries, where private property rights were subject to change.

The industry responded to these challenges by adopting cost reduction programs. From 1980 to 1992, employment at eight major oil companies declined by 63 percent, from 800,000 to 300,000. Headquarters staff at six of the largest firms declined from 3,000 to 800 in the period 1988 to 1992. In addition, companies sought to increase flexibility by leasing rather than owning tankers. But as prices continued to plummet in the late 1990s, oil companies sought other ways to increase efficiency.

The outcome was a series of large mergers and acquisitions that transformed the industry: BP merged with Amoco in 1998 and acquired Arco the following year; Total, a French oil firm, acquired the large Belgian oil firm Petrofina in late 1998 and subsequently purchased Elf Acquitaine in a $49 billion hostile takeover; Texaco was acquired by Chevron in 2000; and Phillips Petroleum acquired Tosco in early 2001, and late during the same year agreed to merge with Conoco.

The management of Exxon and Mobil argued that a merger would provide the new company with three significant benefits. First, as noted above, the combined firm would be able to reduce costs by $2.8 billion per year through efficiency improvements such as streamlining administrative overhead, eliminating excess capacity and duplicate facilities, using purchasing power to reduce raw material costs, and coordinating exploration in regions where the two firms operated separately. These savings were expected to be fully realized by the third year after the merger. Second, management noted that the two companies had complementary assets that would help increase productivity. For example, Exxon was a leader in deepwater exploration in West Africa, which complemented Mobil's production and exploration activities in Nigeria and Equatorial Guinea. In the Caspian, Exxon's presence in Azerbaijan complemented Mobil's strength in Kazakhstan, including a significant interest in the Tengiz field and its presence in Turkmenistan. Complementary exploration and production operations also existed in South America, Russia, and Eastern Canada. Finally, management argued that the merger provided the company with the scale required to manage the risks associated with very sizeable investments involved in new exploration projects.

Analysts and the financial media concurred with management's assessments of the economic benefits that potentially would be derived from the merger. Some analysts nevertheless expressed concern that differences in the cultures of the two companies might make it difficult for them to actually achieve these synergies. Exxon had a reputation for being "tight-lipped and conservative" whereas Mobil was viewed as "more open, both to the public and to new ideas."[7]

ACQUISITION PRICING

A well thought-out economic motivation for a merger or acquisition is a necessary but not sufficient condition for it to create value for acquiring stockholders. The acquirer must be careful to avoid overpaying for the target. Overpayment makes the transaction highly desirable and profitable for target stockholders, but it diminishes the value of the deal to acquiring stockholders. A financial analyst can use the following methods to assess whether the acquiring firm is overpaying for the target.

Analyzing Premium Offered to Target Stockholders

One popular way to assess whether the acquirer is overpaying for a target is to compare the premium offered to target stockholders to premiums offered in similar transactions. If the acquirer offers a relatively high premium, the analyst is typically led to conclude that the transaction is less likely to create value for acquiring stockholders.

Premiums differ significantly for friendly and hostile acquisitions. Premiums tend to be about 30 percent higher for hostile deals than for friendly offers, implying that hostile acquirers are more likely to overpay for a target.[8] There are several reasons for this. First, a friendly acquirer has access to the internal records of the target, making it much less likely that it will be surprised by hidden liabilities or problems once it has completed the deal. In contrast, a hostile acquirer does not have this advantage in valuing the target and is forced to make assumptions that may later turn out to be false. Second, the delays that typically accompany a hostile acquisition often provide opportunities for competing bidders to make an offer for the target, leading to a bidding war.

Comparing a target's premium to values for similar types of transactions is straightforward to compute, but it has several practical problems. First, it is not obvious how to define a comparable transaction. Figure 11-1 shows the mean and median premiums paid for U.S. targets between 1992 and 2001. Average premiums have risen from around 40 percent through the mid-1990s to between 50 and 60 percent in 1999–2001. Median premiums also increased during this period, from around 30 percent to 40 percent. However, mean and median premiums have to be interpreted with caution since there is considerable variation across transactions, making it difficult to use these estimates as a benchmark.

A second problem in using premiums offered to target stockholders to assess whether an acquirer overpaid is that measured premiums can be misleading if an offer is anticipated by investors. The stock price run-up for the target will then tend to make estimates of the premium appear relatively low. This limitation can be partially offset by using target

| Figure 11-1 | Premium Paid for Mergers and Acquisitions, 1992–2001 |

Source: *Mergerstat Review* (W.T. Grimm & Co., Chicago, 2002).

stock prices one month prior to the acquisition offer as the basis for calculating premiums. However, in some cases offers may have been anticipated for even longer than one month.

Finally, using target premiums to assess whether an acquirer overpaid ignores the value of the target to the acquirer after the acquisition. This value can be viewed as

Value of target after acquisition = Value as independent firm +
Value of merger benefits

The value of the target before acquisition is the present value of the free cash flows for the target if it were to remain an independent entity. This is likely to be somewhat different from the firm's stock price prior to any merger announcement since the pre-takeover price is a weighted average of the value of the firm as an independent unit and its value in the event of a takeover. The benefits of the merger include such effects as improvements in target operating performance from economies of scale, improved management, and tax benefits, as well as any spillover benefits to the acquirer from the acquisition. Clearly, acquirers will be willing to pay higher premiums for targets which are expected to generate higher merger benefits. Thus, examining the premium alone cannot determine whether the acquisition creates value for acquiring stockholders.

Analyzing Value of the Target to the Acquirer

A second and more reliable way of assessing whether the acquirer has overpaid for the target is to compare the offer price to the estimated value of the target to the acquirer. This latter value can be computed using the valuation techniques discussed in Chapters 7 and 8. The most popular methods of valuation used for mergers and acquisitions are earnings multiples and discounted cash flows. Since a comprehensive discussion of these techniques is provided earlier in the book, we focus here on implementation issues that arise for valuing targets in mergers and acquisitions. We recommend first computing the value of the target as an independent firm. This provides a way of checking whether the valuation assumptions are reasonable, since for publicly listed targets we can compare our estimate with pre-merger market prices. It also provides a useful benchmark for thinking about how the target's performance, and hence its value, is likely to change once it is acquired.

Earnings Multiples

To estimate the value of a target to an acquirer using earnings multiples, we have to forecast earnings for the target and decide on an appropriate earnings multiple, as follows:

Step 1: Forecasting earnings. Earnings forecasts are usually made by first forecasting next year's net income for the target assuming no acquisition. Historical sales growth rates, gross margins, and average tax rates are useful in building a pro forma income model. Once we have forecasted the income for the target prior to an acquisition, we can incorporate into the pro forma model any improvements in earnings performance that we expect to result from the acquisition. Performance improvements can be modeled as

- Higher operating margins through economies of scale in purchasing, or increased market power;
- Reductions in expenses as a result of consolidating research and development staffs, sales forces, and/or administration; or
- Lower average tax rates from taking advantage of operating tax loss carryforwards.

Step 2: Determining the price-earnings multiple. How do we determine the earnings multiple to be applied to our earnings forecasts? If the target firm is listed, it may be tempting to use the preacquisition price-earnings multiple to value postmerger earnings. However, there are several limitations to this approach. First, for many targets earnings growth expectations are likely to change after a merger, implying that there will be a difference between the pre- and postmerger price-earnings multiples. Postmerger earnings should then be valued using a multiple for firms with comparable growth and risk characteristics. (See discussion in Chapter 7.) A second problem is that premerger price-earnings multiples are unavailable for unlisted targets. Once again it becomes necessary to decide which types of listed firms are likely to be good comparables. Finally, if a premerger price-earnings multiple is appropriate for valuing postmerger earnings, care is required to ensure that the multiple is calculated prior to any acquisition announcement since the price will increase in anticipation of the premium to be paid to target stockholders.

The following table summarizes how price-earnings multiples are used to value a target firm before an acquisition (assuming it will remain an independent entity), and to estimate the value of a target to a potential acquirer:

Summary of Price-Earnings Valuation for Targets

Value of target as an independent firm	Target earnings forecast for the next year, assuming no change in ownership, multiplied by its *premerger* PE multiple.
Value of target to potential acquirer	Target *revised* earnings forecast for the next year, incorporating the effect of any operational changes made by the acquirer, multiplied by its *postmerger* PE multiple.

Limitations of Price-Earnings Valuation

As explained in Chapter 7, there are serious limitations to using earnings multiples for valuation. In addition to these limitations, the method has two more that are specific to merger valuations:

1. PE multiples assume that merger performance improvements come either from an immediate increase in earnings or from an increase in earnings growth (and hence an increase in the postmerger PE ratio). In reality, improvements and savings can come

in many forms—gradual increases in earnings from implementing new operating policies, elimination of overinvestment, better management of working capital, or paying out excess cash to stockholders. These types of improvements are not naturally reflected in PE multiples.

2. PE models do not easily incorporate any spillover benefits from an acquisition for the acquirer since they focus on valuing the earnings of the target.

Discounted Abnormal Earnings or Cash Flows

As discussed in Chapters 7 and 8, we can also value a company using the discounted abnormal earnings and discounted free cash flow methods. These require us to first forecast the abnormal earnings or free cash flows for the firm and then discount them at the cost of capital, as follows.

Step 1: Forecast abnormal earnings/free cash flows. A pro forma model of expected future income and cash flows for the firm provides the basis for forecasting abnormal earnings/free cash flows. As a starting point, the model should be constructed under the assumption that the target remains an independent firm. The model should reflect the best estimates of future sales growth, cost structures, working capital needs, investment and research and development needs, and cash requirements for known debt retirements, developed from financial analysis of the target. The abnormal earnings method requires that we forecast abnormal earnings or net operating profit after tax (NOPAT) for as long as the firm expects new investment projects to earn more than their cost of capital. Under the free cash flow approach, the pro forma model will forecast free cash flows to either the firm or to equity, typically for a period of five to ten years. Once we have a model of the abnormal earnings or free cash flows, we can incorporate any improvements in earnings/free cash flows that we expect to result from the acquisition. These will include the cost savings, cash received from asset sales, benefits from eliminating overinvestment, improved working capital management, and paying out excess cash to stockholders.

Step 2: Compute the discount rate. If we are valuing the target's postacquisition abnormal NOPAT or cash flows to the firm, the appropriate discount rate is the weighted average cost of capital for the target, using its expected *postacquisition* capital structure. Alternatively, if the target equity cash flows are being valued directly or if we are valuing abnormal earnings, the appropriate discount rate is the target's *postacquisition cost of equity* rather than its weighted average cost of capital (WACC). Two common mistakes are to use the acquirer's cost of capital or the target's *preacquisition* cost of capital to value the postmerger abnormal earnings/cash flows from the target.

The computation of the target's postacquisition cost of capital can be complicated if the acquirer plans to make a change to the target's capital structure after the acquisition, since the target's costs of debt and equity will change. As discussed in Chapter 8, this involves estimating the asset beta for the target, calculating the new equity and debt betas under the modified capital structure, and finally computing the revised cost of equity capital or weighted cost of capital. As a practical matter, the effect of these changes on the weighted average cost of capital is likely to be quite small unless the revision in leverage has a significant effect on the target's interest tax shields or its likelihood of financial distress.

The following table summarizes how the discounted abnormal earnings/cash flow methods can be used to value a target before an acquisition (assuming it will remain an independent entity), and to estimate the value of a target firm to a potential acquirer.

Summary of Discounted Abnormal Earnings/Cash Flow Valuation for Targets	
Value of target without an acquisition	(a) Present value of abnormal earnings/free cash flows to target equity assuming no acquisition, discounted at *premerger* cost of equity; or
	(b) Present value of abnormal NOPAT/free cash flows to target debt and equity assuming no acquisition, discounted at *premerger* WACC, less value of debt.
Value of target to potential acquirer	(a) Present value of abnormal earnings/free cash flows to target equity, *including benefits from merger,* discounted at *postmerger* cost of equity; or
	(b) Present value of abnormal NOPAT/free cash flows to target, *including benefits from merger,* discounted at *postmerger* WACC, less value of debt.

Step 3: Analyze sensitivity. Once we have estimated the expected value of a target, we will want to examine the sensitivity of our estimate to changes in the model assumptions. For example, answering the following questions can help the analyst assess the risks associated with an acquisition:

- What happens to the value of the target if it takes longer than expected for the benefits of the acquisition to materialize?
- What happens to the value of the target if the acquisition prompts its primary competitors to respond by also making an acquisition? Will such a response affect our plans and estimates?

Key Analysis Questions

To analyze the pricing of an acquisition, the analyst is interested in assessing the value of the acquisition benefits to be generated by the acquirer relative to the price paid to target stockholders. Analysts are therefore likely to be interested in answers to the following questions:

- What is the premium that the acquirer paid for the target's stock? What does this premium imply for the acquirer in terms of future performance improvements to justify the premium?
- What are the likely performance improvements that management expects to generate from the acquisition? For example, are there likely to be increases in the revenues for the merged firm from new products, increased prices, or better distribution of existing products? Alternatively, are there cost savings as a result of taking advantage of economies of scale, improved efficiency, or a lower cost of capital for the target?
- What is the value of any performance improvements? Values can be estimated using multiples or discounted abnormal earnings/cash flow methods.

Exxon's Pricing of Mobil

Exxon's $74.2 billion price for Mobil represented a 26.4 percent premium to target stockholders over the market value on November 20, 1998, when rumors of a merger first reached Wall Street. This was below the mean and median premiums reported for all acquisitions during that year (41 percent and 30 percent, respectively). However, it was toward the high end of estimates made by J. P. Morgan, Exxon's financial advisor, who reviewed 38 large comparable acquisitions and concluded that a 15–25 percent premium was justified. In comparison, BP had paid a 35 percent premium for Amoco during the same period.

In terms of traditional multiple forms of valuation, Exxon's pricing of Mobil appears to be reasonable. For example, at the time of the announcement of Exxon's offer, the PE value for other firms in the oil industry that were comparable to Mobil ranged from 19.3 to 23.8. Exxon's offer valued Mobil at 22.7 times current earnings.

The market reaction to the acquisition announcement suggests that analysts initially believed that the deal was marginal for Exxon's stockholders—Exxon's stock price dropped by 1.5 percent (adjusted for market-wide changes), or $2.6 billion, during the 11 days prior to the announcement through to the actual announcement day. However, by the tenth trading day after the announcement, Exxon's stock was up 3.6 percent, or $6.3 billion. Given the $15.5 billion premium that Exxon paid for Mobil, investors believed that the merger would create value of $21.8 billion.

Subsequent short-term financial results for Exxon-Mobil support the market's optimism about the merger synergies. In August 2000 Exxon-Mobil announced that merger synergies had reached $4.6 billion, far ahead of projections at the time of the merger. Analysts projected that they would reach $7 billion by 2002.

ACQUISITION FINANCING

Even if an acquisition is undertaken to create new economic value and is priced judiciously, it may still destroy shareholder value if it is inappropriately financed. Several financing options are available to acquirers, including issuing stock or warrants to target stockholders, or acquiring target stock using surplus cash or proceeds from new debt. The trade-offs between these options from the standpoint of target stockholders usually hinge on their tax and transaction cost implications. For acquirers, they can affect the firm's capital structure and provide new information to investors.

As we discuss below, the financing preferences of target and acquiring stockholders can diverge. Financing arrangements can therefore increase or reduce the attractiveness of an acquisition from the standpoint of acquiring stockholders. As a result, a complete analysis of an acquisition will include an examination of the implications of the financing arrangements for the acquirer.

Effect of Form of Financing on Target Stockholders

As noted above, the key financing considerations for target stockholders are the tax and transaction cost implications of the acquirer's offer.

Tax Effects of Different Forms of Consideration

Target stockholders care about the after-tax value of any offer they receive for their shares. In the U.S., whenever target stockholders receive cash for their shares, they are required to pay capital gains tax on the difference between the takeover offer price and their original purchase price. Alternatively, if they receive shares in the acquirer as consideration and the acquisition is undertaken as a tax-free reorganization, they can defer any taxes on the capital gain until they sell the new shares.

U.S. tax laws appear to cause target stockholders to prefer a stock offer to a cash one. This is certainly likely to be the case for a target founder who still has a significant stake in the company. If the company's stock price has appreciated over its life, the founder will face a substantial capital gains tax on a cash offer and will therefore probably prefer to receive stock in the acquiring firm. However, cash and stock offers can be tax-neutral for some groups of stockholders. For example, consider the tax implications for risk arbitrageurs, who take a short-term position in a company that is a takeover candidate in the hope that other bidders will emerge and increase the takeover price. They have no intention of holding stock in the acquirer once the takeover is completed and will pay ordinary income tax on any short-term trading gain. Cash and stock offers therefore have identical after-tax values for risk arbitrageurs. Similarly, tax-exempt institutions are likely to be indifferent to whether an offer is in cash or stock.

Transaction Costs and the Form of Financing

Transaction costs are another factor related to the form of financing that can be relevant to target stockholders. Transaction costs are incurred when target stockholders sell any stock received as consideration for their shares in the target. These costs will not be faced by target stockholders if the bidder offers them cash. Transaction costs are unlikely to be significant for investors who intend to hold the acquirer's stock following a stock acquisition. However they may be relevant for investors who intend to sell, such as risk arbitrageurs.

Effect of Form of Financing on Acquiring Stockholders

For acquiring stockholders the costs and benefits of different financing options usually depend on how the offer affects their firm's capital structure and any information effects associated with different forms of financing.

Capital Structure Effects of Form of Financing

In acquisitions where debt financing or surplus cash are the primary form of consideration for target shares, the acquisition increases the net financial leverage of the acquirer. This increase in leverage may be part of the acquisition strategy, since one way an acquirer can add value to an inefficient firm is to lower its taxes by increasing interest tax shields. However, in many acquisitions an increase in postacquisition leverage is a side effect of the method of financing and not part of a deliberate tax-minimizing strategy. The increase in leverage can then potentially reduce shareholder value for the acquirer by increasing the risk of financial distress.

To assess whether an acquisition leads an acquirer to have too much leverage, financial analysts can assess the acquirer's financial risk following the proposed acquisition by these methods:

- Assessing the pro forma financial risks for the acquirer under the proposed financing plan. Popular measures of financial risk include debt-to-equity and interest-coverage ratios, as well as projections of cash flows available to meet debt repayments. The ratios can be compared to similar performance metrics for the acquiring and target firms' industries. Do postmerger ratios indicate that the firm's probability of financial distress has increased significantly?
- Examining whether there are important off-balance-sheet liabilities for the target and/ or acquirer which are not included in the pro forma ratio and cash flow analysis of postacquisition financial risk.

- Determining whether the pro forma assets for the acquirer are largely intangible and therefore sensitive to financial distress. Measures of intangible assets include such ratios as market to book equity and tangible assets to the market value of equity.

Information Problems and the Form of Financing

As we discuss in Chapter 12, information asymmetries between managers and external investors can make managers reluctant to raise equity to finance new projects. Managers' reluctance arises from their fear that investors will interpret the decision as an indication that the firm's stock is overvalued. In the short term, this effect can lead managers to deviate from the firm's long-term optimal mix of debt and equity. As a result, acquirers are likely to prefer to use internal funds or debt to finance an acquisition, since these forms of consideration are less likely to be interpreted negatively by investors.[9]

The information effects imply that firms forced to use stock financing are likely to face a stock price decline when investors learn of the method of financing.[10] From the viewpoint of financial analysts, the financing announcement may, therefore, provide valuable news about the preacquisition value of the acquirer. On the other hand, it should have no implications for analysis of whether the acquisition creates value for acquiring shareholders, since the news reflected in the financing announcement is about the *preacquisition* value of the acquirer and not about the *postacquisition* value of the target to the acquirer.

A second information problem arises if the acquiring management does not have good information about the target. Stock financing then provides a way for acquiring stockholders to share the information risks with target shareholders. If the acquirer finds out after the acquisition that the value of the target is less than previously anticipated, the accompanying decline in the acquirer's equity price will be partially borne by target stockholders who continue to hold the acquirer's stock. In contrast, if the target's shares were acquired in a cash offer, any postacquisition loss would be fully borne by the acquirer's original stockholders. The risk-sharing benefits from using stock financing appears to be widely recognized for acquisitions of private companies, where public information on the target is largely unavailable.[11] In practice it appears to be considered less important for acquisitions of large public corporations.

Key Analysis Questions

The form of financing has important tax and transaction cost implications for target stockholders. It can also have important capital structure and information effects for acquirers. From the perspective of the analyst, the effect of any corporate tax benefits from debt financing should already be reflected in the valuation of the target. Information effects are not relevant to the value of the acquisition. However, the analyst does need to consider whether demands by target stockholders for consideration in cash lead the acquirer to have a postacquisition capital structure which increases the risk of financial distress to a point that is detrimental for stockholders. Thus, part of the analyst's task is to determine how it affects the acquirer's capital structure and its risks of financial distress by asking the following questions:

- What is the leverage for the newly created firm? How does this compare to leverage for comparable firms in the industry?

- What are the projected future cash flows for the merged firm? Are these sufficient to meet the firm's debt commitments? How much of a cushion does the firm have if future cash flows are lower than expected? Is the firm's debt level so high that it is likely to impair its ability to finance profitable future investments if future cash flows are below expectations?

Exxon's Financing of Mobil

Exxon offered Mobil shareholders 1.32 Exxon shares for each Mobil share. Given Mobil's 780 million shares outstanding, Exxon issued 1,030 million shares, which at $72 per share implied a total offer of $74.2 billion.

The merger was structured as a "tax-free reorganization" for federal income tax purposes. This implied that Mobil shareholders would not recognize any gain or loss for federal income tax purposes from exchanging their Mobil stock for Exxon Mobil stock in the merger.

By using stock to finance the acquisition, Exxon actually reduced its financial leverage. However, initially the market reacted negatively to the offer, lowering Exxon's stock price by 1.5 percent (adjusting for marketwide returns) on the announcement date (December 1, 1998). This reaction could have occurred because investors interpreted Exxon's stock offer as indicating that its stock was overvalued. Yet in the following ten days, Exxon's stock staged a recovery, increasing by 3.6 percent.

It is also worth noting that, under accounting rules in force at the time of the Exxon-Mobil merger, the form of financing had an effect on the acquirer's financial statements following the acquisition. In 1999, when the merger was completed, two methods of reporting for an acquisition were permitted under U.S. accounting—purchase and pooling of interests. Under the *purchase method,* the acquirer wrote up the assets of the target to their market value and recorded the difference between the purchase price and the market value of the target's tangible net assets as goodwill. Goodwill was subsequently amortized to earnings over a period of from 5 to 40 years. The *pooling-of-interests method* of accounting for mergers, which was rarely used outside the U.S., required acquirers to show the target's assets, liabilities, and equity at their original book values. Thus no goodwill was recorded, and subsequent earnings did not need to be reduced by the amortization of goodwill.

An acquirer's decision on a method of financing an acquisition largely determined its method of accounting for the transaction. The pooling-of-interests method was typically used if the acquirer issued voting common shares (not cash) in exchange for at least 90 percent of the voting common shares of the target, and if the acquisition occurred in a single transaction. The acquisition of Mobil satisfied these criteria, and Exxon announced that it therefore would use the pooling-of-interests method.

However SFAS 141 and 142 require that, as of July 2001, the purchase method be used to record all acquisitions no matter how they are financed. In contrast to the old purchase accounting rules, goodwill is no longer to be amortized unless there is evidence of impairment. Under these rules the financial statements of Exxon Mobil would look markedly different from those reported under the pooling-of-interests method. Mobil's equity would be valued at the $74.2 billion purchase price rather than its $19 billion premerger book value. The ROEs for the new firm would therefore seriously overstate the returns to Exxon shareholders from the acquisition. As discussed in Chapter 4, one way for the analyst to deal with this problem is to adjust the financial statements to reflect purchase accounting.

ACQUISITION OUTCOME

The final question of interest to the analyst evaluating a potential acquisition is whether it will indeed be completed. If an acquisition has a clear value-based motive, the target is priced appropriately, and its proposed financing does not create unnecessary financial risks for the acquirer, it may still fail because the target receives a higher competing bid or because of opposition from entrenched target management. Therefore, to evaluate the likelihood that an offer will be accepted, the financial analyst has to understand whether there are potential competing bidders who could pay an even higher premium to target stockholders than is currently offered. They also have to consider whether target managers are entrenched and, to protect their jobs, likely to oppose an offer.

Other Potential Acquirers

If there are other potential bidders for a target, especially ones who place a higher value on the target, there is a strong possibility that the bidder in question will be unsuccessful. Target management and stockholders have an incentive to delay accepting the initial offer to give potential competitors time to also submit a bid. From the perspective of the initial bidder, this means that the offer could potentially reduce stockholder value by the cost of making the offer (including substantial investment banking and legal fees). In practice, a losing bidder can usually recoup these losses and sometimes even make healthy profits from selling to the successful acquirer any shares it has accumulated in the target.

Key Analysis Questions

The financial analyst can determine whether there are other potential acquirers for a target and how they value the target by asking the following questions:

- Are there other firms that could also implement the initial bidder's acquisition strategy? For example, if this strategy relies on developing benefits from complementary assets, look for potential bidders who also have assets complementary to the target. If the goal of the acquisition is to replace inefficient management, what other firms in the target's industry could provide management expertise?

- Who are the acquirer's major competitors? Could any of these firms provide an even better fit for the target?

Target Management Entrenchment

If target managers are entrenched and fearful for their jobs, it is likely that they will oppose a bidder's offer. Some firms have implemented "golden parachutes" for top managers to counteract their concerns about job security at the time of an offer. Golden parachutes provide top managers of a target firm with attractive compensation rewards should the firm get taken over. However, many firms do not have such schemes, and opposition to an offer from entrenched management is a very real possibility.

While the existence of takeover defenses for a target indicates that its management is likely to fight a bidding firm's offer, defenses have typically not prevented an acquisition from taking place. Instead, they tend to cause delays, which increase the likelihood that there will be competing offers made for the target, including offers by friendly parties solicited by target management, called "white knights." Takeover defenses therefore increase the likelihood that the bidder in question will be outbid for the target, or that it will have to increase its offer significantly to win a bidding contest. Given these risks, some have argued that acquirers are now less likely to embark on a potentially hostile acquisition.

Key Analysis Questions

To assess whether the target firm's management is entrenched and therefore likely to oppose an acquisition, analysts can ask the following questions:

- Does the target firm have takeover defenses designed to protect management? Many such defenses were used during the turbulent 1980s, when hostile acquisitions were at their peak. Some of the most widely adopted include poison pills, staggered boards, super-majority rules, dual-class recapitalizations, fair-price provisions, ESOP plans, and changes in firms' states of incorporation to states with more restrictive anti-takeover laws.
- Has the target been a poor performer relative to other firms in its industry? If so, management's job security is likely to be threatened by a takeover, leading it to oppose any offers.
- Is there a golden parachute plan in place for target management? Golden parachutes provide attractive compensation for management in the event of a takeover to deter opposition to a takeover for job security reasons.

Analysis of Outcome of Exxon's Offer for Mobil

Analysts covering Mobil had little reason to question whether Mobil would be sold to Exxon. The offer was a friendly one that had received the approval of Mobil's management and board of directors. There probably was some risk of another major oil company entering the bidding for Mobil. For example, BP had shown an appetite for making major acquisitions with its purchase of Amoco in August 1998. In early 1999 BP also acquired Arco in a second mega-deal. Chevron was also rumored to be open to an acquisition, and in October 2000 it acquired Texaco. In the end, none of these competitors made a bid for Mobil. The acquisition was completed on December 1, 1999, twelve months after announcement of the initial agreement.

SUMMARY

This chapter summarizes how financial statement data and analysis can be used by financial analysts interested in evaluating whether an acquisition creates value for an acquiring firm's stockholders. Obviously, much of this discussion is also likely to be relevant to other merger participants, including target and acquiring management and their investment banks.

For the external analyst, the first task is to identify the acquirer's acquisition strategy. We discuss a number of strategies. Some of these are consistent with maximizing acquirer value, including acquisitions to take advantage of economies of scale, improve target management, combine complementary resources, capture tax benefits, provide low-cost financing to financially constrained targets, and increase product-market rents.

Other strategies appear to benefit managers more than stockholders. For example, some unprofitable acquisitions are made because managers are reluctant to return free cash flows to shareholders, or because managers want to lower the firm's earnings volatility by diversifying into unrelated businesses.

The financial analyst's second task is to assess whether the acquirer is offering a reasonable price for the target. Even if the acquirer's strategy is based on increasing shareholder value, it can overpay for the target. Target stockholders will then be well rewarded but at the expense of acquiring stockholders. We show how the ratio, pro forma, and valuation techniques discussed earlier in the book can all be used to assess the worth of the target to the acquirer.

The method of financing an offer is also relevant to a financial analyst's review of an acquisition proposal. If a proposed acquisition is financed with surplus cash or new debt, it increases the acquirer's financial risk. Financial analysts can use ratio analysis of the acquirer's postacquisition balance sheet and pro forma estimates of cash flow volatility and interest coverage to assess whether demands by target stockholders for consideration in cash lead the acquirer to increase its risk of financial distress.

Finally, the financial analyst is interested in assessing whether a merger is likely to be completed once the initial offer is made, and at what price. This requires the analyst to determine whether there are other potential bidders, and whether target management is entrenched and likely to oppose a bidder's offer.

DISCUSSION QUESTIONS

1. During the early 1990s there was a noticeable increase in mergers and acquisitions between firms in different countries (termed cross-border acquisitions). What factors could explain this increase? What special issues can arise in executing a cross-border acquisition and in ultimately meeting your objectives for a successful combination?

2. In the 1980s leveraged buyouts (LBOs) were a popular form of acquisition. Under a leveraged buyout, a buyout group (which frequently includes target management) makes an offer to buy the target firm at a premium over its current price. The buyout group finances much of the acquisition with debt capital, leading the target to become a highly leveraged private company following the acquisition.
   a. What types of firms would make ideal candidates for LBOs? Why?
   b. How might the acquirer add sufficient value to the target to justify a high buyout premium?

3. Kim Silverman, CFO of the First Public Bank Company, notes: "We are fortunate to have a cost of capital of only 10 percent. We want to leverage this advantage by acquiring other banks that have a higher cost of funds. I believe that we can add significant value to these banks by using our lower cost financing." Do you agree with Silverman's analysis? Why or why not?

4. The Boston Tea Company plans to acquire Hi Flavor Soda Co. for $60 per share, a 50 percent premium over current market price. John E. Grey, the CFO of Boston Tea, argues that this valuation can easily be justified, using a price-earnings analysis. "Boston Tea has a price-earnings ratio of 15, and we expect that we will be able to generate long-term earnings for Hi Flavor Soda of $5 per share. This implies that Hi Flavor is worth $75 to us, well below our $60 offer price." Do you agree with this analysis? What are Grey's key assumptions?

5. You have been hired by GS Investment Bank to work in the merger department. The analysis required for all potential acquisitions includes an examination of the target for

any off-balance-sheet assets or liabilities that have to be factored into the valuation. Prepare a checklist for your examination.

6. Company T is currently valued at $50 in the market. A potential acquirer, A, believes that it can add value in two ways: $15 of value can be added through better working capital management, and an additional $10 of value can be generated by making available a unique technology to expand T's new product offerings. In a competitive bidding contest, how much of this additional value will A have to pay out to T's shareholders to emerge as the winner?

7. In 1995 Disney acquired ABC television at a significant premium. Disney's management justified much of this premium by arguing that the acquisition would guarantee access for Disney's programs on ABC's television stations. Evaluate the economic merits of this claim.

8. A leading oil exploration company decides to acquire an Internet company at a 50 percent premium. The acquirer argues that this move creates value for its own stockholders because it can use its excess cash flows from the oil business to help finance growth in the new Internet segment. Evaluate the economic merits of this claim.

9. Under current U.S. accounting standards, acquirers are required to capitalize goodwill and report any subsequent declines in value as an impairment charge. What performance metrics would you use to judge whether goodwill is impaired?

NOTES

1. In a review of studies of merger returns, Michael Jensen and Richard Ruback, "The Market for Corporate Control: The Scientific Evidence," *Journal of Financial Economics* 11, (April 1983): 5–50, conclude that target shareholders earn positive returns from takeovers, but that acquiring shareholders only break even.

2. Much of our discussion is based on analysis of the acquisition presented by F. Weston, "The Exxon-Mobil Merger: An Archetype," *Journal of Applied Finance* 12, no. 1, Spring/Summer 2002.

3. Of course another possibility is for the profitable firm to acquire the unprofitable one. However, in the U.S. the IRS will disallow the use of tax loss carryforwards by an acquirer if it appears that an acquisition was tax-motivated.

4. See Steven Kaplan, "Management Buyouts: Evidence on Taxes as a Source of Value," *Journal of Finance* 44 (1989): 611–32.

5. Krishna Palepu, "Predicting takeover targets: A methodological and empirical analysis," *Journal of Accounting and Economics* 8 (March 1986): 3–36.

6. Chapter 2 discusses the pros and cons of corporate diversification and evidence on its implications for firm performance.

7. See S. Liesman and A. Sullivan, "Tight-Lipped Exxon, Outspoken Mobil Face Major Image, Cultural Differences," *Wall Street Journal*, December 2, 1998.

8. See Paul Healy, Krishna Palepu, and Richard Ruback, "Which Mergers Are Profitable—Strategic or Financial?," *Sloan Management Review* 38, no. 4 (Summer 1997): 45–58.

9. See Stewart Myers and Nicholas Majluf, "Corporate Financing and Investment Decisions When Firms Have Information That Investors Do Not," *Journal of Financial Economics* (June 1984): 187–221.

10. For evidence see Nicholas Travlos, "Corporate takeover bids, methods of payments, and bidding firms' stock returns," *Journal of Finance* 42 (1987): 943–63.

11. See S. Datar, R. Frankel, and M. Wolfson, "Earnouts: The Effects of Adverse Selection and Agency Costs on Acquisition Techniques," *Journal of Law, Economics, and Organization* 17 (2001): 201–238.

Corporate Financing Policies

In this chapter, we discuss how firms set their capital structure and dividend policies to maximize shareholder value. There is a strong relation between these two decisions. For example, a firm's decision to retain internally-generated funds rather than paying them out as a dividend can also be thought of as a financing decision. It is not surprising, therefore, to find that many of the factors that are important in setting capital structure (such as taxes, costs of financial distress, agency costs, and information costs) are also relevant for dividend policy decisions. We examine how these factors affect capital structure and dividend policy, as well as how the financial analysis tools, discussed in Part 2 of this book, can be used to evaluate capital structure and dividend policy decisions.

A variety of questions are dealt with in analysis of corporate financing policies:

- Securities analysts can ask: Given its capital structure and dividend policy, how should we position a firm in our fund—as a growth or income stock?
- Takeover specialists can ask: Can we improve stockholder value for a firm by changing its financial leverage or by increasing dividend payouts to owners?
- Management can ask: Have we selected a capital structure and dividend policy which supports our business objectives?
- Credit analysts can ask: What risks do we face in lending to this company, given its business and current financial leverage?

Throughout our discussion we take the perspective of an external analyst who is evaluating whether a firm has selected a capital structure and dividend policy that maximize shareholder value. The topic obviously also applies to management's decisions about what debt and dividend policies it should implement.

FACTORS THAT DETERMINE FIRMS' DEBT POLICIES

As discussed in Chapter 5, a firm's debt policy can be represented by comparing its net debt, defined as interest-bearing debt less excess cash and marketable securities, and its equity. In practice, since it is difficult to estimate excess cash and marketable securities, analysts typically use total cash and marketable securities as a proxy. For example, consider the debt policies for Pfizer Inc., a large pharmaceutical company, and Duke Energy Corporation, a large public utility, for the year ended December 31, 2001, reported in Table 12-1.

Table 12-1 Net Interest-Bearing Debt for Pfizer and Duke Energy for the Year Ended December 31, 2001

($ millions, except for net debt to equity ratio)	Pfizer	Duke Energy
Interest-bearing debt	$9,461	$14,198
Less: cash and short-term investments	8,615	290
Net debt	846	13,908
Book shareholders' equity	18,293	12,689
Net interest-bearing debt to book equity	5%	110%

Pfizer's liquid assets (cash and marketable securities) are comparable to its interest-bearing debt. As a result, its net debt is only 5 percent of its book equity. In contrast, Duke Energy has a ratio of net debt to book equity of 110 percent. Throughout the chapter we will examine factors that are relevant to the financing differences for these firms.

When financial analysts evaluate a firm's capital structure, two related questions typically emerge. First, in the long term, what is the best mix of debt and equity for creating stockholder value? And second, if managers are considering new investment initiatives in the short term, what type of financing should they use? Two popular models of capital structure provide help in thinking about these questions. The static model of capital structure examines how trade-offs between the benefits and costs of debt determine a firm's long-term optimal mix of debt and equity. And the dynamic model examines how information effects can lead a firm to deviate from its long-term optimal capital structure as it seeks financing for new investments. We discuss both models, since they have somewhat different implications for thinking about capital structure.

THE OPTIMAL LONG-TERM MIX OF DEBT AND EQUITY

To determine the best long-term mix of debt and equity capital for a firm, we need to consider the benefits and costs of financial leverage. By trading off these benefits and costs, we can decide whether a firm should be financed mostly with equity or mostly with debt.

Benefits of Leverage

The major benefits of financial leverage typically include corporate tax shields on interest and improved incentives for management.

Corporate Interest Tax Shields

In the U.S., and in many other countries for that matter, tax laws provide a form of government subsidy for debt financing which does not exist for equity financing. This arises from the corporate tax deductibility of interest against income. No such corporate tax shield is available for dividend payments or for retained earnings. Debt financing therefore has an advantage over equity, since the interest tax shields under debt provide additional income to debt and equity holders. This higher income translates directly into higher firm values for leveraged firms in relation to unleveraged firms.

Some practitioners and theorists have pointed out that the corporate tax benefit from debt financing is potentially offset by a personal tax disadvantage of debt.[1] That is, since the holders of debt must pay relatively high tax rates on interest income, they require that corporations offer high pretax yields on debt. This disadvantage is particularly severe when interest income is taxed at a higher rate than capital gains on equity. Under current U.S. tax laws, personal tax rates on interest income are higher than on long-term capital gains, implying that personal tax effects at least partially offset the corporate tax benefits of debt. However, most financial managers and financial economists believe that there is a corporate tax advantage to debt financing.

Therefore, the corporate tax benefits from debt financing should encourage firms with high effective tax rates and few forms of tax shield other than interest to have highly leveraged capital structures. In contrast, firms that have tax shield substitutes for interest, such as depreciation, or that have operating loss carryforwards and hence do not expect to pay taxes, should have capital structures that are largely equity.

Key Analysis Questions

To evaluate the tax effects of additional debt, analysts can use accounting, financial ratio, and prospective analysis to answer the following types of questions:

- What is a firm's average income tax rate? How does this rate compare with the average tax rate and financial leverage for its major competitors?
- What portion of a firm's tax expense is deferred taxes versus current taxes?
- What is the firm's marginal corporate tax rate likely to be?
- Does the firm have tax loss carryforwards or other tax benefits? How long are they expected to continue?
- What noninterest tax shields are currently available to the firm? For example, are there sizeable tax shields from accelerated depreciation?
- Based on pro forma income and cash flow statements, what are estimates for the firm's taxable income for the next five to ten years? What noninterest tax shields are available to the firm? Finally, what would be the tax savings from using some debt financing?

Management Incentives for Value Creation

A second benefit of debt financing is that it focuses management on value creation, thus reducing conflicts of interest between managers and shareholders. Conflicts of interest can arise when managers make investments that are of little value to stockholders and/or spend the firm's funds on perks, such as overly spacious office buildings and lavish corporate jets. Firms are particularly prone to these temptations when they are flush with cash but have few promising new investment opportunities, often referred to as "free cash flow" situations. These firms' stockholders would generally prefer that their managers pay out any free cash flows as dividends or use the funds to repurchase stock. However, these payouts reduce the size of the firm and the assets under management's control. Management may therefore invest the free cash flows in new projects, even if they are not valued by stockholders, or spend the cash flows on management perks.

How can debt help reduce management's incentives to overinvest and to overspend on perks? The primary way is by reducing resources available to fund these types of outlays, since firms with relatively high leverage face pressures to generate cash flows to meet payments of interest and principal.

The debt introduced as a result of the 1988 leveraged buyout of RJR Nabisco was viewed by many as an example of debt creating pressure for management to refocus on value creation for stockholders. Under this view, the incentive problems facing the company stemmed from the high cash flows it generated in the tobacco business and the low investment opportunities in this line of business given the decline in popularity of smoking in the U.S. The increased debt taken with the LBO forced RJR Nabisco's management to eliminate unnecessary perks, such as corporate jets and parties with famous sports stars, to slow diversification into the food industry, and to cancel unprofitable projects such as the smokeless cigarette.

Key Analysis Questions

Financial ratio and prospective analysis can help analysts assess whether there are currently free cash flow inefficiencies at a firm as well as risks of future inefficiencies.

Symptoms of excessive management perks and investment in unprofitable projects include the following:

- *High ratios of general and administrative expenses and overhead to sales.* If a firm's ratios are higher than those for its major competitors, one possibility is that management is wasting money on perks.
- *Significant new investments in unrelated areas.* If it is difficult to rationalize these new investments, there might be free cash flow problems.
- *High levels of expected operating cash flows (net of essential capital expenditures and debt retirements) from pro forma income and cash flow statements.*
- *Poor management incentives to create additional shareholder value,* evidenced by a weak linkage between management compensation and firm performance.

Costs of Leverage: Financial Distress

As a firm increases its leverage, it increases the likelihood of financial distress, where it is unable to meet interest or principal repayment obligations to creditors. This may force the firm to declare bankruptcy or to agree to restructure its financial claims.

Financial distress can be expensive, since restructurings of a firm's ownership claims typically involve costly legal negotiations. It can also be difficult for distressed firms to raise capital to undertake profitable new investment opportunities. Finally, financial distress can intensify conflicts of interest between stockholders and the firm's debtholders, increasing the cost of debt financing.

Legal Costs of Financial Distress

When a firm is in serious financial distress, its owners' claims are likely to be restructured. This can take place under formal bankruptcy proceedings or out of bankruptcy. Restructurings are likely to be costly, since the parties involved have to hire lawyers, bankers, and accountants to represent their interests, and they have to pay court costs if there are formal legal proceedings. These are often called the *direct* costs of financial distress.

Costs of Foregone Investment Opportunities

When a firm is in financial distress and particularly when it is in bankruptcy, it may be very difficult for it to raise additional capital for new investments, even though they may be profitable for all the firm's owners. In some cases bankrupt firms are run by court-appointed trustees, who are unlikely to take on risky new investments—profitable or not. Even for a firm whose management supports new investment, the firm is likely to be capital constrained. Creditors are unlikely to approve the sale of nonessential assets unless the proceeds are used to first repay their claims. Potential new investors and creditors will be wary of the firm because they do not want to become embroiled in the legal disputes themselves. Thus, in all likelihood the firm will be unable to make significant new investments, potentially diminishing its value.

Costs of Conflicts Between Creditors and Stockholders

When a firm is performing well, both creditors' and stockholders' interests are likely to coincide. Both want the firm's managers to take all investments which increase the value of the firm. But when the firm is in financial difficulty, conflicts can arise between different classes of owners. Creditors become concerned about whether the firm will be able to meet its interest and principal commitments. Shareholders become concerned that their equity will revert to the creditors if the firm is unable to meet its outstanding obligations. Thus managers are likely to face increased pressure to make decisions which serve the interests of only one form of owner, typically stockholders, rather than making decisions in the best interests of all owners. For example, managers have incentives to issue additional debt with equal or higher priority, to invest in riskier assets, or to pay liquidating dividends, since these actions reduce the value of outstanding creditors' claims and benefit stockholders. When it is costly to completely eliminate this type of game playing, creditors will simply reduce the amount they are willing to pay the firm for the debt when it is issued, increasing the costs of borrowing for the firm's stockholders.

Overall Effects of Financial Distress

The costs of financial distress discussed above offset the tax and monitoring benefits of debt. As a result, firms that are more likely to fall into financial distress or for which the costs of financial distress are especially high should have relatively low financial leverage. Firms are more likely to fall into financial distress if they have high business risks, that is, if their revenues and earnings before interest are highly sensitive to fluctuations in the economy. Financial distress costs are also likely to be relatively high for firms whose assets are easily destroyed in financial distress. For example, firms with human capital and brand intangibles are particularly sensitive to financial distress since dissatisfied employees and customers can leave or seek alternative suppliers. In contrast, firms with tangible assets can sell their assets if they get into financial distress, providing additional security for lenders and lowering the costs of financial distress. Firms with intangible assets are therefore less likely to be highly leveraged than firms whose assets are mostly tangible.

These factors probably largely explain why Pfizer and Duke Energy, the two companies discussed at the beginning of the chapter, have such different financing policies. Pfizer probably keeps its leverage low because many of its core assets are intangibles, such as research staff and sales force representatives. These types of assets can easily be lost if Pfizer gets into financial difficulty as a result of too much leverage. In all likelihood, management would be forced to cut back on R&D and marketing, allowing their most talented researchers and sales representatives to be subject to offers from competitors. Pfizer can reduce these risks by having very low leverage.

In contrast, Duke Energy is a utility. It has very stable cash flows since its revenues are largely regulated. In addition, its major asset is its physical plant, which is less likely to diminish in value if it gets into financial distress. If the debtholders ended up as the new owners of the firm following financial distress, they could continue to use the existing assets. Duke Energy can therefore take advantage of the tax benefits from corporate debt without bearing a high cost of financial distress.

Key Analysis Questions

The above discussion implies that a firm's optimal financial leverage will depend on its underlying business risks and asset types. If the firm's business risks are relatively high or its assets can be easily destroyed by financial distress, changing the mix of debt and equity toward more debt may actually destroy shareholder value. Analysts can use ratio, cash flow, and pro forma analysis to assess a firm's business risks and whether its assets are easily destroyed by financial distress. Their analysis should focus on these activities:

> • *Comparing indicators of business risk for the firm and other firms in its industry with the economy.* Popular indicators of business risk include the ratio of fixed operating expenses (such as depreciation on plant and equipment) to sales, the volatility of return on assets, as well as the relation between indicators of the firm's performance and indicators of performance for the economy as a whole.
> • *Examining competition in the industry.* For firms in a highly competitive industry, performance is very sensitive to changes in strategy by competitors.
> • *Determining whether the firm's assets are largely intangible and therefore sensitive to financial distress,* using such ratios as market-to-book equity.

Determining the Long-Term Optimal Mix of Debt and Equity

The above discussion implies that the optimal mix of debt and equity for a firm can be estimated by trading off the corporate interest tax shield and monitoring benefits of debt against the costs of financial distress. As the firm becomes more highly leveraged, the costs of leverage presumably begin to outweigh the tax and monitoring benefits of debt.

However there are several practical difficulties in trying to estimate a firm's optimal financial leverage. One difficulty is quantifying some of the costs and benefits of leverage. For example, it is not easy to value the expected costs of financial distress or any management incentive benefits from debt. There are no easy answers to this problem. The best that we can do is to qualitatively assess whether the firm faces free cash flow problems, and whether it faces high business risks and has assets that are easily destroyed by financial distress. These qualitative assessments can then be used to adjust the more easily quantified tax benefits from debt to determine whether the firm's financial leverage should be relatively high, low, or somewhere in between.

A second practical difficulty in deciding on a firm's level of financial leverage is quantifying what we mean by high, low, and medium. One way to resolve this question is to use indicators of financial leverage, such as debt-to-equity ratios, for the market as a whole as a guide on leverage ranges.

To provide a rough sense of what companies usually consider to be high and low financial leverage, Table 12-2 shows median debt-to-market equity and debt-to-book equity ratios for selected U.S. industries for the year ended December 31, 2001. Median ratios are reported for all listed companies and for NYSE companies.

Median debt-to-book equity ratios are highest for the electric services and water supply industries. The core assets for firms in these industries include physical equipment and property that are readily transferable to debt holders in the event of financial distress. In addition, firms in the electric power and water supply industries are typically not highly sensitive to economy risk. In contrast, the software and pharmaceutical industries' core assets are their research staffs. Ownership of these types of assets cannot be easily transferred to debt holders if the firm is in financial distress. Researchers are likely to leave for greener pastures if their budgets are cut. As a result, firms in this industry have relatively conservative capital structures. Petroleum refining and hotel firms have leverage in between these extremes, reflecting the need to balance the impact of having extensive physical assets and being subject to more volatile revenue streams.

It is also interesting to note that NYSE firms tend to have higher leverage than non-NYSE firms in the same industries. This probably reflects the fact that larger NYSE firms tend to have more product offerings and to be more diversified geographically, reducing

Table 12-2 Median Net Interest-Bearing Debt-to-Book Equity and Net Interest-Bearing Debt-to-Market Equity for Selected U.S. Industries in 2001

Industry	Net Interest-Bearing Debt-to-Book Equity		Net Interest-Bearing Debt-to-Market Equity	
	All Listed Firms	NYSE Firms	All Listed Firms	NYSE Firms
Prepackaged Computer Software	−64%	−25%	−17%	−7%
Pharmaceutical	−54%	−5%	−8%	−1%
Hotels & Motels	46%	64%	111%	68%
Petroleum Refining	52%	49%	29%	23%
Water Supply	96%	101%	40%	52%
Electric Services	124%	125%	67%	71%

their vulnerability to negative events for a single product or market, and enabling them to take on more debt.

The net debt-to-market equity ratios by and large tell a similar story to the debt-to-book equity ratios. They reflect the fact that most firms have market-to-book equity ratios greater than 1 because companies generally invest in projects that add value for stockholders and because some types of assets, such as R&D, are typically not reflected in book equity.

THE FINANCING OF NEW PROJECTS

The second model of capital structure focuses on how firms make new financing decisions. Proponents of this dynamic model argue that there can be short-term frictions in capital markets which cause deviations from long-run optimal capital structure. One source of friction arises when managers have better information about their firm's future performance than outside investors. This could lead managers to deviate from their long-term optimal capital structure as they seek financing for new investments.

To see how information asymmetries between outside investors and management can create market imperfections and potentially affect short-term capital structure decisions, consider management's options for financing a proprietary new project that it expects to be profitable. One financing option is to use retained earnings to cover the investment outlay. However, what if the firm has no retained earnings available today? If it pays dividends, it could perhaps cut dividends to help pay for the project. But as we see later, investors usually interpret a dividend cut as an indication that the firm's management anticipates poor future performance. A dividend cut is therefore likely to lead to a stock price decline, which management would probably prefer to avoid. Also, many firms do not pay dividends.

A second financing option is to borrow additional funds to finance the project. However, if the firm is already highly leveraged, the tax shield benefits from debt are likely to be relatively modest and the potential costs of financial distress relatively high, making additional borrowing unattractive.

The final financing option available to the firm is to issue new equity. However, if investors know that management has superior information on the firm's value, they are likely to interpret an equity offer as an indication that management believes that the firm's stock price is higher than the intrinsic value of the firm.[2] The announcement of an equity offer is therefore likely to lead to a drop in the price of the firm's stock, raising the firm's cost of capital, and potentially leading management to abandon a perfectly good project.

This discussion implies that if the firm has internal cash flows available or is not already highly leveraged, it is relatively straightforward for it to arrange financing for the new project. Otherwise, management has to decide whether undertaking the new project is worthwhile given the costs of cutting dividends, issuing additional debt, or issuing equity to finance the project. The information costs of raising funds by these means lead to a "pecking order" for new financing. Managers first use internal cash to fund investments, and only if this is unavailable do they resort to external financing. Further, if they have to use external financing, managers first use debt financing. New equity issues are used only as a last resort because of the difficulties that investors have in interpreting these issues.[3]

One way for management to mitigate the information problems of using external financing is to ensure that the firm has financial slack. Management can create financial slack by reinvesting free cash flows in marketable securities so that it doesn't have to go to the capital market to finance a new project. It could also choose to have relatively low levels of debt, so that the firm can borrow easily in the future.

In summary, information asymmetries between managers and external investors can make managers reluctant to raise equity to finance new projects. Managers' reluctance arises from their fear that investors will interpret the decision as an indication that the firm's stock is overvalued. In the short term, this effect can lead managers to deviate from the firm's long-term optimal mix of debt and equity.

Key Analysis Questions

The above discussion implies that in the short term management should attempt to finance new projects primarily with retained earnings. Further, it suggests that management would be well advised to maintain financial slack to ensure that it is not forced to use costly external financing. To assess a firm's financing options, we would ask the following types of questions:

- What is the value of current cash reserves (not required for day-to-day working capital needs) that could be used for new capital outlays? What operating cash resources are expected to become available in the coming few years? Do these internal resources cover the firm's expected cash needs for new investment and working capital?
- How do the firm's future cash needs for investment change as its operating performance deteriorates or improves? Are its investment opportunities relatively fixed, or are they related to current operating cash flow performance? Investment opportunities for many firms decline during a recession and increase during booms, enabling them to consistently use internal funds for financing. Therefore firms with stable investment needs should build financial slack during booms so that they can support investment during busts.
- If internal funds are not readily available, what opportunities does the firm have to raise low-cost debt financing? Normally, a firm which has virtually zero debt could do this without difficulty. However, if it is in a volatile industry or has mostly intangible assets, debt financing may be costly.
- If the firm has to raise costly equity capital, are there ways to focus investors on the value of the firm's assets and investment opportunities to lower any

> information asymmetries between managers and investors? For example, manage-ment might be able to disclose additional information about the value of existing assets, and the uses and expected returns from the new funds.

Summary of Debt Policy

There are no easy ways to quantify the best mix of debt and equity for a firm and its best financing options. However, some general principles are likely to be useful in thinking about these questions. We have seen that the benefits from debt financing are likely to be highest for firms with

- high marginal tax rates and few noninterest tax shields, making interest tax shields from debt valuable;
- high, stable income/cash flows and few new investment opportunities, increasing the monitoring value of debt and reducing the likelihood that the firm will fall into finan-cial distress or require costly external financing for new projects; and
- high tangible assets that are not easily destroyed by financial distress.

The financial analysis tools developed in Part 2 of the book are useful in rating a firm's interest tax shield benefits, its business risk and investment opportunities, and its major asset types. This information can then be used to judge whether there are benefits from debt or whether the firm would be better off using equity financing to support its business strategies.

FACTORS THAT DETERMINE DIVIDEND POLICIES

To assess a firm's dividend policy, analysts typically examine its dividend payout, its divi-dend yield, and any stock repurchases. Dividend payout is defined as cash dividends as a percentage of income available to common shareholders, and it reflects the extent to which a company pays out profits or retains them for reinvestment. Dividend yield is dividends per share as a percentage of the current stock price, and indicates the current dividend return earned by shareholders. Finally, stock repurchases are relevant because many companies use repurchases of their own stock as an alternative way of returning cash to shareholders. Table 12-3 provides information on these variables for Pfizer and Duke Energy.

Table 12-3 Dividend Policy for Pfizer and Duke Energy
for the Year Ended December 31, 2001

	Pfizer	Duke Energy
Dividend payout	35%	64%
Dividend yield	1.1%	3.9%
Cash common dividends	$2,715m	$1,200m
Stock repurchases	$3,603m	$0m

Pfizer appears to be following a more conservative dividend policy. It has a lower pay-out than Duke Energy and a lower dividend yield. However, in 2001 Pfizer returned

$3.6 billion to shareholders through stock repurchases, whereas Duke Energy made no stock repurchases. If this distribution is included with dividends, Pfizer actually paid out 81 percent of income in 2001.

What factors should a firm consider when setting its dividend policy? Do investors prefer firms to pay out profits as dividends or to retain them for reinvestment? As we noted above, many of the factors that affect dividends are similar to those examined in the section on capital structure decisions. This should not be too surprising, since a firm's dividend policy also affects its financing decisions. Thus, dividends provide a means of reducing free cash flow inefficiencies. They also have tax implications for investors and can reduce a firm's financial slack. Finally, lending contracts that are designed to protect lenders' interests can affect a firm's dividend payouts.

Below we discuss the factors that are relevant to managers' dividend decisions and how financial analysis tools can be used in this decision process.

Dividends as a Way of Reducing Free Cash Flow Inefficiencies

As we discussed earlier, conflicts of interest between managers and shareholders can affect a firm's optimal capital structure; they also have implications for dividend policy decisions. Stockholders of a firm with free cash flows and few profitable investment opportunities want managers to adopt a dividend policy with high payouts. This will deter managers from growing the firm by reinvesting the free cash flows in new projects that are not valued by stockholders or from spending the free cash flows on management perks. In addition, if managers of a firm with free cash flows wish to fund a new project, most stockholders would prefer that they do so by raising new external capital rather than cutting dividends. Stockholders can then assess whether the project is genuinely profitable or simply one of management's pet projects.

Key Analysis Questions

Earlier we discussed how ratio and cash flow analysis can help analysts assess whether a firm faces free cash flow inefficiencies, and how pro forma analysis can help indicate the likelihood of future free cash flow problems. The same analysis and questions can be used to decide whether a firm should initiate dividends.

Tax Costs of Dividends

What are the implications for dividend policy if dividends and capital gains are taxed, particularly at different rates? Classical models of the tax effects of dividends predict that if the capital gains tax rate is less than the rate on dividend income, investors will prefer that the firm either pay no dividends, so that they subsequently take gains as capital accumulation, or that the firm undertakes a stock repurchase, which qualifies as a capital distribution. Even if capital gains are slightly higher than dividend tax rates, investors may prefer capital gains to dividends since they do not actually have to realize their capital gains. They can delay selling their shares and thereby defer paying the taxes on any capital appreciation. Of course, if capital gains tax rates are substantially higher than the rates on ordinary income, investors are likely to favor dividend distributions over capital gains.

Today many practitioners and theorists believe that taxes play only a minor role in determining a firm's dividend policy since a firm can attract investors with various tax preferences. Thus a firm that wishes to pay high dividend rates will attract stockholders that are tax-exempt institutions, which do not pay taxes on dividend income. In contrast, a firm that prefers to pay low dividend rates will attract stockholders who have high marginal tax rates and prefer capital gains to dividend income.

Dividends and Financial Slack

We discussed earlier how managers' information advantage over dispersed investors can increase a firm's cost of external funds. One way to avoid having to raise costly external funds is to have a conservative dividend policy which creates financial slack in the organization. By paying only a small percentage of income as dividends and reinvesting the free cash flows in marketable securities, management reduces the likelihood that the firm will have to go to the capital market to finance a new project.

Managers of firms with high intangible assets and growth opportunities are particularly likely to have an information advantage over dispersed investors, since accounting information for these types of firms is frequently a poor indicator of future performance. Accountants, for example, do not attempt to value R&D, intangibles, or growth opportunities. These types of firms are therefore more likely to face information problems and capital market constraints. To compound this problem, high-growth firms are typically heavily dependent on external financing since they are not usually able to fund all new investments internally. Any capital market constraints are therefore likely to affect their ability to undertake profitable new projects.

Because paying dividends reduces financial slack and is thus costly, a firm's dividend policy can help management communicate effectively with external investors. Investors recognize that managers will only increase their firm's dividend rate if they anticipate that the payout does not have a serious effect on the firm's future financing options. Thus, the decision to increase dividends can help investors appreciate management's optimism about the firm's future performance and its ability to finance growth.[4]

Key Analysis Questions

As noted earlier for debt policy, the financial analysis tools discussed in Part 2 of the book can help analysts assess how much financial slack a firm should maintain. The same analysis and questions are relevant to dividend policy analysis. Based on the answers to the earlier questions, analysts can assess whether the firm's projected cash needs for new investments are stable in relation to its operating cash flows. If so, it makes sense for management not to pursue too high a dividend payout and to build financial slack during boom periods to help fund investments during busts. Similarly, if the firm's ability to raise low-cost debt is limited because it is in a volatile industry or has mostly intangible assets, management is likely to avoid high dividend payouts to reduce the risk that it will have to raise high-cost external capital in the future or even forego a profitable new project.

Lending Constraints and Dividend Policy

One of the concerns of a firm's creditors is that when the firm is in financial distress, managers will pay a large dividend to stockholders. This problem is likely to be particularly severe for a firm with highly liquid assets, since its managers can pay a large dividend without selling assets. To limit these types of ploys, managers agree to restrict dividend payments to stockholders. Such dividend covenants usually require the firm to maintain certain minimum levels of retained earnings and current asset balances, which effectively limit dividend payments in times of financial difficulty. However these constraints on dividend policy are unlikely to be severe for a profitable firm.

Determining Optimal Dividend Payouts

One question that arises in using the above factors to determine dividend policy is defining what we mean by high, low, and medium dividend payouts. To provide a rough sense of what companies usually consider to be high and low dividend payouts and yields, Table 12-4 shows median dividend payout ratios and dividend yields for selected U.S. industries for the year ended December 31, 2001. Median ratios are reported for all listed companies and for NYSE companies.

Table 12-4 Median Dividend Payout Ratio and Dividend Yield for Selected U.S. Industries in 2001

	Dividend Payout Ratio		Dividend Yield	
Industry	All Listed Firms	NYSE Firms	All Listed Firms	NYSE Firms
Prepackaged Computer Software	0%	0%	0.0%	0.0%
Pharmaceutical	0%	1%	0.0%	0.8%
Hotels & Motels	0%	0%	0.0%	0.0%
Petroleum Refining	0%	12%	0.9%	1.9%
Electric Services	47%	49%	4.2%	4.3%
Water Supply	58%	61%	3.0%	3.0%

It is interesting to note that many U.S. listed companies do not pay any dividends. This is particularly true for non-NYSE firms, which probably have more attractive growth opportunities. The highest payouts tend to be made by public utilities, such as natural gas, water, and electric services. For these firms the median payouts tend to be roughly 45–60 percent and yields are between 3 and 4.3 percent. In contrast, firms in highly competitive industries with substantial reinvestment opportunities, such as software and pharmaceutical, tend to have very low dividend payouts and dividend yields.

Returning to the cases of Pfizer and Duke Energy, it is interesting to see that Pfizer has a higher dividend payout ratio than its industry median (35 percent versus 0 percent). When stock repurchases are included, Pfizer actually paid out 81 percent of its 2001 profits. Apparently the company believes that it does not have to reinvest all of its profits to maintain its high rate of success in drug development. It is also interesting to note that Pfizer uses stock repurchases as an important way to return funds to shareholders. One potential explanation for this is that Pfizer does not want to commit to the current high rate of payout indefinitely. Its dividend payout therefore represents its long-term payout commitment, and repurchases are used for temporary increases in that rate. Also, Pfizer's use of stock repurchases is probably tax effective for its shareholders since capital gains rates on repurchased stock gains are lower than ordinary income rates on dividends.

A Summary of Dividend Policy

Just as it is difficult to provide a simple formula to compute a firm's optimal capital structure, it is difficult to formalize the optimal dividend policy. However, we can identify several factors that appear to be important:

- High-growth firms should have low dividend payout ratios, and they should use their internally generated funds for reinvestment. This minimizes any costs from capital market constraints on financing growth options.
- Firms with high and stable operating cash flows and few investment opportunities should have high dividend payouts to reduce managers' incentives to reinvest free cash flows in unprofitable ventures.
- Firms should probably not be too concerned about tax factors in setting dividend policy. Whatever their policy, they will be able to attract a clientele of investors. Firms that select high dividend payouts will attract tax-exempt institutions or corporations, and firms that pay low or no dividends will attract individuals in high tax brackets.
- Firms' financial covenants can have an impact on their dividend policy decisions. Firms will try to avoid being too close to their constraints in order to minimize the possibility of cutting their dividend.

SUMMARY

This chapter examined how firms make optimal capital structure and dividend decisions. We show that a firm's optimal long-term capital structure is largely determined by its expected tax status, business risks, and types of assets. The benefits from debt financing are expected to be highest for firms with (1) high marginal tax rates and few non-interest tax shields, making interest tax shields valuable; (2) high, stable income/cash flows and few new investment opportunities, increasing the monitoring value of debt and reducing the likelihood that the firm will fall into financial distress; and (3) high tangible assets that are not easily destroyed by financial distress.

We also show that, in the short term, managers can deviate from their long-term optimal capital structure when they seek financing for new investments. In particular, managers are reluctant to raise external financing, especially new equity, for fear that outside investors will interpret their action as meaning that the firm is overvalued. This information problem has implications for how much financial slack a firm is likely to need to avoid facing these types of information problems.

Optimal dividend policy is determined by many of the same factors—firms' business risks and their types of assets. Thus, dividend rates should be highest for firms with high and stable cash flows and few investment opportunities. By paying out relatively high dividends, these firms reduce the risk of managers investing free cash flows in unprofitable projects. Conversely, firms with low, volatile cash flows and attractive investment opportunities, such as start-up firms, should have relatively low dividend payouts. By reinvesting operating cash flows and reducing the amount of external financing required for new projects, these firms reduce their costs of financing.

Financial statement analysis can be used to better understand a firm's business risks, its expected tax status, and whether its assets are primarily assets in place or growth opportunities. Useful tools for assessing whether a firm's current capital structure and dividend policies maximize shareholder value include accounting analysis to determine off-balance-sheet liabilities, ratio analysis to help understand a firm's business risks, and cash flow and pro forma analysis to explore current and likely future investment needs.

DISCUSSION QUESTIONS

1. Financial analysts typically measure financial leverage as the ratio of debt to equity. However, there is less agreement on how to measure debt, or even equity. How would you treat the following items in computing this ratio? Justify your answers.
   - Revolving credit agreement with bank
   - Cash and marketable securities
   - Deferred tax liabilities
   - Preferred stock
   - Convertible debt

2. Until 1987 Master Limited Partnerships (MLPs) were treated as partnerships for tax purposes. This meant that no corporate taxes were paid by the entity. Instead, taxes were paid by partners (at their individual tax rates) on entity profits (both distributed and undistributed). The marginal tax rate for corporations in 1987 was 34 percent, compared to 33 percent for individuals in the highest tax bracket.
   a. If an entity distributes all after-tax earnings as dividends and generates before-tax earnings of $10 million, what would be the distribution to owners (after entity and personal taxes) if it is organized as (1) a corporation and (2) an MLP?
   b. What would be the optimal capital structure for the MLP discussed in (a)? Justify your answer.
   c. What types of dividend policy do you expect the MLP to follow? Why?

3. Finance theory implies that the debt-to-equity ratio should be computed using the market values of debt and equity. However, most financial analysts use book values of debt and equity to compute a firm's financial leverage. What are the limitations of using book values rather than market values for comparing leverage across industries or firms? For what types of industries/firms are book values likely to be most misleading?

4. One important driver of a firm's capital structure and dividend policy decisions is its business risk. What ratios would you look at to assess business risk? Name two industries with very high business risk and two industries with very low business risk.

5. U.S. public companies with "low" leverage have an interest-bearing net debt-to-equity ratio of 0 percent or less, firms with "medium" leverage have a ratio between 1 and 62 percent, and "high" leverage firms have a ratio of 63 percent or more. Given these data, how would you classify the following firms in terms of their optimal debt-to-equity ratio (high, medium, or low)?
   - a successful pharmaceutical company
   - an electric utility
   - a manufacturer of consumer durables
   - a commercial bank
   - a start-up software company

6. A rapidly growing Internet company, recently listed on NASDAQ, needs to raise additional capital to finance new research and development. What financing options are available, and what are the trade-offs between each?

7. The following table reports (in millions) earnings, dividends, capital expenditures, and R&D for Intel for the period 1990–95:

Year	Net Income	Dividends	Capital Expenditures	R&D
1990	$650	$0	$680	$517
1991	819	0	948	618
1992	1,067	43	1,228	780
1993	2,295	88	1,933	970
1994	2,288	100	2,441	1,111
1995	3,566	133	3,550	1,296

What are the dividend payout rates for Intel during these years? Is this payout policy consistent with the factors expected to drive dividend policy discussed in the chapter? What factors do you expect would lead Intel's management to increase its dividend payout? How do you expect the stock market to react to such a decision?

8. U.S. public companies with low dividend payouts have payout ratios of 0 percent or less, firms with medium payouts have ratios between 1 and 48 percent, and high payout firms have a ratio of 49 percent or more. Given these data, how would you classify the following firms in terms of their optimal payout policy (high, medium, or low)?
   - a successful pharmaceutical company
   - an electric utility
   - a manufacturer of consumer durables
   - a commercial bank
   - a start-up software company

9. It is frequently argued that Japanese and German companies can afford to have more financial leverage and to follow lower dividend payout policies than U.S. companies because they are largely owned by financial institutions that have long-term horizons. Does this argument make economic sense? If so, explain why, and if not, why not. What other factors might explain differences in capital structure and dividend policy across countries?

10. In 1990 U.S. tax law increased capital gains rates from 20 percent to the same level as ordinary income rates, between 28 and 34 percent. What implications does this change have for corporate dividend policy and capital structure?

NOTES

1. See Merton Miller, "Debt and Taxes," *Journal of Finance* 32 (May 1977): 261–76.

2. Paul Healy and Krishna Palepu in "Earnings and Risk Changes Surrounding Primary Stock Offers," *Journal of Accounting Research* 28 (Spring 1990): 25–49, find that announcements of stock issues are interpreted by investors as a signal from management that the firm is riskier than investors expected.

3. These issues are discussed by Stewart Myers and Nicholas Majluf in "Corporate Financing and Investment Decisions When Firms Have Information That Investors Do Not Have," *Journal of Financial Economics* (June 1984): 187–221.

4. Findings by Paul Healy and Krishna Palepu in "Earnings Information Conveyed by Dividend Initiations and Omissions," *Journal of Financial Economics* 21 (September 1988): 149–75, indicate that investors interpret announcements of dividends initiations and omissions as managers' forecasts of future earnings performance.

Communication and Governance

Corporate governance has become an increasingly important issue in capital markets throughout the world following financial market meltdowns in the Asian and U.S. markets. These market collapses exposed problems of accounting misstatements and lack of corporate transparency, as well as governance problems and conflicts of interest among the intermediaries charged with monitoring management and corporate disclosures.

The breakdowns have increased the challenge for managers in communicating credibly with skeptical outside investors, making it more difficult than ever for new (and in some cases even established) firms to raise capital. Financial reports, the traditional platform for management to communicate with investors, are viewed with increased skepticism following a number of widely publicized audit failures and the demise of Arthur Andersen.

The market crashes have also raised questions about improving the quality of governance by information and financial intermediaries. New regulations, such as the Sarbanes-Oxley Act in the U.S., attempt to increase accountability and financial competence for audit committees and external auditors, who are charged with reviewing the financial reporting and disclosure process.

This chapter discusses how many of the financial analysis tools developed in Chapters 2 through 8 can be used by managers to develop a coherent disclosure strategy, and by corporate board members and external auditors to improve the quality of their work. The following types of questions are dealt with:

- Managers ask: Is our current communication strategy effective in helping investors understand the firm's business strategy and expected future performance, thereby ensuring that our stock price is not seriously over- or undervalued?
- Audit committee members ask: What are the firm's key business risks? Are they reflected appropriately in the financial statements? How is management communicating on important risks that cannot be reflected in the financial statements? Is information on the firm's performance presented to the board consistent with that provided to investors in the financial report and firm disclosures?
- External auditors ask: What are the firm's key business risks, and how are they reflected in the financial statements? Where should we focus our audit tests? Is our assessment of the firm's performance consistent with that of external investors and analysts? If not, are we overlooking something, or is management misrepresenting the firm's true performance in disclosures?

Throughout this book we have focussed primarily on showing how financial statement data can be helpful for analysts and outside investors in making a variety of decisions. In this chapter we change our emphasis and focus primarily on management and governance agents. Of course an understanding of the management communication process and corporate governance is also important for security analysts and investors. The approach taken here, however, is more germane to insiders since most of the types of analyses we discuss are not available to outsiders.

GOVERNANCE OVERVIEW

As we discuss throughout this book, outside investors require access to reliable information on firm performance, both to value their debt and equity claims and to monitor the performance of management. Investors require that managers provide information on their company's performance and future plans when they agree to provide capital to the firm.

However, left to their own devices, managers are likely to paint a rosy picture of the firm's performance in their disclosures. There are three reasons for manager optimism in reporting. First, most managers are genuinely positive about their firms' prospects, leading them to unwittingly emphasize the positive and downplay the negative.

A second reason for management optimism in reporting arises because firm disclosures play an important role in mitigating "agency" problems between managers and investors.[1] Investors use firm disclosures to judge whether managers have run the firm in investors' best interests or, on the other hand, have abused their authority and control over firm resources. Reporting consistently poor earnings increases the likelihood that top management will be replaced, either by the board of directors or by an acquirer who takes over the firm to improve its management.[2] Of course managers are aware of this and have incentives to show positive performance.

Finally, managers are also likely to make optimistic disclosures prior to issuing new equity. Recent evidence indicates that entrepreneurs tend to take to their firms public after disclosure of strong reported, but frequently unsustainable, earnings performance. Also, seasoned equity offers typically follow strong, but again unsustainable, stock and earnings performance. The strong earnings performance prior to IPOs and seasoned offers appears to be at least partially due to earnings management.[3] Of course rational outside investors recognize management's incentives to manage earnings and downplay any bad news prior to a new issue. They respond by discounting the stock, demanding a hefty new issue discount, and in extreme cases refusing to purchase the new stock. This raises the cost of capital and potentially leaves some of the best new ventures and projects unfunded.[4]

Financial and information intermediaries help reduce agency and information problems that face outside investors by evaluating the quality of management representations in the firm's disclosures, providing their own analysis of firms' (and managers') performance and making investment decisions on investors' behalf. As presented in Figure 13-1, these intermediaries include internal governance agents, assurance professionals, information analyzers, and professional investors. The importance of these intermediaries is underscored by the magnitude of the fees that they collectively receive from investors and entrepreneurs.

Internal governance agents, such as corporate boards, are responsible for monitoring a firm's management. Their functions include reviewing business strategy, evaluating and rewarding top management, and assuring the flow of credible information to external parties. Assurance professionals, such as external auditors, enhance the credibility of financial information prepared by managers. Information analyzers, such as financial analysts and ratings agencies, are responsible for gathering and analyzing information to provide performance forecasts and investment recommendations to both professional and retail individual investors. Finally, professional investors (such as banks, mutual funds, insurance, and venture capital firms) make investment decisions on behalf of dispersed investors. They are therefore responsible for valuing and selecting investment opportunities in the economy.

In this framework, management, internal governance agents, and assurance professionals are charged with supplying information; individual and professional investors and

Figure 13-1   The Intermediation Chain Between Managers and Investors

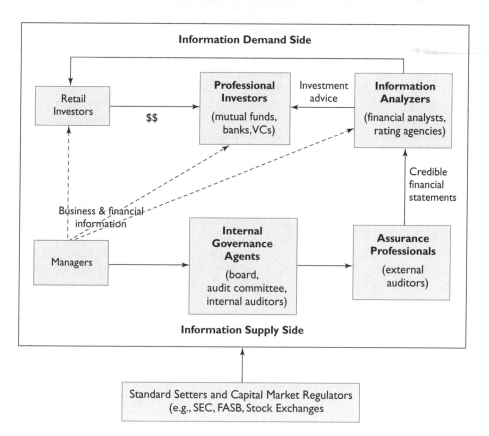

information analyzers make up the demand side. Both the supply and demand sides are governed by a variety of regulatory institutions. These include public regulators, such as the Securities and Exchange Commission and the bank regulators, as well as private sector bodies, such the Financial Accounting Standards Board, the American Institute of Certified Public Accountants, and stock exchanges.

The level and quality of information and residual information and agency problems in capital markets are determined by the organizational design of these intermediaries and regulatory institutions. Key organizational design questions include the following: What are the optimal incentive schemes for rewarding top managers? What should be the composition and charter of corporate boards? Should auditors assure that financial reports comply with accounting standards or represent a firm's underlying economics? Should there be detailed accounting standards or a few broad accounting principles? What should be the organizational form and business scope of auditors and analysts? What incentive schemes should be used for professional investors to align their interests with individual investors?

A variety of economic and institutional factors are likely to influence the answers to these design questions. Examples include the ability to write and enforce optimal contracts, proprietary costs that might make disclosure costly for investors, and regulatory imperfections. The spectacular rise and fall of Enron suggests that these limitations could have a first-order effect on the functioning of capital markets.

While it is interesting to speculate on how to improve the functioning of capital markets through changes in organizational design, that issue goes beyond the scope of this chapter. Instead, we discuss how the financial analysis tools developed in Chapters 2 through 8 can be used to improve the performance of some of the information intermediaries who have been widely criticized following revelations of financial reporting fraud and misstatements at companies such as Enron, Worldcom, Tyco, Xerox, Global Crossing, and Lucent.[5]

We have already discussed the application of financial analysis tools to equity and credit analysts and to professional investors in Chapters 9 and 10. In the remainder of this chapter, we discuss how these tools can be used by managers to develop a strategy for effective communication with investors, by members of boards of directors and audit committees in overseeing management and the audit process, and by audit professionals.

MANAGEMENT COMMUNICATION WITH INVESTORS

Some managers argue that communication problems are not worth worrying about. They maintain that as long as managers make investment and operating decisions that enhance shareholder value, investors will value their performance and the firm's stock accordingly. While this is true in the long run, since all information is eventually public, it may not hold in the short or even medium term. If investors do not have access to the same information as management, they will probably find it difficult to value new and innovative investments. In an efficient capital market, they will not consistently over- or undervalue these new investments, but their valuations will tend to be noisy. This can make stock prices relatively noisy, leading management at various times to consider their firms to be either seriously over- or undervalued.

Does it matter if a firm's stock is over- or undervalued for a period? Most managers would prefer to not have their stock undervalued, since it makes it more costly to raise new financing. They may also worry that undervaluation is likely to increase the chance of a takeover by a hostile acquirer, with an accompanying reduction in their job security. Managers of firms that are overvalued may also be concerned about the market's assessment, since they are legally liable for failing to disclose information relevant to investors.[6] They may therefore not wish to see their stock seriously overvalued, even though overvaluation provides opportunities to issue new equity at favorable rates.

A Word of Caution

As noted above, it is natural that many managers believe that firms are undervalued by the capital market. This frequently occurs because it is difficult for managers to be realistic about their company's future performance. After all, it is part of their job to sell the company to new employees, customers, suppliers, and investors. In addition, forecasting the firm's future performance objectively requires them to judge their own capabilities as managers. Thus many managers may argue that investors are uninformed and that their firm is undervalued. Only some can back that up with solid evidence.

If management decides that the firm does face a genuine information problem, it can begin to consider whether and how this could be redressed. Is the problem potentially serious enough that it is worth doing something to alter investors' perceptions? Or is the problem likely to resolve itself within a short period? Does the firm have plans to raise new equity or to use equity to acquire another company? Is management's job security threatened? As we discuss below, management has a wide range of options in this situation.

Key Analysis Questions

We recommend that before jumping to the conclusion that their firms are undervalued, managers should analyze their firms' performance and compare their own forecasts of future performance with those of analysts, using the following approach:

- *Is there a significant difference between internal management forecasts of future earnings and cash flows and those of outside analysts?*
- *Do any differences between managers' and analysts' forecasts arise because of different expectations about economy-wide performance?* Managers may understand their own businesses better than analysts, but they may not be any better at forecasting macroeconomic conditions.
- *Can managers identify any factors that might explain a difference between analysts' and managers' forecasts of future performance?* For example, are analysts unaware of positive new R&D results, do they have different information about customer responses to new products and marketing campaigns, etc.? These types of differences could indicate that the firm faces an information problem.

Example: Communication Issues for FPIC Insurance Group

FPIC Insurance Group Inc. is the largest provider of liability insurance for doctors and hospitals in Florida. In the period 1996 to 1998, FPIC reported stable returns on equity of 13.8 percent, average growth in both revenues and net income of 28 percent, and growth in book equity of 2.8 percent. On December 31, 1998, the firm had a book value per share of $15.85, a price-to-book value of 2.23, a price to earnings multiple of 15.9, and an equity beta of 1.57.

In August 1999 the firm's stock price declined from $45.25 to $14.25. The stock decline began on August 10, the day the company reported a 48 percent jump in second-quarter profits to $7.4 million. The earnings increase was in part attributable to the FPIC's Florida Physicians unit releasing $8.1 million in reserves it had set aside against future claims, compared with $4 million in the year-ago quarter. In addition, the company reported higher-than-expected claims in a health insurance plan offered to Florida Dental Association members.

Reuters reported that the stock price decline reflected investors' concern about the quality of the firm's earnings. In response, FPIC spokeswoman Amy D. Ryan stated, "As far as we're concerned, we had a great quarter." The company's chief operating officer, John Byers, argued that the company's decision to release the unit's reserves was normal business practice and based on its expectations of future claims. In response to the higher than expected dental claims, the company announced that it had increased its rates for this insurance.

The sharp decline in its price raises questions about the valuation of the company's stock. On September 9, 1999, the price-to-book ratio was less than 1, and the price-to-earnings multiple was 6.0. The market therefore expected that the company would generate a return on equity somewhat lower than its cost of capital. FPIC's management appeared to be puzzled by the sharp drop in price and argued that the market was undervaluing the firm. However, before this can be concluded, a number of questions need to be answered:

- Was the firm previously overvalued? If so, what forces were behind the market's high valuation of the company? If the market expected the company to continue to grow at 2.8 percent, to generate a 13.8 percent return on equity, and the firm's cost of capital is 11.3 percent (consistent with a market risk premium of 4 percent and a risk-free rate of 5 percent), FPIC would be worth around $20.50. Why then was the stock valued at $45 early in August? Had management been painting too rosy a picture for the company's future in its meetings with analysts?
- What events explain the company's sudden drop in stock value? As noted above, the primary question for analysts was the quality of the firm's earnings. However management needs to have a deeper understanding of these issues.
- If management believes that the firm is actually undervalued, what options are available to correct the market's view of the company?

COMMUNICATION THROUGH FINANCIAL REPORTING

Financial reports are the most popular format for management communication. Below we discuss the role of financial reporting as a means of investor communication, the institutions that make accounting information credible, and when it is likely to be ineffective.

Accounting As a Means of Management Communication

As we discussed in Chapters 3 and 4, financial reports are an important medium for management communication with external investors. Reports provide investors with an explanation of how their money has been invested, a summary of the performance of those investments, and a discussion of how current performance fits within the firm's overall philosophy and strategy.

Accounting reports not only provide a record of past transactions, they also reflect management estimates and forecasts of the future. For example, they include estimates of bad debts, forecasts of the lives of tangible assets, and implicit forecasts that outlays will generate future cash flow benefits that exceed their cost. Since management is likely to be in a position to make forecasts of these future events that are more accurate than those of external investors, financial reports are a potentially useful way of communicating with investors. However, as discussed above, investors are also likely to be skeptical of reports prepared by management.

Factors That Increase the Credibility of Accounting Communication

A number of mechanisms mitigate conflicts of interest in financial reporting and increase the credibility of accounting information that is communicated to stockholders. These include accounting standards, auditing, monitoring of management by financial analysts, and management reputation.

Accounting Standards and Auditing

Accounting standards, such as those promulgated by the Financial Accounting Standards Board (FASB) and the Securities Exchange Commission (SEC) in the U.S., provide guidelines for managers on how to make accounting decisions and provide outside investors with a way of interpreting these decisions. Uniform accounting standards attempt to reduce managers' ability to record similar economic transactions in different ways, either over time or across firms. Compliance with these standards is enforced by external auditors who attempt to ensure that managers' estimates are reasonable. Auditors therefore reduce the likelihood of earnings management.

Monitoring by Financial Analysts

Financial intermediaries such as analysts also limit management's ability to manage earnings. Financial analysts specialize in developing firm- and industry-specific knowledge, enabling them to assess the quality of a firm's reported numbers and to make any necessary adjustments. Analysts evaluate the appropriateness of management's forecasts implicit in accounting method choices and reported accruals. This requires a thorough understanding of the firm's business and the relevant accounting rules used in the preparation of its financial reports. Superior analysts adjust reported accrual numbers, if necessary, to reflect economic reality, perhaps by using the cash flow statement and the footnote disclosures.

Analysts' business and technical expertise as well as their legal liability and incentives differ from those of auditors. Consequently, analyst reports can provide information to investors on whether the firm's accounting decisions are appropriate or whether managers are overstating the firm's economic performance to protect their jobs.[7]

Management Reputation

A third factor that can counteract external investors' natural skepticism about financial reporting is management reputation. Managers that expect to have an ongoing relation with external investors and financial intermediaries may be able to build a track record for unbiased financial reporting. By making accounting estimates and judgments that are supported by subsequent performance, managers can demonstrate their competence and reliability to investors and analysts. As a result, managers' future judgments and accounting estimates are more likely to be viewed as credible sources of information.

Limitations of Financial Reporting for Investor Communication

While accounting standards, auditing, monitoring of management by financial analysts, and management concerns about its reputation increase the credibility and informativeness of financial reports, these mechanisms are far from perfect. Consequently there are times when financial reporting breaks down as a means for management to communicate with external investors. These breakdowns can arise when (1) there are no accounting rules to guide practice or the existing rules do not distinguish between poor and successful performers, (2) auditors and analysts do not have the expertise to judge new products or business opportunities, or (3) management faces credibility problems.

Accounting Rule Limitations

Despite the rapid increase in new accounting standards, accounting rules frequently do not distinguish between good and poor performers. For example, current accounting rules do not permit managers to show on their balance sheets in a timely fashion the benefits of investments in quality improvements, human resource development programs, research and development (with the exception of software development costs), and customer service.

Some of the problems with accounting standards arise because it takes time for standard setters to develop appropriate standards for many new types of economic transactions. Other difficulties arise because standards are the result of compromises between different interest groups (e.g., auditors, investors, corporate managers, and regulators).

Auditor and Analyst Limitations

While auditors and analysts have access to proprietary information, they do not have the same understanding of the firm's business as managers. The divergence between managers' and auditors'/analysts' business assessments is likely to be most severe for firms with distinctive business strategies, or firms that operate in emerging industries. In addition, auditors' decisions in these circumstances are likely to be dominated by concerns about legal liability, hampering management's ability to use financial reports to communicate effectively with investors.

Finally, conflicts of interest faced by auditors and analysts make their analysis imperfect. Conflicts can potentially induce auditors to side with management to retain the audit, or to enable the audit firm to sell profitable non-audit services to the client. They can also arise for analysts who provide favorable ratings and research on companies to support investment banking services, or to increase trading volume among less informed investors.

Limited Management Credibility

When is management likely to face credibility problems with investors? There is very little evidence on this question. However, managers of new firms, firms with volatile earnings, firms in financial distress, and firms with poor track records in communicating with investors should expect to find it difficult to be seen as credible reporters.

If management has a credibility problem, financial reports are likely to be viewed with considerable skepticism. Investors will see financial reporting estimates that increase income as evidence that management is padding earnings. This makes it very difficult for management to use financial reports to communicate positive news about future performance.

Example: Accounting Communication for FPIC Insurance Group

FPIC Insurance Group's key financial reporting estimates are for loss reserves for insurance claims using actuarial analysis of its own and other insurers' claims histories. At the end of fiscal year 1998, FPIC reported a loss reserve of $242.3 million. In its 10-K, management warned that "the uncertainties inherent in estimating ultimate losses on the basis of past experience have grown significantly in recent years, principally as a result of judicial expansion of liability standards and expansive interpretations of insurance contracts. These uncertainties may be further affected by, among other factors, changes in the rate of inflation and changes in the propensities of individuals to file claims. The inherent uncertainty of establishing reserves is relatively greater for companies writing long-tail casualty insurance."

To help investors assess its track record in making loss estimates, FPIC is required to provide a detailed breakdown of changes in loss estimates from prior years given actual claim losses. These data indicate that FPIC has actually been quite conservative in prior years' forecasts and has historically incurred fewer losses than it had initially predicted.

It is interesting to note that the area that raised questions for investors about FPIC's record was precisely its conservative estimation of loss reserves and their subsequent reversal. By being conservative, management may have raised questions about its ability to forecast losses reliably in the future, or given investors the impression that it had been managing earnings.

> ## Key Analysis Questions
>
> For management interested in understanding how effectively the firm's financial reports help it communicate with outside investors, the following questions are likely to provide a useful starting point:
>
> - What are the key business risks that have to be managed effectively? What processes and controls are in place to manage these risks? How are the firm's key business risks reflected in the financial statements? For example, credit risks are reflected in the bad debt allowance, and product quality risks are reflected in allowances for product returns and the method of revenue recognition. For these types of risks, what message is the firm sending on the management of these risks through its estimates or choices of accounting methods? Has the firm been unable to deliver on the forecasts underlying these choices? Alternatively, does the market seem to be ignoring the message underlying the firm's financial reporting choices, indicating a lack of credibility?
> - How does the firm communicate about key risks that cannot be reflected in accounting estimates or methods? For example, if technological innovation risk is critical for a company, it is unable to reflect how well it is managing this risk through research and development in its financial statements. But investors will still have questions about this business issue.

OTHER FORMS OF COMMUNICATING WITH INVESTORS

Given the limitations of accounting standards, auditing, and monitoring by financial analysts, as well as the reporting credibility problems faced by management, firms that wish to communicate effectively with external investors are often forced to use alternative media. Below we discuss three alternative ways that managers can communicate with external investors and analysts: meetings with analysts to publicize the firm, expanded voluntary disclosure, and using financing policies to signal management expectations. These forms of communication are typically not mutually exclusive.

Analyst Meetings

One popular way for managers to help mitigate communication problems is to meet regularly with financial analysts that follow the firm. At these meetings management will field questions about the firm's current financial performance as well discuss its future business plans. In addition to holding analyst meetings, many firms appoint a director of public relations, who provides further regular contact with analysts seeking more information on the firm.

In the last ten years, conference calls have become a popular forum for management to communicate with financial analysts. Recent research finds that firms are more likely to host calls if they are in industries where financial statement data fail to capture key business fundamentals on a timely basis.[8] In addition, conference calls themselves appear to provide new information to analysts about a firm's performance and future prospects.[9]

While firms continue to meet with analysts, new SEC rules, called Regulation Fair Disclosure (or Reg FD), have changed the nature of these interactions. Under these new rules, which became effective in the U.S. in October 2000, firms that provide material nonpublic information to security analysts or professional investors must simultaneously (or promptly thereafter) disclose the information to the public. This has reduced the information that managers are willing to disclose in conference calls and private meetings, making these less effective forums for resolving information problems.

Voluntary Disclosure

Another way for managers to improve the credibility of their financial reporting is through voluntary disclosure. Accounting rules usually prescribe minimum disclosure requirements, but they do not restrict managers from voluntarily providing additional information. These could include an articulation of the company's long-term strategy, specification of nonfinancial leading indicators which are useful in judging the effectiveness of the strategy implementation, explanation of the relation between the leading indicators and future profits, and forecasts of future performance. Voluntary disclosures can be reported in the firm's annual report, in brochures created to describe the firm to investors, in management meetings with analysts, or in investor relations responses to information requests.[10]

One constraint on expanded disclosure is the competitive dynamics in product markets. Disclosure of proprietary information on strategies and their expected economic consequences may hurt the firm's competitive position. Managers then face a trade-off between providing information that is useful to investors in assessing the firm's economic performance, and withholding information to maximize the firm's product market advantage.

A second constraint in providing voluntary disclosure is management's legal liability. Forecasts and voluntary disclosures can potentially be used by dissatisfied shareholders to bring civil action against management for providing misleading information. This seems ironic, since voluntary disclosures should provide investors with additional information. Unfortunately, it can be difficult for courts to decide whether managers' disclosures were good-faith estimates of uncertain future events which later did not materialize, or whether management manipulated the market. Consequently many corporate legal departments recommend against management providing much voluntary disclosure.

Finally, management credibility can limit a firm's incentives to provide voluntary disclosures. If management faces a credibility problem in financial reporting, any voluntary disclosures it provides are also likely to be viewed skeptically. In particular, investors may be concerned about what management is not telling them, particularly since such disclosures are not audited.

Selected Financial Policies

Managers can also use financing policies to communicate effectively with external investors. Financial policies that are useful in this respect include dividend payouts, stock repurchases, financing choices, and hedging strategies. One important difference between this type of communication and additional disclosure is that the firm does not provide potentially proprietary information to competitors. The signal therefore indicates to competitors that a firm's management is bullish on its future, but it does not provide any details.

Dividend Payout Policies

As we discussed in Chapter 12, a firm's cash payout decisions can provide information to investors on managers' assessments of the firm's future prospects. This arises because dividend payouts tend to be sticky, in the sense that managers are reluctant to cut dividends. Thus, managers will only increase dividends when they are confident that they will be able to sustain the increased rate in future years. Consequently, investors interpret dividend increases as signals of managers' confidence in the quality of current and future earnings.[11]

Stock Repurchases

In some countries, such as the U.S. and the U.K., managers can use stock repurchases to communicate with external investors. Under a stock repurchase, the firm buys back its own stock, either through a purchase on the open market, through a tender offer, or through a negotiated purchase with a large stockholder. Of course a stock repurchase, particularly a tender offer repurchase, is an expensive way for management to communicate with outside investors. Firms typically pay a hefty premium to acquire their shares in tender offer repurchases, potentially diluting the value of the shares that are not tendered or not accepted for tender. In addition, the fees to investment banks, lawyers, and share solicitation fees are not trivial. Given these costs, it is not surprising that research findings indicate that stock repurchases are effective signals to investors about the level and risk of future earnings performance.[12] Research findings also suggest that firms that use stock repurchases to communicate with investors have accounting assets that reflect less of firm value and have high general information asymmetry.[13]

Financing Choices

Firms that have problems communicating with external investors may be able to use financing choices to reduce them. For example, a firm that is unwilling to provide proprietary information to help dispersed public investors value it may be willing to provide such information to a knowledgeable private investor—which can become a large stockholder/creditor—or a bank that agrees to provide the company with a significant new loan. A firm with credibility problems in financial reporting can sell stock or issue debt to an informed private investor such as a large customer who has superior information about the quality of its product or service.

Such changes in financing and ownership can mitigate communication problems in two ways. First, the terms of the new financing arrangement and the credibility of the new lender or stockholder can provide investors with information to reassess the value of the firm. Second, the accompanying increased concentration of ownership and the role of large block holders in corporate governance can have a positive effect on valuation. If investors are concerned about management's incentives to increase shareholder value, the presence of a new block shareholder or significant creditor on the board can be reassuring. This type of monitoring arises in leveraged buyouts, start-ups backed by venture capital firms, and in firms with equity partnership investments. In Japanese and German corporations, it may also arise because large banks own both debt and equity and have close working relationships with firms' managers.

Of course, in the extreme, management can decide that the best option for a firm is to no longer operate as a public company. This can be accomplished by a management buyout, where a buyout group (including management) leverages its own investment (using bank or public debt finance), buys the firm, and takes it private. The buyout group hopes to run the firm for several years and then take the company public again, hopefully with a track record of improved performance that enables investors to value the firm more effectively.

Hedging

An important source of mispricing arises if investors are unable to distinguish between unexpected changes in reported earnings due to management performance and transitory shocks that are beyond managers' control (e.g., foreign currency translation gains and losses). Managers can counteract these effects by hedging such "accounting" risks. Even though hedging is costly, it may be valuable if it reduces information problems that potentially lead to misvaluation.

Example: Other Communications for FPIC Insurance Group

On August 12, 1999, FPIC Insurance Group announced that it would immediately begin purchasing shares of its common stock. As many as 429,000 shares were to be repurchased under the program. The company argued that the dramatic drop in its stock price was unwarranted and that its stock was now greatly undervalued. William R. Russell, president and chief executive officer of FPIC stated: "We believe the recent drop in our stock price may be linked to certain changes in our reserving policy that were described in our earnings release. We believe that our reserving policy is now and has always been appropriate. We believe that the market has overreacted and that FPIC continues to be an excellent long-term investment. Our repurchases . . . reflect our commitment to enhance shareholder value." (Reuters, August 12, 1999)

The repurchase temporarily arrested FPIC's stock price slide. The price recovered from $21 to around $26 during the repurchase period. However this effect was temporary, and the price subsequently fell further to $14.25.

Key Analysis Questions

For management considering whether to use financing policies to communicate more effectively with investors, the following questions are likely to provide a useful starting point for analysis:

- Have other potentially less costly actions, such as expanded disclosure or accounting communication, been considered? If not, would these alternatives provide a lower cost means of communication? Alternatively, if management is concerned about providing proprietary information to competitors, or has low credibility, these alternatives may not be effective.
- Does the firm have sufficient free cash flow to be able to implement a share repurchase program or to increase dividends? If so, these may be feasible options. If the firm has excess cash available today but expects to be constrained in the future, a stock repurchase may be more effective. Alternatively, if management expects to have some excess cash available each year, a dividend increase may be in order.
- Is the firm cash constrained and unable to increase disclosure for proprietary reasons? If so, management may want to consider changing the mix of owners as a way of indicating to investors that another informed outsider is bullish on the company. Of course another possibility is for management itself to increase its stake in the company.

AUDITOR ANALYSIS

In the U.S. the auditor is responsible for providing investors with assurance that the financial statements are prepared in accordance with Generally Accepted Accounting Procedures (or GAAP). This requires the auditor to evaluate whether transactions are recorded in a way that is consistent with the rules produced by regulators (including the FASB, AICPA, and SEC) and whether management estimates reflected in the financial statements are reasonable. The results of the audit are disclosed in the audit report, which is part of the financial statements. If the firm's financial statements conform to GAAP, the auditor issues an unqualified report. However, if the financials do not conform to GAAP, the auditor is required to issue a qualified or an adverse report that provides information to investors on the discrepancies. Finally, if the auditor is uncertain about whether the firm can survive during the coming year, a going concern report is issued that points out the firm's survival risks.

In contrast, in the UK and countries that have adopted the UK system, such as Australia, New Zealand, Singapore, Hong Kong, and India, auditors undertake a broader review than their U.S. counterparts. UK audits are required to not only assess whether the financial statements are prepared in accordance with UK GAAP, but also to judge whether they fairly reflect the client's underlying economic performance. This additional assurance requires more judgment on the part of the auditor but also increases the value of the audit to outside investors.

The key procedures involved in a typical audit include (1) understanding the client's business and industry to identify key risks for the audit, (2) evaluating the firm's internal control system to assess whether it is likely to produce reliable information, (3) performing preliminary analytic procedures to identify unusual events and possible errors, and (4) collecting specific evidence on controls, transactions, and account balance details to form the basis for the auditor's opinion. In most cases client management is willing to respond to issues raised by the audit to ensure that the company receives an unqualified audit opinion. Once the audit is completed, the auditor presents a summary of audit scope and findings to the Audit Committee of the firm's Board of Directors.

It is worth noting that in both the U.S. and UK systems, the audit is not intended to detect fraud. Of course in some cases it may do so, but that is not its purpose. The detection of fraud is the domain of the internal audit.

Challenges Facing Audit Industry[14]

To understand the current problems facing the audit industry, it is necessary to go back to the mid-1970s, when two critical events created pressures on audit firms to cut costs and seek alternative revenue sources. The first of these was a decision by the Federal Trade Commission, concerned with a potential oligopoly by the large audit firms, to pressure the major firms to compete aggressively with each other for clients. The second was a shift in legal standards that enabled investors of companies with accounting problems to seek legal redress against the auditor without having to show that they had specifically relied on questionable accounting information in making their investment decisions. Instead, they could assert that they had relied on the stock price itself, which has been affected by the misleading disclosures. This change, along with increasing litigiousness, dramatically increased the lawsuit risk for auditors.

Audit firms responded to the new business environment in several ways. They lobbied for mechanical accounting and auditing standards and developed standard operating procedures to reduce the variability in audits. This approach reduced the cost of audits and provided a defense in the case of litigation. But it also meant that auditors were more likely to view their role narrowly, rather than as matters of broader business judgment.

Furthermore, while mechanical standards make auditing easier, they do not necessarily increase corporate transparency.[15] Audit firms decided that profit margins would be thin in a world of mechanized, standardized audits, and they responded in two ways. One way was by aggressively pursuing a high volume strategy, and so audit partner compensation and promotion became more closely linked to a cordial relationship with top management that attracted new audit clients and retained existing clients. This made it difficult for partners to be effective watchdogs. The large audit firms also responded to challenges to their core business by developing new higher margin, higher growth consulting services. This diversification strategy deflected top management energy and partner talent from the audit side of the business to the more profitable consulting part.

The Enron debacle dramatically illustrated many of the problems facing the industry. The use of mechanical, standardized audits encouraged Enron's auditors to take a narrow perspective on their role as financial report watchdogs. Even though they may have believed that Enron's reports met GAAP, they failed to ask big picture questions about their client's strategy, core risks, and the company's overall transparency. Mechanical standards also made it easier for Enron's unscrupulous managers to meet the letter of GAAP (although in the end they did not even do that), but to skirt their spirit, concealing important obligations and overstating profits. Finally, the pressure on Enron's auditors to retain their clients and to grow their firms' consulting businesses reduced their independence, leading them to approve questionable accounting decisions and to work closely with management to meet Enron's financial reporting objectives.

Several recent regulatory changes have been passed to correct the structural problems facing the industry. The SEC has banned audit firms from providing certain types of consulting services to their clients. The Sarbanes-Oxley Act requires the Audit Committee of the Board of Directors to become more active in appointing and reviewing the audit. It also requires the CEO and CFO to sign off that the financials fairly represent the financial performance of the company. These are all likely to improve the dynamics of the industry. It remains to be seen whether they will be sufficient once the current anxiety dies down.

Role of Financial Analysis Tools for Auditing

How can the financial analysis tools discussed in this book be used by audit professionals? The four steps in financial analysis are strategy analysis, accounting analysis, financial analysis, and prospective analysis. We discuss how each of these is relevant to the audit.

Strategy Analysis

One of the fundamental challenges facing auditors is how to narrow the scope of their work. Large corporations undertake millions of transactions each year. It is not possible for any audit to review all of these. So the auditor has to decide where to focus attention and time.

Strategy analysis can help identify those few key areas of the business that are critical to the organization's survival and future success. These are the areas that investors want to understand so that they can evaluate the firm's value proposition and how well it is managing key success factors. They are also likely to be areas worth further testing and analysis by the auditor, to assess their impact on the financial statements. For example, the key success factor for Tyco, a conglomerate that pursued a strategy of acquisitions to consolidate small players in a variety of industries, was managing acquisitions. The key success factor for a financial services firm is managing loan risks, and the key risk for Intel is its product innovation.

Strategy analysis is critical to the first stage to the audit, understanding the client's business, industry, and risks. It is important that the auditor develop the expertise to be able to identify the one or two key risks facing their clients.

Accounting Analysis

For the auditor, accounting analysis involves two steps. First, the auditor must understand how the key success factors and risks are reflected in the financial statements. For Tyco, for example, they are reflected in the valuation of goodwill. If Tyco fails to manage its acquisitions successfully, it will have to take a write-down of goodwill. For financial services companies the key success factors and risks are reflected in loan loss reserves. If a firm fails to manage its loan process properly, it will begin making loans to more risky clients, leading to higher future default rates and requiring higher loan loss estimates. In contrast, for Intel, accounting rules treat its key success factor, product innovation, in a mechanical way by requiring that it expense all R&D when it is incurred. While this probably makes the audit easier to perform, it implies that Intel's financial statements are not a very timely source of information on the company's innovation, and the auditor's service is less valuable. Intel's management will have to use other ways of providing credible information to investors on its product innovation.

The second step in accounting analysis is for the auditor to evaluate management judgment reflected in the key financial statements items. For example, for a financial services company where loan loss reserves are critical, the auditor will need to design tests and collect evidence to evaluate management's forecasts of future loan losses implicit in the reserve. The auditor must assess whether these forecasts are reasonable given the company's historical performance, the current economic climate, and the credit review and collection process in place in the firm. For a firm such as Tyco, where goodwill valuations are critical, the auditor must judge whether the current performance of acquired companies meets forecasts made by Tyco's management at the time of the acquisition and is reflected in the price Tyco paid for the target.

Financial Analysis

Auditors use financial ratio analysis as part of their analytic review. Financial ratios help auditors judge whether there are any unusual performance changes for their client, either relative to past performance or relative to their competitors. Such changes merit further investigation to ensure that the reasons for the change can be fully explained, and to determine what additional tests are required to satisfy the auditor that the reported changes in performance are justified.

For example, financial ratio analysis of Worldcom's financial performance should have revealed a significant decline in the company's cost structure that was not matched by any of its competitors. Such analysis should have been a red flag for the auditor that prompted a detailed examination of Worldcom's costs and capitalization policies, and might have led the auditor to detect the massive fraudulent change in capitalization of network costs at Worldcom.

Careful ratio analysis can also reveal whether clients are facing business problems that might induce management to conceal losses or keep key obligations off the balance sheet. Such information should alert auditors that extra care and additional detailed tests are likely to be required to reach a conclusion on the client's financial statements.

Prospective Analysis

Auditors use prospective analysis to assess whether estimates and forecasts made by management are consistent with the firm's economic position. They typically do not concern themselves with the stock market's valuation of their client. Yet there is valuable information for auditors in the market's valuation. The market's perception of a client's future performance provides a useful benchmark for affirming or disconfirming the auditor's assessment of the client's propsects. If the auditor reaches a different conclusion about a client than the market, it is worth exploring reasons for the differences. Is the client failing to disclose some critical information known to the auditor? Or is the auditor too optimistic or pessimistic?

If the auditor concludes that the market is overly optimistic about a client, is additional disclosure required to help investors get a more realistic view of the company's prospects? Are the estimates and forecasts made by management in preparing the financial statements realistic, or do they seek to avoid disappointing the market?

Alternatively, if the auditors decide that the market is overly pessimistic about their client's prospects, what additional information, if any, can be disclosed to increase transparency? Is the company too conservative in its financial statement estimates and forecasts?

Key Analysis Questions

The following questions are likely to provide a useful starting point for auditors in their analysis of a client's financial statements:

- What are the key business risks facing the firm? How well are these risks managed?
- What are the key accounting policies and estimates that reflect the firm's key risks? What tests and evidence are required to evaluate management judgment that is reflected in these accounting decisions?
- Do key ratios indicate any unusual changes in client performance? What tests and evidence are required to understand the causes of such changes?
- Has firm performance deteriorated, creating pressure on management to manage earnings or record off-balance-sheet transactions? If so, what additional tests and evidence are required to provide assurance that the financial statements are consistent with GAAP and (for UK system auditors) fairly represent the firm's financial position?
- How is the market assessing the client's prospects? If different from the auditor, what is the reason for the difference? If the market is overly optimistic or pessimistic, are there implications for client disclosure or accounting estimates?

Example: Auditing FPIC Insurance Group

For FPIC Insurance Group, how well the company manages claim risk is its most critical success factor. Not surprisingly, the stock market volatility appears to be largely driven by changing perceptions of this risk. In the financial statements, claim risk is reflected in the reserves set aside for future claims. This should be a key focus of the audit.

Questions for the auditor include the following.

- Why did the company change its reserve policy this period? Does the change reflect a change in its business model, such as an attempt to reduce insurance sales for more risky customers? If so, is there evidence of a change in customer demographics and claim patterns?
- Does the change reflect excessive over-reserving by the client in earlier periods? If so, why did the auditors approve this earlier policy? Why did management select this year to release those reserves?
- Is the change in reserve policy justifiable, or is management simply responding to pressure to meet unrealistic market expectations?
- What information is available about a representative sample of outstanding claims? Are estimates of the cost of settling these claims realistic given prior settlements and experiences for other firms in the same industry?

- If the change in claim reserves appears to be reasonable, what additional information can the firm provide to investors to address their concerns? Will this information need to be audited?

AUDIT COMMITTEE REVIEWS

Audit committees are responsible for overseeing the work of the auditor, for ensuring that the financial statements are properly prepared, and for reviewing the internal controls at the company. Audit committees, which are mandated by many stock exchanges, typically comprise three to four outside directors who meet regularly before or after their full board meetings.

In the last few years requirements for audit committee have been beefed up and formalized. In December 1999, the SEC, the national stock exchange(s), and the Auditing Standards Board issued new audit committee rules based largely on recommendations of the Blue Ribbon Committee (BRC) on Improving the Effectiveness of Corporate Audit Committees. The new rules defined best practices for judging audit committee members' independence and their qualifications.

Following the collapse of Enron, additional audit committee requirements have been created under the Sarbanes-Oxley Act. This requires that audit committees take formal responsibility for appointing, overseeing, and negotiating fees with external auditors. Audit committee members are required to be independent directors with no consulting or other potentially compromising relation to management. It is recommended that at least one member of the committee have financial expertise, such as being a CFO or CEO, or being a retired audit partner.

Ideally the audit committee is expected to be independent of management and to take an active role in reviewing the propriety of the firm's financial statements. Committee members are expected to question management and the auditors about the quality of the firm's financial reporting, the scope and findings of the external audit, and the quality of internal controls.

In reality, however, the audit committee has to rely extensively on information from management as well as internal and external auditors. Given the ground that it has to cover, its limited available time, and the technical nature of accounting standards, audit committees are not in a position to catch management fraud or auditors' failures on a timely basis.

How then can the audit committee add value?[16] We believe that many of the financial analysis tools discussed in this book can provide a useful way for audit committees to approach their tasks. Many of the applications of the financial analysis steps discussed for auditors also apply for audit committees.

In its scrutiny of financial statements, the committee should use the 80-20 rule, devoting most of its time to assessing the effectiveness of those *few* policies and decisions that have the *most* impact on investors' perceptions of the company's critical performance indicators. This should not require any additional work for committee members, since they should already have a good understanding of the firm's key success factors and risks from discussions of the full board.

Audit committee members should also have sufficient financial background to identify where in the financial statements the key risks are reflected. Their discussions with management and external auditors should focus on these risks. How well are they being managed? How are the auditors planning their work to focus on these areas? What evidence have they gathered to judge the adequacy of key financial statement estimates?

The audit committee also receives regular reviews of company performance from management as part of their regular board duties. Committee members should be especially proactive in requesting information that helps them evaluate how the firm is managing its key risks, since this information can also help them judge the quality of the financial statements. Audit committee members need to ask: Is information on company performance we are receiving in our regular board meetings consistent with the picture portrayed in the financial statements? If not, what is missing? Are additional disclosures required to ensure that investors are well informed about the firm's operations and performance?

Finally, audit committees need to focus on capital market expectations, not just statutory financial reports. In today's capital markets, the game begins when companies set expectations via analyst meetings, press releases, and other forms of investor communications. Indeed, the pressure to manage earnings is often a direct consequence of Wall Street's unrealistic expectations, either deliberately created by management or sustained by their inaction. Thus it is also important for audit committees to oversee the firm's investor relations strategy and ensure that management sets realistic expectations for both the short and long term.

Key Analysis Questions

The following questions are likely to provide a useful starting point for audit committees in their discussions with management and auditors over the firm's financial statements:

- How are the key business risks facing the firm reflected in its financial statements? How are these risks being managed?
- How are the firm's key risks reflected in the financial statements—what are the key accounting policies and estimates? What was the basis for the external auditor's assessment of these items?
- Is information on the key value drivers and firm performance presented to the full board consistent with the picture of the firm reflected in the financial statements and MD&A?
- What expectations are management creating in the capital market? Are these likely to create undue pressure to manage earnings?

SUMMARY

This chapter discussed how many of the financial analysis tools developed in Chapters 2 through 8 can be used by managers to develop a coherent disclosure strategy, and by corporate board members and external auditors to improve the quality of their work.

By communicating effectively with investors, management can potentially reduce information problems for outside investors, lowering the likelihood that the stock will be mispriced or unnecessarily volatile. This can be important for firms that wish to raise new capital, avoid takeovers, or whose management is concerned that its true job performance is not reflected in the firm's stock.

The typical way for firms to communicate with investors is through financial reporting. Accounting standards and auditing make the reporting process a way for managers to not only provide information about the firm's current performance, but to indicate, through accounting estimates, where they believe the firm is headed in the future. However, financial reports are not always able to convey the types of forward-looking information that investors need. Accounting standards often do not permit firms to capitalize outlays, such as R&D, that provide significant future benefits to the firm.

A second way that management can communicate with investors is through non-accounting means. We discussed several such mechanisms, including meeting with financial analysts to explain the firm's strategy, current performance, and outlook; disclosing additional information, both quantitative and qualitative, to provide investors with similar information as management's; and using financial policies (such as stock repurchases, dividend increases, and hedging) to help signal management's optimism about the firm's future performance.

In this chapter we have stressed the importance of communicating effectively with investors. But firms also have to communicate with other stakeholders, including employees, customers, suppliers, and regulatory bodies. Many of the same principles discussed here can also be applied to management communication with these other stakeholders.

Finally, we examined the capital market role of governance agents, such as external auditors and audit committees. Both have recently faced considerable public scrutiny following a spate of financial reporting meltdowns in the U.S. Much has been done to improve the governance and independence of these intermediaries. We focus on how the financial analysis tools developed in the book can be used to improve the quality of audit and audit committee work. The tools of strategy analysis, accounting analysis, financial analysis, and prospective analysis can help auditors and audit committee members to identify the key issues in the financial statements to focus on and provide commonsense ways of assessing whether there are potential reporting problems that merit additional testing and analysis.

DISCUSSION QUESTIONS

1. Apple's inventory increased from $1 billion on December 29, 1994, to $1.95 billion one year later. In contrast, sales for the fourth quarter in each of these years increased from $2 billion to $2.6 billion. What is the implied annualized inventory turnover for Apple for these years? What different interpretations about future performance could a financial analyst infer from this change? What information could Apple's management provide to investors to clarify the change in inventory turnover? What are the costs and benefits to Apple from disclosing this information? What issues does this change raise for the auditor? What additional tests would you want to conduct as Apple's auditor?

2. a. What are likely to be the long-term critical success factors for the following types of firms?
   - a high technology company such as Microsoft
   - a large low-cost retailer such as Kmart

   b. How useful is financial accounting data for evaluating how well these two companies are managing their critical success factors? What other types of information would be useful in your evaluation? What are the costs and benefits to these companies from disclosing this type of information to investors?

3. Management frequently objects to disclosing additional information on the grounds that it is proprietary. Consider the recent FASB proposals on expanding disclosures on (a) executive stock compensation and (b) business segment performance. Many

corporate managers expressed strong opposition to both proposals. What are the potential proprietary costs from expanded disclosures in each of these areas? If you conclude that proprietary costs are relatively low for either, what alternative explanations do you have for management's opposition?

4. Financial reporting rules in many countries outside the U.S. (e.g., the UK, Australia, New Zealand, and France) permit management to revalue fixed assets (and in some cases even intangible assets) which have increased in value. Revaluations are typically based on estimates of realizable value made by management or independent valuers. Do you expect that these accounting standards will make earnings and book values more or less useful to investors? Explain why or why not. How can management make these types of disclosures more credible?

5. Under a management buyout, the top management of a firm offers to buy the company from its stockholders, usually at a premium over its current stock price. The management team puts up its own capital to finance the acquisition, with additional financing typically coming from a private buyout firm and private debt. If management is interested in making such an offer for its firm in the near future, what are its financial reporting incentives? How do these differ from the incentives of management that are not interested in a buyout? How would you respond to a proposed management buyout if you were the firm's auditor? What about if you were a member of the audit committee?

6. You are approached by the management of a small start-up company that is planning to go public. The founders are unsure about how aggressive they should be in their accounting decisions as they come to the market. John Smith, the CEO, asserts, "We might as well take full advantage of any discretion offered by accounting rules, since the market will be expecting us to do so." What are the pros and cons of this strategy? As the partner of a major audit firm, what type of analysis would you perform before deciding to take on a new start-up that is planning to go public?

7. Two years after a successful public offering, the CEO of a biotechnology company is concerned about stock market uncertainty surrounding the potential of new drugs in the development pipeline. In his discussion with you, the CEO notes that even though they have recently made significant progress in their internal R&D efforts, the stock has performed poorly. What options does he have to help convince investors of the value of the new products? Which of these options are likely to be feasible?

8. Why might the CEO of the biotechnology firm discussed in Question 7 be concerned about the firm being undervalued? Would the CEO be equally concerned if the stock were overvalued? Do you believe that the CEO would attempt to correct the market's perception in this overvaluation case? How would you react to company concern about market under- or overvaluation if you were the firm's auditor? Or if you were a member of the audit committee?

9. When companies decide to shift from private to public financing by making an initial public offering for their stock, they are likely to face increased costs of investor communications. Given this additional cost, why would firms opt to go public?

10. German firms are traditionally financed by banks, which have representatives on the companies' boards. How would communication challenges differ for these firms relative to U.S. firms, which rely more on public financing?

NOTES

1. M. Jensen and W. Meckling, "Theory of the Firm: Managerial Behavior, Agency Costs, and Capital Structure," *Journal of Financial Economics* 3 (October 1976): 305–360, analyzed agency problems between managers and outside investors. Subsequent work by B. Holmstrom and others examined how contracts between managers and outside investors could mitigate the agency problem.

2. Kevin J. Murphy and Jerold L. Zimmerman, "Financial Performance Surrounding CEO Turnover," *Journal of Accounting and Economics* 16 (January/April/July 1993): 273–315, find a strong relation between CEO turnover and earnings-based performance.

3. See S. Teoh, I. Welch, and T. Wong, "Earnings Management and the Long-Run Market Performance of Initial Public Offerings, *The Journal of Finance* 63 (December 1998): 1935–74, and S. Teoh, I. Welch, and T. Wong, "Earnings Management and the Underperformance of Seasoned Equity Offerings," *Journal of Financial Economics* 50 (October 1998): 63–99.

4. This market imperfection is often referred to as a "lemons" or "information" problem. It was first discussed by G. Akerlof in relation to the used car market (see "The Market for 'Lemons': Quality Uncertainty and the Market Mechanism," *Quarterly Journal of Economics* 90 (1970): 629–50. Akerlof recognized that the seller of a used car knew more about the car's value than the buyer. This meant that the buyer was likely to end up overpaying, since the seller would accept any offer that exceeded the car's true value and reject any lower offer. Car buyers recognized this problem and would respond by only making low-ball offers for used cars, leading sellers with high quality cars to exit the market. As a result, only the lowest quality cars (the "lemons") would remain in the market. Akerlof pointed out that qualified independent mechanics could correct this market breakdown by providing buyers with reliable information on a used car's true value.

5. Of course improved analysis alone is unlikely to be sufficient to improve market intermediation if the structural reforms implemented by the Sarbanes-Oxley Act and the stock exchanges fail to correct the serious conflicts of interest for intermediaries that we have witnessed in the last few years.

6. Douglas J. Skinner, "Earnings disclosures and stockholder lawsuits," *Journal of Accounting and Economics* (November 1997): 249–83, finds that firms with bad earnings news tend to predisclose this information, perhaps to reduce the cost of litigation that inevitably follows bad news quarters.

7. For example, G. Foster, "Briloff and the Capital Market," *Journal of Accounting Research* 17, no. 1 (Spring 1979): 262–74, finds firms that are criticized for their accounting by Abraham J. Briloff on average suffer an 8 percent decline in their stock price.

8. See Sarah Tasker, "Bridging the Information Gap: Quarterly Conference Calls as a Medium for Voluntary Disclosure." *Review of Accounting Studies* 3, no. 1-2 (1998): 137–67.

9. See Richard Frankel, Marilyn Johnson, and Douglas Skinner, "An Empirical Examination of Conference Calls as a Voluntary Disclosure Medium," *Journal of Accounting Research* 37, no. 1 (Spring 1999): 133–50.

10. Recent research on voluntary disclosure includes Mark Lang and Russell Lundholm, "Cross-Sectional Determinants of Analysts' Ratings of Corporate Disclosures," *Journal of Accounting Research* 31 (Autumn 1993): 246–71; Lang and Lundholm, "Corporate Disclosure Policy and Analysts," *The Accounting Review* 71 (October 1996): 467–92; M. Welker, "Disclosure Policy, Information Asymmetry and Liquidity in Equity Markets," *Contemporary Accounting Research* (Spring 1995); Christine Botosan, "The Impact of Annual Report Disclosure Level on Investor Base and the Cost of Capital," *The Accounting Review* (July 1997): 323–50; and Paul Healy, Amy Hutton, and Krishna Palepu, "Stock Performance and Intermediation Changes Surrounding Sustained Increases in Disclosure," *Contemporary Accounting Research* 16, no. 3 (Fall 1999): 485–521. This research finds that firms are more likely to provide high levels of disclosure if they have strong earnings performance, issue securities, have more analyst following, and have less dispersion in analyst forecasts. In addition, firms with high levels of disclosure policies tend to have a lower cost of capital and bid-ask spread. Finally, firms that increase disclosure have accompanying increases in stock returns, institutional ownership, analyst following, and stock liquidity. In "The Role of Supplementary Statements with Management's Earnings Forecasts," working paper, Harvard Business School, 2003, A. Hutton, G. Miller, and D. Skinner examine the market response to management earnings forecasts

and find that bad news forecasts are always informative but that good news forecasts are informative only when they are supported by verifiable forward-looking statements.

11. Findings by Paul Healy and Krishna Palepu in "Earnings Information Conveyed by Dividend Initiations and Omissions," *Journal of Financial Economics* 21 (1988): 149–75, indicate that investors interpret announcements of dividend initiations and omissions as managers' forecasts of future earnings performance.

12. See Larry Dann, Ronald Masulis, and David Mayers, "Repurchase Tender Offers and Earnings Information," *Journal of Accounting & Economics* (September 1991): 217–52, and Michael Hertzel and Prem Jain, "Earnings and Risk Changes Around Stock Repurchases," *Journal of Accounting & Economics* (September 1991): 253–76.

13. See Mary Barth and Ron Kasznik, "Share Repurchases and Intangible Assets," *Journal of Accounting & Economics* 28 (December 1999): 211–41.

14. See P. Healy and K. Palepu, "The Fall of Enron," *Journal of Economic Perspectives,* forthcoming; and P. Healy and K. Palepu, "How the Quest for Efficiency Undermined the Market," *Harvard Business Review,* forthcoming.

15. For example, M. Nelson, J. Eliott, and R. Tarpley, in "Evidence from Auditors About Managers' and Auditors' Earnings Management Decisions," *The Accounting Review* 77 (2002 Supplement): 175–202, show that mechanical accounting rules for structured finance transactions lead to more earnings management.

16. See P. Healy and K. Palepu, "Audit the Audit Committees: After Enron Boards Must Change the Focus and Provide Greater Financial Transparency," *Financial Times,* June 10, 2002, p. 14.

INDEX

Note: **Boldface** is used for rule numbers to distinguish them from page numbers; *italics* are used for page numbers for tables and charts.

A

abandonment option, 8-15 – 16
ABC Corp., 4-11
accounting
  accrual, 1-3 – 4, 3-1 – 2, 3-5, 3-14n.4
  aggressive, 3-10
  analysis. *See* analysis, accounting
  bias in. *See* accounting, distortions in
  cash, 1-3, 3-1, 3-14n.4
  changes in, 3-10, 3-12
  clean surplus, 7-18n.1, 8-18n.5
  conservative vs. good, 3-11 – 12, 8-14 – 15, 13-3, 13-16
  conventions in, 1-5
  data, value of, 3-12 – 13
  distortions in, 3-14n.4, 3-15n.5, 4-1, 4-5 – 29
    to undo, 3-1, 3-11, 8-15
    and valuation, 8-14 – 15, 8-18n.6
  flexibility in, 3-7
  formats for statements of, 4-1 – 5, *4-2 – 4-4*
  for mergers and acquisitions, 11-11 – 12
  methods of, and valuation, 7-4 – 5, 11-13
  nomenclature used in, 4-1 – 2
  policies, 3-6 – 7, 3-8
  quality of, 3-4 – 6
  rules of. *See* rules, accounting
  standards of, 1-4 – 5, 3-3 – 4, 13-6 – 7
  strategy, evaluation of, 3-7 – 8
  unbiased, 7-19n.13
  unusual vs. questionable, 3-12
Accounting Principles Board (APB), rules of, **25**, 4-30

accounts payable, 5-12, 5-13
accounts receivable, 2-10, 4-7 – 8, 5-12
  change in, 3-9, 3-12
  discounted, 4-14, 4-22 – 23, 4-24 – 25
  sale of, 3-10
  as security, 10-5
  turnover ratio, 5-13
accrual, current
  distinguished from noncurrent, 5-22
  information on, 5-23
acquisition. *See* mergers and acquisitions; control
Act, legislative
  Clayton (1914), 11-3
  Hart Scott Rodino (1976), 11-3
  Sarbanes-Oxley (2002), 13-1, 13-14, 13-17, 13-21n.5
  Sherman (1890), 11-3
  Tax Reform (1986), 11-2
advantage
  comparative, 9-3
  competitive, 2-7 – 9, *2-8*, 2-9
AICPA. *See* American Institute of Certified Public Accountants
airline industry, 2-4, 4-8, 4-14, 4-15 – 17
ALZA Corp., 4-17 – 18
Amazon.com, 2-13 – 14, 4-31
American Airlines (AMR), 10-10, *10-10*
American Express, *10-10*
American Institute of Certified Public Accountants (AICPA), 3-3, 13-3, 13-12
Amoco, 11-4
amortization
  of goodwill. *See* goodwill
  of long-term assets, 4-8, 4-13
AMR. *See* American Airlines
analysis
  accounting, 1-8, 3-1 – 13, 3-14n.1, 10-6
    auditing and, 13-14 – 15

    financial statements for, 1-7
    and forecasting, 6-1
    pitfalls in, 3-11 – 12
    procedure for, 3-6 – 11
    purpose of, 3-1, 8-1
    value of, 3-13 – 14
  business, 1-1, 1-6 – 9
  cash flow. *See* cash flow, analysis
  credit. *See* credit analysis
  debt, 5-16 – 19, 10-9 – 13
  equity security. *See* equity security analysis
  financial, 1-7, 1-8, 5-5 – 29, 6-1, 10-6, 11-1 – 15, 13-2, 13-14 – 16
  financial statement, 9-3, 10-9
  fundamental, quantitative vs. traditional, 9-4, 9-5, 9-10
  income statement, 5-9 – 11
  industry, 2-1 – 7
  prospective, 1-7, 7-1 – 18, 8-1 – 18
    auditing and, 13-15 – 16
    and forecasting, 6-1 – 16
    see also valuation
  ratio, 5-1 – 22, 8-1, 10-6 – 7, 13-15
  securities, 1-8, 9-5, 9-6 – 10, 10-11, *10-12*
    see also equity security analysis
  sensitivity, 6-10 – 12, 11-9
  statistical. *See* statistics
  strategy
    business, 1-8, 6-1, 8-1, 10-6, 13-14
    competitive, 2-1, 2-7 – 10
    corporate, 2-1, 2-11 – 14
  technical, 9-5
analysts
  financial
    industry expertise of, 13-7
    and management's credibility, 13-7
    meetings of, with management, 13-9
    as monitors, 13-7
  securities
    expectations of, 9-9

analysts, securities (*continued*)
    performance of, 9-10 – 11
Ann Taylor, 7-6
AOL, Time Warner and, 4-11 – 12
APB. *See* Accounting Principles
    Board
Apple Computer, 2-6, 10-10, *10-10*
Arco, 11-4
Arthur Andersen, 13-1
assets
    defined, 3-2, 4-5
    distortions in accounting for, 4-5 –
        21
    estimating value of, 4-6 – 7, 8-11
    fair value of, and book value, 4-6 –
        7
    impaired, 4-6, 4-7
    intangible, 3-12, 4-8, 4-15, 4-20 –
        21, 12-11
    long-term
        assumptions about, and
            valuation, *8-5*
        defined, 5-13 – 15
        depreciation of, 4-8, 4-13,
            4-15 – 17
        fair value of, 4-6
        management of, 5-12
        net, 5-7, 5-13 – 15
        turnover of, 5-12 – 15
        write-downs of, 4-8, 4-11 – 12,
            4-13
    management of, to analyze, 5-12 –
        15, *5-14*
    "negative pledge" on, as security,
        10-5
    net, defined, 5-7
    operating
        net, to define, 5-13
        turnover, 5-7 – 8, *5-21*, *6-15*
    overstated, 4-7 – 12
    return on. *See* return on assets
    sale of, 12-6
    turnover of. *See* turnover, assets
    understated, 4-12 – 21
    valuation of, 4-6 – 12, 7-1, 7-3,
        8-1, 8-2 – 7, *8-7*, 8-11
    write-offs of, 3-8, 3-10
    writing down, 4-7, 4-8 – 9, 4-13
assumption, forecasting, 8-1 – 3, *8-5*,
    8-8
    competitive equilibrium, 8-7 – 8
    constant rate, 8-9
AT&T, debt rating of, *10-10*
audit committee, 13-1, 13-13, 13-14,
    13-17 – 18

auditing
    accounting analysis in, 13-14 – 15
    changes in, 3-10
    changes to practice of, 13-13 – 14
    credit analysis and, 10-1
    defined, 3-3
    external, 3-3 – 4, 13-1, 13-2
    financial analysis and, 13-14 – 16
    industry expertise and, 13-8
    internal, and fraud, 13-13
    and management's credibility, 13-7
    mechanical standards in, 13-13,
        13-14
    procedures in, 13-13
    qualified opinions and, 3-10,
        13-12 – 13
Auditing Standards Board, 13-17
auditor
    analysis by, 13-12 – 16
    reports issued by, 13-12 – 13,
        13-14
    responsibilities of, 13-12 – 13
Australia, auditors in, 13-13
automobile industry, 2-5, 2-17n.10

B

BA. *See* British Airways
balance sheet, 3-1, 3-2
    assets excluded from, 4-14, 4-18 –
        21
    "condensed," 6-2
    forecast of, 6-2, 6-9, *6-10*
    liabilities excluded from, 4-22 –
        23, 4-24 – 25, 13-15
    recasting, 4-1
    standardized format for, *4-3*, *4-41*,
        4-44
banking industry, 3-6, 3-7, 9-6
bankruptcy
    leverage and, 12-4
    predicting, 10-13
banks
    commercial, as suppliers of credit,
        10-1, 10-2, 10-9, 10-11, *10-12*
    as professional investors, 13-2
bargaining power, and competition,
    2-5
Barnes and Noble, 2-13
barriers, and competition, 2-4 – 5, 2-6,
    2-17n.10
benchmarks, 5-1
    efficient markets hypothesis as,
        9-4
    for evaluating operating ROA, 5-8

for forecasts, 6-3 – 7
for fund management, 9-11
historical values of key ratios for,
    5-21 – 22
for performance, 11-6
ROE, 5-5
sustainable growth rate as, 5-19 –
    20
usefulness of, 6-3, 6-5
for valuation, 7-14, 8-14, 13-15 –
    16
benefit, future economic, and expense
    recognition, 4-6
benefits, pension and postretirement
    accounting for, 3-7, 4-23, 4-25 –
        29, 4-39n.19
    management of, 9-11, 9-12
Bezos, Jeff, 2-13
bias
    accounting. *See* accounting,
        distortions in
    in security analysis, 9-11
biotechnology industry, 3-7, 8-15
Black-Scholes model, 4-31,
    4-40n.24
Blue Ribbon Committee (BRC) on
    Improving the Effectiveness of
    Corporate Audit Committees,
    13-17
bonds, 10-2
    rating, 10-12, *10-13*
bonuses, 3-5, 3-8, 3-15n.8
book value
    and asset valuation, 4-6 – 7, 7-3
    negative, 8-15 – 16
    and valuation, 7-7 – 9, 7-18n.6,
        8-10, 8-15 – 16
BP (British Petroleum), 11-4
brands
    accounting for, 4-15
    Amazon.com as, 2-13
BRC. *See* Blue Ribbon Committee
Briloff, Abraham, 3-15n.5, 13-21n.7
British Airways (BA), 4-15 – 17,
    10-10
broadcasting, 2-4
business, activities of, and financial
    statements, 1-3 – 6, *1-4*
business strategy, 1-8, 5-8
    analysis of, 1-8, 6-1, 8-1, 10-6,
        13-14
    auditing industry, 13-13 – 14
    disclosure of long-term, 13-10
buyers, bargaining power and, 2-5,
    2-6

buyout
    leveraged (LBO), 10-2, 10-3, 10-9,
        11-2, 12-3
    management, 13-11
Byers, John, 13-5

C

CA. *See* Computer Associates
Canada, accounting in, 4-39n.12
capacity, and competition, 2-4
capital
    cost of
        model for (CAPM), 8-3 – 4
        postacquisition, 11-8
        and return on equity, 5-4, 13-2
        and valuation, 8-1 – 7
        weighted average (WACC),
            5-8, 7-3, 8-2
    net, 5-7
    structure of, 12-1
        and mergers and acquisitions,
            11-11 – 12
        model, 12-2
        optimal, 12-2 – 7
    see also operating working capital;
        working capital
capital gains, and dividends, 12-10
capital markets, 1-2
    and accounting choices, 3-5 – 6
    expectations of, and audits, 13-18
    intermediaries in, 1-2 – 3
    and savings, 1-2
    transaction costs and, 2-12
CAPM. *See* model, capital asset
        pricing
cash
    for acquisitions, 11-3, 11-10 – 11
    balance, 5-15
    as deferred revenue, 4-22
    excess, 8-16
    from operations, 5-23
    valuation of, 8-16
cash flow
    analysis, 1-8, 3-13, 3-14 – 15n.4,
        5-1, 5-23 – 27, *5-24*, 10-6
    change in, 3-10
    data, to restate, 5-24, *5-24*
    discounted (DCF)
        mergers and acquisitions and,
            11-8 – 9
        and valuation, 7-1, 7-12 – 13, 8-9
    distinguished from net income,
        5-22

excess, and valuation, 8-16
    forecast of, 6-1, 6-3, 6-9 – 10,
        8-6 – 7, *8-7*, 8-10
    free, 5-25
        to debt, 8-1, 8-2
        defined, 8-2, 8-6
        dividends and, 12-10
        and equity, 7-12 – 13, 8-1, 8-2,
            8-6
        inefficiencies in, 12-3 – 4,
            12-10
        use of, 12-8, 12-11
        and valuation, 8-10, 8-11,
            11-8 – 9
    and long-term investments, 5-23,
        5-25
    measures of, *5-24*, 5-25 – 26
    undiscounted, 4-6 – 7
    and valuation, 8-11
    see also loan, "cash-flowing" of
cash flow statement, 3-1, 3-10, 5-22
    direct and indirect formats of, 5-22
    standardized format of, *4-3*, *4-43*,
        4-45
    see also funds flow statement
cellular telephone industry, 5-19
Center for Financial Research and
        Analysis (CFRA), 4-10 – 11
CFRA. *See* Center for Financial
        Research and Analysis
Charming Shoppes, 7-6
Chevron, 11-4
Coca-Cola Inc., 2-3, 2-5, 4-31, *10-10*
collateral, 10-4
commerce, electronic, 2-11
commercial paper, 10-2
communication, corporate
    analysis of, 1-8
    see also managers, reporting
        strategy of
companies, rivalry among, 2-2 – 3,
    2-6, 2-7
Compaq, 2-6, 2-9, 2-10
comparisons
    benchmark and, 5-1
    cross-sectional, 5-1
    mergers and acquisitions and, 11-6
    time-series, 5-1
    see also analysis, ratio
competition
    and accounting choices, 3-6
    for acquisitions, 11-14
    balance in, 2-3
    bargaining power and, 2-4 – 5

barriers to, 2-4 – 5, 2-6, 2-17n.10
    credit analysis and, 10-1
    and disclosures by management,
        13-10
    and long-range growth, 8-8
    perfect, 2-1 – 2
    personal computer industry and,
        2-5 – 6
    regulation and, 2-4
    ROE and, 6-6
    strategy for, 2-7 – 10, 5-2 – 3
CompUSA, 2-6
Computer Associates (CA), 4-24 – 25
concentration ratio, 2-16n.5
conflict of interest
    among financial intermediaries,
        13-21n.5
    between creditors and
        shareholders, 12-4 – 5
    between managers and
        shareholders, 12-3, 12-10,
        13-6
conglomerate. *See* organization,
        multibusiness
Conoco, 11-4
conservatism, convention of, 1-5
construction contract, revenues and,
    3-10
consulting services, auditors', 13-14
Continental Airlines, 10-10, *10-10*
control
    management
        and debt policies, 12-3
        and mergers and acquisitions,
            11-2
    over business entities, accounting
        for, 3-5
corporation
    boards of, 13-2, 13-13, 13-17
    control of, and accounting choices,
        3-5
    governance of. *See* governance
    transparency in dealings of,
        13-13 – 14
    value creation and, 2-11 – 14
cost
    of capital. *See* capital, cost of
    competition and, 2-3
    control, 2-8
    of debt and equity capital
        (WACC), 8-2 – 5
    legal, of financial distress, 12-4
    switching, 2-2, 2-4, 2-6
    transaction, 2-11 – 12, 11-11

cost leadership, and competition,
2-7 – 8, *2-8*, 2-9 – 10
credit
analysis of. *See* credit analysis
evaluation, 1-8
market for, 10-2 – 3
open line of, 10-4
policies, analysis of, 5-14
rating, 8-3
revolving line of, 10-4
suppliers of, 10-2 – 3
trade, 5-14
see also financing; loan
credit analysis, 5-14, 10-1 – 15
borrowers and, 10-1
defined, 10-1
process of, 10-3 – 10
scope of, 10-3
uses for, 10-1
creditors, stockholders and, 12-4 – 5
credit-worthiness, analysis of,
10-5 – 7
customers, credit analysis and, 10-1
CVS, Inc., 2-13

D

data, disaggregated, 5-19
days' inventory, 5-13
days' payable, 5-13
Dayton Hudson. *See* Target
DCF. *See* cash flow, discounted
debt
allowance for bad, 4-7
analyzing, 5-16 – 19, 10-9 – 13
assumptions about, for valuation,
8-2
beta, 8-4 – 5
capital, 5-8
convertible, 4-30
costs of, to weight, 8-2 – 5
covenants. *See* loan, covenants
equity and, 12-6 – 7
forecasting, 6-8, 8-1
free cash flows to, 8-1
interest rate on, 8-2 – 3
investment grade, 10-9
and long-term solvency, 5-16 – 19
market value for, 8-2
negative, 5-6, 5-29n.4
net, 5-7, *8-5*
for new financing, 10-10, 12-7,
12-8
public, 10-2 – 3, 10-8 – 9

ratings of, 10-2, 10-9 – 13, *10-10*,
10-12
models of, 10-12 – 13, *10-12*
ratios for analyzing, 5-17
senior, 10-3
subordination of, and ratings,
10-12, *10-13*
debt financing
cost of, 10-10, *10-10*
mergers and acquisitions and,
11-10
pros and cons of, 5-16, 12-9
debt policy
analysis of, 1-8, 5-16 – 19
factors influencing, 12-1 – 2
summarized, 12-8
Dell, Michael, 2-6, 2-9
Dell Computer Corp., 2-6, 2-9 – 10
Delta Air Lines, 10-10, *10-10*
depreciation, accounting for, 3-7, 4-8,
4-13, 4-15 – 17, 4-39n.16
differentiation, potential for, and
competition, 2-3, 2-6, 2-7,
2-8 – 9, *2-8*, 2-17n.10
Dillard's, 7-6, *7-9*
direct selling, 2-10
disclosure
additional voluntary, 3-9, 13-10
constraints on, 13-10
extent of, 1-6
fair, 9-11
policies on, 3-6
quality of, 3-8 – 9
discount, diversification, 2-12
discount rate
to compute, 8-2 – 7
mergers and acquisitions and, 11-8
performance forecasts and, *8-7*
Disney Corp., 4-11
distortion, in financial statements. *See*
accounting, distortions in
distress, financial
costs of, 12-4 – 6
effects of, 12-6
leverage and, 12-4 – 6
predicting, for debt repayments,
10-13 – 15
distribution, and competition, 2-4, 2-6
diversification, mergers and
acquisitions and, 11-3
divestiture, policy on, 5-14
dividend payout
defined, 12-9
levels of, 12-12, *12-12*

as management communication,
13-10
optimal, 12-12
ratio, 5-19
dividend policy
analysis of, 1-8, 5-20, 5-25
factors influencing, 12-1, 12-9 – 13
loan constraints and, 12-11 – 12
summarized, 12-13
and valuation, 8-16
dividends
and capital gains, 12-10
discounted, valuation and, 7-1,
7-2 – 3
and financial slack, 12-10, 12-11
free cash flow and, 12-10
as preferable to acquisitions, 11-3
preferred, 10-6, 10-16n.1
reductions in, 12-7
taxes and, 12-2, 12-3, 12-10 – 11
dividend yield, *12-12*
defined, 12-9
dot.com industry, 4-8 – 9, 9-10,
10-14 – 15
Down Under Company, valuation for
discounted cash flow, 7-13, *7-13*
earnings-based, 7-4, *7-4*, 7-7
equity, 7-2, *7-2*, 7-8 – 9, *7-8 – 7-9*
Duke Energy Corp.
dividend policy of, 12-8 – 10,
12-9, 12-12
financing policies of, 12-1 – 2,
12-1, 12-5

E

earnings
abnormal
assumptions about, for
valuation, 8-5 – 7
and current earnings, 7-10 – 11
defined, 7-3, 8-6
discounted, and valuation, 7-1,
7-2, 7-4 – 5, 7-10 – 12, 8-9
forecasting and, 6-4 – 5, 6-7 –
10, 8-1, 8-5 – 7, 8-9, 8-10
mergers and acquisitions and,
11-8 – 9
before interest, taxes,
depreciation, and amortization
(EBITDA), 5-11
forecast of, 6-1, 6-3, 7-10 – 11,
9-10 – 11, 11-7
loan covenants and, 10-8

earnings (*continued*)
management of, 3-2, 3-8, 4-8, 13-2
mergers and acquisitions and, 11-7
momentum of, and securities analysis, 9-6
multiples, for valuing mergers and acquisitions, 11-7 – 8
retained, 12-2, 12-7
and valuation, 7-9, 7-10 – 11, 8-11, 11-7 – 8
EBITDA. *See* earnings, before interest, taxes, depreciation, and amortization
electricity services, 12-6, *12-7, 12-12*
Elf Acquitaine, 11-4
employees, credit analysis and, 10-1
Enron, 3-4, 3-8, 4-31, 9-10, 13-3, 13-4, 13-14, 13-17
entities, special purpose, 3-8, 3-10
entrance barriers, and competition, 2-2, 2-3 – 4
equilibrium, assumption of competitive, 8-8, 8-9, 8-10
equity
beta, 8-4 – 5
book value of, 8-2
capital, 5-8
costs of, to weight, 8-3 – 5
credit analysis and, 10-3
debt and, 12-6 – 7
defined, 3-2
distortions in reported, 4-30 – 32
free cash flow and, 7-12 – 13
issue of new, for financing, 12-7 – 8, 13-2
return on. *See* return on equity
valuation of, 7-1, 7-2 – 3, 7-20, 8-1, 8-2, *8-7*, 8-11
equity security analysis
candidates for, to select, 9-6
described, 9-1
expectations and, 9-9
and funds management, 9-4 – 6
and market efficiency, 9-2 – 4
process of, 9-6 – 10
uses for, 9-1
European Commission, 11-3
evaluation, credit, 1-8
exit barriers, and competition, 2-4
expenses
analyzing, 5-10 – 11
defined, 3-2

selling, general, and administrative (SG&A), analyzing, 5-10 – 11
Exxon, merger of, with Mobil, 11-1 – 2, 11-3, 11-4 – 5, 11-9 – 10, 11-13, 11-15

F
FASB. *See* Financial Accounting Standards Board
Federal Trade Commission (FTC), 11-3, 13-13
Federated Department Stores, 7-6
Filene's Basement, business strategy of, 2-7
finance companies, and credit supplies, n, 10-2
Financial Accounting Standards Board (FASB), 1-6, 3-3, 3-4, 4-30, 4-31, 13-3, 13-6, 13-12
130, 7-18n. 1
financial statements
analysis of, 9-3, 10-9 – 13
audit report in, 13-13
and business activities, 1-3 – 6, *1-4*
and business analysis, 1-6 – 9, *1-7*
"condensed," 6-2
described, 3-1
elements of, 1-2 – 7
forecasting. *See* forecasting
institutional framework of, 3-1
limitations of, 13-7 – 8
and management's communications, 1-3, 13-6 – 9
management strategy for, 1-6, 4-5 – 6
recasting, 4-1 – 5, 4-41 – 45
role of, in capital markets, 1-1 – 3
use of, in financial analysis, 1-7 – 9
value of, 3-14 – 15
see also footnotes
financing
cash flow from, 5-22
corporate policies on, 12-1 – 13
lease, 10-5
mechanisms of, 3-10
mergers and acquisitions and, 11-2, 11-10 – 13
for new projects, 12-7 – 9
options for, 12-7 – 8, 13-11
sources of, 10-2 – 3

firm
selecting comparable, for valuations, 7-6
size of
and debt ratings, 10-10 – 11, *10-13*
and leverage, 12-6 – 7
and stock returns, 8-3
first mover advantages, 2-3 – 4
footnotes, to financial statements
on accounting changes, 3-10, 4-4 – 5
accounting policies and, 3-8, 3-11
leases and, 5-15
on liabilities, 4-26, 4-40n.22
off-balance sheet items, 4-18
on reserves, 4-9
on stock options, 4-31
on taxes, 3-10, 5-12
Ford Motor Company, *10-10*
forecasting
abnormal earnings, 8-1
assumptions and, 6-7 – 8
balance sheet, 6-9, *6-10*
cash flows, 8-1
debt, 6-8
detailed, 8-1 – 7
earnings, 6-7 – 10, 9-10
errors in, 3-4, 3-5
financial, 5-1
and financial analysis, 6-1
financial statement, 1-8, *6-10*
horizon for, 8-1, 8-10
interim, 6-11 – 12
long-term, 6-9
by management, 13-10, 13-15
market consensus, 9-7
NOPAT margin and, 6-6, 6-8, 6-9
one year ahead, 6-7 – 8
operating ROA and, 6-6
prospective analysis and, 6-1 – 16
quarterly, 6-11 – 12
ROE and, 6-5 – 7, 8-1
sales, 6-3 – 4, 6-7 – 8, 9-7
structure of, 6-1 – 3
techniques of, 6-1 – 7
of terminal value, 8-1
formula
acquisition premiums, 11-6
asset valuation, 7-3
CAPM, 8-3
cash flow, discounted, 7-12 – 13
cash ratio, 5-15
coverage, 5-17 – 18, 10-6

formula (*continued*)
   current ratio, 5-15
   days' inventory, 5-13
   days' payables, 5-13
   days' receivables, 5-13
   debt to capital, 5-17
   debt to equity, 5-17
   dividend payout, 5-19
   dividends, discounted, 7-3
   earnings
      current abnormal, 7-10 – 11
      discounted abnormal, 7-3,
         7-10 – 11
   EBITDA, 5-11
   equity values, 7-1, 7-2 – 3, 7-7,
      7-8, 7-9, 7-12
   Foster model, 6-11, 6-14n.7
   funds flow coverage, 10-6
   gross profit margin, 5-9
   interest coverage, 5-17
   investment turnover, 5-13
   liabilities to equity, 5-17
   long-term assets, 5-13
   net debt to capital ratio, 5-17
   net debt to equity ratio, 5-17
   net long-term assets turnover, 5-13
   NOPAT margin, 5-11
   operating cash flow, 5-15
   operating ROA, 5-7
   operating working capital, 5-12
   payables turnover, 5-13
   PP&E turnover, 5-14
   quick ratio, 5-15
   random walk model, 7-10 – 11
   receivables turnover, 5-13
   ROA, 5-6
   ROE, 5-4, 7-11
   sustainable growth measure,
      5-19 – 21
   WACC, 8-2
   working capital turnover, 5-13
FPIC Insurance Group
   audit of, 13-16
   communication issues of, 13-5 – 6,
      13-8, 13-12
France, accounting in, 4-39n.12
fraud, auditing and, 13-13, 13-16
FTC. *See* Federal Trade Commission
funds flow statement, 3-1, 5-22 – 23
   see also cash flow statement
funds, investment
   balanced, 9-2
   bond, 9-2
   equity, 9-2

   management of, and securities
      analysis, 9-4 – 6, 9-11 – 12
   money market, 9-2
   mutual. *See* mutual funds
   real estate, 9-2

G

GAAP. *See* Generally Accepted
      Accounting Principles
GAAS. *See* Generally Accepted
      Auditing Standards
Gap, The, 7-6
General Electric, 2-11, 10-9, *10-10*
General Motors, 4-26 – 29, *10-10*
Generally Accepted Accounting
      Principles (GAAP), 1-5, 3-3,
      13-12, 13-14
Generally Accepted Auditing
      Standards (GAAS), 3-4
Germany, accounting in, 3-6,
      4-39n.12, 13-11
GlaxoSmithKline, *10-10*
Global Crossing, 13-4
goodwill
   amortization of, 3-7, 11-13
   exclusion of, 4-13 – 14, 4-17 – 18
   valuation of, 13-15
   write-downs of, 4-8
governance, corporate, 13-1 – 3
   internal, 13-2
growth
   drivers of, *5-2*
   forecasting, 7-11 – 12, 9-9
   sustainable, and analysis, *5-20, 5-21*

H

hedging, stock mispricing and, 13-11
Hewlett-Packard, 2-9
high-technology industry, 8-15, 9-10
Home Depot, 2-17n.10
Hong Kong, auditors in, 13-13
hotel industry, 5-19, 12-6, *12-7, 12-12*
hypothesis
   bonus, 3-15n.8
   efficient markets, 9-2, 9-4

I

IASC. *See* International Accounting
      Standards Committee
IBM
   competition and, 2-3, 2-5, 2-9, 2-10

   valuation of, 9-3, 9-7 – 8, *9-8*
income, comprehensive, 7-18n.1
   see also net income
income smoothing, 3-12, 4-12 – 13
income statement, 3-1, 3-2, 3-14n.2
   analysis of, 5-9 – 11
   common-sized, 5-9, 5-10, *5-10*
   standardized format for, *4-2, 4-42,*
      4-45
index, market, 9-11
India, auditors in, 13-13
indicators, leading, and management
      communications, 13-10
industry
   comparable firms in, 7-6
   concentration in, 2-3
   considerations of, in mergers and
      acquisitions, 11-3
   fragmented, 2-3, 2-6
   growth rate in, 2-3
   leverage of, by type, 12-6 – 7
   structure of, and profitability,
      2-1 – 2, *2-2*
industry analysis, 2-1 – 7
information
   asymmetries of
      and the acquisition of capital,
         12-7, 13-2, 13-21n.4
      and mergers and acquisitions,
         11-2, 11-12
   non-public, and financial
      reporting, 9-11
   proprietary, and financial
      reporting, 13-10
initial public offering (IPO), 13-2
insurance industry
   and credit supplies, 10-2
   and debt ratings, 10-11, *10-12*
   as professional investors, 13-2
   see also FPIC
Intel, 2-6, 2-7, 2-10, 13-15
interest
   accounting for, 4-25, 4-40n.21
   conflict of. *See* conflict of interest
   debt and, 8-2 – 3
   expense, net after tax, 5-7, *8-5*
   pooling of. *See* pooling of interest
   rate
      London Interbank Offer
         (LIBOR), 10-9, 10-10,
         10-10
      prime, 10-9
intermediaries, financial, 1-2 – 3,
      13-2, *13-3*, 13-7

International Accounting Standards
    Committee (IASC), 3-3
Internet firms, 5-19, 8-15
    see also dot.com
inventory, 5-12
    accounting for, 3-5, 3-7
    analyzing management of, 4-8 – 9,
        5-14
    change in, 3-9 – 10, 3-12
    as security, 10-5 – 6
    turnover of, ratio, 5-13
investment opportunity, costs of
        foregone, 12-4
investments
    cash flow and, 5-22, 5-23, 5-25
    long-term assets and, 5-13
    mergers and acquisitions as, 11-1
    time horizon of, 9-10
investors
    and management communications,
        13-2, 13-4 – 6
    objectives of, 9-1 – 2
    professional, 13-2
    use of financial reports by, 13-6
IPO. *See* initial public offering

J

J C Penney, 7-6, *7-9*
JAL. *See* Japan Airlines
Japan
    accounting in, 4-39n. 12, 13-11
    competitiveness in, 2-17n. 10
Japan Airlines (JAL), 4-18 – 20,
    4-39n. 17
jet engine industry, 2-3
Johnson & Johnson, 4-17 – 18, 10-9,
    10-10

K

knight, white, 11-15

L

labor unions, and accounting choices,
    3-6
law
    antitrust, 11-2 – 3
    standards of, and auditing, 13-13
LBO. *See* buyout, leveraged
lease
    accounting for, 4-5, 4-13, 4-14,
        4-18 – 20, 4-23, 4-39n. 17

financing, 10-5
leasing industry, 3-7, 3-8
legal barriers, 2-4
legal liabilities
    and accounting, 1-5, 3-4
    and disclosure, 13-10
"lemons" problem, 1-2, 13-21n.4
Letter to the Shareholders,
        management's use of, 3-8
leverage
    adjusting multiples for, 7-7
    benefits of, 12-2 – 4
    costs of, 12-4 – 6
    and costs of debt and equity,
        8-4 – 5
    and debt ratings, *10-12*, *10-13*
    financial
        behavior of, *6-16*
        evaluating, 5-15 – 19
        and prediction of distress,
            10-14
    indicators of, 12-6 – 7
    measure of, 5-6, *5-21*
    mergers and acquisitions and,
        11-2, 11-11, 11-13
    and options for new financing,
        12-7, 12-8
    quantifying pros and cons, 12-6 – 7
    and size of firm, 12-6 – 7
liabilities
    current, 5-15
    defined, 3-2, 4-21
    distortions in reporting, 4-21 – 29
    interest-bearing, 5-15
    legal. *See* legal liabilities
    loan covenants and, 10-8
    measurement of, 4-21 – 22
    understated, 4-22 – 29
    unreported (off-balance-sheet),
        4-23, 13-15
        mergers and acquisitions and,
            11-11
LIBOR. *See* interest rate, London
        Interbank Offer
Limited, The, 7-6
liquidity
    ratios of, *5-16*
    short-term, 5-16
litigation, accounting for, 1-5, 3-4
LiveBid.com, 2-13
loan
    allowance for losses on, 4-7, 4-13
    amount of, 10-4
    "cash-flowing" of, 10-7

covenants, 3-5, 3-8, 10-7, 10-8,
        10-9 – 10, 12-10, 12-11 – 12
    evergreen, 10-7
    lease financing, 10-5
    mortgage, 10-4
    off-balance sheet, 4-22 – 23
    purpose of, 10-4
    security for, 10-5
    structure, 10-7 – 9
    term, 10-4, 10-5, 10-8
    type of, 10-4 – 5
    unsecured, 10-5
    working capital, 10-4
loss, communicating estimates on,
        13-8
Lucent Technologies
    debt ratings of, 10-10, *10-10*
    distortion in accounts of, 4-8 – 10
    financial fraud and, 13-4
    and prediction of distress, 10-14 –
        15, *10-14*
Lufthansa, 4-15 – 17, 4-39n. 16

M

machinery and equipment, as security,
        10-5
management, financial, evaluating,
        5-15 – 19
Management Discussion, and
        Analysis, evaluating, 3-8 – 9
managers
    analysis of their own firms by,
        13-1
    compensation of, and accounting
        choices, 3-5, 3-15n. 8
    conflicts of interest and, 12-3,
        12-10, 13-6
    credibility of reporting by, 13-1,
        13-3, 13-6 – 7, 13-8, 13-11,
        13-15
    fund, performance of, 9-11 – 12
    leveraged buyout by, 13-11
    meetings with analysts and, 13-9
    mergers and acquisitions and,
        11-2, 11-14 – 15
    reporting strategy of, 1-6
        accounting changes and, 3-4
        and external investors, 13-4 –
            12
        and market efficiency, 9-3 – 4
        and quality of disclosure, 3-1,
            3-2, 3-8 – 9, 4-5, 4-12 – 13,
            13-2

managers, reporting strategy of
  (*continued*)
    and valuation, 4-7, 7-6, 8-14 –
      15
    stock ownership by, 3-8
manufacturing, 2-10, 4-7
margin
    EBITDA, *5-10*, 5-11
    NOPAT, 5-7, 5-8, 5-11
    operating
    supernormal, 8-8, 8-9
    see also profit margin
marketing, expensing, 3-7
markets, security
    collapse of, and corporate
      governance, 13-1
    efficiency of, 9-2 – 4, 9-10
    expectations of, 9-7 – 9
    financial statements and, 13.11-l5
    imperfect, and financing
      constraints, 13-2, 13-21n.4
market value, and valuation, 8-13,
  13-15 – 16
May Department Stores, 7-6
McDonald's Corp., *10-10*
mean, reversion to, 6-3, 6-5, 7-11 –
  12, 8-10
measurability, convention of, 1-5
medical services, 2-4
membership bases, accounting for,
  4-15
Merck & Co. Inc.
    debt rating of, 10-9, *10-10*
    intangibles of, 3-12
    and predictions of distress, *10-14*,
      10-15
mergers and acquisitions
    accounting for, 4-13, 11-13
    analysis of, 1-8, 11-1 – 15
    benefits of, 11-1 – 3, 11-6,
      11-8 – 9
    consummation of, 11-14 – 15
    goodwill and, 4-11 – 12, 4-13 – 14
    loan covenants and, 10-8, 10-9
    motivation for, 11-1 – 5
    oil industry, 11-4
    policy on, 5-14
    pricing, 11-5 – 10
    tax effects of, 11-10 – 11, 11-13
Microsoft
    competition and, 2-4, 2-5, 2-6, 2-7
    debt rating of, *10-10*
    R&D of, 2-10, 4-20 – 21
    stock options and, 4-32

MicroStrategy, 4-10 – 11, 4-23 – 24
mispricing, of securities, 9-1, 9-2, 9-3
Mobil. *See* Exxon, merger of
model
    abnormal earnings, and valuation,
      7-15
    Altman Z-score, 10-14 – 15,
      10-17n.9
    autoregressive, 7-11, 7-18n.9
    Black-Scholes, 4-30, 4-31,
      4-40n.24
    capital asset pricing (CAPM),
      8-3 – 4, 8-17nn.1, 2, 3, 9-11
    capital structure, 12-2, 12-7 – 9
    for cash flow analysis, *5-24*
    classic, of tax effects of dividends,
      12-10
    of debt ratings, 10-12 – 13, *10-12*
    discounted abnormal earnings,
      7-3, 7-15, 7-20
    discounted cash flow, and
      valuation, 7-13, 7-15, 7-19n.12
    dividend discount, *7-2*, 7-3, 7-13,
      7-18n.2, 7-20
    for forecasting, 6-11 – 12
    Foster, 6-11 – 12, 6-14n.7
    Kaplan Urwitz, 10-11, *10-13*
    for predicting distress, 10-13 – 15
    pro forma, 11-8 – 9
    random walk, 6-4, 7-10 – 11,
      7-18n.7
    for security analysis, 9-11
    time-series, 9-10, 9-14n.9
    "Zeta," 10-13
Moody's, 10-2, 10-9
multiples. *See* earnings multiples;
    price multiples
mutual funds (unit trusts), 9-2, 9-11 –
    12, 13-2

N

natural gas industry, 12-12
Neiman Marcus, 7-6
Nestlé, debt ratings of, 10-9, *10-10*
net income
    accruals in, 1-3 – 4, 5-22
    as a performance index, 3-1
    change in, 3-10
    comprehensive, 3-14n.3
    distinguished from operating cash
      flow, 5-22
net worth, loan covenants on, 10-8
New Zealand, auditors in, 13-13

NOPAT. *See* profit, net operating
    after taxes
Nordstrom, Inc., 4-5
    business strategy of, 2-7
    financial analysis of, 5-2 – 5,
      5-29n.1
      asset turnover, 5-14 – 15, *5-14*
      cash flow analysis, *5-24*, 5-26 –
        27
      common-sized income
        statement for, 5-9, *9-10*
      debt coverage, 5-18 – 19, *5-18*
      liquidity, 5-16, *5-16*
      net profit margins, 5-9 – 11
      profitability, 5-10 – 11, *5-10*
      ROE, 5-5, *5-5*, 5-6, 5-8 – 9, *5-8*
      sustainable growth rate, 5-20 –
        21, *5-20*
      taxes, *5-10*, 5-12
    financial statements of,
      standardized, *4-41 – 4-45*
    valuation of, 7-6 – 7
Northwest Airlines, 10-10, *10-10*
note, secured, 10-3

O

obligation, ambiguity about, 4-21,
    4-23
oil industry, 11-4, 12-6, *12-7*, *12-12*
on-line business. *See* commerce,
    electronic
operating working capital, 5-7, 5-12,
    5-13
    management of, 5-12 – 13
    see also working capital
operations
    assessing, 5-9 – 11
    cash flow from, 5-22
organization
    design of, and information, 13-3 – 4
    multibusiness, analysis of, 2-7 –
      10, 3-9, 5-19

P

parachute, golden, 11-14
payables. *See* accounts payable
pensions. *See* benefits, pension
Pepsi, 2-3, 2-5
performance
    assumptions about, *8-5*
    expectations of, 9-9 – 10, 13-2
    forecasts of, 8-5 – 7, *8-5*, *8-7*

performance (*continued*)
  of fund managers, 9-11 – 12
  mergers and acquisitions and, 11-4
  poor, and valuations, 7-6 – 7
  of security analysts, 9-10 – 11
  and security prices, 9-9 – 10
personal computer industry, 2-6 – 7
Petrofina, 11-4
Pfizer
  debt policies of, 12-1 – 2, *12-1*
  dividend policy of, 12-8 – 10,
    12-9, 12-12
  financing policies of, 12-5
pharmaceutical industry, 2-3, 4-15,
  6-5, 7-15, 12-6, *12-7*, *12-12*
Phillips Petroleum, 11-4
plant, accounting for acquisition of, 4-6
policy, financial, as communication,
    13-10
pooling of interest, for asset
    consolidation, in mergers and
    acquisitions, 4-13 – 14, 4-17 –
    18, 11-13
PP&E. *See* property, plant and
    equipment
premium
  comparable, for an acquisition,
    11-5 – 6, *11-6*, 11-9 – 10
  and stock prices, 8-4, 8-17n.1,
    11-5 – 16, *11-6*, 11-9 – 10
price multiples
  discounted abnormal, 7-1
  leading, 7-7
  leverage and, 7-7
  trailing, 7-7
  see also ratio; valuation, price
    multiples for
price, sensitivity to
  and competition, 2-5, 2-6 – 7
  see also cost; stock, price
price-to-book value
  multiples, and ROE, *7-12*
  ratio of, and valuation, 7-1
price-to-earnings (PE), ratio of, and
    valuation, 7-1, *7-9*, 11-7 – 8,
    11-7
price-to-sales, ratio of, and valuation,
    7-1
profit
  defined, 3-2
  margin. *See* profit margin; sales,
    return on
  net operating after taxes
    (NOPAT), 5-9

and asset valuation, 7-3, 8-1,
    8-2
  assumptions about, and
    valuation, *8-5*
  defined, 5-7, 8-6
  margin. *See* profit margin,
    NOPAT
  mergers and acquisitions and,
    11-8 – 9
profitability
  analysis of, 5-1 – 11, 9-9
  and debt ratings, 10-12, *10-12*,
    10-13
  decomposing, 5-6 – 9
  drivers of, 5-2 – 3, *5-2*
  industry structure and, 2-1 – 2, *2-2*
  measuring overall, 5-4 – 5
  and prediction of distress, 10-14
  ratios of, 5-9, *5-10*
profit margin
  decomposing net, 5-9 – 11
  forecast of, 6-2
  gross, 5-8 – 9, *5-10*
  NOPAT, 5-7, *5-10*, 5-11
    behavior of, *6-15*
    forecasting and, 6-6, 6-8, 6-9,
      6-14n.5, 8-8 – 12
  see also sales, return on
property, plant and equipment
    (PP&E), 5-13 – 15
proxy fight, 3-6, 3-8
purchase accounting, for mergers and
    acquisitions, 11-13

R

R&D. *See* research and development
random walk, 6-4, 7-10 – 11, 7-18n.7
rate
  interest. *See* interest rate
  tax. *See* tax rate
ratings
  agency, 13-2
    see also Moody's; Standard &
      Poor's
  bond, 10-12, *10-13*
  credit, 8-3
  debt, 10-2, 10-9 – 13, *10-10*, *10-11*
ratio
  accounts payable turnover, 5-13
  accounts receivable turnover, 5-13
  analysis. *See* analysis, ratio
  asset management, *5-14*
  asset turnover, 5-6

capital expenditures to earnings
    before depreciation, 10-8
  cash, 5-15, 5-16, *5-16*
  concentration (four-firm), 2-16n.5
  coverage, 5-17 – 18, *5-18*, 10-6 –
    7, 10-8, 10-12, 10-13
  current, 5-15, *5-16*, 10-8
  days' inventory, 5-13
  days' receivables, 5-13
  debt, 5-16 – 19, *5-18*
  debt to capital, 5-17
  debt to equity, 5-17, 12-6 – 7, *12-7*
  disaggregated data, 5-19
  dividend payout, 5-19, *12-12*
  EBITDA, 5-11
  equity to book, 7-7 – 8, 7-10
  financial, and debt ratings, 10-11,
    10-11
  funds flow coverage, 10-6 – 7, 10-8
  historical patterns of, 5-21 – 22
  interest coverage, 5-17, 10-12,
    10-13
  inventory turnover, 5-13
  liabilities to equity, 5-17
  liabilities to net worth, 10-8
  liquidity, 5-16, *5-16*
  net debt to equity, 5-17
  net debt to net capital, 5-17
  net financial leverage., 5-21
  net long-term asset turnover, 5-14
  NOPAT, 5-7 – 8, 5-11, *5-21*
  operating asset turnover, *5-21*
  operating cash flow, 5-15
  operating ROA, 5-7, *5-21*
  operating working capital
    turnover, 5-13
  PE, 7-1
  physical data, to operations, 5-19
  PP&E turnover, 5-14
  price-to-book value, 7-1
  probability, 2-1 – 2
  quick, 5-15
  ROA, 5-6, *5-21*
  ROE, 5-3 – 4, *5-21*
  sales to assets. *See* ratio, asset
    turnover
  SG&A expense to sales, 5-11
  solvency, 10-6
  spread, 5-7, 5-8, *5-21*, 6-6
  sustainable growth rate, *5-21*
  "target" for debt and equity, 8-2
  tax expense, 5-12
  value to earnings, 7-9
  see also price multiples

real estate
    investment funds, 9-2
    as security, 10-5
receivables. *See* accounts receivable
red flags, identifying potential,
    3-9 – 11
regulation
    and accounting choices, 3-5
    and competition, 2-4
    and corporate governance, 13-3
    and securities analysis, 9-11
Regulation Fair Disclosure (Reg FD),
    9-11, 13-9
rent
    lease arrangements as, 4-14
    product-market, mergers and
        acquisitions and, 11-2
repayment
    assessing prospects for, 10-7,
        10-13 – 15
    schedule, 10-7
reports
    auditor's, 13-12 – 13
    financial. *See* financial statements
research and development (R&D)
    accounting for, 3-7, 4-15, 4-20 –
        21, 7-15
    expensing, 3-4, 4-6, 4-12,
        4-39n.12
    investment in, 2-10
    partnerships, 3-10
reserves
    overestimated, 4-13
    underestimated, 4-7, 4-9 – 10
resources
    complementary, mergers and
        acquisitions and, 11-2
    control of, 4-4 – 6
restructuring, leverage and, 12-4 – 6
retailing industry, 4-7, 5-19, 6-7, 7-6 –
    7, 7-9, 7-9
    see also Nordstrom, Inc.; TJX
        Companies
retirement benefits, accounting for.
    See benefits, pension
return on assets (ROA), 5-5 – 9
    and debt ratings, 10-12, *10-12*
    operating, 5-7 – 9, *5-21*, 8-1
        abnormal, defined, 8-6
        behavior of, *6-15*
        forecasting, 6-6
    valuation and, 7-8, 8-1, 8-2, 8-11
return on equity (ROE), 1-8, 3-12 –
    13, 5-1, *5-3*, 7-9, *7-9*

abnormal, 8-1, 8-6
    assumption about, 8-7
    behavior of, *6-15 – 6-16*
    and cost of capital, 5-4
    decomposing, 5-5 – 6, *5-5*, *5-8*
    defined, 5-4, 5-29nn.2, 3, 7-18n.5
    forecasting, 8-1, *8-5*, 8-7, 10-5 – 7
    patterns of, 6-6, 6-8
    price-to-book multiples and, *7-12*
    valuation and, 7-9, *7-9*, 7-11 – 12,
        7-14 – 19, 7-18n.5, 8-11
revenue
    defined, 3-2
    recognition of, 4-5, 4-6, 4-7 – 8,
        4-10 – 11, 4-22, 4-23 – 24
risk
    banking and, 10-2
    business and capital structure,
        5-16
    debt ratings and, 10-9, 10-11,
        10-11, 10-13
    evaluating, 9-9, 10-11 – 13,
        13-16
    financial analysis and, 9-10, 10-7
    financial distress and, 12-5
    leverage and, 5-16 – 18
    loan covenants and, 10-9 – 10
    measuring, 11-11 – 12
    mergers and acquisitions and,
        11-11 – 12
    pro forma, 11-11 – 12
    unavoidable, 9-2
RJR Nabisco, 12-4
ROA. *See* return on assets
ROE. *See* return on equity
ROS. *See* sales, return on
rules, accounting, 3-4, 4-5
    on asset values, 4-13
    on disclosure, 3-8, 13-9
    on liabilities, 4-22, 4-27
    limitations of, 13-7 – 8
    on securities, 4-30
    on stock options, 4-30
Ryan, Amy D., 13-5

S

Saks, Inc., 7-6
sales
    assumptions about, and valuation,
        8-5
    and forecasting, 6-2, 6-7 – 8, 6-9,
        8-7 – 9, *8-12*
    growth of, 6-3 – 4, *6-4*, *8-5*

incremental, 8-8 – 9
    ratio of, to assets (asset turnover),
        5-6
    return on (ROS), 5-9
        see also profit margin
savings, national, and business
    investments, 1-2 – 3
scale, economies of, 2-3, 11-1 – 2
screening, securities analysis as, 9-5,
    9-6
Sears Roebuck & Co., 2-11, *10-10*
seasonality, effects of, 6-11 – 12
SEC. *See* Securities and Exchange
    Commission
securities
    analysis of, 6-1, 9-6 – 11, 10-11,
        10-12
        see also equity security
            analysis
    hybrid, 4-30, 4-31
    marketable, free cash flow and,
        12-8
    prices for, 9-3, 9-7, 9-9
    see also analyst, securities; stock
Securities and Exchange Commission
    (SEC), 3-3, 3-13, 4-8, 4-24,
    9-11, 13-3, 13-6, 13-9, 13-13,
    13-14, 13-17
security, for loans, 10-5
sellers, as suppliers of credit, 10-3
sensitivity. *See* analysis, sensitivity
service, low-cost, 2-10
SFAS. *See* Statement of Financial
    Accounting Standards
SG&A. *See* expenses, selling, general,
    and administrative
shareholders, creation of value for
    corporate financing and, 12-1,
        12-2
    defining, 7-1, 7-2 – 3
    mergers and acquisitions and,
        11-1, 11-5, 11-6
    by Nordstrom Inc., 5-9
Singapore, auditors in, 13-13
slack, financial
    dividends and, 12-10
    financing choices and, 12-8
soft-drink industry, 2-3, 2-5
    see also Coca-Cola; Pepsi
software industry, 3-7, 4-15, 12-6,
    12-7, *12-12*
solvency, long-term. *See* debt,
    analyzing
Sony Corp., *10-10*

spread
  behavior of, *6-16*
  ratio, 5-7, 5-8, *5-21*, 6-6
stakeholders, and accounting choices,
    3-6
Standard & Poor's, 10-2, 10-9,
    10-10
standards, auditing, 13-13, 13-14
Statement of Financial Accounting
    Standards (SFAS)
  2, 3-4
  13, 4-14, 4-39n.10
  86, 4-38n.1
  87, 4-27
  95, 5-22, 5-23
  123, 4-30, 4-32
  140, 4-14
  141, 4-13, 11-13
  142, 4-12, 4-13, 11-13
  144, 4-6
statistics
  and debt ratings, *10-13*
  and prediction of financial
    distress, 10-14, *10-14*
  techniques in, and securities
    analysis, 9-4, 9-5
status, financial, analysis of, for
    credit, 10-5 – 7
stock
  acquisition for, 11-10, 11-12,
    11-13
  overvalued, 11-12
  ownership of, by management, 3-8
  portfolio, management of, 9-5
  price
    financial statement data and,
      3-15n.5
    and legal redress, 13-13
    and market efficiency, 9-3, 9-4,
      9-10
    mergers and acquisitions and,
      11-12, 11-13
    movements of, 9-6
    and valuation, 7-1, 8-13, 8-15,
      9-7 – 8, *9-8*, 13-2, 13-4,
      13-11
  recommendations to purchase,
    9-10
  repurchases of, 5-25, 12-9, 12-12,
    13-10 – 11, 13-12
  returns on
    financial statement data and,
      3-13
    and firm size, 8-3, *8-4*

undervalued, 13-4, 13-5 – 6
  see also securities
stock exchange, 13-3, 13-17
stock options, valuing, 4-30 – 32, 8-15
strategy, analyzing
  competitive, 2-1, 2-7 – 10
  corporate, 2-1, 2-7, 2-11 – 14
  see also business strategy
substitution, and competition, 2-4
suppliers
  bargaining power of, 2-5, 2-6
  credit extended by, 10-3
switching costs, 2-3, 2-4, 2-6

T

takeover, hostile, 3-5, 11-3, 11-5,
    11-14 – 15, 13-4
Target, 7-6, *7-9*
taxes
  and accounting changes, 3-10
  capital gains, 11-10, 11-11
  considerations of, and accounting
    choices, 3-5
  debt financing and, 12-2
  deferred, 11-10
  dividends and, 12-10 – 11, 12-12
  as expenses, to evaluate, 5-12
  leverage and, 12-2
  mergers and acquisitions and,
    11-2, 11-4, 11-10 – 11, 11-13,
    11-17n.3
  and reported income, 3-9
  and unearned revenue, 4-24
taxi services, 2-4
tax planning, analyzing, 5-12
tax rate, 5-12, 8-3
telecommunications industry, 2-3,
    2-4, 8-15
tender offer, for stocks, 13-11
Texaco, 11-4
theorem, Modigliani-Miller, 8-16
Time Warner, AOL and, 4-11 – 12
TJX Companies, Inc.
  financial analysis of, 5-2 – 5, 5-5,
    5-5, 5-29n.1, 6-1
    asset turnover, 5-14 – 15, *5-14*
    cash flow analysis, *5-24*, 5-26 –
      27
    common-sized income
      statement for, 5-9, *5-10*
    cost of capital, 8-5
    debt coverage, 5-18 – 19, *5-18*
    liquidity, 5-16, *5-16*

net profit margins, 5-9 – 11
    ROE, *5-6*, 5-8 – 9, *5-8*, 5-10 –
      11, *5-10*, 5-29n.6
    sustainable growth rate, 5-20 –
      21, *5-20*
    taxes, *5-10*, 5-12
  forecasts for, 6-3, 8-5 – 7, *8-5*
    financial statements, *6-10*, 8-6
    income statements, 6-7 – 8,
      6-10
    performance, 8-7
    terminal values, 8-10 – 13,
      8-12
    stock prices of, 8-13
    valuation of, 7-6, *7-9*, 8-7, 8-11,
      8-12
Tosco, 11-4
Total (oil company), 11-4
transactions
  costs of
    capital markets and, 2-11 – 12
    in mergers and acquisitions,
      11-10
  related-party, 3-10
  unexplained, 3-9
turnaround, predicting, 10-13
turnover
  accounts payable, 5-13
  accounts receivable, 5-13
  assets, 5-6 – 8, 5-7 – 8, 5-12 – 15,
    5-14, *5-21*, 6-16
  formulas for calculating. *See*
    formula
  inventory, 5-13
  investment, 5-13
  PP&E, 5-14
  ratios for calculating. *See* ratio
  working capital, 5-13
Tyco, 13-4, 13-14 – 15

U

UAL. *See* United Airlines
UK. *See* United Kingdom
union. *See* labor unions
United Airlines (UAL), 10-10,
    10-10
United Kingdom
  accounting in, 4-39n.12, 13-10
  auditing in, 13-13
United States, accounting in, 5-22,
    13-10
unit trusts. *See* mutual funds
utility industry, 4-8, 12-12

V

valuation, 1-8
  and accounting distortions, 8-14 –
    15, 8-18n.6
  of assets, 4-6 – 12, 7-1, 7-3, 8-1,
    8-2 – 7, 8-7, 8-11
  defined, 7-1
  of equity, 8-1
  forecasting and, 6-1
  formal vs. informal, 9-5 – 6
  implementation of, 8-1 – 18
  marginalist, 9-5 – 6
  and market value, 8-13
  of mergers and acquisitions,
    11-7 – 8
  methods of, 7-1 – 2
    compared, 7-14 – 16
  of poorly performing firms,
    7-6 – 7
  price multiples for, 7-1, 7-2, 7-5 –
    10, 8-10
  procedure for making, 7-6
  of stock options, 4-30 – 32, 8-15
  uses of, 7-1
value
  creation of, by mergers and
    acquisitions, 11-1, 11-2 – 3,
    11-6 – 9

defined, 1-3
fair, 4-6 – 7
shareholder. *See* shareholders
terminal, and valuation methods,
  7-14 – 15, 8-1, 8-7 – 11, *8-12*,
  8-13
values
  present, 8-7
  residual, 3-7
  terminal
    competitive equilibrium
      assumption and, 8-7 – 8
    defined, 8-7
venture capital industry, 2-11, 13-2
volatility, and prediction of distress,
  10-14

W

WACC. *See* capital, cost of, weighted
  average
Wal-Mart Stores, Inc., 2-13,
  2-17n.10, 6-5, 8-8, *10-10*
warrants, debt, 4-30
warranty, accounting for, 3-7
Washington Post, 4-31
water supply industry, 12-6, *12-7*,
  12-12

working capital
  defined, 5-12
  flows of, in funds flow statement,
    5-23, 5-29n.9
  forecasting, *8-5*
  loan covenants and, 10-8
  management of, 5-12 – 13,
    5-29n.8
  operating. *See* operating working
    capital
Worldcom, 3-4, 9-10, 13-4, 13-15
worth. *See* net worth
write-downs, 4-7, 4-8
write-off, 3-8, 3-10

X

Xerox, 13-4

Y

year, terminal, 8-7

AUTHOR INDEX

A

Aboody, D., 4-39
Akerlof, G., 1-9, 13-21
Altman, Edward, 10-16, 10-17
Amir, E., 4-39

B

Barth, Mary, 4-39, 4-40, 9-15, 13-22
Beatty, A., 3-15, 3-16
Beaver, William, 10-16
Bell, Marie, 2-17
Beneish, M. D., 3-16
Berger, Phillip, 2-17, 3-16
Bernard, Victor, 3-16, 6-14, 9-14
Besanko, David, 2-16
Bhushan, R., 9-14
Botosan, Christine, 13-21
Brown, Lawrence, 6-14, 9-14, 9-15
Bruns, Jr., W., 3-16
Bublitz, B., 4-39

C

Carhart, M., 9-15
Chamberlain, S., 3-15
Chan, S., 4-39
Chang, J., 3-16
Claus, James, 8-17
Clement, M., 9-15
Coase, Ronald, 2-17
Coggin, T., 9-16
Collins, J., 3-15
Collins, W. E., 3-16
Collis, David J., 2-16
Copeland, T., 8-17
Cuny, C., 4-40

D

Dann, Larry, 13-21
Datar, S., 11-17
DeAngelo, L., 3-15
Dechow, P., 3-15, 3-16, 4-40, 7-18, 9-15

Doherty, Jacqueline, 2-17
Dranove, David, 2-16
Dukes, R., 4-39
Dyckman, T., 4-39

E

Eccher, E., 4-39
Elliott, J., 3-16, 4-38, 4-39, 13-22
Ettredge, M., 4-39
Exstein, Michael, 5-3

F

Fabozzi, F., 9-16
Fama, Eugene, 6-14, 9-14
Feltham, G., 7-19
Ferson, W., 9-16
Fields, T., 3-15
Foster, George, 3-15, 3-16, 6-14, 9-15, 13-21
Francis, J., 3-16, 4-38, 7-19, 9-15
Frankel, R., 9-14, 11-17, 13-21
Freedman, Corinna, 5-4
Freeman, Robert, 6-14
French, Kenneth, 6-14

G

Gebhardt, William R., 8-17
Ghemawat, Pankaj, 2-16
Gilson, S., 9-15
Givoly, D., 9-14
Gordon, E., 4-39
Grant, Robert, 2-16
Griffin, P., 9-14
Grinblatt, M., 9-15
Guidry, F., 3-15

H

Hagerman, R., 9-14
Hammel, Gary, 2-17
Hand, John, 3-16, 10-16
Hanna, D., 4-38

Healy, Paul, 2-17, 3-15, 3-16, 4-38, 4-39, 9-14, 9-15, 11-17, 12-15, 13-21, 13-22
Hemmer, T., 4-40
Hendricks, D., 9-15
Hertzel, Michael, 13-21
Hirschey, M., 4-39
Holthausen, Robert, 3-15, 9-14, 10-16
Hood, Wayne, 5-3
Howe, C., 4-38, 4-39
Huddart, S., 4-40
Hutton, Amy, 4-40, 7-18, 9-15, 13-21

I

Imhoff, E., 4-39

J

Jacob, J., 9-15
Jaffe, Richard, 5-4
Jain, Prem, 13-21
Jensen, Michael, 9-15, 11-17, 13-20
Johnson, Marilyn, 13-21
Jones, J., 3-15
Jorion, P., 4-40
Justynski, Jennifer, 5-3

K

Kaplan, Robert, 3-16, 10-16
Kaplan, Steven, 11-17
Kasznik, Ron, 13-22
Kensinger, J., 4-39
Khang, K., 9-16
Khanna, Tarun, 2-17
Koller, T., 8-17
Kothari, S., 9-14

L

Lakonishok, J., 9-14, 9-16
Lang, Larry, 2-17
Lang, Mark, 3-16, 13-21
Larcker, D., 3-15, 9-14

Lee, Charles, 7-18, 8-17, 9-14
Leftwich, Richard, 10-16
Leone, A., 3-15
Lev, B., 4-39
Liesman, S., 11-17
Lilien, L., 4-39
Lin, H., 9-15
Linsmeier, T., 4-39
Lintner, J., 7-18
Lipe, R., 4-39
Lundholm, Russell, 3-16, 13-21
Lys, T., 3-15, 4-39, 9-15

M

Macedo, Laura, 5-3
McGahan, Anita M., 2-16
McNichols, Maureen, 4-39, 9-15
McNichols, W., 3-16
Magliolo, J., 3-15, 3-16
Majluf, Nicholas, 11-17, 12-15
Malkiel, M., 9-15
Martin, J., 4-39
Martinez-Jarad, A., 4-38
Masulis, Ronald, 13-21
Matsumoto, D., 9-15
Matsunaga, S., 4-40
Maydew, E., 3-16
Mayers, David, 13-21
Meckling, W., 13-20
Mendenhall, R., 3-16
Michaely, R., 9-15
Miller, G., 13-21
Miller, Merton, 7-18, 12-15
Modigliani, F., 7-18
Montgomery, Cynthia, 2-16, 2-17
Moyer, S., 3-15
Murphy, Kevin J., 13-20
Murrin, J., 8-17
Myers, J., 7-18
Myers, Stewart, 4-38, 4-39, 11-17, 12-15

N

Narayandas, Das, 2-17
Neale, M., 9-15
Nelson, M., 13-22
Nichols, W., 3-16
Nissim, Doron, 5-29
Noe, C., 9-15
Noel, J., 3-16
Noreen, E., 9-15

O

O'Brien, Patricia, 6-14, 9-14, 9-15
Ofek, Eli, 2-17
Ohlson, James, 6-14, 7-18, 7-19, 10-16
Olsson, P., 7-19
Oswald, D., 7-19
Ou, J., 9-14

P

Palepu, Krishna, 2-17, 3-15, 3-16, 4-38, 9-14, 9-15, 11-17, 12-15, 13-21, 13-22
Pastena, V., 4-39
Patel, J., 9-15
Penman, Stephen, 5-29, 6-14, 7-19, 9-14
Petroni, K., 3-15
Porter, Michael E., 2-16, 2-17
Poulsen, A., 2-17
Prahalad, C. K., 2-17

R

Rahman, S., 9-16
Rangan, V. Kasturi, 2-17
Rao, G., 3-16
Richardson, G., 4-39
Robinson, J., 4-38
Rock, S., 3-15
Rozeff, Michael, 6-14, 9-14
Ruback, Richard, 2-17, 4-38, 11-17

S

Scharfstein, D., 9-15
Scherer, F. M., 2-16
Schipper, Katherine, 2-17, 3-16
Scholes, Myron, 3-15, 5-29
Shackelford, D., 3-15
Shane, P., 4-38
Shanley, Mark, 2-16
Shaw, W., 3-16
Shevlin, T., 4-40
Shivakumar, Lakshmanan, 4-39
Shleifer, A., 9-14, 9-15, 9-16
Skinner, Douglas, 13-21
Sloan, R. G., 3-15, 3-16, 4-40, 7-18, 9-14, 9-15
Smith, Abbie, 2-17
Soffer, L., 9-15
Sohn, S., 9-15

Sougiannis, T., 4-39, 7-19
Stein, J., 9-15
Stewart, Bennett, 7-19
Stulz, Rene, 2-17
Sullivan, A., 11-17
Swaminathan, Bhaskaran, 8-17
Sweeney, A., 3-15, 3-16

T

Tarpley, R., 13-22
Tasker, Sarah, 13-21
Teece, David, 2-17
Teoh, S. H., 3-16, 13-21
Thaler, R., 9-14
Thomas, Jacob, 4-39, 8-17, 9-14
Titman, S., 9-15
Travlos, Nicholas, 11-17

U

Urwitz, G., 10-16

V

Vincent, L., 3-15, 4-38, 4-39
Vishny, R., 9-14, 9-15, 9-16

W

Wahlen, J., 3-15
Wasley, C., 4-39
Watts, B., 3-15
Weber, J., 4-38
Weiss, I., 3-16
Welch, I., 3-16, 13-21
Welker, M., 13-21
Wermers, R., 9-15
Weston, F., 11-17
Weygandt, R., 4-39
Williamson, Oliver, 2-17
Wilson, G. P., 3-15
Wilson, P., 3-16
Wolfson, Mark, 3-15, 5-29, 11-17
Womack, K., 9-15
Wong, T. J., 3-16, 13-21
Wright, D., 4-39

Z

Zeckhauser, R., 9-15
Zimmerman, Jerold, 3-15, 13-20
Zmijewski, M., 9-14, 10-16, 10-17

IMPORTANT FORMULAS

Ratio Analysis

(1) ROE = Operating ROA + Spread × Net financial leverage

(Operating margin × Asset turnover) + Spread × Net financial leverage

$$ROE = \frac{\text{Net income}}{\text{Equity}}$$

$$\text{Operating ROA} = \frac{\text{Net operating profit after tax}}{\text{Operating working capital} + \text{Net long-term assets}}$$

$$\text{Spread} = \text{Operating ROA} - \frac{\text{Net interest expense after tax}}{\text{Debt} - (\text{Cash} + \text{Short-term investments})}$$

$$\text{Net financial leverage} = \frac{\text{Interest-bearing debt} - (\text{Cash} + \text{Short-term investments})}{\text{Equity}}$$

$$\text{Operating margin} = \frac{\text{Net operating profit after tax}}{\text{Sales}}$$

$$\text{Asset turnover} = \frac{\text{Assets} - (\text{Cash} + \text{Short-term investments})}{\text{Sales}}$$

(2) Sustainable growth rate = ROE × (1 − Dividend payout rate)

$$\text{Dividend payout rate} = \frac{\text{Dividends}}{\text{Net income}}$$

Equity Valuation

(1) Equity value $= BVE_0 + \dfrac{NI_1 - r_e \cdot BVE_0}{(1 + r_e)} + \dfrac{NI_2 - r_e \cdot BVE_1}{(1 + r_e)^2} + \dfrac{NI_3 - r_e \cdot BVE_2}{(1 + r_e)^3} + \ldots$

where BVE_t = book value of equity at the end of year t

NI_t = net income available to common shareholders for year t

r_e = cost of equity capital